BREATHING FOR YOGA

Also by Patrick McKeown

The Breathing Cure
Atomic Focus
The Oxygen Advantage
Anxiety Free: Stop Worrying and Quieten Your Mind
Sleep with Buteyko: Stop Snoring, Sleep Apnoea and Insomnia
Buteyko Meets Dr. Mew: Buteyko Method for Children and Teenagers
Always Breathe Correctly (children's book)
Asthma-Free Naturally
Close Your Mouth

Support App

Download the Oxygen Advantage® App to support your
practice of the Oxygen Advantage® technique

BREATHING FOR YOGA

RESTORING THE ANCIENT SCIENCE OF THE BREATH

BY
PATRICK MCKEOWN
AND
ANASTASIS TZANIS

OXYAT BOOKS

Breathing for Yoga. Copyright ©2023 by Patrick McKeown.

For information address: Patrick McKeown, Loughwell, Moycullen, Co Galway, H91H4C1, Ireland

Email: info@oxygenadvantage.com

FIRST EDITION PUBLISHED 2023.

Publisher: OxyAt Books

ISBN: 978-1-909410-33-6

Illustrations by Bex Burgess
Typeset by Karl Hunt
Cover design by Svitlana Stefaniuk

QUICK START REFERENCE GUIDE

This is admittedly a BIG book. We wanted to make it as comprehensive as possible so that it can cater to yogis and yoga teachers of all levels and backgrounds and operate as a complete manual for yoga and the breath. Certain sections of this book may not interest you or apply to you, and some of the science may feel a little heavy at times. But not to worry, because aside from the first four chapters which formulate a solid basis from which to understand the rest, this book can be read out of sequence. The quick reference guide below will allow you to quickly locate what interests you the most.

IF YOU WANT TO LEARN . . .

CONTENTS

FOREWORD

If you happen to find yourself in New Delhi, India, amble over to the National Museum. Skip the library and decorative arts displays and swing a left at the Harrappan collection. There, you will see relics of what is arguably the oldest and most advanced ancient civilization yet discovered. Toys made of copper. Meticulously detailed bronze statues. And a dozen terracotta figurines in unmistakable poses: one of a man sitting erect with arms outstretched and thumbs placed on his knees. Another with eyes barely open in a state of deep meditation. Another with legs outstretched, arms crossed, and chest and abdomen filled with air.

These artifacts are approximately 5,000 years old and constitute what many researchers believe to be the first evidence of ancient conscious breathing practices, or what is better known today as 'yoga'.

The Sanskrit word for asana means "seat" and "posture." Back then, as far as we can tell, yoga was very different from the yoga we practice today. There were no standing salutations or stretching repetitions, and no Jack Johnson playing softly through a Sonos. Yoga was a system of sitting and breathing.

Not much changed in yoga for the next few thousand years. Even in the earliest texts of the Yoga Sutras, written around 300 AD, there is no mention of moving between postures or repeating poses.

Today, the most popular form of yoga is a "vinyasa flow," where one pose flows to the next and back again for several intervals. It feels great, and the science is clear that it has innumerable benefits – from decreasing stress, to building muscles, to supporting a more robust cardiovascular system. This style of yoga is about 100 years old and was developed mostly in the west.

I've been flowing in yoga classes, vinyasa and otherwise, for half my life. The more I learned about ancient yoga practices, and the more

I learned about the science of proper breathing, the more I began to realise something was missing in the instruction of most modern yoga classes. Few were ever talking about breathing, and when they did mention it, their advice was often misguided.

To wit: How often during classes did I hear (and sometimes feel) my fellow urban yogis huffing and puffing through hard poses, taking big gulps of air through their mouths and shallow breaths out? How often did instructors not only encourage it, but egg us all on: "C'mon! Get all that carbon dioxide out; get more oxygen in! Breathe deeper!"

I came to realise much later that breathing this way while practicing yoga could have been hurting as much as it was helping. I spent an embarrassing amount of time (several years) attempting to piece together a conscious breathing practice based on ancient techniques and modern science. I do not recommend this path! It's long and arduous and filled with frustrations.

Luckily, you don't have to. In your hands is the operating manual for new and old yogis alike.

For the past 21 years, McKeown has researched why so many of us breathe so poorly and how we can do it better and improve our lives. He's spent several more years piecing together this carefully constructed compendium of yoga knowledge and distilling it into step-by-step directions, illustrations, scientific context, biomechanics, biochemistry, and more!

My advice: Take a seat, shut your mouth, breathe it in.

James Nestor

INTRODUCTION

This book is different from others you'll find about yoga and the breath in a modern bookstore. In this book, we weave respiratory science and the Oxygen Advantage® approach together with yoga theory and provide a practical and detailed guide to restoring original yogic healthy breathing to your yoga practice.

This book is for all yogis who want to improve their breathing and yoga instructors who want to support their students in establishing healthy breathing patterns for healthier lives.

Our hope with this book is to empower more people every day to breathe better, feel better and achieve their potential . . . both on and off the yoga mat!

MEET THE AUTHORS

Patrick McKeown

During filming for a Channel Four documentary by Julia Bradbury, she surmised that "training my breathing saved my life". I immediately retorted that "I wouldn't go that far". But that evening, I pondered on her statement and reflected on what 25 years of breath training had done for my own life.

In 1998, after reading a newspaper article about the work of Ukrainian Doctor Konstantin Buteyko, I began practising breath holds and breathing less air. One exercise I practiced involved exhaling through my nose and then pinching my nose with my fingers to hold my breath. As I held my breath, I nodded my head up and down to generate a moderate to strong sensation of air hunger. I resumed breathing through my nose and could immediately feel my nose opening up.

I was astonished that nasal congestion which wreaks havoc on sleep and concentration could be alleviated by simply holding one's breath.

The second exercise I practised while breathing in and out through my nose, was inhaling about 30% less air and allowing a slow and prolonged exhalation. This again generated a feeling of air hunger. In two to three minutes, the temperature of my hands improved, and I felt notably calmer. There and then, I knew it worked!

I felt an immediate difference when I changed my breath. This, plus the discovery that I could decongest my nose, and improve blood circulation and oxygen delivery is what got me into breath training. I was accredited as a Buteyko instructor by Dr Konstantin Buteyko, eventually becoming Director of Education and Training at Buteyko Clinic. I then created the Oxygen Advantage® a science-based series of unique breathing exercises for optimal physical and emotional health, mental clarity and performance.

Looking back over my career and the importance of training my breath – did it save my life? Yes, I now believe so . . . and it could do the same for you!

Anastasis Tzanis

As a boy, I struggled with seasonal hay fever, insomnia, and difficulty concentrating – all symptoms I would later realise are associated with dysfunctional breathing. The importance of the breath really crystallised at age 12, when I was pushed by another boy and landed flat on my back. I fell so hard my diaphragm collapsed. Decades later, my memory of being unable to breathe is still crushingly vivid.

The importance of healthy breathing became increasingly apparent throughout my career, first serving in the special forces as a paratrooper and later, working as a trader at an investment bank. Whilst working in those highly competitive environments I observed first-hand the cost that stress can have on the body. And stress always affects our breathing.

My career temporarily stalled in 2008 when laser eye surgery triggered glandular fever. Instead of a week's recovery, it took two months to get my eyesight back. At a loss as to how to best help my recovery, and placate a very demanding manager, I began studying nutritional therapy and attending yoga classes. For the next three years, I immersed myself deeply in yoga. I trained as a yoga teacher. I travelled around the world, learning everything I could from leading yoga teachers.

My true path opened up to me when I was made redundant. At the time, it intuitively felt right to take a break from banking . . . I never found the desire to go back!

I knew that breathing was important in my practice, and I had learned that different prāṇāyāmas create different results; but prāṇāyāma was not covered in any real depth in my training. On a quest for better understanding, I attended training on the Wim Hof Method and Oxygen Advantage® with Patrick McKeown. By midday of the first day of Patrick's workshop, I had learned more about breathing than I had in nine years of yoga practice!

The breath is incredibly powerful. Once you know how it works and really understand how to use it, its potential is limited only by how much work you're prepared to put in – just like any other worthwhile practice. I wanted to discover how I could apply the principles of respiratory physiology to prāṇāyāma and to be clear about the purposes of the different prāṇāyāma techniques.

When I could not find a book or teacher that offered adequate answers, I began my own research alongside Patrick – and so this book was born!

OXYGEN ADVANTAGE®
RESOURCES AND
SUPPORT

This book provides a practical guide to allow you to incorporate the Oxygen Advantage® approach into your yoga practice and daily life. We also have a number of resources available to guide and support you on this journey.

- Many of our Oxygen Advantage® Instructors are trained yoga instructors and are ideally placed to guide you through breathing and asanas. Please see our website, where you may search the list of instructors by country, language, background, and gender to find an instructor to work with.
- If you wish to delve even deeper into the Oxygen Advantage® approach and are interested in becoming a certified Oxygen Advantage® Instructor, a range of types of training, including a course specifically for yoga, are available via our website.
- The Oxygen Advantage® app is an excellent support tool and is available free of charge to both instructors and students alike. It is available on both Android and Apple devices.
- We have a library of breathing exercises and videos on our YouTube channel.
- There is an Oxygen Advantage® podcast featuring interviews with breath training experts, elite athletes, biohackers, yogis and doctors. You will also find helpful guided breathing exercises with relaxation as spoken by Patrick.
- Finally, you may also wish to check out our various social media channels for updates and information.

http://www.oxygenadvantage.com/

THE BREATH IN YOGA & OXYGEN ADVANTAGE®

CHAPTER ONE

THE BREATH IN YOGA & OXYGEN ADVANTAGE®

If there was a powerful, safe, and free tool that you could use to optimise not only your yoga practice but also your mental and physical health, would you use it?

If you teach yoga, would you want to understand this tool so that you could share it with your students and create dramatic changes in their lives as well?

Since you're reading this book, you likely know precisely what this "tool" is that we are referring to and have answered "yes" to at least one of the above questions. However, some of you may be wondering, what's wrong with how the breath is currently taught in yoga?

As James Nestor observed in the foreword to this book, breath practices in many modern yoga classes, particularly those in the West, have drifted away from their origins. Ancient yogis weren't scientists, but they did understand the body/mind connection. They worked with this for thousands of years before science caught up. Only in recent decades have researchers been able to demonstrate that humans can influence their own nervous systems and regulate bodily functions once thought to be outside of our control.

Unfortunately, by the time our scientific understanding of the body/mind connection had caught up, the general understanding of healthy breathing in yoga had already shifted from its origins. Much of the shift occurred in the late 1800s, partly through the influence of the Hygienic and self-help movements. At that time, yoga breathing practices began to deviate from being highly diverse, with a focus on breathing less and breath retention, towards the present-day focus on large, deep breaths. Ironically, this shift was partially motivated by a desire to help practitioners confront the health dangers of the time. Please see Appendix One for a more in-depth historical perspective by Magdalena Kraler, an academic specialising in the history of modern prāṇāyāma.

Fast-forward to today, and while many yoga teachers around the world advise paying attention to breathing, the shift away from the original yogic understanding of healthy breathing is apparent. Misleading ideas about the breath are widely and frequently shared.

DISPELLING COMMON BREATH MYTHS

Many of us think we know about the breath, especially in the yoga community, but there are many misconceptions. We are told that carbon dioxide is a waste gas. We assume that mouth breathing is normal. We believe that it's enough to focus on "belly breathing" in class. And we believe that we need to breathe more air to get more oxygen into the body. In fact, it's common in yoga to hear the instructor encourage students to "breathe big, full breaths into the belly", or "exhale through the mouth".

You may well know that faster, harder breathing increases brain activity and contributes to anxiety – but did you know that big, full breaths cause the same negative effects? Imagine the scene for a minute – a yoga instructor guides the students to take big, deep, audible breaths. The class responds with gusto. Little do they realise the harm this breathing could do to their bodies.

Until we understand the many facets and functions of the breath and how it interacts with the body, we cannot truly use it effectively. We can't be sure we are practising beneficial techniques. We cannot guide others in using even the simplest breath practice to support their asana practice and their lives. Worse, we may unwittingly contribute to injury, stress, and disease in ourselves as well as our students.

Breathing is a complex and vital process. If we replace common myths with a correct and clear understanding of functional breathing, from a multidimensional perspective, we can transform our yoga practice, our health, and our lives.

Some truths about breathing that you will learn in this book:

- **Carbon dioxide (CO_2) is not a waste gas.** It has many crucial functions in the body. It is actually what makes oxygen available to your cells via the Bohr Effect, which we'll look at later. CO_2 also has healing properties in the body.
- **Belly breathing is not the same as diaphragm breathing.** The abdominal muscles can move independently of the breathing muscles.
- **Slow breathing is not always relaxing.** If you breathe a disproportionate volume of air or encourage a student with dysfunctional breathing to slow their breathing too much, you can tip them into the stress response and even trigger anxiety and panic symptoms.
- **Persistent mouth breathing is dysfunctional breathing.** It encourages over-breathing, bypasses the immune defences of the nose, creates upper chest breathing, and is associated with stress and disease states.
- **Less is more.** Breathing lighter and slower through the nose and at a personalised rate that creates a comfortable air hunger, is the key to increasing oxygenation.

OUR GOAL WITH THIS BOOK

We believe this book is different from other books about breathing for yoga. It provides a practical and detailed guide to respiratory science from a multidimensional perspective. As we progress through the book, we will explore how to bring the current scientific understanding of the breath into your yoga practice and restore the original yogic understanding of healthy breathing. We will also explain our approach to breathing and how to utilise the Oxygen Advantage® in your yoga practice.

As a student or teacher of yoga, you will learn how to adjust your practice to get the most benefit from breathing, physical movement, and the mental stillness that results. You will also gain answers to some of the most commonly asked questions, including:

- Should we breathe through the nose or mouth?
- How much air should we take in and out of the body?
- Should we shake the walls with the strength of our ujjayi prāṇāyāma, or not?
- Why do we sometimes snore so loudly in savasana?

We encourage you to take these learnings off the yoga mat and to incorporate functional breathing practices into your everyday life – just as the early yogis did. By retraining yourself to breathe optimally 24/7, you will improve mobility and reduce the risk of injury during your yoga practice. Perhaps more importantly, you will gain greater control over your mental, emotional, and physical health. And if you suffer with asthma, anxiety, panic disorder, chronic fatigue syndrome, snoring, or sleep apnea, you could experience a profound reduction in symptoms.

––––––––––

Disclaimer: we would like to make it clear that we don't claim to have all the answers or to be able to interpret the ancient yogic texts in a new way. There is a complex history and philosophy behind each school of yoga, and there are plenty of people who are better equipped to explain those ideas. However, what we do know is that many of the concepts that are commonly shared about breathing today are misleading or selective.

The goal of this book is not to challenge tradition but to understand it, question it, and apply it, so you can experience deeper, more lasting benefits from your practice. Yoga instructors already teach breathing and adapt the physical poses for each student. In this book, we will go a little deeper and provide the tools to tailor breathing practices for each student. There is tremendous potential here to marry the two.

WHY BREATH TRAINING MATTERS ON & OFF THE MAT

The majority of yogis, no matter how advanced, could benefit from having a teacher who understands the breath and can help improve breathing both on and off the mat. Learning to breathe optimally in everyday life is critical to ensuring that your breath matches the metabolic needs of your body. If it doesn't, over time, this will likely impact your physical and emotional wellbeing.

Unfortunately, because breathing is something we do continuously from the moment we are born, there is a misconception that breathing is not something we can get "wrong" and a cynicism around breathing exercises. When the topic of breath training comes up, there's always one person keen to joke, "I've been breathing my whole life!" Yes, if you are healthy, automatic processes like breathing are naturally in-tune from birth. However, when any system in the body gets out of balance, compensatory functions kick in, and these can become our norm. And because breathing affects and is affected by every other system in the body, many of us are stuck in a cycle of dysfunction.

While it's common to be taught to acknowledge the importance of the breath during a yoga class, how often do you think about breathing outside the studio? During your day-to-day life, whether you are practising yoga, working, exercising, or playing with your children, your breathing either supports your strength, balance, movement, and overall health or compromises it. Moreover, breathing during rest directly influences breathing during asana. The lighter the breath, the easier the asana. But breathing lightly during challenging postures does not come naturally to us. It requires training. Nothing will improve your focus and progress during yoga practice more than training yourself to breathe optimally in everyday life.

YOGA ORIGINS & HIERARCHY

There is disagreement on when yoga originated. Some sources say it dates back to 10,000 years ago, while others state it originated 8,000, 5,000, or 2,500 years ago. In his 2021 book, *The Truth of Yoga*, the scholar Daniel Simpson states: "Yoga is neither five thousand years old, as is commonly claimed, nor does it mean 'union,' at least not exclusively." Simpson says the earliest evidence of yogic practice dates back only around 2,500 years.[1] He uses his book to give a precise history and analysis of the various yogic texts and philosophies. He sheds light on the fact that, while much of modern yoga is credited to the sage Patanjali, it is unclear who Patanjali was or even if he practised what is taught.

---

1 Simpson, D. (2021). *The truth of yoga: A comprehensive guide to yoga's history, texts, philosophy, and practices*. North Point Press.

Some researchers attribute the core teachings of yoga to the ancient Hindu scriptures, the *Upanishads*.[2] Breath control is described in that text as a mechanism to refine and transcend consciousness and it is regarded as the key to the mental control essential for spiritual growth.[3] Breath control is the act of exercising, restraining, or influencing our breathing. It involves slowing and sometimes suspending the breath. This affects the nervous system and areas of the brain, allowing us better control over our thoughts and emotions. It gives us tools to step outside negative, repetitive thinking, clear the mind, and look at our problems with a fresh perspective.

Nowadays, the core focus of yoga is rarely breath control; instead, it is focused on posture and asanas. The flowing sequences so familiar today were not recognized as yoga until the modern era. For instance, Simpson says: "The earliest reference to a sun salutation in yogic texts appears in Brahmananda's nineteenth-century commentary on *Hatha Yoga Pradipika*." Even there, it is mentioned in a cautionary context, as a warning against excessive physical stress. Simpson goes on to identify convincing connections between our familiar dynamic forms of yoga and gymnastics.

Our modern pursuit of outward bodily perfection, our filtered Instagram posts with their honed, toned, polished yoga bodies with a side-helping of personal or spiritual growth – all this is new. Even the focus on relaxation is recent. While traditional texts may discuss the benefits of a comfortable seated or supine pose, in Western yoga, fitness or stress relief have become the primary goals for most practitioners.[4]

There is a hierarchy in yoga and the breath creates a fundamental base. The fifteenth-century Sanskrit manual *Hatha Yoga Pradipika*

---

2 Courtney, Rosalba. "Dysfunctional Breathing: Its Parameters, Measurement and Relevance." *Dissertation*. RMIT University, 2011.

3 Feuerstein, Georg. *The Yoga Tradition: Its History, Literature, Philosopy and Practise*. Prescott, Arizona: Hohm Press, 2008.

4 "Why Does Anyone Do Yoga, Anyway?" *Psychology Today Ireland*. 06. Published 2015. http://www.psychologytoday.com/ie/blog/urban-survival/201506/why-does-anyone-do-yoga-anyway.

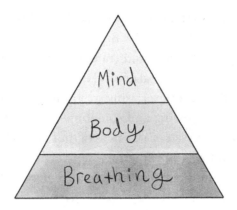

The Hierarchy of Yoga

explains that the mind is the king of the senses and that breath is the king of the mind.[5] The way we think and move and the way we breathe are intimately connected. As long as breathing is dysfunctional, your mind will continue to race and chatter, no matter how much you crave stillness. With a cluttered mind, you will struggle to focus on your physical postures. This affirms that functional breathing should always come first in the hierarchy of a yoga practice.

It is common for books and articles about yogic breathing to open with this verse from *Hatha Yoga Pradipika*:

> *When the breath is unsteady, the mind is unsteady. When the breath is steady, the mind can become steady.*[6]

In yoga, this idea of steadiness of the breath is presented as our first challenge. However, defining this steadiness is somewhat subjective, and there is little guidance on what it means or how to achieve it. A google search of the meaning of the word *steady* will return: "regular,

---

5 *BKS Iyengar Prāṇāyāma.* Accessed July 5, 2022. http://www.youtube.com/watch?v= fcPjvp4La8A.

6 Simpson, Daniel. *The Truth of Yoga: A Comprehensive Guide to Yoga's History, Texts, Philosophy, and Practices.* North Point Press, 2021.

even, and continuous in development, frequency, or intensity." Steady breathing goes hand in hand with functional breathing. When breathing is optimal across a number of dimensions, steadiness naturally occurs in everyday breathing.

BREATH BASICS & THE THREE DIMENSIONS OF BREATHING

Quite simply, the main reason any animal breathes is to get oxygen into the body's cells. Oxygen is needed for aerobic respiration – the chemical process by which we get energy from the food we eat. Humans average between 10 and 14 cycles of breath per minute. For each breath we take during rest, we draw half a litre of air into the lungs. Every 60 seconds, we inhale three to seven litres of air, and we take around 20,000 breaths each day.[7]

Often, our basic understanding of breathing is that we inhale oxygen and exhale carbon dioxide (CO_2). We are taught to believe oxygen is useful, and CO_2 is not. However, oxygen can be toxic and corrosive, while too little carbon dioxide can cause fainting, seizures, and even death. As with anything in the body, it's about achieving balance or homeostasis to maintain an internal environment that supports life.

The oxygen in the air we breathe must take a long journey to get to our cells. The human body contains around 60,000 miles of blood vessels through which oxygen travels[8]. For much of this extraordinary distance, you would expect that we have little or no control over what happens to the oxygen we inhale, but the way we breathe in and out has a dramatic effect on what happens next. We explore this further in the next chapter. With a correct understanding of breathing, we can

---

7 Sherwood, Lauralee. *Fundamentals of Physiology: A Human Perspective*. Cengage Learning, 2005.
8 "Heart & Blood Vessels: Blood Flow | Cleveland Clinic." Published 2000. my.cleveland clinic.org/health/articles/17059-how-does-blood-flow-through-your-body (accessed July 2, 2022).

influence blood circulation and oxygen delivery to the cells and organs, as well as many facets of our mental and physical health.

When we teach Oxygen Advantage® breathing exercises, we are interested in improving breathing patterns from three dimensions:

1. **Biochemical (or metabolic)** – this refers to how the breath affects the balance of carbon dioxide in the body.
2. **Biomechanical** – this refers to the functioning of the diaphragm and other breathing muscles.
3. **Nervous System (or psycho-physiological)** – this is the connection between breathing and the autonomic nervous system, and it explains how stress and relaxation responses can be influenced through breathing rates.

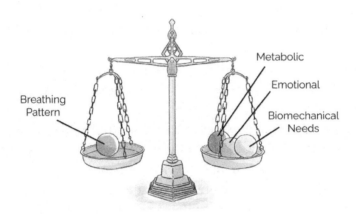

Optimal Breathing

In other words, to get an understanding of any breathing exercise, we need to ask three questions:

1. What does it do to the biochemical dimension?
2. What does it do to the biomechanical dimension?
3. What does it do to the nervous system?

In a broad sense, all breathing exercises are targeting one or more of the above dimensions, but in what way? Understanding this is the key to teaching breathing and it forms the basis of the Oxygen Advantage® method which we will share in this book. What's more, understanding this will allow you to finetune the breathing exercises to adequately target the dimensions in yourself and/or your students.

Dysfunctional Breathing & Stress

The optimal way to breathe is through the nose, in a light, slow and regular breathing pattern, driven by the diaphragm. Without realizing it, many people develop breathing patterns that are less than ideal. There's no denying that we live in an environment that is vastly different from our evolutionary norm. Chronic stress is at an all-time high and this affects our breathing. As a result, breathing pattern disorders are common in our modern world. Your body can start to get used to this altered inefficient breathing pattern without you even noticing.

Between 50% to 80% of adults have some form of dysfunctional breathing patterns.[9] And rates are reported to rise as high as 90% in athletes[10] and 75% in people with anxiety.[11] Females are more prone to poor breathing patterns than males, partly due to hormonal changes. The reported ratios of those with dysfunctional breathing vary from 2:1 females to males, to as high as 7:1 females to males.[12] Please see Chapter Six for further detail on breathing pattern disorder.

Many of us initially turn to yoga to reduce the impact of stress. However, there are signs that all is not well in the modern practice of yoga. Between 2001 and 2014, hospital emergency departments in

9 Kiesel K, et al. "Development of a Screening Protocol to Identify Individuals with Dysfunctional Breathing." *J Sports Phys Ther.* 2017 Oct;12(5):774-786.

10 Shimozawa Y, et al. "Point Prevalence of the Biomechanical Dimension of Dysfunctional Breathing Patterns Among Competitive Athletes." *J Strength Cond Res.* 2023 Feb 1;37(2):270-276.

11 Courtney, Rosalba. "Multi-dimensional model of dysfunctional breathing and integrative breathing therapy–commentary on the functions of breathing and its dysfunctions and their relationship to breathing therapy." *J Yoga Phys Ther* 6.4 (2016): 257.

12 Chaitow et al. "Multidisciplinary Approaches to Breathing Pattern Disorders." Churchill Livingstone. 2002 (Chapter 2, page 44).

the US treated 29,590 yoga-related injuries. Meanwhile, research has established a significant relationship between injury, dysfunctional movement, and dysfunctional breathing (from a biochemical or biomechanical standpoint). One 2014 study from The International Journal of Sports Physical Therapy states: "If breathing is not normalised, no other movement pattern can be."

All of this leads us to ask:

- Is there something more we could do for ourselves and our yoga students?
- Is there a way we can learn to directly reverse the stress response and support a healthier, more effective yoga practice?

Is there a breathing technique that will:

- Balance blood chemistry and encourage proper function of the breathing muscles?
- Optimise the benefits of yoga, on and off the mat, for better wellbeing?
- Support our efforts to build a healthier, fitter body for a longer, healthier life?

In our experience, the answer to all the above is "yes!".

Assessing your breathing

So how might you know if you have dysfunctional breathing patterns? Common signs include breathing through your mouth rather than your nose, noisy breathing, yawning or sighing regularly, breathing into your upper chest and waking up with a dry mouth.

You can assess the functionality of your breathing patterns using a simple breath hold measurement known as the Body Oxygen Level Test (BOLT). To take your BOLT, sit down and breathe normally for a few minutes. Then exhale normally through your nose and pinch your nose with fingers to stop breathing. Time in seconds how long you can hold your breath until you experience the first definite desire to breathe. When you resume breathing, the breath in should be normal – you shouldn't have to take in a big breath.

A BOLT score of over 25 seconds indicates functional breathing. A BOLT score of 40 seconds is the goal. In Chapter Four, we explore the BOLT in more detail. With the right breathing exercises, your breath hold time (and thus BOLT score) will likely increase by 3 or 4 seconds during the first few weeks. Within 5 or 6 weeks, breathing both on and off the mat will become easier and more stable.

The Challenges of Breathing in a Yoga Pose

Breathing regularly and keeping the breath soft during an asana practice is not easy. The diaphragm and many other breathing muscles work much harder than they do at rest. Many of us hope to gain control of our breath as we practice, with little real understanding of how to achieve this goal. First, we try to make sure our breathing is not disrupted. Over time, we expect the breath to soften and become easy. But for some practitioners, this never happens, even after years of practice, and this is because they are missing key information on how to breathe functionally.

To make sure that yoga is effective and beneficial for you and your students and that it doesn't produce any unwanted effects, there are some simple steps that you can take:

- Integrate functional breathing from three dimensions into your practice (this includes breathing through the nose at all times).
- Adjust your breathing speed and volume in line with your breathing capacity.
- Understand what causes air hunger and how to work with it.
- Learn to lead with your breathing, rather than forcing your breathing to match your physical practice.

We'll cover how to do these things in due course. But to take it right back to the basics, remember that the exercise-based physical practices of Western yoga are relatively new. Yogic breathing techniques are traditionally done in a seated posture. Yet, in the same way that we now expect pop stars to perform choreographed dance workouts while they sing and then wonder why they lip sync on stage, we expect ourselves to be able to breathe in a controlled way during flow yoga. And we expect this without first training or even understanding our breath.

Yes, we've all seen examples of yogis with phenomenal breath holding ability and incredible physical fitness. For example, the Ukrainian doctor and inventor of the Buteyko Method, Dr. Konstantin Buteyko, recorded a comfortable breath hold time of 180 seconds following a normal exhalation. This corresponded with a physical condition he described as "super endurance."[13]

You can also find videos on YouTube showing the yogi, B.K.S. Iyengar performing an almost 50-second inhalation. Similarly, in his book, *Taoism, the Road to Immortality*, John Blofeld describes yogis who held their breath for as many as a thousand seconds. But this is a "highly dangerous proceeding," he cautions, "for the yogically untrained."[14] These people were able to breathe very slowly and hold their breath for a long time because they had a reduced sensitivity to the build-up of carbon dioxide in the lungs and blood – as you will learn in the coming chapters.

Your Breathing Pattern is as Unique as You Are

Every one of us is unique. Your metabolic status, emotional state, and hormonal profile all affect your breath. This means that the breathing pattern your body needs will be different from that of anyone else reading the same paragraphs. Still, every human body is subject to the same scientific principles. The same techniques can be adapted to help

---

13 Altukhov, Sergei. *Doctor Buteyko's Discovery, Volume 1: The Destruction of the Laboratory.* Novosibirsk: Altmilla, 1993.
14 Blofeld, John. "Taoism--The Road to Immortality." *Philosophy East and West* 31.2 (1981).

each of us get more oxygen to the brain, alter the heart rate, change states of consciousness, and support functional movement in both everyday life and asana practice.

Modern life often gets the blame for the unwanted health challenges we face. It's true that our lifestyles are very different from those of our ancestors, even just a few generations back. This affects our breathing. However, our twenty-first century lifestyle offers as many opportunities as it does challenges. If we embrace these challenges and adapt, we can achieve our highest potential. Functional breathing can help make us resilient against stress, less reactive, and better able to respond to the stress of modern living.

IMPORTANT: SAFETY FIRST

Breath training, like any other activity that challenges the body, comes with some risks. To stay safe, it is always advisable to work with an experienced instructor, particularly if undertaking practices that involve hyperventilation. The Oxygen Advantage® app, available on Android and Apple devices includes a free daily plan, exercises, and a list of trained instructors. Whether working independently with this book as your guide, or with an instructor, build up your breathing practice gradually, initially performing each exercise for no more than two minutes. After each exercise, take care to recover your breath, ensuring breathing and heart rate have returned to normal before continuing with another exercise.

Be particularly aware that the breathing practises which carry most risk are hyperventilation paired with extreme breath holds. Hyperventilation is "big" breathing. It is often described as breathing hard or deep. This breathing pattern forms the basis of several popular breathing techniques. Unfortunately, it is also already present in many people with anxiety, cardiovascular problems, and chronic fatigue.

Hyperventilation and long breath holds stress the body and mind. No doubt, they can be helpful for many people. But, often, what we need to do is to down-regulate our stress response and activate recovery. For someone who is already hyperventilating chronically, it doesn't make much sense to deliberately increase breathing volume. Instead, the intent should be to normalise the volume of air you breathe – every minute, every hour, every day.

Hyperventilation with long breath holding can be described as an "extrovert" breathing technique. It's the type of practice that draws a lot of attention. However, just as the introvert personality has value for society, so do "introvert" breathing techniques. They are subtle and quieter – and incredibly effective. There is nothing for people to see, but they bring a stillness in body and mind. This is powerful. It develops inner strength without a bold outward display.

Please note – if you have any neurological, cardiovascular, metabolic (such as diabetes), or respiratory conditions, you must

be extra cautious when practicing. Do not practice long breath holds or hyperventilation. If you suffer with any chronic or acute health conditions, you must **consult your doctor** before embarking on any breathing practice. Even with medical approval, breathing exercises should first be approached with the supervision of an instructor.

Finally, if you are a yoga instructor, it is important that you ensure your students are in good health before offering breath training guidance. If they have a medical condition, advise them to talk to their medical provider before implementing any new breath training program.

What to Do if Focusing on the Breath is Challenging

We must be realistic here – when your mind is in turmoil, it is very challenging, and often frustrating, to pay attention to your breath. But don't worry. You can still get all the benefits from breath training.

If you are having difficulty paying attention to your breath, simply go for a walk or practice yoga with your mouth closed. Don't pay any attention to your breathing. Simply breathe through your nose and walk or move at a pace where you feel a comfortable degree of breathlessness. This alone will help to improve your breathing from a biochemical and biomechanical standpoint.

You can also practice breathing recovery exercises, which involve holding your breath for short periods of time during rest or light movement. This won't require much, if indeed any, attention to be placed on the breath. Simply focus on the count.

Breathing in through the nose and humming gently on the exhale slows down the speed of the exhalation to help activate the body's rest and digest response. This too is a great exercise to help improve breathing without having to place attention on the breath.

Short-term, the goal is to be able to change states by altering our breathing in order to understand the power we have over our own physiology. This is a tool that is rarely discussed or used to its full advantage – as we can see from the number of people who live with daily anxiety, high stress, and panic disorder. Ultimately, one long-term goal of breathing exercises is to give us control over our mind, so we become less reactive to difficult situations. As a result, we come full circle and become more able to pay conscious attention to our breathing.

BENEFITS OF YOGA & FUNCTIONAL BREATHING

Before we explore the science of breathing, why it's important, and how it relates to yoga, let's take a moment to think about why we do yoga in the first place. Whether you're reading this to deepen your own practice or to offer better advice to your students, it's worth acknowledging what brought you here and whether that motivation is different now than it was at the outset.

More than 90% of students first come to yoga for health, stress relief, flexibility, and physical fitness. However, for 66% of students and 85%

of yoga teachers,[15] it becomes a path to self-actualization and spiritual growth. In all these areas, the breath is a gateway to possibility. Used correctly, it provides deeper insight, greater mental clarity, optimal physical movement, and a means to rid the body and mind of stress.

As yoga has grown in popularity, there has been a corresponding increase in research studies. Scientists have examined the impact of yoga on chronic disease risk and diseases, mental health, and physical wellbeing.[16] A quick search of the online research library, PubMed, shows nearly 7,049 studies involving yoga in 2021, compared with just 39 two decades earlier. At the same time, scientific interest in breathing exercises has also increased – 5,205 studies were published between 2012 and 2022. We are entering a new paradigm in personal health and wellness. It's a great time to learn more about our yoga and breathing practices.

Some of those many and various research studies have found that yoga can decrease heart rate and systolic and diastolic blood pressure. It can relieve symptoms of mental disorders including anxiety, panic disorder, depression, schizophrenia, and obsessive-compulsive disorder. It has a beneficial impact on blood glucose levels in people with diabetes, and can lessen the symptoms of menopause, kidney disease, and multiple sclerosis. It improves fitness too, enhancing flexibility, dynamic muscle strength, and endurance.[17]

When it comes to breathing, one study of healthy young adults reported an increase in maximal oxygen uptake of 7% after practising yoga twice a week for two months.[18] Maximal oxygen uptake (or VO_2 max) is the amount of oxygen your body consumes during intensive

15 "Why Does Anyone Do Yoga, Anyway?" *Psychology Today Ireland*. 06. Published 2015. http://www.psychologytoday.com/ie/blog/urban-survival/201506/why-does-anyone-do-yoga-anyway.

16 Forseth, Bethany, Hunter Stacy D. "Range of Yoga Intensities from Savasana to Sweating: A Systematic Review." *Journal of Physical Activity and Health* 17.2 (2020): 242-249.

17 Gordon, Julianne. "The Metabolic Demand of a Vinyasa Yoga Session." *Dissertation*. University of Saskatchewan, 2014.

18 Tran MD, Holly RG, Lashbrook J, Amsterdam EA. Effects of Hatha Yoga Practice on the Health-Related Aspects of Physical Fitness. *Prev Cardiol*. 2001;4(4):165-170.

exercise. An improvement in VO_2 max is highly beneficial for any athlete who wants to push the upper limits of their performance.

As we noted, 66% of those who do yoga turn to it as a path to self-actualization and spiritual growth. In a spiritual sense, yoga is about transcending judgement and learning to be in the now. On a day-to-day basis, it is impossible to be present, for yourself or others, when your mind is racing into the future or dwelling on past events or conversations. When it comes to being truly present, the breath is a powerful anchor to the present moment, with the ability to change the body's physiology to bring stillness to the mind.

As we will learn in the subsequent chapters of this book, we can use our breath to influence our physiology and change our states. A routine of simple breathing exercises and cultivating healthy everyday breathing can create physiological shifts that move you out of stress or anxiety states in a proactive, accessible, and reliable way. In fact, if your mind is busy, or difficult emotions are near the surface, breathing exercises can help, whereas mindfulness or meditation may initially be too challenging or confronting. When the nervous system is balanced, the mind is naturally quieter. With improved breathing patterns and sleep, agitation of the mind reduces. Only then is it easier to be breath, body, and mind aware.

Practical Reasons for Understanding the Science of Breathing

There are purely practical reasons to understand the science behind breathing when practicing or teaching yoga. During an asana practice, the metabolic needs of your body change significantly. Your cardiovascular system must adjust to meet the demands of your heart, breathing muscles, and active skeletal muscles. Breathing must adapt too, as oxygen extraction from the blood to the working muscles increases.[19] Your physical balance

---

19 Korthuis, Ronald J. "Exercise Hyperemia and Regulation of Tissue Oxygenation During Muscular Activity." In *Skeletal Muscle Circulation.* San Rafael, CA: Morgan and Claypool Life Sciences, 2011.

depends on good diaphragm function, and dysfunctional breathing leaves you more vulnerable to injury.

From a metabolic perspective, you may be surprised to know that fast-flowing styles of yoga including ashtanga are classified in one review as "light intensity" exercise, and vinyasa yoga as only "moderate intensity,"[20] though this classification depends on the speed at which, for example, sun salutations are performed.[21] However, this ease in practice demands strength, stamina, balance, and persistent practice. Standing poses, inversions, and backbends use more oxygen than seated or supine poses. Intensive sequences such as sun salutations will require the heart to pump faster, and the more vinyasas or sun salutations are performed during practice, the more energy is expended.[22]

We could second-guess, analyse, and question every move we make, but what we really want to know is this: can we improve our yoga practice by understanding the science of breathing? Absolutely! (It's much simpler than it looks at first glance . . .)

OUR RECOMMENDATION FOR NAVIGATING THIS BOOK

This book is for all yogis who want to improve their breathing and yoga instructors who want to support their students in establishing healthy breathing patterns for healthier lives. Unfortunately, commonly repeated ideas about how to do that are vague. "Breathe deeper." "Practise conscious breathing all the time!" "Use the diaphragm." There is nothing inherently wrong with these ideas, but there's nothing specific about them either. If you want to make effective change, you need something more definitive that you can track.

20   Forseth, Bethany, Hunter Stacy D. "Range of Yoga Intensities from Savasana to Sweating: A Systematic Review." *Journal of Physical Activity and Health* 17.2 (2020): 242-249.
21   Pryor, J. Luke, et al. "Metabolic Demands of Yoga at Varying Tempos and Compared with Walking." *Journal of Physical Activity and Health* 16.7 (2019): 575-580.
22   Gordon, Julianne. "The Metabolic Demand of a Vinyasa Yoga Session." *Dissertation.* University of Saskatchewan, 2014.

We feel it's imperative to have an understanding of the science of the breath and how it affects the body before going out and utilising or sharing these techniques. As such, we have dedicated several sections of the book to the science of the breath. Some of the science in this book may feel a little heavy. At times, the topics move away from the yogic tradition. Try to keep an open mind. To appreciate any breathing technique, whatever its roots, we first need to understand the effect it has on the body. Science allows us to gain this understanding.

As Daniel Simpson says in *The Truth of Yoga*, "Everyone is free to create a new version of yoga philosophy. However, it seems wise to engage with tradition before going freestyle."[23] The same can be said when it comes to understanding the science behind your practices: it is wise to understand the practical science before "going freestyle."

We do, however, appreciate that not everyone is excited by science and if certain sections of the book feel too heavy, feel free to skip that section. Most of this book can be read out of sequence and you can refer to the "Quick Start Reference" guide at the beginning of the book, to locate what interests you the most.

In the Appendices, we have included a series of interviews with Oxygen Advantage® Instructors, each discussing their journey to breath training and how they integrate the OA® techniques in their practice. The interviews provide a rich insight into the practice of functional breathing in varying personal practices of yoga, Aurveyda, Qigong and chiropractic therapy. We have also included a section on breathing for cold exposure practice. While this is not of immediate relevance to yoga, we thought many readers may be interested in the topic.

A final thought for this first chapter

Our hope is that this book will inform enough people about the power and importance of functional breathing and breath holding, that there

---

23 Simpson, Daniel. *The Truth of Yoga: A Comprehensive Guide to Yoga's History, Texts, Philosophy, and Practices.* North Point Press, 2021.

will be a breath revolution in the yoga world – a bold aspiration! We envision yoga studios offering not only asana classes but also breath training classes that teach students how to improve breathing from a multidimensional perspective. If you own a yoga studio, this could open up a whole new avenue for you. If you are a yoga instructor, incorporating Oxygen Advantage® into your classes will make you stand out from other instructors and help you to really make a difference in your students' lives.

Now, let's dive into Chapter Two – *The Science of Breathing*.

THE SCIENCE OF BREATHING

In Chapter One we mentioned the importance of understanding and integrating functional breathing from three dimensions: biochemistry, biomechanics, and the nervous system. As a reminder, the biochemistry of breathing refers to the balance of blood gas carbon dioxide (CO_2). The biomechanics of breathing refers to the functioning of the breathing muscles, including the diaphragm. The nervous system (or psychophysiological) dimension of breathing encompasses the two-way connection between breathing and the autonomic nervous system.

THE BIOCHEMISTRY OF BREATHING

There are two reasons why the biochemistry of breathing is so important:

1. Oxygen(O_2) is essential for life. But many people aren't aware that oxygen's vital functions in the human body depend on two other chemical compounds: carbon dioxide and nitric oxide.
2. Many, many functions in the body are affected directly or indirectly by breathing. Your heart rate, metabolism, circulation, immune system, and even your ability to release toxins and body fat, all rely on healthy, functional breathing.

Because of this, breathing biochemistry has knock-on effects on multiple organs and systems within and throughout your body; essentially opening the door for wellness or disease.

Oxygen (O_2)

Every cell in the human body uses biochemical reactions (cellular respiration) to stay alive. This process, called aerobic respiration, takes place in tiny organelles, called mitochondria, inside each cell in the body. Aerobic respiration uses oxygen to convert glucose, amino acids, and fatty acids from food into the energy storage molecule, Adenosine Triphosphate or ATP.

Human cells can also produce energy anaerobically. This happens when we need a sudden burst of energy or when oxygen may be less available, for instance, during intensive exercise. Professional sprinters must rely on anaerobic respiration during a race, as they do not have time to breathe and fully replenish the oxygen used. People suffering with conditions like obstructive sleep apnea, breathing disorders, and chronic fatigue also regularly operate in an anaerobic state. They experience dis-ease because a large and complex organism like a human being needs a high level of energy to stay alive.

Aerobic respiration produces 15 times the energy of anaerobic respiration.[24] Scientists have only identified one animal on Earth that does not breathe – an almost single-celled parasite that feeds on fish. In fact, it is believed that this unusual creature may import the missing ATP directly from its host.

Because it is so essential for life (unless you're a single-celled fish parasite), humans have evolved to ensure oxygen is always available. Therefore, the blood is almost fully saturated with oxygen, at around 95% to 99%. Once inhaled, oxygen passes from the lungs to the blood.

---

24 "Could We Have Evolved Without Oxygen?" *Science Focus.* http://www.sciencefocus. com/the-human-body/could-we-have-evolved-without-oxygen/ (Accessed July 2, 2022).

Nearly all (98%) of it travels around the body in a protein in red blood cells called haemoglobin, while 2% is dissolved directly into the blood plasma. You can easily test how much oxygen is currently circulating in your blood using a pulse oximeter, an inexpensive, non-invasive device that attaches to the tip of your finger.

So, just how does all that oxygen get from the blood to the mitochondria, where it can be used?

Oxygen (O2):

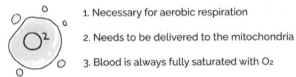

1. Necessary for aerobic respiration

2. Needs to be delivered to the mitochondria

3. Blood is always fully saturated with O2

Carbon Dioxide (CO_2)

Inhaled air contains 21% oxygen, 79% nitrogen, and just 0.4% CO_2. Exhaled air contains 5% CO_2. This difference occurs because CO_2 is produced in the body as a by-product of cellular respiration. The more energy we produce, the more CO_2 is released. During rest, CO_2 production slows down. During exercise, it speeds up.

The CO_2 we produce is carried back to the lungs, either dissolved in the blood or in the haemoglobin molecules that were carrying oxygen. There it is extracted by the alveoli (small air sacs where gas exchange takes place) for us to breathe out excess CO_2.

School science lessons leave many of us with the idea that carbon dioxide is a toxic waste gas and serves no function in the body. The most readily available online information will confirm this belief. A quick Google search of, "carbon dioxide waste gas," will lead to results about CO_2 poisoning. This oversimplification of the role of CO_2 underpins and perpetuates the common misunderstanding of breathing.

Five Important Facts About CO_2:

1. **CO_2 is necessary for oxygenation.** Without it, even if our blood is fully saturated with oxygen, our bodies cannot adequately access the oxygen to produce energy. We've already described how O_2 is carried around the blood in haemoglobin in red blood cells. The next important piece in the puzzle is that CO_2 is the *key* or *catalyst* that unlocks O_2 from the haemoglobin, releasing it to the cells.

    When blood CO_2 is low, the bond between O_2 and haemoglobin becomes stronger – which means that your body can't access the oxygen it needs. This is called the Bohr effect, named after the Danish biochemist Christian Bohr. In 1904, Bohr wrote that when CO_2 increases in the blood, the blood becomes more acidic and the affinity of haemoglobin for O_2 decreases. (This leads us to the second truth.)

2. **CO_2 is important for pH (acidity/alkalinity) balance in the body.** In a healthy person, the body contains a constant level of CO_2 (around 40 mmHg). This helps maintain a blood pH of 7.35 to 7.45.[25] This narrow margin represents optimal functioning for the human body.

    Breathing exercises can alter blood pH for short periods of time to cause adaptations. Breathing fast and hard causes a lowering of CO_2 in the blood to increase blood pH, while breathing light or breath holding increases carbon dioxide to lower blood pH.

3. **CO_2 provides your brain with its primary stimulus to breathe.** The brain monitors O_2 levels, but it is much more sensitive to CO_2. When CO_2 increases in the blood, breathing speeds up. Faster breathing gets rid of more CO_2, so blood levels of CO_2 return to normal. If we are overly sensitive to the accumulation of CO_2 in the blood, our breathing is habitually faster and harder. This can produce disease states. Chronic hyperventilation – consistently breathing more air than the body needs – reduces levels of CO_2 in the blood. This is linked to many acute and chronic health conditions.

---

25 Brinkman JE, Sharma S. Respiratory Alkalosis. In: *StatPearls*. Treasure Island (FL): StatPearls Publishing; July 25, 2022.

4. **CO_2 dilates smooth muscle.** Smooth muscle is found throughout the body and performs many functions. In her book, *Restoring Prana*, Robin Rothenberg describes how some of her clients experienced relief from constipation, mildly elevated blood pressure, gastroesophageal reflux, and breathlessness simply by changing their breathing patterns to increase CO_2.[26]

5. **CO_2 reduces oxidative stress, decreasing inflammation.** Despite our first impression that it is a toxin, the free radicals that cause oxidative stress and contribute to ageing target the mitochondria where ATP is produced. CO_2 acts as an antioxidant, protecting the cells that produce our life-giving energy.[27]

6. **CO_2 helps to activate the body's relaxation response by stimulating the vagus nerve.** This helps balance the body and mind, to make you more resilient.[28]

Carbon Dioxide (CO_2)

1. It's a byproduct of aerobic respiration

2. It has an acidic effect

3. Due to the Bohr effect, it is needed for O_2 to enter the cells

4. It plays a key role in the breathing cycle

5. It decreases inflammation

6. It promotes relaxation

A method called capnometry is used to indirectly measure levels of blood CO_2 in laboratory experiments and medical settings. However, it

26 Rothenberg, Robin L. *Restoring Prana: A Therapeutic Guide to Prāṇāyāma and Healing Through the Breath for Yoga Therapists, Yoga Teachers, and Healthcare Practitioners.* Singing Dragon, 2019.

27 Vasela, A., and J. Wilhem. "The Role of Carbon Dioxide in Free Radical Reactions of the Organism. *Physiological Research* 51.4 (2002): 335-339.

28 Singh, Umesh Pal. "Evidence-Based Role of Hypercapnia and Exhalation Phase in Vagus Nerve Stimulation: Insights Into Hypercapnic Yoga Breathing." *Journal of Yoga & Physical Therapy* 7.3 (2017).

is possible to get an idea of whether your CO_2 levels are higher or lower than normal based on a few common symptoms:

- When CO_2 is elevated, you will feel air hunger (the need to take in more air, or the feeling you can't take a big enough breath). You may feel suffocated or want to breathe faster.
- When CO_2 is low, you can feel light-headed or dizzy or even experience epileptic seizures.

While you can't directly measure CO_2, it is possible to measure your sensitivity to CO_2 using a simple measure of breathlessness called the BOLT, which you can find in Chapter Four.

Nitric Oxide

When you breathe through your nose, nitric oxide (NO) is produced in the sinuses surrounding your nasal airway and carried into your lungs.

Of the three gases important for respiration, we know the least about NO. This is hardly surprising, given that the existence of NO in the exhaled breath of humans was only discovered in 1991.[29] Then, in 1995, scientists found that NO is produced in the sinuses around the nose and in the nasal cavity.[30]

The many functions of NO are still being discovered – the gas has a half-life of only a few seconds, making it difficult to track in laboratory settings.[31] (A half-life is the time it takes for the gas to reduce by half.) However, we do know it acts as a neurotransmitter, a hormone, and even a free radical.

29 Selimoglu, Erol. "Nitric Oxide in Health and Disease from the Point of View of the Otorhinolaryngologist." *Current Pharmaceutical Design* 11.23 (2005): 3051-3060.

30 Lundberg, J., *et al.* High nitric oxide production in human paranasal sinuses. *Nat Med* 1, 370–373 (1995).

31 Ricciardolo, Fabio Luigi Massimo. "Multiple Roles of Nitric Oxide in the Airways." *Thorax* 58.2 (2003): 175-182.

NO also sterilises inhaled air, directly supporting your immune system. It has anti-bacterial, anti-allergenic, anti-fungal, and even anti-viral properties, preventing viruses from replicating in common airborne diseases like flu and COVID-19. That, by itself, is reason enough to breathe through your nose!

NO dilates blood vessels in the lungs, performing a vital role in helping oxygen reach the blood and can lower blood pressure.[32]

You can harness the superpowers of NO simply by breathing through your nose. In fact, "the concentration of NO originating from the nose is 100 times higher than in the lower airways."[33]

Nitric Oxide (NO)

1. It's produced primarily in the nose

2. It sterilizes the air we inhale

3. It dilates blood vessels, and helps oxygenate the blood

4. It's a neurotransmitter and a signaling molecule of the immune system

We think it's mind-blowing that something as simple as the *way* we breathe allows us to manipulate our body's levels of O_2, CO_2, and NO, to produce specific results.

While it is unclear how much the ancient yogis knew about respiratory biochemistry, prāṇāyāma exercises were developed to achieve the desirable physical and psychological effects of altered blood gas levels. Many centuries later, the Oxygen Advantage® method was developed for the same purpose.

32 Hermann, M., et al. "Nitric oxide in hypertension." *The Journal of Clinical Hypertension* (2006) 8, 17-29.

33 Shapiro, A.J., et al. "Nasal nitric oxide measurement in primary ciliary dyskinesia. A technical paper on standardized testing protocols." *Annals of the American Thoracic Society* 17.2 (2020): e1-e12.

THE JOURNEY OF OXYGEN IN THE BODY

The journey of oxygen to the cells happens in four stages:

1. External respiration
2. Internal respiration
3. Cellular respiration
4. Mitochondrial respiration

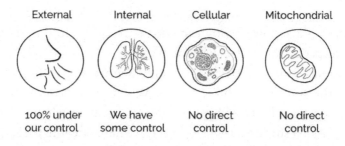

External	Internal	Cellular	Mitochondrial
100% under our control	We have some control	No direct control	No direct control

External Respiration: Functions of the Nose

Of the four stages of breathing, we have the most control over external respiration. By consciously choosing *how* we breathe air into the body, we can influence what happens next. External respiration impacts our health in diverse ways, from mouth hygiene to brain function, and circulation, to sleep. Right from the outset, it affects the quality and the quantity of air we inhale.

You inhale air into your lungs either through your nose or mouth. The breathing route you choose affects your body in many ways.

The air you breathe naturally varies from one moment to the next. Sometimes it is warm, sometimes cold. It may be humid, dry, heavily air conditioned, or full of dust particles, pollutants, or allergens. To keep the lungs safe so they can fulfil their role in getting oxygen to the blood, air needs to be filtered, humidified, and warmed.

What's Wrong with Mouth Breathing?

We still have a long way to go before oxygen reaches our cells, but first let's look at mouth breathing. If you've read James Nestor's bestseller, *Breath: The New Science of a Lost Art,*[34] or flipped through the pages of *The Breathing Cure* by Patrick McKeown,[35] you already will have a pretty good idea that habitual mouth breathing is bad for you. While researching for his book, Nestor performed a series of experiments on himself, where he plugged his own nose to force himself to breathe through his mouth for ten days. Before long, he was groggy, stressed, irritable, and experiencing sleep apnea – a serious disorder in which breathing stops periodically during sleep, causing oxygen levels to plunge.

The mouth is best used as a backup when nasal breathing cannot support the body's metabolic needs. When your nose is blocked, for instance, your body will get air into the body in whatever way is available. As Nestor experienced, when humans breathe through the mouth long-term (or even relatively short-term) there are a series of unpleasant consequences. The most obvious is that you don't get the benefits of nose breathing . . . but it doesn't stop there.

Mouth breathing generally involves breathing a larger volume of air than your body needs. *Over-breathing* in this way is considered a disease state and contributes to a huge range of common physical and mental health problems, including insomnia, sleep apnea, cardiovascular disease, sexual dysfunction, headaches, back pain, brain fog, PMS, nasal congestion . . . and the list goes on.

Mouth breathing causes saliva to dry up,[36] creating acidity that dissolves your tooth enamel.[37] It contributes to dental decay, excessive

34 Nestor, James. *Breath: The New Science of a Lost Art*. Penguin, 2010.

35 McKeown, Patrick. *The Breathing Cure: Develop New Habits for a Healthier, Happier, and Longer Life*. Humanix Books, 2021.

36 Triana, B.E. et al. "Mouth Breathing and Its Relationship to Some Oral and Medical Conditions; Physiopathological Mechanisms Involved." *Revista Habanera de Ciencias Medicas* 15.2 (2016): 200-212.

37 Choi, J. E., et al. "Intraoral PH and Temperature During Sleep with and Without Mouth Breathing." *Journal of Oral Rehabilitation* 43.5 (2016): 356-363.

bacterial growth, and smelly breath. In turn, poor mouth hygiene leads to bad gut health, and so the problem can permeate every system in the body.

Many of us are accustomed to breathing through the nose during asana practice. Indeed, it's a familiar feature of most styles of yoga that breathing should be only through the nostrils. But how many of us take this idea into our everyday lives? Healthy breathing is through the nose, 24 hours a day, during exercise, rest, and sleep.

The bottom-line is this: the way you inhale air into your body has a powerful effect on what happens inside the body.

Air Conditioning for the Whole Body

When you inhale through your nose, air is efficiently heated to within a few degrees of core body temperature. The nose contains a high number of capillaries that warm the air as it enters the nostrils. Nasal nitric oxide contributes to thermoregulation in the nasal cavity by dilating nasal capillaries.[38] The result is that air temperature increases by more than 10°C between the nostrils and the back of the nose.[39] When you exhale through the nose, the air is cooled, and its warmth is reabsorbed by the nasal mucosa. This prevents you from losing too much body heat.[40] (A comprehensive list of the functions of the nose is available from OxygenAdvantage.com)

In contrast, if you breathe through your mouth, the air you take in arrives in the lungs cold. This causes the blood vessels and capillaries surrounding the lungs to constrict, reducing the exchange of oxygen

---

38 Holden, William E., et al. "Temperature Conditioning of Nasal Air: Effects of Vasoactive Agents and Involvement of Nitric Oxide." *Journal of Applied Physiology* 87.4 (1999): 1260-1265.

39 Elad, David, Michael Wolf, and Tilman Keck. "Air-conditioning in the Human Nasal Cavity." *Respiratory Physiology & Neurobiology* 163.1-3 (2008): 121-127.

40 Holden, William E., et al. "Temperature Conditioning of Nasal Air: Effects of Vasoactive Agents and Involvement of Nitric Oxide." *Journal of Applied Physiology* 87.4 (1999): 1260-1265.

into the blood. The negative impact of cold air in the lungs depends on how much air you breathe. When airflow increases, the cooling effect of inhaled air increases too.

In 2018, scientists in Italy made a direct connection between over-breathing and cold-induced airway damage. They reported:

> *Breathing of + 20° C air at 15 litres per minute decreases the tracheal temperature to 34° C whereas breathing similar air at 100 litres per min decreases this temperature to 31° C.* [41]

Breathing a large volume of air produces similar negative effects as inhaling cold air, even when the air is temperate. When we explore prāṇāyāma techniques, we'll discover how certain breathing exercises can alter body temperature. Changes in breathing control and thermoregulation directly affect each other. It is important to understand that nasal breathing keeps the temperature inside your body within a healthy range. In high temperatures, such as a sweltering hot yoga studio, nasal breathing even helps keep your brain cool. [42]

Nose breathing also prevents dehydration. When you breathe out through your mouth, 42% more moisture is lost from the body than when exhaling through the nose.[43] The upper part of your respiratory system is moist. This humid atmosphere captures dust, dirt, bacteria, and viruses before they reach your lungs. Because nasal exhalation preserves the humidity of the airway, it indirectly supports your immune system.

41 D'Amato, Maria, et al. "The Impact of Cold on the Respiratory Tract and Its Consequences to Respiratory Health." *Clinical and Translational Allergy* 8.1 (2018): 1-8.

42 Zila, I., Calkovska, A. "Effects of Elevated Body Temperature on Control of Breathing." *Acta Medica Martiniana* 11.1 (2011): 24.

43 Svensson, S. et al. "Increased Net Water Loss by Oral Compared to Nasal Expiration in Healthy Subjects." *Rhinology* 44 (2006).1: 74.

How Much Air Should You Breathe? Air Volume

Because the nose is smaller than the mouth, nasal breathing adds resistance to inhaling and exhaling, reducing the volume of air you exchange with the environment. During exercise, this resistance increases significantly.[44] This extra resistance has been shown to improve lung capacity (the volume of air in your lungs when you make a maximum-effort inhalation). A good lung capacity potentially means more oxygen is available and breathing is more efficient. Contrary to what we are often told, large inhalations through the mouth may result in *decreased* lung capacity and *less* oxygen getting to the blood.

Try it for yourself – take a full breath of air through your mouth. Place your hands on your ribcage to check whether the air enters the upper or lower parts of the lungs. Wait a minute or so and repeat, this time breathing through your nose. The resistance imposed by the nose will allow the air to enter more slowly, so it has more time to circulate throughout the lungs, and for the body to extract oxygen from that air.

When we talk in yoga classes about the importance of keeping the breath light, a few eyebrows always raise. So many of us are taught to believe that more is better when it comes to breathing, even though we're quick to accept that more isn't better when it comes to food. Yet, for breathing, there is simply *no* evidence to support this "more is better" belief.

On the contrary, there is an optimal breathing volume, and anything that deviates from it is considered pathological – the cause or effect of illness. The volume of air we breathe is so significant that it is detailed in every book about the physical processes and disease states of breathing.

So, what is an optimal breathing volume? The volume of air you need is determined primarily by your metabolic state. When your body needs more energy, for instance during exercise (or more long-term,

---

44   Trevisan, ME, et al. "Diaphragmatic Amplitude and Accessory Inspiratory Muscle Activity in Nasal and Mouth-Breathing Adults: A Cross-Sectional Study." *Journal of Electromyography and Kinesiology* 25.3 (2015): 463-468.

when you're pregnant), your demand for oxygen increases. When you sit still on your mat or lie down in savasana, you need less oxygen.

During normal breathing, your breathing volume should match your metabolic needs. If you are breathing *more* air than you require, you are *hyperventilating*, and this results in a lowering of CO_2 in the lungs and blood. If you do this habitually, you may have something called hyperventilation syndrome (or chronic hyperventilation). This can occur in response to trauma, stress, perfectionism, and many other factors. It is very common for people to hyperventilate and not know they are doing it. On the other hand, if you breathe *less* air than you require, such as during sleep apnea, you are *hypoventilating*, resulting in an increased amount of CO_2 in the blood.

Simply put, optimal breathing is the breathing pattern that meets your current biochemical (metabolic), biomechanical, and nervous system demands.

Minute Volume

Minute volume is the volume of air that is inhaled and exhaled from the lungs during one minute. This is calculated by multiplying the respiratory rate (the number of breaths per minute) by the tidal volume (the volume of air drawn into the lungs during one breath).

$$RR * TV = MV$$

Normal ventilation for a resting adult is between five and eight litres per minute. Tidal volumes can vary from 500ml to 600ml, with respiratory rates of twelve to fourteen breaths per minute.

Medical textbooks describe normal minute volume during rest as between four and six litres of air per minute. During light physical exercise, minute ventilation can double, and during intense physical exercise minute volume can be as high as 150 or more litres per minute.

During an acute panic attack, your respiratory rate and especially the tidal volume increases, leading to excessive minute volume. While doctors are aware of the dangers of *acute* hyperventilation, little

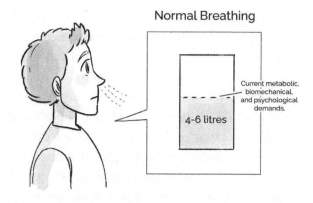

Normal Breathing

Current metabolic, biomechanical, and psychological demands.

4-6 litres

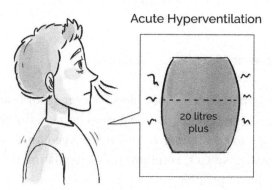

Acute Hyperventilation

20 litres plus

attention is paid to *chronic* hyperventilation. While your breathing may not look exaggerated, chronic hyperventilation is common and will have negative effects on mind and body.

Supporting Internal Respiration

As well as performing important "air conditioning" functions, nose breathing decreases dead space, even when you breathe a lot of air fast.[45] Dead space is air that is inhaled but doesn't get down into the alveoli,

---

45 Moller, Winfried, et al. "Nasal High Flow Reduces Dead Space." 122.1 (2017): 191-197.

the small air sacs in the lungs where the exchange of oxygen and carbon dioxide actually takes place. This is normally assumed to be 150 ml. Of every breath that is drawn into the lungs, the final 150 ml of air remains in the nasal cavity, throat, trachea, bronchi, and first 16 branches of the airways. This has implications in terms of breathing. It means faster breathing is less economical than slow breathing. The less air that remains in dead space, the more oxygen that is available from every inhale.

Nose breathing also increases diaphragm movement and strength,[46] and helps to ensure the tongue sits in its proper resting position, where it will not hinder the airway. It also results in higher levels of CO_2 and NO in the airways. Both gases dilate blood vessels and keep the airway open, supporting O_2 on the next stage of its journey.

Why Your Tolerance to CO_2 Matters

The level of carbon dioxide in your blood triggers your brain's drive to breathe. When CO_2 increases, the breathing centre in the brain signals to the diaphragm to contract. It is CO_2, not oxygen, that provides this stimulus to breathe, so CO_2 is important in regulating the speed and volume at which you breathe.

Carbon dioxide is also important for regulating the acidity or alkalinity of the blood. When there is too much CO_2 in the blood, it becomes too acidic for a short period of time. The kidneys compensate by retaining bicarbonate, which normalises blood pH and helps improve buffering capacity. When you breathe harder and faster, CO_2 levels decrease in the blood, making it more alkaline. To balance this alkalosis, your body gets rid of the alkaline buffer, bicarbonate, through the kidneys. This leads to an imbalance of calcium and magnesium, and can reduce your bicarbonate reserves, making you more susceptible to the symptoms of elevated CO_2.

---

46 Trevisan, Maria Elaine, et al. "Diaphragmatic Amplitude and Accessory Inspiratory Muscle Activity in Nasal and Mouth-Breathing Adults: A Cross-Sectional Study." *Journal of Electromyography and Kinesiology* 25.3 (2015): 463-468.

If your body is very sensitive to changes in CO_2, you will experience breathlessness and feel the need to breathe more air. You'll feel constant air hunger, and the disrupting levels of CO_2 will keep you in a constant negative cycle of over-breathing and breathlessness. One of the things that separates outstanding endurance athletes from the rest of us is a heightened tolerance to CO_2.[47]

Like most things in human physiology, the body works best when CO_2 is within a certain range. Too much or too little, and there's a domino effect on other systems. End-tidal carbon dioxide (etCO$_2$) is the pressure of CO_2 at the end of an exhaled breath and represents blood CO_2 levels. EtCO$_2$ in a healthy adult should be, on average, around 40 mmHg.[48] This will support the supply of oxygen to the cells and aerobic respiration. You can achieve this by breathing softly through your nose.

Internal Respiration: The Role of the Diaphragm

Now, let's return to the journey of O_2 in the body and follow the oxygen molecules into your lungs and on into the cells.

When you breathe in, air travels down your windpipe (trachea). The trachea splits off into branches. These end with the tiny air sacs where the lungs and blood exchange O_2 and CO_2. These air sacs, called alveoli, have a combined surface area of 70 to 100 square metres.

Inhaling occurs when muscles including your diaphragm and external intercostals (the small muscles between each of your ribs) contract. Exhaling is largely passive, happening when your breathing muscles relax. As your diaphragm contracts on inhalation, it moves into the abdomen, pulling air into the lungs. The lungs inflate in every

---

47 Woorons, X., et al. "Moderate Exercise in Hypoxia Induces a Greater Arterial Desaturation in Trained Than Untrained Men." *Scandinavian Journal of Medicine & Science in Sports* 17.4 (2007): 431-436.

48 Rowley, Janet. "Recognizing and Treating Breathing Disorders: A Multidisciplinary Approach." *New Zealand Journal of Physiotherapy* 42.2 (2014): 110-111.

direction, but their expansion downward is most important. The lowest part of your lungs contains the highest concentration of alveoli. Blood is heavier than air, and this downward expansion allows more oxygen to reach that lower blood.

While muscles in the back, neck, abdomen, and ribcage contribute to breathing, the efficiency of internal respiration depends largely on how well the diaphragm works. The more the diaphragm contracts, the more lung volume increases. In this sense, diaphragm activation is key to functional breathing.

As your diaphragm contracts and descends during inhalation, your ribs move out to the sides. Because of the pressure around your navel, the abdomen pushes out laterally. The important thing to note here is that diaphragm breathing is *not* synonymous with belly breathing. The muscles of the abdomen can move independently of the diaphragm. What you're looking for is lateral expansion and contraction of the ribs. As you inhale, check whether the lower ribs move outwards and as you exhale, that the lower ribs move inwards.

The journey of oxygen from the lungs to the blood also relies on CO_2 and NO. These gases help relax the tissue that surrounds and protects the lungs. CO_2 and NO also both dilate the blood vessels and airways,[49] allowing more oxygen to get to the blood.

In yoga, we often tend to focus on the biomechanics of breathing, because our primary concern is the movement of muscles and joints in the body. But, to breathe correctly, it's important to understand that breathing biomechanics and biochemistry are interconnected and of equal importance. Nasal breathing helps maintain optimal levels of both CO_2 and NO, and it improves diaphragm function.[50] The common instruction to "breathe through your mouth and use the diaphragm," flies in the face of respiratory science.

49 Villanueva, Cleva, and Cecilia Giulivi. "Subcellular and Cellular Locations of Nitric Oxide Synthase Isoforms as Determinants of Health and Disease." *Free Radical Biology and Medicine* 49.3 (2010): 307-316.
50 Trevisan, Maria Elaine, et al. "Diaphragmatic Amplitude and Accessory Inspiratory Muscle Activity in Nasal and Mouth-Breathing Adults: A Cross-Sectional Study." *Journal of Electromyography and Kinesiology* 25.3 (2015): 463-468.

At the same time, poor diaphragm activation is associated with unhealthily low levels of blood CO_2. Scientists have shown that chest breathers have much lower blood CO_2 levels at rest than diaphragm breathers (32.4 mmHg and 35.47 mmHg). During exercise, diaphragm breathing supports normal CO_2 levels and reduces injury risk.[51] We have devoted a whole chapter to the diaphragm as it is fundamental to healthy breathing (see Chapter Eleven).

Cellular Respiration: The Journey of Oxygen in the Cells

For O_2 to take part in aerobic respiration, it needs to get to the mitochondria inside the cells. The mitochondria are the energy generators of the cell. The only cells in the human body that do not have mitochondria and, therefore, do not directly contribute to energy production are the red blood cells that carry O_2 around the body.

While the O_2 is in those red blood cells, it can't participate in energy production.[52] In the red blood cells, oxygen bonds with haemoglobin, attaching itself to the iron atoms within the haemoglobin molecule. Around 70% of all the iron in your body is found in haemoglobin. This makes iron an essential building block for oxygenation. An iron-rich diet will support good O_2 uptake. Iron supplements can support the making of haemoglobin and new red blood cells. This can be especially relevant after heavy menstruation. (Before taking iron supplements, talk to your health care provider first as taking too much iron is not good for your health).

Carbon dioxide and nitric oxide also bind to haemoglobin for transport in the blood. The biochemist, Christian Bohr, discovered that how strongly O_2 binds with haemoglobin is inversely related to

51 Bradley, Helen, and Dr. Joseph Esformes. "Breathing Pattern Disorders and Functional Movement." *International Journal of Sports Physical Therapy* 9.1 (2014): 28.
52 *UCSB Science Line*. scienceline.ucsb.edu/getkey.php?key=4831 (accessed July 14, 2022).

the acidity of the blood and the concentration of CO_2.[53] When CO_2 is low, more O_2 will attach to the haemoglobin, so less O_2 is available for release to the cells. When CO_2 levels increase, blood pH drops releasing the O_2 to the cells where it can participate in energy production.

Remember, the harder and faster you breathe the less oxygen is delivered throughout the body including to the heart and brain.

Mitochondrial Respiration: Converting Oxygen to Energy

Once oxygen is released from the blood to the tissues, it must cross the membrane of those cells. Cell membranes regulate the exchange of nutrients and signals between the cell and its environment. By "environment," we mean the fluids outside the cell and the other cells that belong to the same tissue or organ. Oxygen crosses the cell membrane by diffusion, a passive process in which a molecule dissolves in the membrane, passes through it, then dissolves in the solution on the other side of that membrane.[54]

Once across the cell membrane, the O_2 finds its way to the mitochondria inside the cells. The mitochondria are the only places within the cell where aerobic respiration can occur. However, there can be several thousand mitochondria in every cell. These tiny organelles can fuse and divide, forming ever-changing tubular networks within the cell. Mitochondria are normally depicted as long cylinders, but, in reality, they are shape shifters, constantly changing and morphing.[55]

Because mitochondria are responsible for most of the oxygen consumption in the cell, it is believed that they also act as O_2 sensors.

53 Bohr, Chr, K. et al. "Ueber Einen in Biologischer Beziehung Wichtigen Einfluss, den die Kohlensäurespannung des Blutes auf dessen Sauerstoffbindung übt 1." *Skandinavisches Archiv Für Physiologie* 16.2 (1904): 402-412.

54 Cooper, Geoffrey M. "Transport of Small Molecules," *NIH.* (2015) http://www.ncbi. nlm.nih.gov/books/NBK9847/ (Accessed July 14, 2022).

55 Alberts, Bruce, et al. "Drosophila and the Molecular Genetics of Pattern Formation: Genesis of the Body Plan." in *Molecular Biology of the Cell.* New York: Garland Science, 2002.

A review in the *Journal of Applied Physiology* in 2000 explains that mitochondria do more than just generate energy. When blood oxygen saturation is low, they initiate a series of chemical reactions that allow the body to adapt to hypoxia (low oxygen).[56] The mitochondria are also key players in sensing CO_2 levels.

The process by which mitochondria signal their need for a higher or lower supply of oxygen is complex. Each mitochondrion is bound by two separate membranes, an outer and inner membrane that contain the mitochondrial matrix.[57] During aerobic respiration, reactive oxygen species are produced. These are better known as *free radicals* – which are just molecules containing oxygen that react easily with other molecules in a cell. When O_2 levels in the mitochondria go down, the number of free radicals increases.[58] This triggers a chain of events that causes O_2 to flood into the cells.

One study suggests that the metabolic processes within the mitochondria correlate with real-time inhalation and exhalation[59] – which means that the rhythm of our external breathing may be in concert with the trillions of mitochondria, all breathing together, inside the 100 trillion energy-producing cells in the human body!

In a resting state, a healthy adult consumes about 550 litres of O_2 every day. In the same 24 hours, we breathe out around 500 litres (nearly a kilo) of CO_2.[60,61] Oxygen travels to the mitochondria to be

56 Chandel, Navdeep S., and Paul T. Schumacker. "Cellular Oxygen Sensing by Mitochondria: Old Questions, New Insight." *Journal of Applied Physiology* 88.5 (2000): 1880-1889.
57 Alberts, Bruce, et al. "Drosophila and the Molecular Genetics of Pattern Formation: Genesis of the Body Plan." In *Molecular Biology of the Cell*. New York: Garland Science, 2002.
58 Waypa, Gregory B., Kimberly A. Smith, and Paul T. Schumacker. "O2 Sensing, Mitochondria and ROS Signaling: the Fog is Lifting." *Molecular Aspects of Medicine* 47 (2016): 76-89.
59 Jerath, R. et al. "Widespread Depolarization During Expiration: A Source of Respiratory Drive?" *Medical Hypotheses* 84.1 (2015): 31-37.
60 Jequier, Eric, Kevin Acheson, and Yves Schutz. "Assessment of Energy Expenditure and Fuel Utilization in Man." *Annual Review of Nutrition (USA)* (1987).
61 Withers, Nikki. *How Much Does Human Breathing Contribute to Climate Change*. (2013) http://www.sciencefocus.com/planet-earth/how-much-does-human-breathing-contribute-to-climate-change/ (accessed July 14, 2022).

converted into energy while CO_2 begins its journey out of the body from the mitochondria.[62] It is no coincidence that CO_2 takes almost the same route as O_2 but in reverse. As we've seen, CO_2 is intimately involved in the journey of O_2 through the body at every stage – during external, internal, cellular, and mitochondrial respiration.

The good news is that you don't need to sign up for science classes to improve your breathing. Far from it! You now have the information you need to understand the science behind prāṇāyāma exercises. The most important takeaway from this detailed journey is this:

To support the optimal transport of oxygen, you must Breathe Light, slow and low through your nose, on and off your mat, during rest, exercise, and sleep.

---

62   Yang, Shao-hua, and Ran Liu. "For the Pursuit of Oxygen and Carbon Dioxide Channels in Mitochondria." *Medical Gas Research* 6.4 (2016): 237.

CHAPTER THREE

PRĀṆĀYĀMA: BREATH CONTROL

Prāṇāyāma, which is about controlling the breath in order to control the life force, provides the obvious link in yoga between breathing and the asanas. These traditional breathing practices are an important component of practice, but they are not commonly used during asana or meditation and are generally considered advanced techniques. This is surprising, given that breathing naturally continues during these practices and the way we do it affects us physically, mentally, and emotionally.

You may already have some ideas about the breath from your yoga practice, but please put that to the side as you read this book. Many misconceptions have been handed down, learned, and re-learned, until the purpose of certain exercises is all but lost. As Robin Rothenberg explains in her book, *Restoring Prana: A Therapeutic Guide to Prāṇāyāma and Healing Through the Breath for Yoga Therapists, Yoga Teachers, and Healthcare Practitioners*:

> "There is so much more written about prāṇāyāma in the *Yoga Sutra* and *Hatha Yoga Pradipika* than what I was being taught. In my therapeutic yoga training, increasing exhalation and inhalation was emphasised as the first step towards health . . . This concept feeds directly into the myth that bigger is better, and likely has gone

far to fertilise the big breathing practice observed in many of our contemporary yoga classes."[63]

So, let's start looking at what's really going on when we breathe as we practise yoga.

PRANA AND THE EIGHT LIMBS OF YOGA

Yoga consists of eight limbs or stages, designed to serve as guides for living a meaningful life. Through practice, the yogi progresses step-by-step from the known – the body – to the unknown – the highest state achievable while still bound to the body. These eight stages of yoga are:

1. Yama – attitude toward our environment
2. Niyama – attitude toward ourselves
3. Asana – physical postures
4. Prāṇāyāma – restraining or expansion of the breath
5. Pratyahara – withdrawal of the senses
6. Dharana – concentration
7. Dhyana – meditation
8. Samadhi – enlightenment

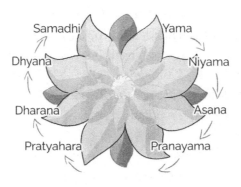

63 Rothenberg Robin L. *Restoring Prana: A Therapeutic Guide to Prāṇāyāma and Healing Through the Breath for Yoga Therapists, Yoga Teachers, and Healthcare Practitioners.* Singing Dragon, 2019.

The fourth stage, *prāṇāyāma,* is commonly translated as *breath control.* The way you breathe impacts every system in your body. On a more metaphysical level, air has substance, just as water does. If you think of yourself as living in an "air ocean," just as a fish swims in the sea, your connection with the air, with the breath, becomes more tangible. Breathing unites us with each other and with nature. Life is therefore a continual exchange, and we are truly part of the universe.

Prana can be used to mean both breath and vital energy. prāṇ āyāma is about more than the exchange of air. It is really about the expansion or extension of primal energy. As Swami Rama elegantly puts it in his practical guide *Science of Breath,* "Prana is the vital energy of the universe." Rama explains that respiration is the most outward manifestation of this cosmic or absolute energy and that, by guiding the breath, the yogi learns to control more subtle energy layers within the body. So, prāṇāyāma is perhaps more accurately defined as the science related to the control of prana. "One who has learned to control prana," Rama says, "has learned to control all the energies of the universe."[64]

This concept echoes *the Upanishads,* where the word prana refers to both life force and breath and to the breath as "lord of all." In the *Brihad Aranyaka Upanishad,* the breath equates to "immortality" (6.1.1) and a timeless source of vitality (1.6.3). Geshe Michael Roach and Christie McNally illustrate this idea in their *Essential Yoga Sutra:*

> "Although our breath is not the inner wind, the two are intimately connected. Whatever happens with one resonates with the other, like guitar strings tuned to the same note."[65]

Yogi Ramacharaka highlights the importance of prana as something separate from the individual. "Prana must not be confounded with the

---

64   Rama, Swami, Rudolph Ballentine, and Alan Hymes. *Science of Breath: A Practical Guide.* Himalayan Institute Press, 1998.

65   Roach, Geshe Michael, and Lama Christie McNally. *The Essential Yoga Sutra: Ancient Wisdom for Your Yoga.* Harmony, 2009.

Ego," he cautions. "Prana is merely a form of energy used by the Ego in its material manifestation."[66]

On a spiritual level, this idea is echoed in different cultures, including the Bible's book of Genesis. Our inhalation happens without conscious effort, supporting life. In our exhalation, we let go, releasing a small part of ourselves to the universe. In Genesis, Chapter One, the Hebrew words *ruach Elohim* mean *breath of God*, which translates as *spirit of life*. This conveys the same meaning as prana.

The Jewish scholar and mindfulness teacher, Rabbi Jill Zimmerman, explains that the different Hebrew words for breath found in Genesis, Chapters One and Two, poetically express the idea that the breath forms our connection with the Divine.[67] In Taoism the word is *Ch'i*, and, in traditional Chinese medicine, it's *Qi*.

In his bestselling book on Celtic Spirituality, *Anam Cara*, John O'Donohue writes:

> "Traditionally the breath was understood as the pathway through which the soul enters the body. Breaths come in pairs, except the first breath and the last breath. At the deepest level, breath is sister of spirit."[68]

In each, the underlying truth is the same, that the breath connects us with the intangible.

WHAT IS PRĀṆĀYĀMA?

As with other aspects of yoga, there are plenty of questions about the origin and purpose of prāṇāyāma and its breathing practices.

66 Ramacharaka, Yogi. *Science of Breath: A Complete Manual of the Oriental Breathing Philosophy of Physical, Mental, Psychic and Spiritual Development.* Book Tree, 2007.

67 Zimmerman, Rabbi Jill. *Connecting with Breath and Spirit.* (August 2, 2013). http://www.ravjill.com/connecting-with-breath-and-spirit/ (Accessed July 2, 2022).

68 O'Donohue, John. *Anam Cara: A Book of Celtic Wisdom.* New York: Cliff Street Books, 1997.

When it comes to understanding how and why we practice, varying interpretations passed from teacher to student can create confusion. In Indian, Chinese, and Tibetan yoga, emphasis is placed on special types of breathing.[69]

In *Restoring Prana*, Robin Rothenberg describes learning about prāṇāyāma as –

> "... a splatter of mixed techniques, and conflictual explanations that were incongruent with one another, even among those with Ayurvedic and medical knowledge."

However, she describes a thread common to many of the breathing techniques she learned. They were "dramatic, noisy, and required a great deal of muscular heaving." She was left frustrated by the results.

> "Though I found these practices intriguing ... none transformed my mind or energy dimension in the way the texts spoke was possible. I assumed this was because I was spiritually unfit or emotionally unable to sustain practices that required that level of intensity."[70]

On a practical level, we can say that prāṇāyāma is a type of conscious breathing practice in which attention and intention are harnessed to control inhalation, exhalation, and retention. In this practice, there are four phases of the breath:

- Puraka – inhalation
- Antara or Puraka Kumbhaka – retention or breath hold after inhalation

---

69 Blofeld, John. "Taoism--The Road to Immortality." *Philosophy East and West* 31.2 (1981).
70 Rothenberg, Robin L. *Restoring Prana: A Therapeutic Guide to Prāṇāyāma and Healing Through the Breath for Yoga Therapists, Yoga Teachers, and Healthcare Practitioners.* Singing Dragon, 2019.

- Rechaka – exhalation
- Bahya or Rechaka Kumbhaka – retention or breath hold after exhalation

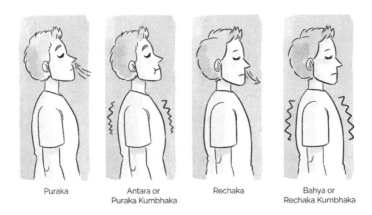

Puraka   Antara or   Rechaka   Bahya or
          Puraka Kumbhaka   Rechaka Kumbhaka

In *The Physiological Essentials of Yogic Relaxation*, Dr. Umesh Pal Singh describes prāṇāyāma as "an art of re-patterning of breathing mechanics used for the optimization of the blood chemistry." He explains that it "allows for the maturation of the nervous system, that determines the health to all parts of the body."[71]

Similarly, B.K.S. Iyengar writes:

"Asanas, together with the practice of prāṇāyāma, or the control of the breath, rectify physical, physiological, and psychological disorders. They have a positive impact on the effects of stress and disease."[72]

Likewise, in *Yoga, The Iyengar Way*, by Sylva, Mera, and Shyam Mehta, the authors explain that "prāṇāyāma calms and strengthens the mind . . . Once the lungs are strong, it increases their capacity."[73]

---

71 Singh, Dr. Umesh Pal. *The Physiological Essentials of Yogic Relaxation: Body Mind Breath & Stress*. Partridge Publishing, India, 2015.
72 Iyengar, Bellur Krishnamukar Sundara. *BKS Iyengar Yoga: The Path to Holistic Health*. Penguin, 2007.
73 Mehta, Silva, Mira Mehta, and Shyam Mehta. *Yoga: The Iyengar Way*. Knopf, 1990.

The importance of functional everyday breathing is talked about in Indian and Taoist literature, both in terms of prāṇāyāma and overall health. More recently, Dr. Singh explains that breathing therapy can be used to correct dysfunctional breathing and enhance respiratory function beyond "normal" parameters. "Breathing," he says, "unlike most physiological functions, can be controlled voluntarily and it can serve as an entry point for physiological and psychological regulation." In fact, he goes on to explain that most prāṇāyāma is not appropriate because it does not allow the practitioner to first learn about healthy, natural breathing that is not consciously controlled.[74] This resonates with one of the most important ideas behind the Oxygen Advantage®: *Get your functional breathing right before you stress the body trying more extreme breathing exercises.*

The link between breathing and health is frequently mentioned by scholars and yogis alike. In his article, "Breathing in Yoga," Daniel Pinault echoes research that demonstrates cardiovascular fitness does not necessarily equate with overall wellbeing. "Total wellbeing," explains Pinault, "would include psychological and mental health and would have to be addressed by using appropriate breathing."[75]

When thinking stops, the breath naturally pauses too. prāṇāyāma was originally designed as a method to control thought and develop introspection, to prevent the dualistic thinking that distorts our reality and keeps us from enlightenment.

Alan Fogel, Professor of Psychology Emeritus at the University of Utah explains it like this: "The breath is the most reliable indicator of our embodied state of awareness." While aspects like body image and pain take a long time to change, we can change our breathing in the moment. So, Fogel says, "Learning to notice our breath is one of the simplest means of assessing our state of embodied self-awareness."[76]

74 Singh, Umesh Pal. *The Physiological Essentials of Yogic Relaxation: Body Mind Breath & Stress.* Partridge Publishing, India, 2015.
75 Pineault, D. "Breathing in Yoga: Role, Relevance and Technique."
76 Fogel, Alan. *Restorative Embodiment and Resilience: A Guide to Disrupt Habits, Create Inner Peace, Deepen Relationships, and Feel Greater Presence.* North Atlantic Books, 2021.

WHAT IS OPTIMAL BREATHING?

There is an agreement in yogic literature that optimal breathing in a person in good physical and emotional health is slow, regular, even, diaphragmatic, and through the nose.[77,78,79] In *Yoga, The Path to Holistic Health*, B.K.S. Iyengar writes, "prāṇāyāma is not deep breathing." In *Light on Prāṇāyāma*, he describes it as the respiratory art that consists of long, sustained, and subtle breathing. Iyengar points to the breath as the link between the physiological and spiritual body, with the diaphragm as a meeting point. He explains that, during prāṇ āyāma, you must be totally absorbed in "the fineness of inhalation, exhalation and the naturalness of retention." It is important not to disturb or jerk the nerves or vital organs, or to stress the brain cells. "Deep breathing," Iyengar says, "creates hardness in the fibres of the lungs and chest, preventing the percolation of breath through the body."[80]

Taoism stresses proper breathing too. Taoist yogis believe the breath should be inaudible and "so smooth that the fine hairs within the nostrils remain motionless."[81] Indeed, Taoist wisdom is that breathing that is from the diaphragm and through the nose, with full and complete exhalations, is fundamental to meditation and to medical therapy. Going further, Jolan Chang says, in *The Tao of Love and Sex*, concerning complete exhalations and upright posture:

77 Ramacharaka, Yogi. *Science of Breath: A Complete Manual of the Oriental Breathing Philosophy of Physical, Mental, Psychic and Spiritual Development.* Book Tree, 2007.

78 Rama, Swami, Rudolph Ballentine, and Alan Hymes. *Science of Breath: A Practical Guide.* Himalayan Institute Press, 1998.

79 Sovik, Rolf. "The Science of Breathing—The Yogic View." *Progress in Brain Research* 122 (2000): 491-505.

80 Iyengar, Bellur Krishnamukar Sundara. *BKS Iyengar Yoga: The Path to Holistic Health.* Penguin, 2007.

81 Blofeld, John. "Taoism—The Road to Immortality." *Philosophy East and West* 31.2 (1981).

"Naturally you will not breathe this way all the time, but you should do it for at least a few minutes daily so that deep and slow diaphragmatic breathing will become a natural habit even when you are asleep."[82]

Those definitions are all in line with the descriptions of healthy breathing given by scientists and with the Oxygen Advantage® fundamentals of good breathing: functional breathing is silent, soft, nasal, regular, and diaphragmatic, 24/7.

Scientists say breathing should be steady and rhythmic. The word "steady" echoes that much-quoted verse from the *Hatha Yoga Pradipika*. To meet the body's metabolic demands, we should be taking no more than 10 to 14 breaths in and out every minute. The tidal volume, which is the volume of air drawn into the lungs during inhalation, should be normal. The exhale should be 1.5 or 2 times longer than the inhale with a natural pause after exhalation. Breathing should involve minimal effort from the breathing muscles, and the diaphragm must be free to move.[83,84]

Under the microscope of respiratory science, the yogic ideas from different continents measure up. Yet, somehow, the important messages about subtleness, health, and reduced volume breathing are often lost in translation. Popular modern breathing practices are often about big, noisy breaths, and much of prāṇāyāma is viewed through that same lens, especially by students who search for 'truths' on YouTube.

So, where did these dramatic breathing exercises come from? The fact is that there are many types of prāṇāyāma. Each evolved to meet the changing physical, mental, intellectual, and spiritual needs of the practitioner.[85]

82 Chang, Jolan. *The Tao of Love and Sex: The Ancient Chinese Way to Ecstasy.* Penguin Books, 1977.

83 Chaitow, L., D. Bradley, and C. Gilbert. *Recognizing and Treating Breathing Disorders.* E-book, 2014.

84 Sovik, Rolf. "The Science of Breathing—The Yogic View." *Progress in Brain Research* 122 (2000): 491-505.

85 Iyengar, Belur Krishnamacharya Sundaraja. *Light on Prāṇāyāma: The Yogic Art of Breathing.* Crossroad, 1981.

When Robin Rothenberg learned to reduce her breathing volume, everything changed for her. At first, she found her efforts suffocating. Over time, she was able to comfortably hold her breath and felt less breathless throughout the day. But the most profound shift was an internal one, something she could only describe as a feeling of contentment. "It was as if," she says, "by learning to need less breath, my entire system was feeling less need to need."[86] Please see Appendix Two for an interview with Robin on teaching yoga and the role of functional breathing.

As with any process, breath training begins with awareness. By becoming conscious of your breathing, and, by practising the breathing exercises described in this book, it is possible to control your body's response to internal and external challenges, to use your breath as a tool, rather than be at the mercy of its "unsteadiness." It is possible to control your experience and to improve your practice and your wellbeing.

ACHIEVING STEADINESS IN BREATH AND MOVEMENT

"Controlling the breath is a prerequisite to controlling the mind and the body."[87]

— Swami Rama

Silent, soft regular breathing is challenging enough during day-to-day life, let alone while holding strenuous asanas. But it is possible. To build strength in any muscle, we must push the ability of our muscles to contract against resistance. To run faster, we must extend our endurance,

---

86 Rothenberg, Robin L. *Restoring Prana: A Therapeutic Guide to Prāṇāyāma and Healing Through the Breath for Yoga Therapists, Yoga Teachers, and Healthcare Practitioners.* Singing Dragon, 2019.

87 Rama, Swami, Rudolph Ballentine, and Alan Hymes. *Science of Breath: A Practical Guide.* Himalayan Institute Press, 1998.

training ourselves to run further, or for longer, in different terrains. In the same way, to improve our breathing capacity and achieve this subtlety of breath, we must challenge our breathing.

From a biochemical perspective, we do this in two ways:

1. Increasing the level of CO_2 in the blood to bring the body into a state called hypercapnia, or
2. Intermittently reducing blood oxygen saturation to bring the body into a state called hypoxia.

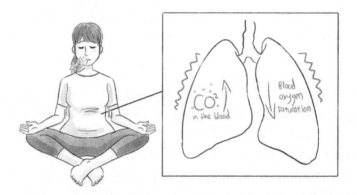

These two states can be achieved using the Oxygen Advantage® breathing exercises. They can also be reached through prāṇāyāma. The Oxygen Advantage® has 25 unique breathing exercises. These include exercises to improve functional breathing as well as exercises to stress the body and mind for positive adaptations. Just as in yoga or any physical training, it is important that exercises are tailored to each person. This is both safer and more effective and can be achieved by working in alignment with your BOLT score, which we will explore in the next chapter.

Safety Reminder:

The breathing exercises outlined in this book are powerful and with this is mind, there are a few important guidelines:

- Don't practise any of the exercises other than nasal breathing with relaxation if pregnant.
- If you have a serious medical condition, it's safer to avoid holding your breath for a long duration of time, and also avoid practising faster and harder breathing (hyperventilation). Instead, focus on breathing through your nose during rest, sleep, and physical activity. Also, practise the **Breathe Light** exercise by gently softening breathing to achieve a comfortable shortage of air.
- If you are over 60 years of age, have a BOLT score of less than 25 seconds, or have any serious medical condition it is important to proceed gently. This includes neurological, cardiovascular, and metabolic conditions such as diabetes.

If you are a newcomer to breathing, dip your toe into the water and listen to your body. Breathing should not be in any way stressful. Even the long breath holds should be under good control and performed under a feeling of relaxation. You will find it helpful to download the free OxygenAdvantage® app, which will provide a daily plan based on your state of health and breathing patterns. If you are a yoga instructor, the app will provide support for your students' breathing outside of yoga practice.

If you are inexperienced with breathing exercises, it is always best to work with a breathing instructor or prāṇāyāma teacher.

As Blofeld writes:

> "Before that yoga (prāṇāyāma) is embarked upon, the adept should have made himself proficient in the simpler types of breathing, but even these can be dangerous if performed without supervision from a competent teacher."[88]

---

88 Blofeld, John. "Taoism--The Road to Immortality." *Philosophy East and West* 31.2 (1981).

Swami Rama also cautions:

"Kumbhakas (breath holds) should be practised carefully under a competent guide, never by reading manuals alone. Nor should they be practised without applying the bandhas."[89]

It deals with your very life force. If you make a mistake during asana practice, you might tear a muscle. Mistakes made in breathing exercises can negatively impact the brain and the nervous system.[90]

For the same reason, it is important to understand that stressor exercises involving hyperventilation and long breath holds should always be undertaken with caution. There is a fine line between *good* stress and *bad* stress. Ideally, you should only practice hyperventilation and long breath holds if you are fit and young and once your BOLT score is over 25 seconds.

A final note of caution – it can be tempting to ignore this advice, as the image of these strong exercises is very enticing, but there are documented cases of heart problems, tinnitus (ringing in the ears), facial tics, and even death by drowning as the result of practicing the wrong exercises at the wrong time.

89 Rama, Swami, Rudolph Ballentine, and Alan Hymes. *Science of Breath: A Practical Guide.* Himalayan Institute Press, 1998.
90 Mehta, Silva, Mira Mehta, and Shyam Mehta. *Yoga: The Iyengar Way.* Knopf, 1990.

CHAPTER FOUR

APPLYING OXYGEN ADVANTAGE® FUNDAMENTALS TO YOGA

In this Chapter we will share several breath training exercises which formulate the basis of the Oxygen Advantage® method. However, it's important to first understand the Body Oxygen Level Test (BOLT). This understanding will allow you to customise your training to fit your current biochemistry and breathing functionality levels, and also to track your progress.

THE BOLT SCORE

The BOLT is a simple measurement of breath hold time after an exhalation. It gives feedback about breathlessness and sensitivity to carbon dioxide (CO_2). The breathing exercises in this chapter work by increasing tolerance to changes in CO_2 in the blood. This makes breathing slower, easier, and steadier. For now, here's what you need to know . . .

A higher BOLT score equates to ease of breathing. A low BOLT score indicates breathing that is dysfunctional – fast, hard, and into the upper chest. When the BOLT score is less than 25 seconds, you may be able to **breathe slowly**, but your breath will quickly become unbalanced during asana practice. Once the BOLT score is more than 40 seconds, you will be able to maintain breathing that is slow and light during physical exercise. This is the goal if you want to achieve peak physical fitness.

The BOLT score offers yoga teachers and students alike a novel way to assess breathing patterns and functionality. Regardless of whether the yogi is a beginner or not, if the BOLT score is below 25 seconds there is work to be done.

How to Measure Your BOLT Score

To get the most accurate measurement, take your BOLT score in the morning before you begin your day. You may either follow the instructions on the Oxygen Advantage® app for measuring your BOLT score, or you may follow the directions below. Note – you will need a timer or stopwatch that counts seconds.

- Sit upright in a straight-backed chair or on your mat.
- Allow your breathing to settle.
- When you feel your breathing is quiet and steady, take a normal silent breath in and out through your nose.
- After the exhalation, pinch your nose to hold your breath.
- Start the timer or stopwatch.
- When you feel the first definite desire to breathe, let go of your nose and breathe in through it.
- Stop the timer or stopwatch.

After the breath hold, breathing should immediately be calm and quiet. You may notice your first definite desire to breathe as a contraction in your diaphragm or throat, or just a psychological need for air. This is not a perfect measure of breathing. In fact, measuring the BOLT can be an interesting challenge, given that people with perfectionist natures often push themselves past their limits. These same people are highly prone to dysfunctional breathing patterns, including hyperventilation and it's important to emphasise that the BOLT score should not be forced. It is not a "test" to be done competitively. It simply indicates how functional your breathing is today. If you find yourself (or your students) getting obsessed with the BOLT score, forget about it for a few weeks.

Take your BOLT score in the morning.
You will need a timer or stopwatch.

Sit upright.

Lift up through the crown of your head.

Allow your breathing to calm.

Take a normal breath in and out through your nose.

After the exhale, pinch your nose to hold your breath.

Start the timer.

When you feel the first definite desire to breathe, inhale.

Stop the timer. The result is your BOLT score.

As you begin to practise the breathing exercises in this book, you will notice an improvement of between three and four seconds in your BOLT score during the first few weeks. Thereafter, progress slows but with consistent practice, improvement in the BOLT score does take place. Integrate the breathing techniques into your physical yoga practice to increase your BOLT score above 20 seconds. Work consistently and gently with the breath. It is incredibly powerful. Remember, it takes a lifetime for breathing to become dysfunctional. And it takes gentle, consistent practice to learn to breathe optimally again.

Here's what to expect (breathing patterns relative to BOLT score):

BOLT Score of 11 Seconds	BOLT Score of 25 Seconds
Faster respiratory rate	Normal respiratory rate
Irregular breathing, including frequent sighing and yawning	Regular breathing with less breathlessness
Harder breathing	Normal, light breathing
Upper chest breathing	Breathing is driven by the diaphragm
Feeling of air hunger/suffocation	Effortless breathing
A mixture of mouth and nose breathing	Full-time nasal breathing
No natural pause following exhalation	Natural pause following exhalation

The main thing to remember is that the degree of breathlessness you feel during practice and your ability to **breathe slow**ly enough to follow your teacher's cues is primarily governed by your sensitivity to carbon dioxide – and that is something you can improve with breath training.

TAILORING YOUR PRACTICE ACCORDING TO THE BOLT

The BOLT score gives feedback on functional breathing, fitness levels, and exercise tolerance. A rule of thumb is the lower the BOLT score, the lighter the intensity of physical, yoga, and breathing exercises should be. If you have a low BOLT score, you will need to go gently during practice and only experience an air hunger that is comfortable for you.

For teachers, it's important to know that some people have an exaggerated alarm response to the build-up of carbon dioxide. If they push a little too hard during practice with a lower BOLT score, there is a risk of them losing control of breathing patterns. It is always better to encourage the student to be guided by their breath than to impose what can be intense and frightening feelings of strong air hunger during practice. If a student is finding breathing during practice too challenging, advise them to return to normal breathing for a few minutes. When ready, they may return to Breathe Light with gentle air hunger to acclimatise their body to a tolerable feeling of breathlessness.

It is helpful to think of breathing in the same vein as physical exercise. If you are over 60 years of age, have poor breathing patterns, or have any serious medical conditions you are hardly going to sprint with all-out intensity. Instead, you might walk, light jog, or practice gentle yoga as part of your physical training.

As a guide:

BOLT Score	Intensity	Physical Movement	Breathing Exercises
to 10 seconds	Gentle	• Very slow walking	• Nose breathing • Humming • Breathing Recovery
10 to 15 seconds	Light	• Walking • Dancing • Yoga • Pilates • Household chores	• Nose breathing • Humming • *Breathe Light* • *Breathe slow* • *Breathe low*
15 to 20 seconds	Moderate	• Brisk walking • Riding a bike • Easy jogging • Light weightlifting	• Breath holding during rest or physical exercise until moderate air hunger • Brisk walking or jogging with mouth closed
20 to 25 seconds	Strong	• Running • Lap swimming • Cycling fast	• Breath holding during rest or physical exercise to achieve moderate to strong air hunger (blood O_2 saturation lowers between 94% and 80%)
25 seconds plus	Extreme	• Sprinting – HIIT	• Hyperventilation followed by breath holding (blood O_2 saturation to below 70%)

BREATHING THROUGH THE NOSE IF YOUR NOSE IS BLOCKED

One of the foundations of the Oxygen Advantage® method is breathing through the nose 24/7. Unfortunately, many of us struggle to breathe through the nose at times. If you're not used to full-time nasal breathing, your nose is likely to be congested. If you have a deviated septum or another physical nasal obstruction, nose breathing can leave you feeling like you just aren't getting enough air. So, how do you switch to nasal breathing during exercise, rest, and sleep?

There are five things you can do to get started:

1. If breathing through the nose is uncomfortable for you, then try wearing a nasal dilator during physical exercise and sleep. A simple internal nasal dilator (available at www.OxygenAdvantage.com) will open your airways, helping you breathe more easily.
2. It sounds counterintuitive but breathe through your nose as much as you can. With nasal breathing, as with most things, there's an element of "use it or lose it." Full-time nose breathing encourages the airway to open.
3. Tape your mouth before going to bed. Closing the mouth with a medical paper tape or a specialist lip tape such as MyoTape is the ONLY way to ensure you breathe through your nose during sleep.
4. Practise the Nose Unblocking Exercise. If you have any chronic health condition such as cardiovascular issues or high blood pressure, use the Breathing Recovery, Sitting exercise instead.
5. Regularly practise the *Breathe Light* exercise to normalise your breathing volume. Over time, you will observe improvements to your breathing patterns reflected in a higher BOLT score.

If you are in good health, try the following Nose Unblocking Exercise:

*   Sit upright in a straight-backed chair or cross-legged on your yoga mat.
*   Take a normal breath, in and out through your nose.
*   Pinch your nose to hold your breath.
*   With your breath held, gently nod your head, or sway your body from side to side.
*   Continue the breath hold and the gentle movement for as long as you can hold the breath.
*   When you feel a moderate-to-strong need for air, let go of your nose and breathe in through it.

- Allow your breathing to calm.
- Repeat this exercise 5 or 6 times until your nose feels completely clear.

You will find that as you improve your everyday breathing by using the five steps outlined above, your BOLT score will increase, and in turn, your nose will become less congested. To alleviate nasal congestion long term, the goal is to maintain a BOLT score of over 20 seconds.

OXYGEN ADVANTAGE® BREATHING EXERCISES: THE FOUNDATION

OA™ Exercise: Breathing Recovery, Sitting

This is a great starting exercise. It increases carbon dioxide in the blood in very small doses and is ideal for anyone prone to anxiety, panic disorder, or fear of suffocation (see Chapter Six for more on the connection between anxiety and the breath). Begin very gently. If your BOLT score is very low, start with a two or three second breath hold. With this exercise, never extend the breath holds for longer than five seconds. The aim here is not breath suspension. The goal is to stabilise the breathing.

- Sit upright in a straight-backed chair or in any easy seated asana on your mat.
- Take a normal breath in through your nose and out through your nose.
- Pinch your nose to hold your breath for between 2 and 5 seconds.
- Let go of the nose and breathe in silently through it.
- Breathe normally for around three rounds of breath, in and out.
- After a normal exhale, pinch your nose to hold your breath for between 2 and 5 seconds.
- Let go of the nose and breathe in through it.
- Breathe normally for approximately three rounds of breath, or 15 seconds.

- Repeat the breath hold.
- Continue the exercise, performing many small breath holds for 4 or 5 minutes or until breathing symptoms stop.

Breathing Exercise: Breathing Recovery, Sitting

Sit upright.

Lift up through the crown of your head.

Take a normal breath in through your nose and out through your nose.

Hold your breath for 2-5 seconds.

Breathe in through your nose.

Breathe normally for 3 breaths.

Repeat the breath hold followed by 3 normal breaths.
Continue performing the exercise for 4 or 5 minutes.

OA™ Exercise: *Breathe Light* (Biochemistry)

This exercise supports optimal breathing from a biochemical perspective. By reducing the volume of air you breathe in, you create a tolerable air hunger. This signifies that carbon dioxide has accumulated in the lungs and blood. Exposing the body to slightly higher CO_2 for short periods of time reduces the body's sensitivity to the gas, and this is beneficial. Remember – one of the functions of CO_2 is to act as a catalyst for the release of O_2 from the red blood cells. Breathing slowly and lightly also enables nitric oxide (NO) to accumulate in the nasal cavity and travel to the lungs. This lighter, slower, and effortless breathing allows blood vessels to open, and more O_2 to be released into your blood, tissues and organs.

- Sit up tall in a straight-backed chair or cross-legged or in a half-lotus on your mat.
- Lift up through the crown of your head, as if a piece of string were pulling you up toward the ceiling.
- Place your hands in your lap and allow your neck, shoulders, and jaw to relax.
- Become aware of your breath as it enters and leaves your nose.
- Observe the slightly colder air as it comes into your nose and the slightly warmer air that leaves your nose. Start to slow the speed of each breath as it enters and leaves your nose.
- Allow your breathing to become quiet, light, and calm. You should feel hardly any air entering or leaving your nostrils. Let your breathing become so quiet that the fine hairs inside your nose barely move.
- You will get a slight feeling you would like to take in more air or bigger breaths. This means you are performing the exercise correctly. This feeling of air hunger should be tolerable. There is no benefit from pushing it any further.
- Do not interfere with or tense your breathing muscles to reduce the breath. Just allow the breath to become still. If, at any point, your breathing becomes chaotic, or you feel stressed (your mouth may

go dry, or your hands may feel cold) stop practicing the exercise for around a minute and allow your breathing to normalise.

- You can practise the exercise for about 3 minutes. If your BOLT score is very low, begin gradually with 30 seconds of air hunger. Rest for 1 minute, then repeat the 30 seconds of air hunger. Repeat this sequence 4 or 5 times.

Breathing Exercise: Breathe Light (Biochemistry)

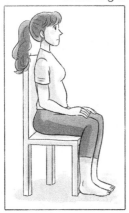

Sit upright.

Lift up through the crown of your head.

Place your hands in your lap and relax your shoulders.

Become aware of your breath.

Observe the air that enters and leaves your nose.

Start to slow the speed of each breath.

Allow your breathing
to become quiet,
light, and calm.

You will get a slight
feeling you would like
to take in more air
or bigger breaths.

Do not interfere with
or tense your breathing
muscles to reduce the breath.

If your BOLT score is very low, begin gradually
with 30 seconds of air hunger. Rest for 1 minute,
then repeat the 30 seconds of air hunger.

You can practise the exercise for about 3 minutes.

OA™ Exercise: *Breathe low* (Biomechanics)

This exercise supports optimal breathing from a biomechanical perspective. More specifically, it improves the functioning of the breathing muscles, including the diaphragm, which is important for postural control and spinal stabilization.

During inhalation, the diaphragm moves downwards, and intra-abdominal pressure is generated. When breathing patterns are healthy, there is also lateral expansion of the lower rib cage. This only occurs when there is sufficient generation of intra-abdominal pressure.

Diaphragmatic breathing helps slow the breathing, improves gas exchange as air is drawn deep into the lungs, and supports functional breathing for functional movement.

- Sit up tall in a straight-backed chair or cross-legged or in a half-lotus on your mat.
- Lift up through the crown of your head, as if a piece of string were pulling you up toward the ceiling.
- Place your hands on your lower ribs, and relax your hands into your sides, softening your jaw and shoulders.
- Bring your attention to the movement of your lower ribs.
- As you breathe in silently through your nose, feel your hands moving gently out.
- And, as you breathe out silently through your nose, feel your hands moving gently in.
- Allow your breathing to be smooth. Your hands should not move a great deal, and they should move smoothly in and out.
- The movement of your hands indicates that your diaphragm is working as it should. When the diaphragm descends during the inhalation, pressure is created in the abdomen, pushing the ribs out.
- When the diaphragm returns to its resting position during the exhale, pressure in the abdomen reduces, and your ribs move back in.
- Be aware of your breathing volume during this exercise. Do not take in an excessive volume of air to make the hands move more. Keep your breathing light and observe the subtle movement in and out.
- Practise the exercise for about 3 minutes.

Breathing Exercise: Breathe Low

Sit upright.

Lift up through the crown of your head.

Place your hands in your lower ribs and relax hands into sides.

Bring attention to lower ribs.

Breathe silently through your nose, feel your hands moving gently in and out.

Breathing should be smooth, hands should not be moving much.

You can practise the exercise for about 3 minutes.

The Buteyko Belt is a helpful and inexpensive support to assist with improving breathing from a biomechanical dimension. It is available from the website **www.OxygenAdvantage.com**.

OA™ Exercise: *Breathe slow* (Nervous System)

This exercise allows you to down-regulate the nervous system and reduce stress and anxiety by modifying the cadence of the breath. "Cadence," refers to the practice of controlling the respiratory rate. The goal is to slow the rhythm of breathing to between 4.5 and 6.5 breaths per minute. This maximizes vagal tone and balances the autonomic nervous system. See Chapter Eleven for more information.

Slowing the breathing rate also improves breathing efficiency – with a reduced respiratory rate, a greater volume of air per minute arrives at the alveoli (the small air sacs in the lungs where gas exchange takes place).

- Sit up tall in a straight-backed chair or cross-legged or in a half-lotus on your mat.
- Lift up through the crown of your head, as if a piece of string were pulling you up toward the ceiling.
- Place your hands on your lower ribs and relax your shoulders.
- Bring your attention to your breath. Begin to slow down and quieten your breathing.
- Breathe in, 2, 3, 4, 5.
- And out, 2, 3, 4, 5.
- In, 2, 3, 4, 5.
- Out, 2, 3, 4, 5.
- You are slowing the breath to around 6 breaths per minute to activate your relaxation response.
- As you breathe in, your hands move out. As you breathe out, your hands move in.
- In, 2, 3, 4, 5.
- Out 2, 3, 4, 5.
- As you slow the breath, do not increase your breathing volume disproportionately. Breathing should be light, quiet, and still.
- You can practise the exercise for around 3 minutes. If this breathing rate is too slow for you, breathe in for 3 seconds and out for 3 seconds instead.

Breathing Exercise: Breathe Slow

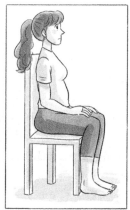

Sit upright.

Lift up through the crown of your head.

Place your hands in your lower ribs and relax hands into sides.

Bring attention to your breath.

Slow down your breathing to 6 breaths per minute, to activate relaxation response.

Breathing should be light, quiet, and still.

You can practise the exercise for about 3 minutes.

OXYGEN ADVANTAGE® RESOURCES AND SUPPORT

As a reminder, we have a range of supplementary resources to guide and support you as you progress through this book:

- Many of our Oxygen Advantage® Instructors are trained yoga instructors and are ideally placed to guide you through breathing and asanas. Please see our website, where you may search the list of instructors by country, language, background, and gender to find an instructor to work with.
- If you wish to delve even deeper into the Oxygen Advantage® approach and are interested in becoming a certified Oxygen Advantage® Instructor, a range of types of training, including a course specifically for yoga, are available via the website.
- The Oxygen Advantage® app is an excellent support tool and is available free of charge to both instructors and students alike. It is available on both Android and Apple devices.
- We have a library of breathing exercises available on our YouTube channel.
- We have an Oxygen Advantage® podcast with interviews and exercises.
- Finally, you may also wish to check out our various social media channels for updates.

http://www.oxygenadvantage.com/

CHAPTER FIVE

USING SIMPLE BREATHING TECHNIQUES IN YOUR ASANA PRACTICE

You can benefit by practicing each of the exercises in the former chapter: **Breathe Light**, **Breathe low**, and **Breathe slow**, for three minutes before you begin your physical yoga practice. If you are teaching a class, consider guiding students through the breathing exercises before you begin cuing the postures. You can then continue to use the breathing techniques during the asanas, from a place of physical and mental readiness.

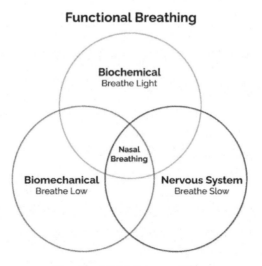

Functional Breathing

Biochemical
Breathe Light

Nasal Breathing

Biomechanical
Breathe Low

Nervous System
Breathe Slow

Breathe Light, Low and Slow

The following sequence uses breathing from the three dimensions, along with breath holds:

1. Biochemistry (**Breathe Light**)
2. Biomechanics (**Breathe low**)
3. Nervous System (**Breath Slow**)

The poses in this sequence relieve tension in the breathing muscles, while getting more oxygen to the brain and working muscles. Some of the postures add a load to the diaphragm to strengthen it. Each pose is active but will relax the body and mind. By bringing awareness out of the mind and into the body/breath, you will centre your practice. Remember to breathe only through the nose throughout all the poses.

First, a word of caution: If you are pregnant, do not practice breath holds. If you have cardiovascular issues or one or more chronic health conditions, do not practice strong breath holds. If you have any concerns, speak to your medical doctor before trying the practice.

Exercises: OA in asana – breathe light, low & slow

Side Head Tilt, Seated

Get into a comfortable seated position on your mat or on a chair.

- Allow your shoulders to relax.
- Imagine a piece of string pulling you up from the crown of your head.
- Now move your head slowly toward your right shoulder.
- As you move your head to the right, breathe in through your nose and out through your nose, and pinch your nose to hold your breath.
- Hold your breath for 5, 4, 3, 2, 1.

- Let go of your nose, and breathe in through it.
- Return your head to the centre, and breathe normally for 10-15 seconds.
- Repeat the exercise on the left side, tilting your head toward your left shoulder.
- As you move your head, breathe in through your nose and out through your nose, and pinch your nose to hold your breath.
- Hold for 5, 4, 3, 2, 1.
- Now let go and breathe in through your nose, returning your head to the centre.
- Breathe normally for 10-15 seconds.
- Repeat the exercise on the right side and then the left side.
- Continue the exercise for 4 minutes.

Exercise: Shoulder Flexion, Seated

- Maintain your upright seated position (on your mat or on a chair).

Pose 1:

- Bring your left arm out in front of you, supporting your elbow with your right hand.
- Apply a little pressure to your arm with your right hand to pull the arm across your body.
- Keep your head and shoulders facing forward.
- As you hold the pose, take a normal breath in and out through your nose.

- After the exhalation, hold your breath for 10-15 seconds, maintaining the pose.
- Come out of the pose and resume normal, nasal breathing for 15-20 seconds.

Pose 2:

- Bring your left arm up toward the ceiling.
- Hold your left elbow gently with your right hand.
- Bend your left elbow, bringing your left hand behind your head.
- Pull gently on the elbow with your right hand, to bring the hand further down your back.
- Keep your head straight and your neck and shoulders relaxed.
- Once in the pose, take a normal breath in and out through your nose.
- After the exhalation, hold your breath for 10-15 seconds, maintaining the pose.
- Come out of the pose and resume normal, nasal breathing for 15-20 seconds.
- Repeat Pose 1 on the right side. Follow the same pattern of breath holding.
- Come out of the pose and breathe normally for 15-20 seconds.
- Repeat Pose 2 on the right side. Follow the same pattern of breath holding.
- Come out of the pose and breathe normally for 15-20 seconds.

Breathe Light, Seated

- Sit up on your mat with your knees bent and your feet flat on the floor.
- Place your arms behind you with your fingers facing away from you.

- Shift your hips forward.

Alternative: If you are hypermobile, you can bend your elbows and turn your fingers to face your body. Shift your hips forward.

During this pose, you will practise *Breathe Light* for approximately two minutes. The purpose of *Breathe Light* is to take less air into your body. You can monitor this in four different ways. You can observe the air as it enters and leaves the nose or feel the air at the back of your throat.

You may notice your chest rising and falling or feel the movement of your abdomen.

- Get yourself into the pose, whichever version works for you.
- Now, begin to slow down the speed of the air as it enters and leaves your nose.
- Can you breathe in so softly, the breath is almost imperceptible?
- Take a very soft, light inhalation through your nose.
- Allow a relaxed, slow, prolonged exhalation through your nose.
- Bring your attention to your breathing.
- At the top of the inhalation, allow a total feeling of relaxation.
- Allow each exhalation to leave the body in a relaxed, slow way. Your exhalation should be longer than your inhalation.
- Continue taking a very soft, slow breath in, and allow a relaxed, slow, gentle exhalation out until you feel a sense of air hunger.
- If the air hunger gets too strong for you or you begin to lose control of your breathing, take a rest from the exercise, and breathe normally.
- Continue with this light breathing for 2 minutes.
- Then come out of the pose and resume normal breathing.
- Sit or kneel on your mat and breathe normally for 2 minutes before moving on to the next pose.

Lunge with Slow, Lateral Breathing

To get into the pose, kneel on your mat and bring your right leg up to place your foot on the floor in front of you. Ensure your front knee is in line with your ankle. If you have any pain in the front knee, you can bring your foot a little further forward. Once you have positioned your front knee correctly, bring the back foot a little further back. Uncurl your toes and tilt your tailbone forwards. Bring the navel in.

Place your hands on the front thigh to help you balance in the pose and observe the sensation in the front part of your back thigh. If you have sensitive knees, you may need to place some padding under the knee that is on the floor.

During this pose, focus on the lateral expansion and contraction of your lower ribs. As you focus on your balance, it can be easy to breathe from the upper chest. Instead, we will activate the diaphragm to **breathe low**.

- As you breathe in through your nose, you will feel your lower ribs gently moving outwards.
- As you breathe out, you will feel your lower ribs gently moving inwards.
- Keep your focus on this lateral expansion and contraction of the lower ribs.
- Breathe silently, in and out through your nose.
- Now, slow down your breathing.
- Breathing in, 2, 3, 4, 5.
- Out, 2, 3, 4, 5.
- In, 2, 3, 4, 5.
- And out, 2, 3, 4, 5.
- Continue this for about a minute.
- Then, come out of the pose and resume normal breathing.
- Now, find the pose on the other side and get settled.
- Repeat the breathing exercise, starting with the lateral expansion and contraction of the lower ribs.
- Then, slow down your breathing, counting in for 5 seconds and out for 5 seconds.

- If this is too challenging for you, breathe in for 3 seconds and out for 3 seconds.
- Resume normal breathing and come out of the pose.

Twisting Lunge

The next pose is another lunge. Start by bringing your right leg forward. Place your left hand on the floor for support. Allow your left leg to move back into a wider lunge, lengthening the distance between the front and back knee. Now lift your left foot and catch hold of it with your right hand or a belt. Gently pull the left foot in toward your body as far as is comfortable.

In this pose, you will practise slow breathing.

- Breathe in, 2, 3, 4, 5, and out, 2, 3, 4, 5.
- As you breathe in, take the air silently in through your nose.
- Breathe light, slow, and low.
- Light breathing means you're taking less air into the body. You will feel a light hunger for air.
- Slow breathing means you are breathing in for 5 seconds and out for 5 seconds.

- Low breathing means you have optimal movement of the diaphragm. You can tell if this is the case by observing the lateral expansion and contraction of the lower ribs.
- Breath in, 2, 3, 4, 5, and out, 2, 3, 4, 5.
- Continue the exercise for 2 minutes.
- Now resume normal breathing.
- Slowly straighten your front leg and switch sides.

- When you are settled in the pose, repeat the light, slow, and deep breathing for 2 minutes.
- When you are ready to come out of the pose, resume normal breathing as you slowly extend the front leg.

Alternative: If you are unable to reach your foot with your hand, you may use the wall for support:

Standing Forward Bend

For this pose, you may be able to have your hands on the floor. Or you may need to support your hands on your shins, or use blocks or a chair, depending on your flexibility.

For this exercise, we will *Breathe Light*. This exercise targets the biochemistry, to open the airways and improve oxygen delivery. Use the pose to explore the resistance to your breathing. During a forward bend, your diaphragm is upside down and must work harder against gravity. In this pose, you may sometimes feel you are running out of air. Do not open your mouth to breathe. Breathe lightly in the pose as follows:

- As you settle into the pose, begin to focus on the airflow as it comes in and out of your nose.
- Begin to gently soften the breath, slowing down each inhalation and exhalation.
- Each inhalation is an almost imperceptible breath in through the nose.
- Each exhalation is light, slow, and gentle.
- When you breathe in, you feel hardly any air move inside your nostrils.

- Can you breathe so softly that the fine hairs in the nostrils do not move?
- Can you have a really relaxed, slow, gentle exhalation, allowing the air to leave your body effortlessly?
- You are taking hardly any air into your nose. And, with each breath, there is a total feeling of relaxation.
- You should be breathing less air than you were at the start of the exercise.

You will know you are doing the exercise correctly when you feel a light hunger for air. This signifies that carbon dioxide has increased in the blood. As we show throughout this book, carbon dioxide is not just a waste gas. It has many important roles in the body.

When you are ready to come out of the pose, resume normal breathing.

Inversion with Breathe Light

The final active pose in this sequence is an inversion. This is another opportunity to work on your breathing muscles as they move against gravity. Choose the inversion that is most comfortable for you. You may select a shoulder stand, headstand, or handstand, depending on your level of physical practice. If none of those are options for you, lie on your back with your hips on a bolster or pillow and your legs up the wall.

- As you settle into the pose, bring your attention out of your mind and into your body.
- Notice the slightly colder air as it

enters your nostrils and the slightly warmer air as it leaves your nose.

- Keep your focus on light, slow, and deep breathing. You can think of the mantra, "Nose, Slow and Low."
- Light breathing is about conserving the breath. It's about increasing carbon dioxide in your lungs and blood. Take the lightest breath into your lungs. Keep your focus on the airflow entering and leaving your nose.
- Can you breathe so lightly that you breathe in hardly any air?
- At the top of the inhale, bring a total feeling of relaxation to your body and allow a relaxed and gentle breath out.
- You will feel a sense of air hunger. This signifies that carbon dioxide has increased in the blood.
- At the same time, think about breathing slow.
- Breathing in for 5 seconds and out for 5 seconds.
- Breathing in, 2, 3, 4, 5, and out, 2, 3, 4, 5.
- Continue the exercise for several minutes, depending on your experience in the pose.
- When you are ready to come out of the pose, resume normal breathing.

Breathing in the Final Resting Pose: Savasana

Make yourself comfortable in savasana. Use a bolster, pillows or cover yourself with a blanket if you like.

Once you are comfortable, close your eyes and bring your attention inward. Place your tongue to rest on the roof of your mouth behind your upper front teeth. In this position, you can practise a body scan meditation. Bring your attention to each small part of your body in turn, allowing your body to relax. Allow your mind to relax in the same way, letting unwanted thoughts leave your mind. As you relax deeply, your breathing will automatically reduce by about 20% and this is good.

After about five minutes or so in the pose, once your body and mind are fully relaxed, bring your attention to your breath. Observe your breath as it enters and leaves your body. When you place attention on your breathing, you take a rest from any mental chatter. You might feel the breath as it enters the nostrils or hits the back of your throat. Or you might feel the movement of your chest and abdomen. Imagine your breathing becoming even more gentle, quiet, and calm, just like a still ocean, with the sun setting across the water.

As your breathing slows, you might feel a slight shortage of air. The feeling of air hunger is something you experience many times a day when you get slightly out of breath. However, in this exercise, the goal is to achieve a light air hunger from a state of deep relaxation. You can do this by gently slowing down the air as it enters and leaves your body. Breathe so smoothly that you feel hardly any movement of air inside your nostrils.

The need for air should feel safe and comfortable. When you create a light need for air by relaxing the muscles of your chest and tummy, your breathing volume reduces, and carbon dioxide builds up in the body. This improves circulation, allowing oxygen to reach every cell of your body. You may sense that your hands are becoming warm or tingly – this is a sign of improved circulation.

You may also notice an increase in watery saliva in your mouth. This indicates the vagus nerve is activated, bringing your body into the parasympathetic rest and digest state. The impact of these exercise on the autonomic nervous system is further explained in Chapter Nine.

If you find your mind wanders during the practice, gently acknowledge your thoughts, and bring your attention back to your breath. Follow your breath and keep your breathing quiet and calm. The more you practice this, the stiller your mind becomes.

Enjoy this part of the exercise for at least ten minutes. Give yourself the time to rest and restore body and mind. When you come out of the pose, remember to take this feeling with you off your mat and into your day.

As you go about your day, if you do find yourself becoming stressed or tense at any point, gently return your attention to your breathing. Quieten and slow your breath to effortlessly improve circulation and calm the mind. A simple but effective way to bring balance to your day.

You will find helpful guided breathing exercises with relaxation as spoken by Patrick on the Oxygen Advantage® and Buteyko Clinic YouTube channels and on Spotify. There are guided breathing practices for: insomnia, perfectionist tendencies, exam preparation, achieving flow states and preparation for musicians prior to concert. Each session is about 20 minutes long and incorporates relaxation and breathing. Google: "patrick mckeown guided breathing".

SECTION TWO

CREATING A BREATHING PRACTICE

HYPERVENTILATION, HYPERCAPNIA, & HYPOXIA: WHAT YOU NEED TO KNOW TO CREATE A BREATHING PROGRAM

To develop your own safe and effective breathing program, you need to understand breathing from the three dimensions, biochemistry, biomechanics, and the nervous system (psycho-physiological). Don't fall into the trap of focusing only on the biomechanics. It also crucial to be conscious of how you breathe not just during yoga, but also during sleep, rest, and exercise – so you can integrate optimal breathing in your everyday life. It's important also to understand why you shouldn't be able to "hear" breathing. And then take all that you've learned back to enrich your yoga practice.

No matter how old you are, or what your level of health, your body strives to find balance. Breath training offers an easy way to support this process, but you do still need to put the work in. It is better to practise patiently and focus on steady progress. Try to resist the temptation to use hacks and shortcuts. Don't rely on extreme breathing techniques that use hyperventilation to "alter your state." Remember – hyperventilation involves breathing more air than the body needs and is linked to many acute and chronic health conditions. After all, breathing is for life. What's the rush? The time commitment is not substantial. You can make great strides just by establishing a morning breathing routine.

A ten-year study demonstrated the positive impact of a morning breath practice in lung and throat cancer survivors. The 122 patients in the study practised breathing exercises in the mornings and had significantly greater survival rates at five and ten years than those in the control group who did not practice breathing exercises. It is thought that the improvement in long-term survival was due to correcting hyperventilation. Those with a morning breathing routine had a BOLT score of 3.3 seconds higher on average. Their everyday breathing was much slower too. They were taking about 4.3 fewer breaths every minute than the patients who had no breathing practice.[91]

The morning breathing program in the study focused on two concepts that are also central to the Oxygen Advantage® method:

1. Normal everyday breathing.
2. Shifting mental states toward a "stress-free mind."

The balance of oxygen and carbon dioxide that results from functional "normal breathing" is crucial for health. The study authors note that any disturbance of this balance "may cause many disorders, especially cancers" (possibly due to tissue hypoxia which occurs when you have low oxygen in the tissues of your body.)"[92] Stress reduction is important too. When you have received a diagnosis of cancer, it's normal to feel highly stressed. Long-term cancer survivors are also much more likely to have psychological problems than people who have never been diagnosed with cancer. Acute and chronic stress will both exacerbate hyperventilation.

---

91 Wu, Wei-Jie, et al. "Morning Breathing Exercises Prolong Lifespan by Improving Hyperventilation in People Living with Respiratory Cancer." *Medicine* 96.2 (2017).
92 Wu, Wei-Jie, et al. "Morning Breathing Exercises Prolong Lifespan by Improving Hyperventilation in People Living with Respiratory Cancer." *Medicine* 96.2 (2017).

The results of the ten-year study indicate that positive benefits are possible from a morning breathing practice – even in those who have been very unwell. A morning breathing routine may well benefit you too.

THE RISKS OF OVERBREATHING: HYPERVENTILATION

Although hyperventilation is used deliberately in certain breathing techniques, such as the Wim Hof Method, in medical terms, it is classed as a breathing pattern disorder. It is synonymous with poor health, and it is at the root of many chronic illnesses. By correcting it, you can reduce the symptoms of many common illnesses.

If you are in good health, deliberate hyperventilation does have some value as part of a breathing practice, but, before we explore that, we need to look at the problems it can cause. Much of this book advocates silent, soft, reduced-volume breathing. So, it makes sense to find out what happens when you deliberately do the opposite.

Chronic Over-breathing

Hyperventilation is a normal physical response. It happens when the body needs to compensate for imbalance, pain, or disease. However, lifestyle, diet, stress, and chronic illness can contribute to habitual over-breathing. We end up breathing more air than the body needs all the time. Labelled as hyperventilation syndrome, this can cause many common symptoms including exhaustion, panic disorder, anxiety, migraine, burnout syndrome, impaired memory and performance, breathlessness, allergies, cold hands and feet, headaches, and back pain.

The respiratory physician, Claude Lum (who is known for his research into hyperventilation) called the hyperventilation syndrome the "fat folder" syndrome. He was referring to the fact that patients are often passed from one specialist to another without getting a clear diagnosis. The patient's medical file gets fatter as they struggle to find answers for symptoms that come and go in many systems in their body.[93]

Chronic hyperventilation doesn't necessarily look or feel like the classic image of hyperventilation. Deep, fast, audible breathing and breathing patterns, such as frequent sighing, can increase your breathing volume by as much as 10%.[94] When you breathe too much air, CO_2 levels in the blood decrease and the blood becomes too alkaline. Hyperventilation can occur whenever breathing is just a little bit faster and harder than necessary. The person standing right next to you may not even be able to tell that you are over-breathing.

Hyperventilation

93 Lum, L. C. "Hyperventilation: the tip and the iceberg." *J Psychosom Res* 19.5-6 (1975): 375-383.

94 Saltzman, Herbert A., Albert Heyman, and Herbert O. Sieker. "Correlation of Clinical and Physiologic Manifestations of Sustained Hyperventilation." *New England Journal of Medicine* 268.26 (1963): 1431-1436.

When hyperventilation is ongoing, the balance of your blood gases is affected. This means the acidity/alkalinity (pH) of your blood is also out of balance. To compensate for the excess acidity caused by chronic over-breathing, your body must constantly excrete bicarbonate to restore pH levels to normal. Over time, your body's reserves of bicarbonate become depleted, leaving you less able to tolerate anything that increases acidity in your body, including breath holding.[95]

What does chronic hyperventilation feel like? You will be more sensitive to air hunger and to constriction in your blood vessels. Your everyday breathing will be faster and harder. You will be more prone to breathlessness, especially during exercise. Your exercise tolerance will be low.[96] And you'll be more likely to breathe into your upper chest. All these breathing habits perpetuate the problem. Hyperventilation then creates an imbalance in your autonomic nervous system and your body gets stuck in the stress response.

As with most chronic conditions, hyperventilation syndrome exists within a spectrum. Some people constantly breathe too much. Others do so occasionally. Hyperventilation syndrome is not a disease. Yet, even from the short list of symptoms above, you can see that it contributes to illness. Many conditions linked with hyperventilation are covered in detail in Patrick McKeown's *The Breathing Cure*. They include sleep apnea, cardiovascular disease, asthma, poor seizure control in epilepsy, poor diabetes control, irritable bowel syndrome, and PMS.[97] Left uncorrected, faster, harder breathing could affect the quality and length of your life.

This connection between hyperventilation and poor health may worry you. If slightly faster, harder breathing can cause so many problems, how can you tell if you hyperventilate? The answer is to have a simple measurement that indicates your body's sensitivity to the build-up of carbon dioxide. In medical settings, blood CO_2 is measured using a

95 Gilbert, Christopher. "Hyperventilation and the Body." *Journal of Bodywork and Movement Therapies* 2.3 (1998): 184-191.

96 Gilbert, Christopher. "Hyperventilation and the Body." *Journal of Bodywork and Movement Therapies* 2.3 (1998): 184-191.

97 McKeown, Patrick. *The Breathing Cure: Exercises to Develop New Breathing Habits for a Healthier, Happier and Longer Life.* OxyAt Books, 2021.

method called capnography. This is expensive and not accessible to most of us. Another problem with capnography is that not everyone with the symptoms of hyperventilation syndrome has low CO_2. Symptoms can occur when resting CO_2 levels are normal.[98,99]

For an objective assessment of your breathing and your sensitivity to CO_2, the answer is to measure with the BOLT (refer back to Chapter Four for a reminder of how to take this measurement).

There are also several observable indicators that you may be suffering from chronic hyperventilation, and they include:

- Mouth breathing
- Stubborn nasal congestion
- Early breathlessness
- Daytime fatigue and yawning
- High levels of anxiety, physical tension, and headaches

When you sense air hunger, your body is giving you the all-important feedback that your CO_2 levels are increasing. When you practise breathing exercises or are doing physical movement, if you have a feeling that you would like to take a bigger breath, it is a good sign that CO_2 is accumulating in your lungs and blood. Over time, experiencing increasing levels of CO_2 until you feel a tolerable air hunger helps to improve your tolerance to the gas. And, as that happens, your BOLT score will increase, and your breathing symptoms will diminish.

It's so important to pay attention to breathing both on and off your yoga mat. Yoga has enormous potential to transform your breathing in general. If your breathing is dysfunctional, the controlled breathing you practice during your asana class will help. The physical poses will to some extent stretch and strengthen the breathing muscles. But remember, you cannot *strengthen* dysfunction. When you push for flexibility instead

---

98 Folgering, H. "The Pathophysiology of Hyperventilation Syndrome." *Monaldi Archives for Chest Disease (Archivio Monaldi per le Malattie del Torace)* 54.4 (1999): 365-372.

99 Magarian, Gregory J. "Hyperventilation Syndromes: Infrequently Recognized Common Expressions of Anxiety and Stress." *Medicine* 61.4 (1982): 219-236.

of stability and steadiness, there will come a point when injury forces you to go back to basics. What's more, if breathing is never assessed and breathing exercises are not tailored, asana practice alone won't be enough to restore functional breathing for lasting wellbeing.

This is especially true if your teacher constantly asks you to breathe audibly and cues your breathing at a speed that causes you to take in a large volume of air. Often, in a yoga class, students are encouraged to hear their breathing, but this can cause them to hyperventilate. When you dig deeper into yogic literature, it seems clear that the focus in ujjayi was never meant to be loud breathing. So, perhaps it is time to stop encouraging students to externalise their focus. Instead, ask them to "listen" for the subtle qualities that occur when breathing is light and breathing volume is slightly restricted.

BREATHING VOLUME: PREVENTING HYPERVENTILATION DURING PRACTICE

The key to preventing hyperventilation during yoga practice (or at any time off the mat) is understanding breathing volume.

Hyperventilation doesn't always look like a panic attack. You can hyperventilate during very slow Prāṇāyāma practice. Or when the breath is cued too slowly during a physical yoga class. You can hyperventilate just by slowing the breath down to six breaths per minute. Unless you pay attention to breathing volume, you are likely to breathe in too much air. Hyperventilation may just feel like breathing that is forced. This is a common feeling when breathing is incorrectly taught. The sense of pushing the abdomen out so the belly swells with each breath, the sore throat after loud ujjayi, or the light-headedness that comes from big, deep breaths, all indicate hyperventilation.

At six breaths per minute, your focus is on the speed of the breath. You are breathing in for five seconds and out for five. It sounds simple, but three different students may experience three different outcomes from the same exercise – if you don't also pay attention to the volume of the breath.

Student A takes big breaths, breathing as much as three litres of air per breath. At six breaths per minute, they will breathe 18 litres of air every minute. This student is hyperventilating. They probably feel lightheaded and stressed, with a dry mouth and cold hands.

Student B inhales the same amount of air they normally would per minute. As they slow their breathing, they increase their volume of air per breath proportionately. They normally breathe six litres of air per minute and continue to do so during the exercise. They will feel calmer.

Student C is more experienced. They take very minimal breaths of only 500 ml, still at six breaths per minute. They are breathing three litres of air and *hypo*ventilating. They will experience air hunger that will help increase their tolerance to CO_2. They will notice an increase of watery saliva in the mouth, a sense of mental calm, and warm, tingly palms.

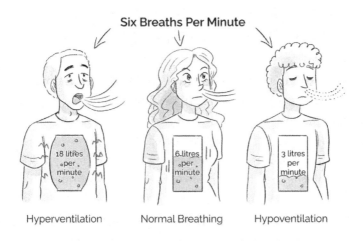

Six Breaths Per Minute

18 litres per minute

6 litres per minute

3 litres per minute

Hyperventilation   Normal Breathing   Hypoventilation

To make sense of breathing volume, it is helpful to think in terms of food volume. If you have an oversized portion of food on your plate, it doesn't matter how many fewer spoons of food you take into your mouth if the spoonfuls are too big. You can still end up overeating. In the same way, when we focus only on the number of breaths, without looking at how much air we are breathing, we still end up over-breathing.

Just as habitual overeating leaves you constantly feeling hungry, one of the symptoms of chronic over-breathing is constant air hunger.

Air hunger comes with a feeling of suffocation that prompts you to breathe faster and into the upper chest. With this type of breathing, exhalations are often incomplete. This means the diaphragm never moves back to its normal resting position. Incomplete exhalations have a knock-on effect. They make it difficult to inhale normally. Breathing remains chaotic, and the feeling of suffocation never really leaves you.

The solution is to breathe through your nose, light, slow, and deep, and to practise breathing exercises that create a tolerable air hunger and improve your BOLT score. Yogis often talk about breathing purely in terms of the diaphragm (biomechanics). However, poor breathing biochemistry contributes to fast, upper chest breathing. This leads to poor diaphragm recruitment. Unless you address the biochemistry, feelings of suffocation will continue to be experienced and diaphragm breathing exercises will not help achieve better breathing long-term. We recommend you begin by restoring nasal breathing to engage the diaphragm and building up the BOLT score to at least 12-15 seconds. Then, it will be a lot easier to focus on working with the breathing muscles.

Tailoring Exercises to Different Yoga Students

What if you have 60 students in your class? How can you teach breathing in a way that works for everyone?

First, ask your students to measure their BOLT, so you can adjust the instructions for each student. The focus should be on creating a *tolerable* air hunger. To begin with, keep the focus only on the biochemistry.

Take time to notice how the students are breathing during physical movement. Can you see signs of strain or tension? This will be reflected in the breath. Guide your class to take a breathing-first approach, adapting their physical movement to the breath. This will feel very different from a practice in which they strain the breath to synchronise it with the postures.

During asana practice, ask your students to breathe in and out silently through the nose. As yoga teachers, we often encourage loud breathing to give the students a clear focus. Instead, use the feeling of tolerable air hunger as your focal point.

Be aware that some students will not be able to slow the breath down to six breaths per minute to begin with. Tailor the exercises accordingly. This is where "standardised" breathing patterns like 4-7-8 breathing are not always helpful. The breathing pattern 4-7-8 produces a 19-second breath phase or a respiratory rate of around three breaths per minute. A student with anxiety or asthma, who normally breathes at around 16 to 18 breaths per minute, is likely to struggle during this exercise. If you reduce the breathing rate so significantly, the student will experience stronger feelings of air hunger. This can be frightening, demotivating, and counterproductive.

What about breathing off the mat? Remind students they don't need to breathe at six breaths per minute all the time. The normal respiratory rate during rest is between 10 and 14 breaths per minute. A good rule of thumb is to maintain silent, nasal breathing as much as possible. The purpose of a breathing practice is to work with a technique so that the benefits carry on as your everyday breathing adapts. The primary objective is to restore functional breathing so that everyday breathing volume is in line with metabolic needs.

RESOLVING HYPERVENTILATION: THE TWO PILLARS OF BREATH TRAINING

Breathing exercises have two "pillars." These are the states we work with to activate different biochemical, biomechanical, and psychophysiological responses within the body. These pillars are *hypercapnia* and *hypoxia*. Hypercapnia is a state in which carbon dioxide levels are higher than normal. Hypoxia is a state in which oxygen is not available in sufficient amounts at the tissue level. Sometimes these states can be induced simultaneously. At other times, you will work only with hypercapnia.

The First Pillar of Breath Training: Hypercapnia

The first step to correcting chronic hyperventilation is to practise light, soft, nasal breathing to achieve a tolerable air hunger and hypercapnia (higher CO_2 levels).

Hypercapnic breathing exercises aim to temporarily build up CO_2 in the lungs and blood. Any time CO_2 leaves the body more slowly than normal, levels of CO_2 will increase in the blood. The type of exercises that induce hypercapnia include reduced volume breathing, physical exercise with the mouth closed, and breath holding after a normal inhalation or exhalation. When the breath is held, CO_2 cannot leave the blood via the lungs. If you add physical movement to light, nasal breathing, or breath holding, CO_2 levels rise even more.

Benefits of Hypercapnic Exercises

Hypercapnic exercises train the respiratory and nervous systems to tolerate higher levels of CO_2. When you train the body in this way, your breathing becomes slower and softer. It takes longer to reach your CO_2 threshold. During yoga practice and other physical exercise, this delays the point at which you become breathless. It improves your capacity for physical exercise and your fitness. Ultimately, a higher tolerance for CO_2 is the secret to the steadiness of breath which is every yogi's goal.

Another notable benefit of hypercapnic exercises is that the increase in carbon dioxide improves blood flow in the brain.[100] This is because CO_2 causes blood vessels to dilate, improving blood flow and oxygen delivery. This effect is so powerful that blood supply to the brain increases by 3-4% per every mmHg increase of $PaCO_2$ (partial pressure of carbon dioxide) in the blood. The **Breathe Light** exercise (see page 69) has an expected increase of $PaCO_2$ by 3 mmHg, resulting in improved blood supply to the brain by 9-12%. During a long breath hold following an

---

100   Reivich, Martin. "Arterial PCO2 and Cerebral Hemodynamics." *American Journal of Physiology – Legacy Content* 206.1 (1964): 25-35.

exhalation, $PaCO_2$ can increase by 10 mmHg resulting in as much as a 30-40% increase in blood supply to the brain.[101]

Over time, the practice of slow, light, and soft breathing has many benefits:

- You will feel calmer.
- Your concentration will improve.
- You will perform better at cognitive tasks.
- Your circulation will improve.
- Your body will be better able to digest the food you eat.
- Organs including your brain and heart will receive optimal levels of oxygen.

People often ask about changes in blood acidity during breathing exercises. There is a common belief that it is always good to avoid acidity in the body, however, as CO_2 increases in the blood, the body does become slightly more acidic. This acidity (called acidosis) is temporary. Blood pH returns to normal within about one minute of normal breathing. Small doses of respiratory acidosis can be deliberately induced to cause positive adaptations in the body. Hypercapnic breathing exercises that induce low levels of temporary acidosis will be of particular benefit to you if one or more of the following applies:

- Your BOLT score is less than 25 seconds.
- You are new to breath training.
- You have a low tolerance to CO_2.
- You become breathless easily during aerobic exercise.

Light breathing exercises should never be stressful. When they are practised correctly, the vagus nerve activates,[102] bringing the nervous

---

101 Battisti-Charbonney A, Fisher J, Duffin J. The cerebrovascular response to carbon dioxide in humans. J Physiol. 2011 Jun 15;589(Pt 12):3039-48.

102 Singh, U. P. "Evidence-Based Role of Hypercapnia and Exhalation Phase in Vagus Nerve Stimulation: Insights into Hypercapnic Yoga Breathing Exercises." *Journal of Yoga & Physical Therapy* 7.3 (2017): 1000270-1000276.

system into a parasympathetic state. At the same time, tissues, muscles, and organs become better oxygenated due to the Bohr effect.

You will know that you have achieved hypercapnia when you feel air hunger. You may also notice watery saliva in your mouth, drowsiness, and an increase in body temperature. Often your hands and fingers feel warmer. Watery saliva is produced as the body prepares for digestion. This only happens when your nervous system is relaxed. The goal is to feel calm and centred, during and after practice. If your mouth feels dry and your hands are cold, take the exercise very gently. This is particularly important if you have anxiety or panic disorder, or a strong reaction to the feeling of suffocation.

How to Practise Hypercapnia

As previously mentioned, it is not easy to measure levels of CO_2 in the lungs or bloodstream without sophisticated scientific equipment. However, an elevated level of CO_2 will send a strong signal to the brain to breathe more, so it's easy to identify hypercapnia by the feeling of air hunger. This might be a slight sense that you would like to take a bigger breath, or, after a strong breath hold, it might feel like a very strong desire to breathe, during which you may notice your diaphragm contract.

You can work with the sensation of air hunger using the Oxygen Advantage® exercise **Breathe Light**, which you will find on page 69. It's a good idea to practise this seated so you get used to the feeling of light breathing and air hunger. You can then bring this exercise into your asana practice. This is an effective way to increase tolerance to CO_2.

The Second Pillar of Breath Training: Hypoxia

Hypoxia is a state where blood oxygen saturation drops. It is a feature of many health conditions, including sleep apnea. It also happens when we travel to high altitude where the pressure of the atmosphere is less. Controlled hypoxia has many benefits, in contrast to the chronic, uncontrolled hypoxia specific to disease states. These benefits can be achieved and maintained using breathing exercises. (Please note the contraindications for hypoxia exercises on page 112).

This is key: Healthy blood oxygen levels are normally between 95% and 100%, meaning that the blood is almost fully saturated with oxygen. It's important to understand this because we need to get rid of the idea that we can somehow get more oxygen by taking bigger breaths. In other words, all the oxygen we need is already in the blood. The issue is getting the oxygen from the blood to where it is needed (and that is where CO_2 plays a crucial role).

In fact, when less oxygen is available, such as at high altitudes, the body adapts to use oxygen more efficiently. The study of these adaptations began in earnest in 1878, with a Frenchman named Paul Bert. Bert was the first to study "mountain sickness," and record how the body adapts to high altitudes, both in the short and long-term. In his *Pression Barométrique*, he laid the foundations for the study of high-altitude physiology and the idea that the partial pressure of atmospheric gases is responsible for certain responses in the body.[103]

Bert's work was inspired by fellow Frenchman, the physician Denis Jourdanet. Jourdanet had practised medicine in Mexico for almost 20 years. Much of his work focused on the effects of high altitude on the human body. He observed a consistent increase in blood thickness at high altitudes. This prompted Bert to theorise that the concentration of red blood cells in the bloodstream increases as we ascend from sea level.[104]

In 1890, another French physiologist, Francois-Gilbert Viault confirmed Bert's hypothesis. Viault spent time hiking in the Peruvian mountains. He found that, after 23 days at 4,392 metres above sea level, his own red blood cell count had increased significantly, from five to eight million per cubic millimetre. In later research, he verified a fact we now take almost for granted – that the concentration of haemoglobin in the blood increases at high altitude, improving the body's oxygen-carrying capacity. [105]

A century after Viault's discoveries, research demonstrated that hypoxia stimulates the release of the hormone erythropoietin (EPO) which is responsible for the production and maturation of new red blood cells. EPO is known to have many therapeutic and performance-enhancing benefits. A 2018 rodent study even suggests it may protect the brain against the damaging effects of chronic stress.[106]

Hypoxia triggers a series of valuable responses in the body:

- The spleen contracts to release its reserves of red blood cell-rich blood. The spleen is the body's blood bank. The blood it contains has a very high concentration of red blood cells and haemoglobin.

103 Rudolph, G. "In Memory of Paul Bert (1833-1886) and the Development of High Altitude Physiology in Switzerland." *Gesnerus* 50 (1993): 79-95.

104 Windsor, Jeremy S., and George W. Rodway. "Heights and Haematology: The Story of Haemoglobin at Altitude." *Postgraduate Medical Journal* 83.977 (2007): 148-151.

105 Viault, F. "On the Large Increase in the Number of Red Cells in the Blood of the Inhabitants of the High Plateaus of South America." *High Altitude Physiology* (1981) 333-4.

106 Dik, Andre, et al. "Contradictory Effects of Erythropoietin on Inhibitory Synaptic Transmission in Left and Right Prelimbic Cortex of Mice." *Neurobiology of Stress* (2018) 113-123.

- The kidneys produce the hormone EPO, which matures new red blood cells.
- During short-term hypoxia, new stem cells are generated.[107] Stem cells are the building blocks of all cell types in the body. They are involved in normal muscle growth and the repair of muscle after injury or disease.
- New blood vessels grow,[108] producing permanent new pathways by which your tissues and organs can receive oxygen.
- Collagen synthesis is stimulated.[109] This can be helpful in early wound repair.
- The p53 gene (tumour-suppressant) is activated.[110,111]

The p53 gene, discovered in 1979, is a tumour-suppressant and is the most frequently mutated gene in human cancer.[112] It plays a key role in cell division and cell death and is sometimes referred to as the "guardian of the genome" because it protects cells from DNA damage.[113] It's important to underline that we are *not* suggesting controlled hypoxia has therapeutic benefits in cancer. A cancerous tumour is already a hypoxic, acidic microenvironment. However, in healthy adults, the p53 gene is thought to contribute to cardiovascular adaptation to exercise and may enhance aerobic capacity.[114]

---

107 Yoshida, Yoshinori, et al. "Hypoxia Enhances the Generation of Induced Pluripotent Stem Cells." *Cell Stem Cell* 5.3 (2009): 237-241.

108 Pugh, Christopher W., and Peter J. Ratcliffe. "Regulation of Angiogenesis by Hypoxia: Role of the HIF System." *Nature Medicine* 9.6 (2003): 677-684.

109 Pugh, Christopher W., and Peter J. Ratcliffe. "Regulation of Angiogenesis by Hypoxia: Role of the HIF System." *Nature Medicine* 9.6 (2003): 677-684.

110 Lowe, S. W. "Activation of p53 by Oncogenes." *Endocrine-Related Cancer* 6.1 (1999): 45-48.

111 Zhao, Yang, Xue-qun Chen, and Ji-zeng Du. 2009. "Cellular Adaptation to Hypoxia and p53 Transcription Regulation." *Journal of Zhejiang University Science B* 10.5 (2009): 404-410.

112 Jing, Xinming, et al. "Role of Hypoxia in Cancer Therapy by Regulating the Tumor Microenvironment." *Molecular Cancer* 18.1 (2019): 1-15.

113 Matthew, Elizabeth M., et al. "The p53 Target Plk2 Interacts with TSC Proteins Impacting mTOR Signaling, Tumor Growth, and Chemosensitivity Under Hypoxic Conditions." *Cell Cycle* 8.24 (2009): 4168-4175.

114 Kim, Boa, et al. "Functional Study of Tumor Suppressor p53 Gene Variation: Effect on Cardiovascular Adaption to Exercise Training." *FASEB Journal Supplement* 26.1 (2012): 1138-5.

Humans have evolved to adapt to low levels of oxygen at high altitudes, while diving, and in certain disease states. We have also developed ways to use these adaptations to our advantage, especially in the fields of sports performance and human optimization. This is the logic behind the illegal and dangerous blood doping with synthetic EPO. It's also why many athletes train at high altitudes as part of their preparation for competition.

Achieving Beneficial Hypoxia at Sea Level

It is possible to bring the body into hypoxia without diving or climbing to a high altitude. This is done through the practice of five consecutive strong breath holds. Five maximal breath holds will cause the spleen to contract, releasing red blood cells-rich blood into circulation.[115,116] The practice also strengthens your diaphragm, as strong breath holding causes the diaphragm to contract vigorously. You can prepare for the exercise with two easy breath holds, with a break of 30 seconds to one minute between each. You can also practise breath holding during your asana sequences, although it is a good idea to accustom yourself to the exercise before trying it during your yoga practice.

Hypoxia is defined as a drop in blood oxygen saturation to below 92%. You can measure your blood oxygen saturation using a pulse oximeter, a simple tool that is readily and affordably available. It is possible to achieve hypoxia within four days of practising strong breath holds. Over time, you will develop an intuitive feeling for hypoxia and will no longer need the oximeter.

115 Schagatay, Erika, et al. "Selected Contribution: Role of Spleen Emptying in Prolonging Apneas in Humans." *Journal of Applied Physiology* 90.4 (2001): 1623-1629.
116 Schagatay, Erika, Johan Andersson, and Bodil Nielsen. "Hematological Response and Diving Response During Apnea and Apnea with Face Immersion." *European Journal of Applied Physiology* 101.1 (2007): 125-132.

Exercise: How to Practise Hypoxia to Simulate High Altitude Training

The following exercise should only be practised if you are in good health. Also, you should never practise breath holding during pregnancy, as hypoxia may harm your unborn baby.

- Breathe normally, in and out through your nose.
- After exhaling, pinch your nose with your fingers and hold your breath.
- With your breath held, start walking.
- Increase your pace to a fast walk, a jog, and then a fast jog.
- As your breathing muscles contract, relax into the contractions.
- When you reach the point where the air hunger feels strong, let go of your nose and breathe in through it.
- Slow to a walk and stop.
- For the next 6 breaths, practise minimal breathing. Take very small breaths in and out through your nose. This helps prolong the hypoxia and allows the body to recover.
- Breathe normally for between 12 and 18 breaths, until your breathing feels comfortable.
- Repeat the sequence of breath holding and recovery 5 times.

How to Practice Hypoxia

Breathe normally, in and out through your nose.

After the exhalation, pinch your nose with your fingers and hold your breath.

With your breath held, start walking.

Increase your pace to a fast walk, a jog and then a fast jog.

As your breathing muscles contract, relax into the contractions.

When the air hunger feels strong, breath in through your nose.

Slow to a walk and stop.

For the next 6 breaths, practise minimal breathing.

Breathe normally until your breathing feels comfortable.

Repeat the sequence of breath holding and recovery five times.

A Word of Caution

Hypoxia and breath holds are sometimes perceived as dangerous, especially when they are viewed through the lens of sleep apnea. This signals a confusion between voluntary, controlled hypoxic episodes that are practised between 3 and 20 times a day and frequent involuntary hypoxia that causes severe oxygen desaturation many times a night. It is also common to overlook the psychological, biomechanical, and biochemical benefits of some forms of conscious breath holding. That said, it is important to proceed with caution and with correct guidance. Improper practice of strong breath holds can worsen dysfunctional breathing.

Don't practise strong breath holds if: you have any medical disorders including cancer, neurological and cardiovascular disorders, and conditions involving blood sugar dysregulation.

CHAPTER SEVEN

BREATHING EXERCISES THAT USE DELIBERATE HYPERVENTILATION

We have explored the problems that come with hyperventilation and the benefits of developing greater tolerance to CO_2. Now, imagine that you add deliberate hyperventilation to the mix. Deliberate hyperventilation exercises involve breathing harder and or faster for a period of time, ranging from a few minutes to an hour or more. This reduces CO_2 – which can be a problem for some people. In certain practices such as the Wim Hof Method, deliberate hyperventilation is followed by breath holding, layering one stressor on top of another. Does this mean you should avoid exercises that require you to hyperventilate at all costs? Not necessarily.

Many people can experience great benefits from exercises involving hyperventilation, but these exercises are very powerful, and for some people, they can be too much. As previously mentioned, they are also contraindicated with certain health conditions.

As such, if you plan to do these breathing practices, you should be in good health and fully informed about how they affect your body. Proceed very carefully. Hyperventilating and holding the breath for long periods of time are where most problems with breathing practices emerge. In this chapter, we will explore the effects, drawbacks, and potential benefits of deliberate hyperventilation exercises so you can decide for yourself whether to practise them.

WHAT HAPPENS DURING DELIBERATE HYPERVENTILATION

In breathing exercises that use hyperventilation followed by breath holding, the main purpose of hyperventilation is to create *hypo*capnia – a reduction in blood CO_2. Because CO_2 operates as the signal to breathe, hypocapnia allows the practitioner to hold their breath for much longer, achieving a significant drop in blood oxygen. Holding the breath for several minutes can lower blood oxygen saturation from a normal level of 98%, to as low as 40%. Such a strong decrease in blood oxygen reduces blood supply to the brain.

Hyperventilation Breath Exercises: The Drawbacks

Voluntary hyperventilation has a number of potential drawbacks. Even under medical supervision, the use of hypocapnia, which is the hallmark of hyperventilation, has become considered questionable due to its many adverse side effects.[117]

A review of the literature reveals a number of concerning findings associated with voluntary hyperventilation. Studies show it can increase the risk of cardiac arrhythmia[118] and epileptic seizures,[119] and cause unfavourable symptoms including dizziness, tinnitus and light-headedness. It may also cause cramps or spasms in the hands during the hyperventilation phase.[120,121] This symptom is called "tetany." It is caused

---

117 Curley, Gerard, Brian P. Kavanagh, and John G. Laffey. "Hypocapnia and the Injured Brain: More Harm Than Benefit." *Critical Care Medicine* 38.5 (2010): 1348-1359.

118 King, J. C., S. D. Rosen, and P. G. F. Nixon. "Failure of Perception of Hypocapnia: Physiological and Clinical Implications." *Journal of the Royal Society of Medicine* 83.12 (1990): 765-767.

119 Kane, Nick, et al. "Hyperventilation During Electroencephalography: Safety and Efficacy." *Seizure* 23.2 (2014): 129-134.

120 Kasperk, C. "Hypercalcemic Crisis and Hypocalcemic Tetany." *Der Internist* 58.10 (2017): 1029-1036.

121 Bansal, Teena, and Sarla Hooda. "Hyperventilation Causing Symptomatic Hypocalcaemia During Labour in a Parturient." *Egyptian Journal of Anaesthesia* 29.4 (2013): 333-335.

by the blood becoming more alkaline than normal.[122] Hyperventilation can also lead to low blood phosphate[123] and trigger symptoms including muscle weakness, numbness, and an altered mental state.[124]

Another drawback of the hypocapnic state that voluntary hyperventilation causes, is that it can reduce breathing and muscle efficiency, and negatively affect physical stamina and recovery. This is because CO_2 is not only vital for oxygen delivery, but also important for muscle repair and endurance. A 2017 rodent study concluded that CO_2 promotes muscle fibre switching from fast-twitch to slow-twitch. Slow-twitch muscle fibres are the most efficient. They rely on aerobic respiration (oxygen) for energy. The adult diaphragm is made up of around 60% slow-twitch muscle fibres.[125,126] Hypocapnic alkalosis limits the ability of muscles to use oxygen when transitioning to moderate-intensity exercise.[127] When muscles do not get enough oxygen, they tire sooner and take longer to repair.

Interestingly, the impact of hyperventilation may depend on your personality type. In a study that attempted to test the relationship between the effects of hyperventilation and personality, researchers found that those with neuroticism (a tendency to experience the world as negative, distressing, and unsafe[128]), were negatively affected while extroverts showed no adverse reaction.[129]

122 Macefield, Gary, and David Burke. "Paraesthesiae and Tetany Induced by Voluntary Hyperventilation: Increased Excitability of Human Cutaneous and Motor Axons." *Brain* 114.1 (1991): 527-540.

123 Paleologos, M., E. Stone, and S. Braude. "Persistent, Progressive Hypophosphataemia After Voluntary Hyperventilation." *Clinical Science* 98.5 (2000): 619-625.

124 "What Is Hypophosphatemia?" *Web MD.* (n.d.) http://www.webmd.com/a-to-z-guides/what-is-hypophosphatemia (Accessed July 4, 2022).

125 Gollnick, P. D., et al. "Enzyme Activity and Fiber Composition in Skeletal Muscle of Untrained and Trained Men." *Journal of Applied Physiology* 33.3 (1972): 312-319.

126 Banner, Michael J. "Respiratory Muscle Loading and the Work of Breathing." *Journal of Cardiothoracic and Vascular Anesthesia* 9.2 (1995): 192-204.

127 Chin, Lisa M. K., et al. "Hyperventilation-Induced Hypercapnic Alkalosis Slows the Adaptation of Pulmonary O2 Uptake During the Transition to Moderate-Intensity Exercise." *The Journal of Physiology* 583.1 (2007): 351-364.

128 Weed, Nathan C., and Sangil Kwon. "Neuroticism | Psychology." *Britannica.* (January 2, 2019). http://www.britannica.com/science/neuroticism (Accessed July 4, 2022).

129 Clark, D. M., and D. R. Hemsley. "The Effects of Hyperventilation; Individual Variability and Its Relation to Personality." *Journal of Behavior Therapy and Experimental Psychiatry* 13.1 (1982): 41-47.

If you hyperventilate before a breath hold, the blood vessels in your brain constrict as CO_2 levels drop. This causes the oxygen supply to reduce more rapidly as hypoxia kicks in. It also allows you to hold your breath for much longer, as the urge to breathe in is dulled. This produces even more extreme hypoxia.

During some hyperventilation and breath holding techniques, blood oxygen saturation (SaO_2) can drop to 50%. At this point, alarmingly, circulation to the brain will reduce. Unfortunately, the exact effects of this are currently unknown and it may be some years before the true effects are realised.

Is there any benefit to reducing blood flow to the brain and temporarily depriving it of oxygen? To answer this, we need to look at the science behind apneas (breath cessation) and brain function.

Research into nocturnal hypoxia tells us there's a 70% greater risk of developing dementia if you have sleep apnea.[130] However, along with involuntary breath holding, sleep apnea also involves sleep fragmentation and deprivation of slow-wave sleep. To get a clearer picture, we need to look at the breath holds in apneas in isolation without the other effects. To do this, it is useful to explore the science around free diving. Research from 2009 shows that long breath holds affect the integrity of the central nervous system, and this may cause damage to the brain over time. Divers who held their breath for several minutes showed elevated levels of a protein called S110B, which can signal brain damage.[131]

However, it is known that elite breath hold divers who train intensively adapt physically and develop a higher concentration of red blood cells.[132] This limits the impact of hypoxia by increasing the oxygen-carrying capacity of the blood. There are even entire populations

130 Bubu, Omonigho M., et al. "Obstructive Sleep Apnea, Cognition and Alzheimer's Disease: A Systematic Review Integrating Three Decades of Multidisciplinary Research." *Sleep Medicine Reviews* 50 (2020): 101250.

131 Andersson, Johan P. A., et al. "Increased Serum Levels of the Brain Damage Marker S100B After Apnea in Trained Breath-Hold Divers: A Study Including Respiratory and Cardiovascular Observations." *Journal of Applied Physiology* 107.3 (2009): 809-815.

132 Ostrowski, Andrezej, et al. "The Role of Training in the Development of Adaptive Mechanisms in Freedivers." *Journal of Human Kinetics* 32 (2012): 197.

that have adapted. For instance, the Bajau, a nomadic people who live in the Southeast Asian seas and fish using freediving, are known to have unusually large spleens compared to their nearest geographic neighbours. Researchers concluded that these people had undergone unique adaptations associated with the diving response and spleen size. They have evolved to be able to hold their breath for longer.[133] However, science also tells us that the adaptations elite free divers experience from breath hold training are not easily transferable to non-elite, recreational athletes.[134] This would imply that if you are new to breath training, you will not safely achieve long breath holds, nor should you try.

What's more, another study from 2018 suggests that several years of breath hold dive training may cause memory impairment. The study's authors write, "Despite an increasing number of practitioners, the relationship between apnea-induced hypoxia and neurocognitive functions is still poorly understood."[135]

If you are tempted to practise hyperventilation to prolong your breath holds to super-human lengths, this statement alone should be enough to elicit caution. These exercises should never be practised competitively, and you must always listen to your body. Also, use a pulse oximeter where possible to monitor your blood oxygen saturation.

Hyperventilation Breath Exercises: Potential Benefits

Despite the potential dangers outlined above, voluntary hyperventilation techniques are very popular among yoga practitioners and can lead to positive effects. The benefit of these practices is likely due to hormones,

---

133 Ilardo, Melissa A., et al. "Physiological and Genetic Adaptations to Diving in Sea Nomads." *Cell* 173.3 (2018): 569-580.
134 Dolscheid-Pommerich, Ramona C., et al. "Hematologic Changes After Short Term Hypoxia in Non-Elite Apnea Divers Under Voluntary Dry Apnea Conditions." *Plos One* 15.8 (2020): e0237673.
135 Billaut, Francois, et al. "Do Elite Breath-Hold Divers Suffer from Mild Short-Term Memory Impairments?" *Applied Physiology, Nutrition, and Metabolism* 43.3 (2018): 247-251.

to the hypoxia achieved in the subsequent long breath holds, or to something called physical repatterning.

Hyperventilation causes a unique hormonal response. It stimulates the release of the stress hormones noradrenaline and adrenaline. In one study, during which participants performed voluntary hyperventilation for 20 minutes, noradrenaline increased by 151% and adrenaline by 360%.[136]

Levels of beta-endorphins also increase. Beta endorphins are normally released during physical or emotional stress. They regulate stress, anxiety, appetite, body temperature, and other functions.[137] Beta endorphins are opioids. This means they regulate pain and may improve your mood. Compliance can be a problem with any breathing practice, particularly if your mood is low. However, opioids are addictive, so you may find the release of beta-endorphins motivates you to hyperventilate.

Finally, when you hyperventilate, your trunk moves in an exaggerated way. This can repattern your breathing muscles, reminding you to breathe when you find yourself inadvertently holding your breath. Because the breathing muscles are intimately linked with your posture, hyperventilation can also repattern your physical posture in a positive way.

The Wim Hof Breathing Technique

We are often asked about Wim Hof breathing at Oxygen Advantage®. Wim Hof breathing is part of the Wim Hof Method and involves cold exposure and meditation. Some of our instructors teach both methods. So, what is the difference between the OA® & Wim Hof methods?

In Oxygen Advantage®, breath holds to simulate high altitude training are hypoxic and _hyper_capnic. In contrast, Wim Hof breathing

---

136 Folgering, H., H. Rutten, and Y. Roumen. "Beta-Blockade in the Hyperventilation Syndrome. A Retrospective Assessment of Symptoms and Complaints." *Respiration* 44.1 (1983): 19-25.

137 Felten, David L. *Netter's Neuroscience Flash Cards E-Book*. Elsevier Health Sciences, 2022.

is hypoxic and _hypo_capnic. As a reminder, hypercapnic means _higher_ than normal CO_2 levels in the blood, while hypocapnic means _lower_ than normal levels.

Any form of hyperventilation will cause disturbances depending on:

- The intensity of hyperventilation.
- Your body's reserves of the alkaline buffer bicarbonate.[138,139]
- Your emotional state.[140,141,142]
- And your sensitivity to low CO_2 and respiratory alkalosis.

These features are typical of all hyperventilation techniques.

Some of the benefits of controlled hypoxic hypocapnic breathing exercises include:

- Better motor function in the breathing system (and non-respiratory systems too).
- Better learning, memory, and brain function.[143]
- Production of the hormone erythropoietin, which is needed to mature new red blood cells.
- Anti-inflammatory effects.[144]

138 Lum, L. C. "The Syndrome of Chronic Habitual Hyperventilation." _Modern Trends in Psychosomatic Medicine_ 3 (1976): 196-230.

139 Ley, Ronald. "Panic Attacks During Sleep: A Hyperventilation-Probability Model." _Journal of Behavior Therapy and Experimental Psychiatry_ 19.3 (1988): 181-192.

140 Groen, J. J. "The Measurement of Emotion and Arousal in the Clinical Physiological Laboratory and in Clinical Practice." in _Emotions: Their Parameters and Measurement_, 727-746. New York, New York: Raven Press, Publishers, 1975.

141 Schaefer, Karl Ernst. "Respiratory Pattern and Respiratory Response to CO2." _Journal of Applied Physiology_ 13.1 (1958): 1-14.

142 King, Jenny C. "Hyperventilation – A Therapist's Point of View: Discussion Paper." _Journal of the Royal Society of Medicine_ 81.9 (1988): 532-536.

143 Dale, E. A., F. Ben Mabrouk, and G. S. Mitchell. "Unexpected Benefits of Intermittent Hypoxia: Enhanced Respiratory and Nonrespiratory Motor Function." _Physiology_ 29.1 (2014): 39-48.

144 Kox, Matthijs, et al. "Voluntary Activation of the Sympathetic Nervous System and Attenuation of the Inate Immune Response in Humans." _Proceedings of the National Academy of Sciences._ (n.d.) 7379-7384.

- Better metabolism and reduced cholesterol, body weight, and blood sugar levels.
- Physiological adaptations that enhance athletic performance.[145]

However, as we already discussed, extra-long breath holds that produce severe hypoxia are risky. You can achieve intermittent hypoxia more safely by practising strong breath holds without hyperventilating before. It may not be as gratifying, but, if you tend to be competitive, that's not necessarily a bad thing. Remember what the yogic literature says about taming the lion gradually to avoid being destroyed? It's important to take that seriously.

ANASTASIS'S VIEWPOINT ON VOLUNTARY HYPERVENTILATION

My personal experience with hyperventilation is limited to the Wim Hof Method training. While practising the breathing technique, I felt scared. I also felt much less conscious afterwards. This discouraged me from continuing to practise it once I was certified. I am still asked to guide clients through a hyperventilation process, and I aim to minimise the duration and the intensity of these sessions. I also combine them with meditation and/or a breathing technique that activates the parasympathetic relaxation response.

I have gathered evidence documenting the risks of hyperventilation, but first I want to clarify one thing. Even highly vulnerable individuals may be able to hyperventilate without any side effects. When I was leading workshops that involved hyperventilating exercises, I had participants diagnosed with schizophrenia and bipolar disorder attend. I advised them to modify the breathing sequence slightly, and I am grateful that no one reported any adverse effects. That is not to say it was

---

145 Navarrete-Opazo, Angela, and Gordon S. Mitchell. "Therapeutic Potential of Intermittent Hypoxia: A Matter of Dose." *American Journal of Physiology – Regulatory, Integrative and Comparative Physiology* 307.10 (2014): R1181-R1197.

safe to perform. If you decide to practise a hyperventilation breathing exercise, I suggest you are clear on what you are trying to achieve, and you get guidance from an experienced instructor.

PATRICK'S VIEWPOINT ON VOLUNTARY HYPERVENTILATION

For me personally, breath holding in controlled doses to generate a strong stress response is extremely beneficial, and I have seen some wonderful results. Unfortunately, I have also seen some side effects including panic attacks, severe fatigue and anxiety. And yes, these effects were with my own students, and I had guided them through the exercises. I have made some mistakes teaching long breath holds to students, and the breath holding I taught to generate severe hypoxia was much milder than the Wim Hof Method. Experience can be a wonderful teacher, and it doesn't make sense for you to repeat the same mistakes that I made with some of my clients.

I have always been conservative when it comes to the deliberate practice of hyperventilation, probably because I have spent the last 21 years teaching exercises to address the issues of chronic hyperventilation. Also, feedback from clients and students practising hyperventilation has taught me to proceed with caution. For example, at a recent OA instructor training in Poland, one of the participants who was a fit and healthy male in his mid-thirties explained to the group how he developed heart arrhythmia from practising hyperventilation followed by breath holding. Despite stopping these breathing exercise practices many months ago, he continues to have arrhythmia and while the *breathe light* exercise is helping him reduce the severity of the condition, the problem hasn't gone away. For clarity, I would like to point out that this person's issues didn't arise from the OA° training.

For these reasons, I always apply a tailored approach with my clients, altering the dose and duration of air hunger, based on their age, state of health, and breathing patterns. I have learned over the years to also be particularly cautious when working with people over 60, and people who have cardiac issues, anxiety, panic disorder, etc.

OUR ADVICE

Our advice to anyone who would like to practise stressor breathing techniques such as hyperventilation or long breath holds, is to do so with caution, and to dip your toes into the water gradually. If possible, monitor your blood oxygen saturation to ensure it stays above 60%. The decrease in CO_2 from hyperventilation also strengthens the bond between CO_2 and O_2, which means that less oxygen is readily available to the muscles and organs. At the same time, the longer the breath is held, the more NO is produced. For these reasons, Oxygen Advantage® primarily uses breath holds *after* exhaling and *without* any hyperventilation techniques in order to get the best hypoxic/hypercapnic results.

CHAPTER EIGHT

PRACTICAL APPLICATIONS OF THE BREATH

In this chapter, you will find specific protocols for applying breathing exercises for specific purposes, to prevent fainting, to moderate pain, to detoxify the body, as a warm-up for physical exercise including yoga, and to enter meditation.

USING THE BREATH TO PREVENT FAINTING

"Fainting can occur very quickly, but it can also happen gradually. I have been vulnerable to fainting for a big part of my life. While a few times it was caused by dehydration, it was very common for me to pass out during routine injections and blood tests. When I became familiar with the Buteyko Method, I realised I have much more control than I originally thought. The technique described below has worked for clients of mine who were also susceptible to fainting."

— Anastasis

If you are in a situation where you tend to pass out, you can follow these three steps:

1. Sit or lie down in a comfortable position.
2. Bring your attention to your breath. Intentionally slow your breathing. Be purposeful with both the inhalation and the exhalation and maintain a reduced breathing volume to create a tolerable hunger for air.
3. Continue to breathe intentionally for 1 to 2 minutes or until the feeling that you may faint has passed. Only then should you stand up and proceed with your day.

USING BREATH TO MODERATE PAIN

Scientists have repeatedly shown that breathing modulates our perception of unpleasant stimuli, including pain.[146,147] Slow breathing reduces pain,[148] specifically when the exhalation is longer than the inhalation. Breath holds also moderate pain perception. In a study of 38 healthy adults, breath holding after inhaling was shown to improve pain tolerance more than slow inhalations.[149]

Breathing volume also plays a role in how much pain we feel. Pain perception changes depending on how much air you inhale before the breath hold. In this instance, scientists have shown that inhaling to 80% of your maximum chest expansion suppresses pain more effectively than a 50% inhalation or breath holding after exhaling.[150] You know

146 Iwabe, Tatsuya, Isamu Ozaki, and Akira Hashizume. "The Respiratory Cycle Modulates Brain Potentials, Sympathetic Activity, and Subjective Pain Sensation Induced by Noxious Stimulation." *Neuroscience Research* 84 (2014): 47-59.

147 Wells, Rebecca E., et al. "Attention to Breath Sensations Does Not Engage Endogenous Opioids to Reduce Pain." *Pain* 161.8 (2020): 1884.

148 Jafari, Hassan, et al. "Respiratory Hypoalgesia? Breath-Holding, But Not Respiratory Phase Modulates Nociceptive Flexion Reflex and Pain Intensity." *International Journal of Psychophysiology* (2016) 101: 50-58.

149 Reyes del Paso, Gustavo A, et al. "Breathholding During Exhalation as a Simple Manipulation to Reduce Pain Perception." *Pain Medicine* (2015) 16.9: 1835-1841.

150 Jafari, Hassan, et al. "Respiratory Hypoalgesia? Breath-Holding, But Not Respiratory Phase Modulates Nociceptive Flexion Reflex and Pain Intensity." *International Journal of Psychophysiology* 101 (2016): 50-58.

this instinctively. When you stub your toe or bang your shin, the first response, even before you yell in pain, is a sharp intake of breath followed by a short breath hold. It is likely that the phrenic and vagus nerve, both of which innervate the diaphragm, are also involved in reducing pain through breathing.[151]

With this research in mind, the two best approaches to dealing with pain using your breath are to either hold your breath at the end of a full inhalation or to **breathe slow**ly with an inhalation-to-exhalation ratio of 1:2 (see Chapter Twenty for more info on the connection between pain and breathing patterns).

BREATH TRAINING TO DETOXIFY THE BODY

All breathing exercises will support detoxification in the body, but our attraction to breath training as a form of detox is often driven by our fascination with hyperventilation techniques. For example, in 2020, Canadian researchers proved that deliberate hyperventilation could eliminate alcohol from the body three times faster than the liver can excrete it. Each forceful exhalation releases alcohol that has evaporated from the blood into the lungs. The more you breathe, the more alcohol will evaporate. This finding may provide a novel way to treat alcohol poisoning, but, before you tune in to your Wim Hof breathing after a night out, it's important to remember the negative side-effects of hyperventilation. The researchers in that study prevented dizziness and light-headedness by administering CO_2 during the exercise to maintain normal levels of the gas in the blood.[152]

---

151 Bordoni, Bruno, et al. "Depression, Anxiety and Chronic Pain in Patients with Chronic Obstructive Pulmonary Disease: The Influence of Breath." *Monaldi Archives for Chest Disease* 87.1 (2017).
152 Klostranec, Jesse M., et al. "Accelerated Ethanol Elimination Via the Lungs." *Scientific Reports* 10.1 (2020): 1-7.

Alcohol withdrawal can itself cause severe hyperventilation,[153] leaving you with respiratory alkalosis and panic symptoms. Severity of hyperventilation and anxiety symptoms increase with alcohol dependency.[154] Serious alcohol withdrawal symptoms include seizures and hallucinations.[155] Voluntary hyperventilation is also known to trigger seizures.[156,157] If you want to use breathing exercises to help with alcohol dependency, it is best to work with a certified Oxygen Advantage® instructor who can give you a safe program to follow (see **https://oxygenadvantage.com/instructors**).

Nevertheless, because breathing affects every other system in the body, it does aid in the detoxification of many substances in several different ways. As air enters the body, the nose provides a first line of defence against airborne toxins. Nitric oxide, produced in the sinuses around the nose, kills viruses, bacteria, and fungi as you inhale. Lower down in the respiratory tract, hairlike cells called cilia collect dust and other pathogens in mucus, for you to cough or sneeze out of the body.

Ingested toxins such as metals, alcohol, and drugs are cleared by the liver, kidneys, and digestive system. This process is aided by the diaphragm, which sits above the liver and the small intestines. As the diaphragm oscillates during breathing, it massages the liver. This supports the elimination of waste, including toxins.

Slow, diaphragm breathing also helps detoxification by activating the parasympathetic nervous system, the body's relaxation mode which is known as "rest and digest" because it allows the body to process food

---

153 "How Can Alcohol Make Anxiety Worse?" *Life Skills South Florida.* (April 12, 2019). http://www.lifeskillssouthflorida.com/mental-health-blog/how-can-alcohol-make-anxiety-worse/ (Accessed July 4, 2022).

154 Roelofs, Sarah M. G. J. "Hyperventilation, Anxiety, Craving for Alcohol: A Subacute Alcohol Withdrawal Syndrome." *Alcohol* 2.3 (1985): 501-505.

155 "Management of Moderate and Severe Alcohol Withdrawal Syndromes." *UpToDate.* (n.d.) http://www.uptodate.com/contents/management-of-moderate-and-severe-alcohol-withdrawal-syndromes/print (Accessed July 4, 2022).

156 Salvati, Kathryn A., and Mark P. Beenhakker. "Out of Thin Air: Hyperventilation-Triggered Seizures." *Brain Research* 1703 (2019): 41-52.

157 Indranada, Alaric M., et al. "The Association of Panic and Hyperventilation With Psychogenic Non-Epileptic Seizures: A Systematic Review and Meta-Analysis." *Seizure* 59 (2018): 108-115.

efficiently. When you practise relaxing breathing exercises, you may notice an increase of saliva in your mouth. This is because activating the vagus nerve increases salivation and swallowing,[158] both of which are essential for digestion.[159] Saliva is vital for oral health, which in turn is important for gut health. Gum disease, for instance, can affect the gut microbiome.[160] Saliva is loaded with antibacterial compounds and friendly bacteria,[161] all of which aid the digestive process. What's more, scientists have discovered that the salivation response to food is lower in people who are obese. People who salivate more quickly in response to food tend to consume fewer calories than those who show slower rates.[162] This suggests that habituation of the salivation response helps regulate the point at which we stop eating.

The lungs can also excrete toxins. When the liver is overtaxed, the body uses the breath as a secondary detox pathway. In a 2006 study of people with liver disease, scientists found high levels of metabolites (the end process of metabolism) in the breath.[163] In a healthy person, these metabolites would normally be excreted through the liver.

Nose breathing also supports detoxification by helping to maintain hydration. If the body is dehydrated, the kidneys will hold onto water. This prevents toxins from leaving your body in urine. For the same reason, using a sauna to sweat toxins out of your body can be counterproductive.

158 Ueda, Hirotaka, et al. "Vagal Afferent Activation Induces Salivation and Swallowing-like Events in Anesthetized Rats." *American Journal of Physiology – Regulatory, Integrative and Comparative Physiology* 311.5 (2016): R964-R970.

159 Pedersen, Anne Marie Lynge, et al. "Salivary Functions in Mastication, Taste and Textural Perception, Swallowing and Initial Digestion." *Oral Diseases* 24.8 (2018): 1399-1416.

160 "Oral Dysbiosis: How the Oral Microbiota Affects Your Gut Health." *Atlas Biomed.* (March 31, 2020). http://www.atlasbiomed.com/blog/oral-dysbiosis-affects-gut-health/ (Accessed July 4, 2022).

161 "Saliva: More Than Just Drool." *Bad Gut.* (n.d.) http://www.badgut.org/information-centre/a-z-digestive-topics/saliva-more-than-just-drool/ (Accessed July 4, 2022).

162 Bond, D. S., et al. "Salivary Habituation to Food Stimuli in Successful Weight Loss Maintainers, Obese and Normal-Weight Adults." *International Journal of Obesity* 34.3 (2010): 593-596.

163 Solga, S. F., et al. "Breath Biomarkers and Non-Alcoholic Fatty Liver Disease: Preliminary Observations." *Biomarkers* 11.2 (2006): 174-183.

Exercise for detoxification: Nauli Kriya

An effective detox exercise is nauli kriya. Nauli kriya is a cleansing/purification technique that uses uddiyana bandha to massage the lower back and digestive organs. It can be performed on all fours, or kneeling, seated, or standing, with your hands pressed into your knees. This is a useful practice that works the lower abdominals and connects you with muscles that can be difficult to activate.

- Stand with your feet shoulder-width apart and your knees slightly bent.
- Lean forward and place your hands on your thighs, just above your knees.
- Straighten your arms and lean your weight into your hands.
- Exhale slowly and fully through your mouth.
- Hold your breath.
- With your breath held, draw your abdominal wall in and up toward your spine.
- Continue the breath hold for as long as you can.
- Slowly release your abdominal muscles.
- As you relax your abdomen fully, inhale.
- Repeat the exercise several times.

Once this version of the exercise is mastered, you can practise drawing on one side of the abdomen at a time. This creates a "stirring" movement in the abdominal muscles.

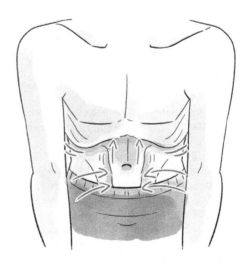

Words of Caution

- Nauli kriya should be practised on an empty stomach.
- Do not attempt this exercise if you are pregnant.
- If you have heart disease, hypertension, hernia, abdominal pain, gallstones, acute peptic ulcer, constipation, or have recently had surgery, do not practise it.

Does Fasting Affect the Breath?

Regular fasting impacts the metabolism. That means we can expect it to influence breathing patterns. Research into intermittent fasting and breathing is currently limited, but there are some interesting findings:

- Intermittent fasting promotes better cardiovascular health, lowering heart rate and blood pressure, and increasing post-exercise heart rate variability (HRV).[164] A systematic review of 19 studies on intermittent fasting found that it reduced bodyweight, lowered systolic blood pressure and glucose concentration and was deemed a promising therapeutic strategy for controlling weight and improving metabolic dysfunctions.[165]
- In one study of non-athletes, maximum breath hold time increased 14.2% after 18 hours of fasting.[166]
- In another study, elite divers were able increase their maximum breath hold time by 22% after an overnight fast.[167]

164 Ahmed, Aftab, et al. "Impact of Intermittent Fasting on Human Health: An Extended Review of Metabolic Cascades." *International Journal of Food Properties* 21.1 (2018): 2700-2713.

165 Moon, Shinje, et al. "Beneficial effects of time-restricted eating on metabolic diseases: a systemic review and meta-analysis." *Nutrients* 12.5 (2020): 1267.

166 Lindholm, Peter, et al. "Effects of Fasting and Carbohydrate Consumption on Voluntary Resting Apnea Duration." *European Journal of Applied Physiology* 100.4 (2007): 417-425.

167 Schagatay, Erika, and Angelica Lodin-Sundstrom. "Fasting Improves Static Apnea Performance in Elite Divers Without Enhanced Risk of Syncope." *European Journal of Sport Science* 14.sup1 (2014): S157-S164.

- A cohort study of people fasting during Ramadan found that intermittent fasting increases lung volume and may improve pulmonary function.[168]

It is important to know that fasting naturally increases the breakdown of fat for energy. Breath holds practised in this metabolic state intensifies the drop to blood oxygen saturation[169] – which makes breath holding less safe during this time.

If you have any underlying health conditions, you should consult your doctor before undertaking intermittent fasting. Please see *https:// joinzoe.com/learn/covid-the-big-if-study* for more information.

Breathing Exercises to Warm Up for Physical Exercise

Before you exercise, you can include some breath training and asanas. This is particularly important if you have asthma, as it prepares the lungs for more intensive exercise. You may like to use this protocol before a vigorous asana practice or before athletic training.

168 Moosavi, Seyyed Alij, et al. 2007. "Evaluation of the Effect of Islamic Fasting on Lung Volumes and Capacities in the Healthy Persons." *Saudi Medical Journal* 28.11 (2007): 1666-1670.
169 Lindholm, Peter, and Mikael Gennser. 2005. "Aggravated Hypoxia During Breath-Holds After Prolonged Exercise." *European Journal of Applied Physiology* 93.5 (2005): 701-707.

Standing Sequence	Short Sequence	Long Sequence
Neck side flexion	Hold for 5-10 seconds on each side	Hold for 5 seconds on each side, then for 10, then 15 seconds
Chin-to-chest neck rotation		Hold for 5 seconds, release, then hold for 10, then 15 seconds
Spine side flexion	Hold for 5-10 seconds on each side	Hold for 5 seconds on each side, then for 10, then 15 seconds
Shoulder horizontal abduction (standing)	Hold for 30 seconds	Hold for 60 seconds
Happy cat vacuum, angry cat standing (with ADIM)	3 rounds	6 rounds
High lunge	Hold for 30 seconds	Hold for 60 seconds
Straight back pike	Hold for 30 seconds	Hold for 60 seconds
Straight back pike, side to side		Hold for 60 seconds

After the physical warm-up sequence, practise two to five minutes of anuloma breathing (see page 269). Keep your exhalation two to three times longer than your inhalation. Or practise *Breathe Light* (see page 69) followed by three to five maximal breath holds after exhaling.

Exercise: Neck Side Flexion

Exercise: Spine Side Flexion

Exercise: Chin-to-Chest Neck Rotation

Exercise: Shoulder Horizontal Abduction (Standing)

*Exercise: Happy Cat
(with Vacuum)*

Exercise: High Lunge

*Exercise: Angry Cat Standing
(with ADIM)*

Exercise: Straight Back Pike

*Exercise: Straight Back Pike,
Side to Side*

Breathing Exercises for Cooling Down

The same exercises that you used to warm up for your physical training can be used to cool down after training.

As part of your cool down after exercise, you can include breath training and asanas. The benefits of this include better oxygenation of the whole body and quicker recovery.

After the physical poses, practise between two and five minutes of Nadi sodhana (alternate nostril breathing, see page 283), **Breathe Light** (page 69), or Samavritti (page 267). Follow this with three to five minutes of diaphragm breathing, either lying on your back with a two-to-five-kilogram weight on your abdomen, or lying on your front, propped on your elbows, with a small block beneath your belly.

THE PHYSICAL STRUCTURES OF BREATHING

CHAPTER NINE

THE NERVOUS SYSTEM AND ITS INTERCONNECTION WITH THE BREATH

Let's consider the nervous system in a little more detail before we dig into its interconnection with the breath. The nervous system is a complex system comprising the brain, spinal cord, and nerves. It plays an important role in generating sleep, wakefulness, creativity, stress, and calm. It allows us to perceive, comprehend, and respond to the world around us.

THE AUTONOMIC NERVOUS SYSTEM

Breathing is controlled by the autonomic nervous system (ANS) which is part of the peripheral nervous system. The ANS regulates numerous other involuntary or automatic processes, including your heartbeat, body temperature, and blood pressure. The ANS has two subdivisions – the sympathetic and the parasympathetic nervous systems, which have opposite actions that continually fluctuate to maintain balance in your body.

The sympathetic nervous system (SNS) is responsible for the "fight or flight" stress response, such as an increase in heart rate and pupil dilation. In evolutionary terms, this innate response was essential for survival. Modern-day stressors such as financial pressures, stress at work, or anything that causes high anxiety, can also stimulate the SNS response.

More recently, the sympathetic response has been dubbed the "fight-flight-freeze-fawn" response. According to Peter Walker, in his book on complex PTSD and recovering from trauma: [170]

> "A **fight** response is triggered when a person suddenly responds aggressively to something threatening. A **flight** response is triggered when a person responds to a perceived threat by fleeing, or by launching into hyperactivity. A **freeze** response is triggered when a person gives up, numbs out into dissociation and/or collapses as if accepting the inevitability of being hurt. A **fawn** response is triggered when a person responds to a threat by trying to be pleasing or helpful in order to appease and forestall an attacker."

In contrast, the parasympathetic nervous system (PNS) is responsible for regulating resting responses, such as your heart rate, salivation, tear secretion, and digestion. It is sometimes referred to as the "rest and digest" response.

The vagus nerve

The vagus nerve moderates the activity of the PNS. This important nerve is the most wide-ranging cranial nerve in your body (vagus means *wandering* in Latin). It controls organ functions such as digestion, heart rate, respiratory rate, perspiration, and muscle sensations. The vagus nerve also regulates reflex actions, such as sneezing, swallowing, coughing, and vomiting.

---

170 Walker, P. *Complex PTSD: From Surviving to Thriving*. Lafayette, California: Azure Coyote Publishing, 2013.

Stimulating the vagus nerve can activate your PNS, balancing out the fight or flight response elicited by the sympathetic nervous system and shifting your body into the rest and digest mode. A variety of breathing exercises found in this book can be used to stimulate your vagus nerve to help manage stress, anxiety, and other parasympathetic responses.

Conscious manipulation of the breath can be used to override autonomic processes via the somatic nervous system.[171] The somatic nervous system is also part of your PNS.[172] It connects the central nervous system (the brain and spinal cord) to the muscles, allowing you to control movements and reflexes. Breathing serves as a "back door" by which we can access the ANS. The breath is really the only function of the ANS that can be both automatic and voluntarily controlled.

While the ANS provides motor and sensory nerves to the entire respiratory tract, it is specifically the movement of muscles involved in breathing that we can control. By consciously altering the breath, we can influence other autonomic functions such as heart rate and blood pressure. This is something that most people know intuitively. It is also the reason breathing exercises support traditional treatment protocols for many diseases.

THE INFLUENCE OF THE ANS ON CARDIOVASCULAR & RESPIRATORY SYSTEMS

The cardiovascular and the respiratory systems are tightly connected and are influenced by the autonomic nervous system in a number of ways.

---

171 McConnell, Alison. *Respiratory Muscle Training: Theory and Practice.* Elsevier Health Sciences, 2013.

172 "Motor and Sensory Function of the Somatic Nervous System." *Very Well Mind.* (2019) http://www.verywellmind.com/what-is-the-somatic-nervous-system-2795866 (accessed July 2, 2022).

Heart rate variability (HRV)

While heart rate is the number of times your heart beats per minute, HRV is the measure of the change in timing, or fluctuations, between successive heartbeats. HRV is affected by the sympathetic and parasympathetic nervous systems. People are more resilient, physically and emotionally, when HRV is higher and more complex.[173] Higher HRV can be a sign that your body adapts well to changes in your environment and different levels of stress.

HRV is also considered a reliable measure of how well the vagus nerve is working, that is, *vagal tone*. Vagal tone, itself, is frequently used to assess heart function and is also useful in assessing emotional regulation and other processes that alter, or are altered by, changes in parasympathetic activity.

How is HRV measured?

Heart rate variability is most accurately measured with an electrocardiogram (ECG or EKG) that uses electrodes to sense the electrical signals in your heart that cause it to beat. You may also measure your HRV at home. Technology has provided a number of wearable devices, and apps that go along with them, that can assess and monitor HRV.

In the absence of a wearable device, you can get a feel for your own HRV simply by locating your pulse at the carotid artery in your neck. As you feel your heartbeat, also pay attention to your breathing. When your heartbeat cycles with your breath, this is called *respiratory sinus arrythmia*. As you focus your attention on your breath, have a soft inhalation and a slow, relaxed exhalation. As you slow your breath, do you notice the timing of the heartbeats gets longer? This slowing of the heartbeat is due to activation of the vagus nerve. When body and mind

---

173 Lehrer, P. M., and R. Gevirtz. "Heart Rate Variability Biofeedback: How and Why Does It Work?" *Frontiers in Psychology* 756 (2014).

are in a state of balance, the time between heart beats is longer during exhalation.

Please be aware that HRV varies from person to person and there isn't a "normal" range that applies to everyone. One person's normal could be abnormal for you. An individual's HRV is influenced by many factors, including genetics, height, sex, age, lifestyle factors and medication. I advise that individuals are not overly concerned by what their HRV figure is. It's more important that they understand that practicing breathing exercises is one way to help optimize HRV and counter stress.

The baroreflex & chemoreflexes

The baroreceptor reflex (otherwise known as the baroreflex) is a homeostatic function that helps maintain blood pressure at healthy, near-constant levels. All major blood vessels contain pressure baroreceptors. When blood pressure rises, the baroreflex immediately causes the blood vessels to dilate and the heart rate to drop. Conversely, when blood pressure falls, the baroreflex ensures the blood vessels constrict and heart rate increases.[174].

The baroreflex is optimized when the relationship between breathing and heart rate is at its most efficient with regard to blood gas exchange. The major influence on the reflex drive to breathe comes from the need to maintain balance by matching ventilation with metabolic demand and maintaining blood O_2, CO_2, and pH within narrow ranges.

Chemoreflexes are a respiratory control system that change ventilation in response to fluctuations in blood gasses and pH.[175] As explained in the earlier part of the book, carbon dioxide accumulation in the blood is the main driver of breathing. In general, people with

---

174 Lehrer, P. M., and R. Gevirtz. "Heart Rate Variability Biofeedback: How and Why Does It Work?" *Frontiers in Psychology* 756 (2014).

175 https://pressbooks.lib.vt.edu/pulmonaryphysiology/Chapter/control-of-breathing/ (Accessed June 25, 2023).

optimal breathing are less sensitive to the accumulation of carbon dioxide, while those who are sedentary, stressed and or have poor health are more sensitive to the gas. The chemoreflex exerts powerful influences over breathing as well as cardiac and vascular control. Interestingly, there is an *inverse* relationship between chemoreflex sensitivity and baroreflex sensitivity:

Poor blood pressure control   =   Increased stimulation of breathing
(low baroreflex sensitivity)   (high chemoreflex sensitivity)

Improved blood pressure control   =   Reduced stimulation of breathing
(high baroreflex sensitivity)   (low chemoreflex sensitivity)

According to Luciano Bernardi, professor of internal medicine:

"When there is reduced control of the blood pressure (low baroreflex sensitivity) there is high stimulation of breathing (high chemoreflex sensitivity). In the long term, this can mean a high risk of cardiovascular disease.

Yoga, physical training and breathing exercises, can all improve blood pressure control, as they can increase the sensitivity of the baroreflex, which in turn reduces the stimulation of breathing (lowers chemoreflex sensitivity). In the long term, this can mean lower blood pressure along with other benefits".[176]

Slow breathing reduces the chemoreflex response to both low oxygen (hypoxia) and high carbon dioxide (hypercapnia). When the baro-receptors are more sensitive to fluctuations in blood pressure, this helps to reduce the sensitivity of the body to carbon dioxide.

Practising light and slow breathing may be of benefit in conditions such as chronic heart failure that are associated with inappropriate

---

176 Excerpt from Luciano Bernardi's presentation "Yoga, Chemoreflex and Barorelex". (Department of Internal Medicine, University of Pavia, and Institute of Respiratory Diseases, University of Catania, Catania, Italy).

chemoreflex activation.[177] An example of this would be that patients with chronic heart failure have exercise intolerance. Essentially, the more the person's breathing is stimulated during exercise, the more breathless they feel, which can deter them from doing exercise, even yoga, altogether. A skilled yoga instructor will be able to identify the student with excessive or disproportionate breathlessness and guide them to train their reflexes and reduce the excessive stimulus to ventilate, allowing them to exercise.

The common denominator in all these systems is the breath, especially slow breathing. In 2017, Russo et al. undertook a review of the effects of slow breathing in the healthy human. They concluded:

"Investigations into the physiological effects of slow breathing have uncovered significant effects on the respiratory, cardiovascular, cardiorespiratory and autonomic nervous systems. Key findings include effects on respiratory muscle activity, ventilation efficiency, chemoreflex and baroreflex sensitivity, heart rate variability, blood flow dynamics, respiratory sinus arrhythmia, cardiorespiratory coupling, and sympathovagal balance."[178]

Interestingly, it has been shown that yoga reduces chemosensitivity to carbon dioxide.[179] Incorporating breathing exercises that target the biochemical dimension of breathing into yoga practice can offer a more direct approach to improve breathing from a biochemical dimension.

177 Bernardi, Luciano, et al. "Slow breathing reduces chemoreflex response to hypoxia and hypercapnia, and increases baroreflex sensitivity." *Journal of hypertension* 19.12 (2001): 2221-2229.

178 Russo, Marc A et al. "The physiological effects of slow breathing in the healthy human." *Breathe (Sheffield, England)* vol. 13,4 (2017): 298-309.

179 Spicuzza, Lucia, et al. "Yoga and chemoreflex response to hypoxia and hypercapnia." *The Lancet* 356.9240 (2000): 1495-1496.

HOW THE BRAIN CONTROLS THE BREATH

Several regions in the brain help to regulate the breath. The central computer resides in your brainstem. The brain stem is shaped like a stalk and connects the brain to the spinal cord. The brain stem is located at the bottom part of the brain and sends signals from the brain to the rest of the body. The basic rhythm of breathing, which at rest only requires muscle activity during inhalation, is set by the medulla in your brainstem.

To regulate the breath in line with the body's metabolic demands, the brainstem has a two-way line of communication with many parts of the body. The incoming signals come from muscles and from specialised nerve cells in the brain called chemoreceptors. The chemoreceptors monitor levels of CO_2, O_2, and blood pH. These body-to-brain signals arrive via *afferent* nerve fibres. They are processed by the brainstem, which then communicates to the diaphragm to contract. The brain-to-body signals travel through *efferent* nerve fibres.

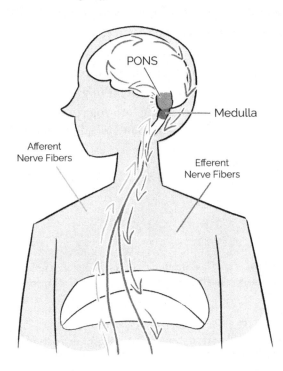

PONS

Medulla

Afferent
Nerve Fibers

Efferent
Nerve Fibers

Afferent and efferent neurons are part of the ANS. They are not classified as part of the sympathetic or parasympathetic nervous systems, but they are found within sympathetic or parasympathetic nerves. For instance, the vagus nerve, which modulates some functions in the lungs, is made up of around 80% afferent (body-to-brain) nerve fibres. The vagus nerve is the main driver of the parasympathetic nervous system – which is why breathing exercises that stimulate the vagus nerve have a calming effect.

The table below lists the different groups of afferent neurons and their impact on breathing.

Stretch receptors (in the lungs)	Pulmonary stretch receptors are located in the smooth muscle of the airways. Stretch receptors regulate the volume of breathing via the vagus nerve.[180]
Irritant receptors (in the lungs)	Irritant receptors are activated through the inhalation of noxious gases, cold, and dust, and cause an increase in breathing rate, volume of breathing, or stimulate coughing.[181] They also transmit information to the respiratory center via the vagus nerve.
Receptors (in the muscles and joints)	When activated, these receptors cause the breathing rate to increase.
Peripheral chemoreceptors (in the neck and the heart base)	When the peripheral chemoreceptors detect increased CO_2, decreased blood pH, or low O_2, breathing rate increases, to remove carbon dioxide from the blood at a quicker rate.
Central chemoreceptors (in the brain stem)	Central chemoreceptors primarily sense and respond to pH changes in the central nervous system caused by alterations in arterial carbon dioxide.[182] When the central chemoreceptors detect high CO_2 or decreased blood pH, breathing rate increases and vice versa.

180 Brinkman, Joshua E., Fadi Toro, and Sandeep Sharma. "Physiology, respiratory drive." *StatPearls [Internet]*. StatPearls Publishing, 2021.
181 Daly, Meredith L. "Hypoventilation." in *Small Animal Critical Care Medicine*, edited by Deborah C. Silverstein and Kate Hopper, 2015, 86-92.
182 https://www.ncbi.nlm.nih.gov/books/NBK482414/. Accessed May 07, 2023.

In the lungs, the ANS controls dilation and constriction of the airway via both the parasympathetic and sympathetic nervous system.[183] Sensory nerve fibres arise out of the vagus nerve, which is the main component of the parasympathetic nervous system.[184] Further sensory nerve fibres innervate the lungs, arising from clusters of nerve bodies positioned along the spinal cord.[185] This bundle of intersecting nerves arrives in the lung via the same route as the veins, arteries, and bronchi. The nerve bundle is made up of the pulmonary branches of the vagus nerve (which mediates the PNS) and the sympathetic trunk[186] (which mediates the SNS). Inside the lungs, the nerves follow the bronchi and branch off to innervate muscle fibres, blood vessels, and glands.

In simple terms, parasympathetic motor nerve fibres regulate the bronchoconstriction (tightening of the airways) while the sympathetic motor nerve fibres regulate bronchodilation (expanding of the airways). The parasympathetic nerves secrete the neurotransmitter acetylcholine into the smooth muscle and mucus-secreting glands in the airways.[187] This causes bronchoconstriction and mucus production. Acetylcholine also controls other functions in the respiratory tract, such as regulating inflammation.[188]

The diaphragm is the motor muscle of breathing – the pump in the respiratory system. It works automatically, but its movement can also be "forced" or controlled. Diaphragm movement is controlled by the phrenic nerve which passes through the third to fifth thoracic vertebrae

183 Kuntz, Albert. "The Autonomic Nervous System in Relation to the Thoracic Viscera." *Diseases of the Chest* 10.1 (1944): 1-18.
184 Breit, Sigrid, et al. "Vagus Nerve as Modulator of the Brain-Gut Axis in Psychiatric and Inflammatory Disorders." *Frontiers in Psychiatry* 44 (2018).
185 Vaillancourt, Mylene, et al. "Autonomic Nervous System Involvement in Pulmonary Arterial Hypertension." *Respiratory Research* 18.1 (2017): 1-15.
186 "Pulmonary Plexus." *Widkipedia*. (December 8, 2019). http://www.widkipedia.com (Accessed July 2, 2022).
187 Hakim, Amir, and O. S. Usamani. "Structure of the Lower Respiratory Tract" in *Reference Module in Biomedical Sciences*, 2014.
188 Borger, Peter, et al. "Beyond the Immune System: The Role of Resident Cells in Asthma and COPD." *Journal of Allergy* (2012).

of the spine. It's no coincidence that some mental health conditions also contain the word "phrenic" for example, schizophrenic.

The diaphragm is also connected to the vagus nerve,[189] which innervates the crural area – the region of the diaphragm responsible for correct breathing.[190] By consciously altering the breath, we can influence autonomic functions such as heart rate and blood pressure and down-regulate our nervous system into a more relaxed rest and digest PNS state. This is something that ancient yogis knew intuitively.

---

189 Young, Richard L., et al. "Sensory and Motor Innervation of the Crural Diaphragm by the Vagus Nerves." *Gastroenterology* 138.3 (2010): 1091-1101.

190 Bordoni, Bruno, and Emiliano Zanier. "Anatomic Connections of the Diaphragm: Influence of Respiration on the Body System." *Journal of Multidisciplinary Healthcare.* 6 (2013): 281.

CHAPTER TEN

BREATHING BIOMECHANICS: A 3D APPROACH

Three physical systems support breathing:

1. **The respiratory tract**
2. **The supportive muscles** (including connective tissue that attaches to the rib cage and the diaphragm)
3. **Posture**

The following Venn diagram illustrates the interconnectedness of these three systems.

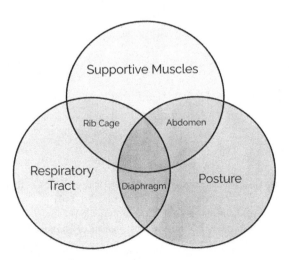

1. PHYSICAL SYSTEMS: THE RESPIRATORY TRACT

The respiratory system is the network of organs and tissues that allow you to breathe. It includes your airways, lungs, blood vessels and the breathing muscles that power your lungs.

The respiratory system contains two tracts: the upper respiratory tract and the lower respiratory tract:

- **Upper respiratory tract** – the nasal cavity, sinuses, pharynx (throat) and larynx (voice box) above the vocal cords.
- **Lower respiratory tract** – the larynx below the vocal cords, the trachea (windpipe) and the bronchi and bronchioles in the lungs. Air travels through the bronchi, which branches out into smaller tubes called bronchioles. At the end of the bronchioles, the air enters one of the many millions of alveoli where gas exchange takes place.

Many yoga practices can affect the function of the upper and the lower airways. For example, neti kriya, which involves either the bathing of the nasal passage in a saline solution (jala neti) or the passing of a thread through the nostrils and out of the mouth (sutra neti), can cleanse the nasal airway. Ujjayi breathing can reduce dead space in the lungs, increasing oxygen diffusion to the bloodstream. Dead space is the volume of air that is inhaled but does not take part in gas exchange. Many asanas promote the full use of the lungs by facilitating the delivery of air to one part of the lungs and restricting it in another. Also, the diaphragm, which sits at the bottom of the lungs, can be strengthened through the practice of breathing exercises and/or asanas.

2. PHYSICAL SYSTEMS: THE SUPPORTIVE MUSCLES

Although the diaphragm is the main respiratory muscle, other muscles, fascia, and nerve cells all play an active role in supporting breathing. These tissues and cells are not technically part of the respiratory system, but, if they fail or become dysfunctional, breathing will be compromised. When breathing is dysfunctional, the body relies on small muscles to get enough air into the lungs. When any small muscle is overused, this often contributes to pain.

The intercostal muscles are positioned between the ribs (the name *intercostal* literally means *between ribs*). They form two thin layers that span the spaces between the ribs – an outer layer (external intercostals) and an inner layer (internal intercostals). These muscles play an intricate role in breathing, and they support trunk stability during movement. Because they're located between the ribs, they share functions with other muscles in this space.

Of these small muscles, the external inter-costals work to lift the ribs and increase the chest cavity. Auxiliary muscles engage when metabolic demands significantly increase, for instance, during high-intensity exercise. If your breathing is dysfunctional, this can also occur during mental stress.

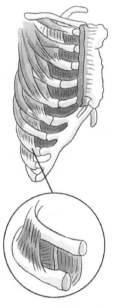

We have little ability to voluntarily control the function of the intercostal muscles through breathing. However, it is possible to strengthen them using load-bearing stretches. Parighasana (gate pose), a strong side bend, can be used to stretch the intercostal muscles and improve lung expansion.[191,192] Be aware, however, that if you pull an intercostal muscle, it can be incredibly painful.

Intercostal Muscles

There are numerous other secondary or accessory breathing muscles. These activate

191 "Why You Should Start to Exercise Your Intercostals Muscles." *Expand-a-Lung.* (n.d.) http://www.expand-a-lung.com/how-to-increase-stamina-improving-your-breathing/ (Accessed July 2, 2022).
192 "Taking Sides: Gate Pose. Yoga Journal." (August 28 2007). http://www.yogajournal.com/practice/beginners/how-to/gate-pose/ (Accessed July 2, 2022).

during different phases of the breath, depending on the intensity of physical activity. As with any movement pattern, the activation of these secondary breathing muscles can sometimes get out of balance.

Above the rib cage, the scalenes and sternocleidomastoid muscles sit on either side of the neck. The scalenes attach to the first and second rib. The sternocleidomastoids attach to the sternum (breastbone) and collarbone. The recruitment of these two pairs of muscles is often considered synonymous with upper chest breathing. It is our observation that when these muscles, alongside the trapezius, are tight, zero movement is possible in the upper chest and upper back. This limits the expansion of the lungs.

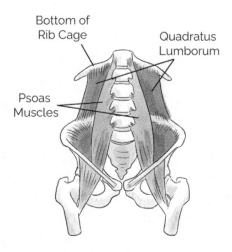

Bottom of Rib Cage

Quadratus Lumborum

Psoas Muscles

Below the rib cage at the rear of the body, the psoas muscle and quadratus lumborum sit either side of the spine. These two pairs of muscles attach to the back of the diaphragm. We have reviewed hundreds of scientific papers and have yet to see these muscles mentioned in studies and articles related to breathing. Nonetheless, their structure and function are, in our opinion, pivotal in breathing. Both muscles attach to the diaphragm. When they are tight, weak, or unevenly balanced, they will restrict diaphragm movement. Both muscles also play an important role in posture – and, when posture is compromised, breathing is restricted.

The table below shows which breathing muscles are active during quiet or vigorous breathing:

	Quiet Breathing			Active Breathing
Breathing Muscles	Primary	Secondary	Auxiliary	Abdominal
Inspiration	Diaphragm	External & internal intercostals	Sternoclei-domastoid & scalenes	Transversus & Rectus Abdominis, Internal & External Obliques
Expiration		Internal intercostals		Rectus abdominis, external & internal obliques, & transversus abdominis

The intercostal muscles and the abdominal obliques have various things in common. Both muscle groups contain two layers that take part in respiration. Both also play a role in the stability of the rib cage and trunk. During contraction, these two muscle groups bring rigidity to the rib cage and trunk, allowing you to pull, push, and lift. Just as the diaphragm has more than one function, these muscles have a double role.

In physical activities such as competitive sports, where the respiratory, muscular, and metabolic demands are high, the body will always prioritise respiration over posture.[193] If your diaphragm becomes too tired to work properly, smaller breathing muscles activate to compensate. This keeps you alive. But it can have negative consequences too.

193 Hodges, Paul W., Inger Heijnen, and Simon C. Gandevia. "Postural Activity of the Diaphragm is Reduced in Humans When Respiratory Demand Increases." *The Journal of Physiology* 537.3 (2001): 999-1008.

If, for instance, your breathing capacity is low, you will get breathless easily. Smaller muscles that usually support your posture will engage to support breathing instead. When small muscles engage to do the work of larger muscles, you are more likely to experience pain as they become overused. When the diaphragm muscle tires easily, you are also more likely to get injured. Proper diaphragm function is vital for stabilisation of the spine and functional movement. What's more, the diaphragm itself forms an integral part of the core, working in concert with abdominal and pelvic floor muscles. This means "core" work can be considered in the same category as breath training and vice versa. The next chapter is dedicated to the diaphragm.

The Structure of the Breathing Muscles

A fundamental concept in understanding living systems is that structure always reflects function. Breathing is vital for life, so it is critical for breathing muscles to be resilient to fatigue. Imagine how fragile life would be if your breathing muscles collapsed under the strain of a short run or a poor night's sleep.

Skeletal muscles are a vital part of your musculoskeletal system. They are attached to bones by tendons and control the voluntary movements of your body. They serve a variety of functions, including expanding and contracting your chest cavity so you can inhale and exhale at will, maintaining body posture, moving the bones in different parts of your body and protecting joints and holding them in place.[194]

Skeletal muscles are made up of three types of muscle fibre:

1. **Type I** are "slow twitch" muscle fibres and contract slowly. They are relatively weak but resistant to fatigue. They are good for long lasting activities, like holding a posture. These fibres rely on aerobic respiration to produce ATP (energy).[195]

194 https://my.clevelandclinic.org/health/body/21787-skeletal-muscle (Accessed May 7, 2023).
195 "Muscle Fibre Types." *Physiopedia*. (n.d.) http://www.physiopedia.com/Muscle_Fibre_Types (Accessed July 2, 2022).

2. **Type IIa** are "fast twitch" muscles fibres. They fire more quickly and are more powerful than type I fibres. They primarily use aerobic respiration but can switch to anaerobic respiration (glycolysis), making them highly resistant to fatigue.
3. **Type IIb** are also "fast twitch" muscle fibres. They are the most powerful but are also very inefficient. They primarily rely on anaerobic respiration. They tire quickly and are only useful for short, intense, bursts of activity.

Type I fibres are synonymous with endurance. They are found in high concentrations in marathon runners and long-distance cyclists.[196] Types IIa and IIb are abundant in weightlifters, sprinters, and other elite power athletes. It should be no surprise that the adult human diaphragm is made up of around 60% type I muscle fibres (that are good for long lasting activities) and only 40% type IIa and IIb fibres,[197,198] with around 20% of each fast-twitch muscle type.

Fascial Tissue Involved in Breathing

As we learned earlier, fascia is a band or sheet of connective tissue that sits under the skin. It's mostly made from collagen, and it attaches to, stabilises, encloses, and separates muscles and other internal organs. It's just as important to assess the structure of fascia involved in breathing as it is to assess the muscles.

---

196 Plotkin, Daniel L., et al. "Muscle Fiber Type Transitions with Exercise Training: Shifting Perspectives." *Sports* 9.9 (2021): 127.
197 Gollnick, P. D., et al. "Enzyme Activity and Fiber Composition in Skeletal Muscle of Untrained and Trained Men." *Journal of Applied Physiology* 33.3 (1972): 312-319.
198 Banner, Michael J. "Respiratory Muscle Loading and the Work of Breathing." *Journal of Cardiothoracic and Vascular Anesthesia* 9.2 (1995): 192-204.

The fascia that connects to the diaphragm is of critical importance to breathing. It can be divided into four sections:

1. **The inter-fascial plane.** This attaches to a series of muscles and organs, including the psoas, quadratus lumborum, liver, and kidneys.[199]
2. **The fascia transversalis.** This is connected to the transversus abdominis (TrA).[200]
3. **The thoracolumbar fascia.** This covers the thoracic and sacral regions. It is attached to the latissimus dorsi, trapezius, gluteus maximus, and the external oblique muscles. It also attaches to the sacrum bone in the pelvis, which belongs to the pelvic floor.[201,202]
4. **The lateral raphe.** This is associated with the quadratus lumborum and iliac crest, the largest of the three bones in the pelvis.[203]

The superficial fascia of the neck is also relevant to breathing because the phrenic nerve passes through it. The phrenic nerve is responsible for motor control of the diaphragm.[204,205]

199 Lee, Su Lim, Young Mi Ku, and Sung Eun Rha. "Comprehensive Reviews of the Interfascial Plane of the Retroperitoneum: Normal Anatomy and Pathologic Entities." *Emergency Radiology* 17.1 (2010): 3-11.
200 Peiper, C., et al. "Abdominal Musculature and the Transversalis Fascia: An Anatomical Viewpoint." *Hernia* 8.4 (2004): 376-380.
201 Willard, F. H., et al. "The Thoracolumbar Fascia: Anatomy, Function and Clinical Considerations." *Journal of Anatomy* 221.6 (2012): 507-536.
202 Soljanik, Irina, et al. "Functional Interactions Between the Fossa Ischioanalis, Levator Ani and Gluteus Maximus Muscles of the Female Pelvic Floor: A Prospective Study in Nulliparous Women." *Archives of Gynecology and Obstetrics* 286.4 (2012): 931-938.
203 Schuenke, M. D., et al. "A Description of the Lumbar Interfascial Triangle and Its Relation With the Lateral Raphe: Anatomical Constituents of Load Transfer through the Lateral Margin of the Thoracolumbar Fascia." *Journal of Anatomy* 221.6 (2012): 568-576.
204 Bordoni, Bruno, and Emiliano Zanier. "Anatomic Connections of the Diaphragm: Influence of Respiration on the Body System." *Journal of Multidisciplinary Healthcare* 6 (2013): 281.
205 Warshafsky, Daniel, David Goldenberg, and Sangam G. Kanekar. "Imaging Anatomy of Deep Neck Spaces." *Otolaryngologic Clinics of North America* 45.6 (2012): 1203-1221.

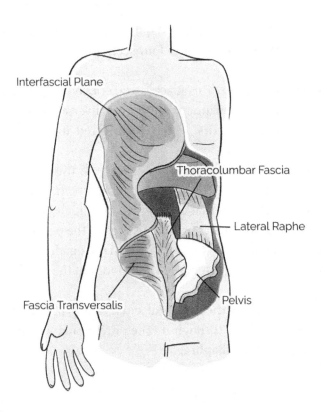

Interfascial Plane

Thoracolumbar Fascia

Lateral Raphe

Fascia Transversalis

Pelvis

3. PHYSICAL SYSTEMS: POSTURE

When it comes to respiratory function, posture is vital but often overlooked. You may be aware that when you slump in your chair, your diaphragm is not free to move. Or that, when you breathe through an open mouth, the extra weight produced by the forward thrust of your head will contribute to neck pain. But it goes deeper than that. Think, for a moment, of an elderly man who has for years habitually put more weight on one foot. Perhaps one of his shoulders is higher than the other. What about a woman with a pronounced scoliosis – a sideways curve in her spine? Or a tennis player or violinist whose upper body muscles have developed unevenly? These physical asymmetries will all affect the ideal symmetrical movement of the rib cage and diaphragm.

Three Connected Systems

Yoga can improve the biomechanics of the breath in most elements in the Venn diagram shared earlier. This is why yogis with respiratory problems often benefit from their practice, even when they pay little attention to the volume of air they breathe. Nevertheless, breathing volume is crucial. It determines how much oxygen gets to your cells. You can amplify the benefits of yoga by bringing attention to both biomechanics *and* biochemistry during your practice.

Now, let's revisit the Venn diagram and look at the overlapping structures, to see why these are all integral components of good breathing:

1. **the rib cage**
2. **the diaphragm**
3. **the abdominals (and pelvic floor)**

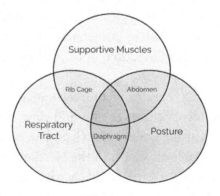

STRUCTURES OF BREATHING: THE RIB CAGE

The rib cage is important in breathing because it houses the lungs. The ribs are designed to move with the breath in a three-dimensional way.

- The 1st and 2nd ribs move upward toward your face. There is a gentle expansion backward in the 1st and 2nd vertebrae.

- Ribs 3 through 12 will move forward, backward, and out to the sides.
- The diaphragm muscle contracts and moves down into the abdomen.

As the five lobes of the lungs are filled with air during inhalation, the ribs move away from the heart, which sits just above the diaphragm.

The structure of the rib cage is determined by the tone and flexibility of the muscles and fascia that attach to it. If these muscles and tissues are tight, they prevent the ribs from expanding in all directions. They may create uneven movement between the left and right sides of the rib cage, compromising breathing.

Two Ways of Moving

This three-dimensional movement of the ribs (up, down, and outward in all directions) occurs during an ideal breathing pattern. During healthy breathing, the ribs move with a "bucket handle" action. They swing out and up, like the handle of a bucket. This involves high recruitment of the diaphragm.

In contrast, when breathing biomechanics are compromised, the rib cage movement reflects the up-and-down motion of a pump handle. Ribs one-through-seven attach to the back of the sternum (breastbone) via pliable cartilage. In the "bucket handle" movement, as the sternum moves forward, so do the ribs. In the "pump handle" movement, however, the sternum moves upward toward the head, and the ribs develop an up and down motion. In this movement, the diaphragm is less active. There is an over-reliance on the scalenes and sternocleidomastoid (neck muscles) to lift the ribs and allow enough air into the lungs via the chest.

During optimal diaphragmatic breathing, the ribs remain in more or less the same position on the horizontal plane. In suboptimal breathing, when the ribs move up instead of outward, the entire chest will move with every inhalation.

Why Does Rib Movement Matter?

A functional mechanical action is critical for the delivery of oxygen to the blood. Both types of rib movement support the increase in lung volume needed for breathing. However, the bucket handle movement, with its optimal diaphragm function, supports a greater increase in lung volume.

To explain further, the lungs always have a slight negative pressure within the chest cavity. This means that there is greater pressure in the atmosphere than there is inside the lungs. This pressure difference helps move air into the lungs and keep the airways open. During inhalation, as the rib cage expands and the diaphragm descends, lung volume increases. This causes pressure in the lungs to decrease further. The difference in air pressure between the lungs and the environment is now greater. Because air moves from areas of high pressure to low pressure, this pressure change facilitates inhalation.

During inhalation, expansion of the lungs is accommodated by both the opening of the rib cage and diaphragm activation. This allows for a deeper influx of air into the body. This means that more air reaches the air sacs in the lungs where gas exchange takes place. Since the lungs are elastic, exhalation occurs when the elastic recoil of the lungs pushes the air back out.

Recruitment of the diaphragm is key for efficient breathing. It is partly responsible for mobilising the rib cage, and it is vital for many aspects of breathing function. However, adequate expansion of the rib cage is equally important, and, for this, you need a functional bucket handle rib movement. Manual therapy and/or physical exercises can be used to improve the mobilisation of the rib cage. In a yoga class, both can be achieved by executing poses accompanied by relevant adjustments from the teacher.

An Energetic Perspective

The manual therapist Tom Myers, founder of *Anatomy Trains* and author of the book of the same name, [206] provides a nice way to segment the rib cage. Myers links parts of the rib cage with the functions of the organs they surround.

Based on this approach, he divides the rib cage into four sections:

1. **The first and second ribs attach to the manubrium, the broad upper part of the sternum/breastbone.**
   The manubrium (meaning *handle* in Latin) is the thickest, strongest section of the breastbone. These ribs can be called *neck ribs*, as the scalenes attach to them. The larynx (voice box) sits just above. This part of the body is associated with how we project ourselves to our environment. The throat is the location of the fifth chakra, Vishudda, which is responsible for self-expression, communication, and your ability to speak your personal truth.

2. **The next three ribs attach to the body of the breastbone.**
   They embrace the lungs and heart. The lungs and heart attach to the shoulder through the pectoralis minor muscle. The heart is where the fourth chakra, Anahata, sits. This chakra is your centre of unconditional love and compassion.

3. **Ribs six to nine attach to cartilage beneath the ribs.**
   Inside these ribs we find the diaphragm, stomach, liver, and pancreas – the organs responsible for assimilation. These ribs can expand sideways, facilitating lateral breathing. The solar plexus (about three fingers' width above your belly button) is where the third chakra, Manipura, is located. Manipura relates to your sense of self.

---

206 Myers, Thomas W., and Susan K. Hillman. *Anatomy Trains.* Primal Pictures Limited, 2004.

4. **The tenth rib attaches to cartilage in the preceding ribs.**
   Ribs 10 to 12 surround the kidneys and the adrenals. In a metaphorical sense, this area can be associated with elimination – what you need in your body and what you should secrete. The second, or sacral chakra, Svadhisthana, sits here.

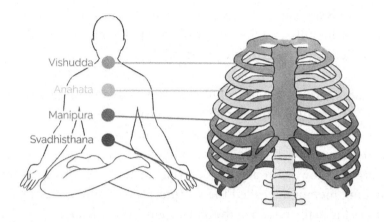

Ribs can be classified according to their attachments. They are called *true ribs* if their costal cartilage attaches directly to the sternum. Ribs one to seven are true ribs. If their cartilage attaches to the cartilage of the rib above, they are known as *false ribs*. Ribs eight to ten are false ribs. Where there is no costal cartilage connection, they are called *floating ribs*. Ribs 11 and 12 are floating ribs.[207]

207 Talbot, Brett S., et al. "Traumatic Rib Injury: Patterns, Imaging Pitfalls, Complications, and Treatment." *Radiographics* 37.2 (2017): 628-651.

STRUCTURES OF BREATHING: THE DIAPHRAGM – THE HEART'S TWIN SISTER

A 2017 review in the *Journal of Bodywork and Movement Therapies* emphatically states:

> "There is arguably no other muscle in the human body that is so central literally and figuratively to our physical, biochemical and emotional health as the diaphragm."[208]

The heart and diaphragm originate from the same tissue. At conception, the fertilised human embryo consists of a single cell. As the foetus develops, the diaphragm grows from various sources. In very early development, the spaces that hold the heart, lungs, and abdominal organs grow from a single internal cavity.[209] As these separate, a dividing membrane called the septum transversum develops. This becomes the main tendon of the diaphragm. Through an intricate folding process, like the splitting of two socks that are wrapped together, the cavities separate during gestation, and the heart and diaphragm emerge.[210,211]

The diaphragm is the primary muscle of *inhalation*. This is in contrast where, during quiet breathing, exhalation is passive, occurring through the elastic recoil of the diaphragm, lungs, and rib cage to their original resting position. The lungs themselves are passive during breathing. They are not involved in initiating or creating the movement that leads to inhalation or exhalation. They are elastic and move in response to

208 Wallden, Matt. "The Diaphragm--More Than an Inspired Design." *Journal of Bodywork and Movement Therapies* 21.2 (2017): 342-349.

209 Saremi, Farhood. "20 the Pericardium." *Thoracickey*. (March 16, 2021). http://www.thoracickey.com/20-the-pericardium/ (Accessed July 2, 2022).

210 Sharma, Ram Prakash. *Embryology: An Illustrated Colour Text*. London: Churchill Livingstone, 2009.

211 Corrin, Bryan., and Andrew G. Nicholson. "Development of the Lungs; Perinatal and Developmental Lung Disease" in *Pathology of the Lungs*, by Bryan Corrin and Andrew G. Nicholson, 35-78. London: Harcourt Publishers Limited, 2000.

pressure changes created by the breathing muscles, primarily the diaphragm, and the muscles between the ribs.[212]

This means that there is no muscle primarily responsible for *exhalation*. During intensive exercise or in conditions such as emphysema where the elasticity of the lung is reduced, active exhalation can be achieved by contracting the muscles of the abdominal wall.[213]

The secondary breathing muscles always participate in respiration,[214] but, in healthy breathing, they have minimal effect.[215] No muscle in the body works independently, and many muscles contribute in some small way to breathing.

The diaphragm has many functions that go far beyond its role in breathing. It is also important for urination, swallowing, speech (phonation), sexual function, vomiting, and defecation. It influences the balance of the metabolism and helps maintain the correct relationship between the stomach and oesophagus, preventing gastric reflux. It is vital for correct posture and functional movement. It even influences pain perception and emotional regulation.[216]

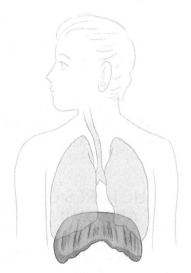

Diaphragm

212 The Process of Breathing | Anatomy and Physiology II. *Lumen Learning.* (2019) courses.lumenlearning.com/suny-ap2/Chapter/the-process-of-breathing-no-content/ (Accessed July 2, 2022).
213 "Muscles of Respiration." *Wikipedia.* (June 27, 2022) www.wikipedia.com (Accessed July 2, 2022).
214 Negro, Del, A. Christopher, Gregory D. Funk, and Jack L. Feldman. "Breathing Matters." *Nature Reviews Neuroscience* 19.6 (2018): 351-367.
215 Maramattom, Boby Varkey, and Eelco F. M. Wijdicks. "Neurology of Pulmonology and Acid Base Disturbance." in *Neurology and Clinical Neuroscience*, Mosby, 2007, 1569-1576.
216 Bordoni, Bruno, et al. "The Influence of Breathing on the Central Nervous System." *Cureus.* 10.6 (2018).

The very fact you are reading this book suggests that you are probably aware of the idea of diaphragmatic breathing. And the truth is that your diaphragm has functioned continuously throughout your life unless you had an unfortunate incident like Anastasis. Even so, it is common for yogis to misunderstand how the diaphragm works and to confuse belly breathing or even chest breathing with a functioning diaphragm.

Unfortunately, low diaphragmatic recruitment has significant and far-reaching consequences. The diaphragm is responsible for between 70-80% of inhalation force.[217] When diaphragm function is suboptimal, we overuse the secondary breathing muscles. Overusing the small muscles in the neck and upper chest shifts the rib cage movement from bucket handle to pump handle. This reduces our lung capacity and contributes to physical tension and pain. Because of the incredible importance of the diaphragm, the following chapter is dedicated entirely to this respiratory muscle and will outline its benefits, as well as how to recruit, strengthen, and stretch it.

STRUCTURES OF BREATHING: THE ABDOMINALS AND PELVIC FLOOR

To understand the role of the abdominal muscles in breathing, take a moment to visualise a runner who has just finished a race. She is on her knees, trying to recover her breath, supporting her upper body with her hands. Her abs are moving vigorously. However, despite this image, not all abdominal muscles participate in breathing. While inner abdominal muscles (including the transversus abdominis) do, the outer abs (such as the rectus abdominis and external obliques) do not.[218]

Why is this? It comes down to the role of the diaphragm as an abdominal, core, and postural muscle. The diaphragm is one of the four

---

217 McNamara, Christine A. "Travell & Simons' Myofascial Pain and Dysfunction: The Trigger Point Manual, Volume 1: Upper Half of Body, Ed 2." *Physical Therapy* 80.5 (2000): 542.

218 Montes, Antonio Mesquita, et al. 2017. "Abdominal Muscle Activity During Breathing in Different Postural Sets in Healthy Subjects." *Journal of Bodywork and Movement Therapies* 21.2 (2017): 354-361.

muscles of an inner unit called the deep core (along with the multifidus, transverse abdominis, and pelvic floor). The diaphragm and transversus abdominis are connected via fascia. Scientists have shown that these four muscles move in concert during postural activity.[219]

The transversus abdominis are active during exhalation but not during inhalation.[220] It is not possible to voluntarily control or modify

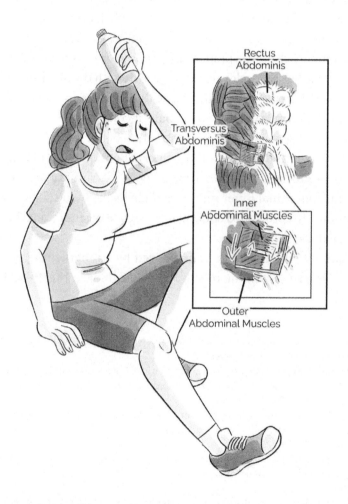

219 Hodges, Paul W., et al. "Intra-Abdominal Pressure Increases Stiffness of the Lumbar Spine." *Journal of Biomechanics* 38.9 (2005): 1873-1880.

220 Jenkin, Sarah E. M., and William K. Milsom. "Expiration: Breathing's Other Face." *Progress in Brain Research* 212 (2014): 131-147.

this synergy.[221] However, by strengthening the abdominal muscles, we can, nonetheless, support breathing.

The abdominal muscles mainly engage during exhalation, but they also contribute to inhalation via slow-twitch muscle activity. They support diaphragm function by preventing excessive contraction of the diaphragm during inhalation. The transversus abdominis muscle wraps around the trunk, which makes it ideally positioned to perform this task. What's more, as the abdominals contract during exhalation, intra-abdominal pressure increases. This optimises the length-to-tension relationship of diaphragm muscle fibres, preparing the body for your next inhalation.[222]

The pelvic floor muscles also work in sync with the diaphragm during breathing. When you inhale, the pelvic floor relaxes and descends as the diaphragm contracts. When you exhale, it contracts and ascends as the abdominal muscles contract.[223] Contraction of the pelvic floor activates the transversus abdominis and the internal obliques, increasing intra-abdominal pressure by up to 10 mmHg.[224] If you have a weak pelvic floor and abdominal inner unit, your belly is likely to stick out during exhalation. This protruded abdomen is a sign of dysfunctional breathing biomechanics.[225]

Breathing efficiency can be improved by strengthening the pelvic floor.[226] Unfortunately, the role of the pelvic floor in breathing is often

221 Gilbert, Chris, Leon Chaitow, and Dinah Bradley. *Recognizing and Treating Breathing Disorders.* Elsevier Health Sciences, 2014.

222 Montes, Antonio Mesquita, et al. "Abdominal Muscle Activity During Breathing in Different Postural Sets in Healthy Subjects." *Journal of Bodywork and Movement Therapies* 21.2 (2017): 354-361.

223 Bartelink, Dil. "The Role of Abdominal Pressure in Relieving the Pressure on the Lumbar Inervertebral Discs." *The Journal of Bone and Joint Surgery.* British Volume 39.4 (1957): 718-725.

224 Neumann, Pelvic, and V. Gill. "Pelvic Floor and Abdominal Muscle Interaction: EMG Activity and Intra-Abdominal Pressure." *International Urogynecology Journal* 13.2 (2002): 125-132.

225 Talasz, Helena, et al. "Breathing With the Pelvic Floor? Correlation of Pelvic Floor Muscle Function and Expiratory Flows in Healthy Young Nulliparous Women." *International Urogynecology Journal* 21.4 (2010): 475-481.

226 Gordon, Kate Emerich, and Ona Reed. "The Role of the Pelvic Floor in Respiration: A Multidisciplinary Literature Review." *Journal of Voice* 34.2 (2020): 243-249.

overlooked, even though between 33-49% of women are unable to voluntarily contract their pelvic floor.[227,228]

This intimate relationship between the transversus abdominis, pelvic floor, and diaphragm has been clearly demonstrated in numerous studies. In one such study, men with urinary incontinence were found to benefit just as much from exercise programs, whether they focused on strengthening the diaphragm, abs, or pelvic floor muscles.[229]

The Pelvic Floor, Breathing, and Pelvic Floor Dysfunction

Before we move on, it's worth taking a closer look at the link between pelvic floor function and breathing. Many students start a yoga practice to increase strength in the core and mobility in the hips and pelvis. But, as the statistic above indicates, sometimes there may be underlying pelvic floor dysfunction.

Pelvic floor dysfunction occurs when the muscles and connective tissues around the pelvis become weak or injured. Although this problem is frequently associated with women, it is also a common issue for men. It manifests as urinary leakage or incontinence, faecal incontinence, and even prolapse. It can also show up as erectile or sexual dysfunction.[230] Most studies examining the relationship between the pelvic floor and other disorders relate to double incontinence (both bladder and bowel incontinence), though research in men also links it

227 Park, Hankyu, Byoungha Hwang, and Kim Yeoungsung. "The Impact of the Pelvic Floor Muscles on Dynamic Ventilation Maneuvers." *Journal of Physical Therapy Science* 27.10 (2015): 3155-3157.

228 Sapsford, Ruth. "Rehabilitation of Pelvic Floor Muscles Utilizing Trunk Stabilization." *Manual Therapy* 9.1 (2004): 3-12.

229 Zachovajeviene, Brigita, et al. "Effect of Diaphragm and Abdominal Muscle Training on Pelvic Floor Strength and Endurance: Results of a Prospective Randomized Trial." *Scientific Reports* 9.1 (2019): 1-9.

230 "Roughly One Quarter of U.S. Women Affected by Pelvic Floor Disorders." *NIH* (27 September 27, 2015). http://www.nih.gov/news-events/news-releases/roughly-one-quarter-us-women-affected-pelvic-floor-disorders (Accessed July 2, 2022).

to erectile dysfunction.[231] In women, sexual dysfunction and pelvic pain are rarely studied.

Pelvic floor dysfunction can also take the form of overly tight muscles. This can make it difficult to insert a tampon or empty your bladder or bowel, even though you may have a more frequent urge to go to the bathroom. Over-active (hypertonic) pelvic floor muscles can be as troublesome as weak ones, and hypertonicity can co-exist with weakness. When pelvic floor muscles are too tight, you may experience haemorrhoids, fissures, and persistent lower back or hip pain. In men, urinary dysfunction and prostatitis can result from hypertonicity in the pelvic floor muscles. This is something to be aware of during yoga practice. If you have perfectionist tendencies, the common instruction to engage mula bandha (your root lock) could contribute to an overly tight pelvic floor. Indeed, one article in *Yoga International* goes as far as to describe mula bandha as "essentially a marathon Kegel."[232]

According to research funded by the National Institutes of Health, nearly 24% of women in the US are affected by at least one pelvic floor disorder.[233] Other studies report that between 1-14% of men are also affected.[234] Pelvic floor dysfunction causes physical discomfort, contributes to a range of health problems, and limits activity and quality of life. The problem increases as we get older. By the ages of 60 to 79 years, more than 40% of women struggle with pelvic floor issues. And pelvic floor disorders affect around half of all women aged 80 and over.[235]

231 Knol-de Vries, Grietje E., and Marco H. Blanker. "Prevalence of Co-existing Pelvic Floor Disorders: A Scoping Review in Males and Females." *Continence* 2 (2022): 100028.

232 Hall, Colin, and Sarah Garden. "Lost in Translation: Is Mulabandha Relevant for Modern Yogis?" *Yoga International*. (n.d.) https://yogainternational.com/article/view/lost-in-translation-is-mulabandha-relevant-for-modern-yogis (Accessed July 2, 2022).

233 "Roughly One Quarter of U.S. Women Affected by Pelvic Floor Disorders." *NIH* 27 September 27, 2015. http://www.nih.gov/news-events/news-releases/roughly-one-quarter-us-women-affected-pelvic-floor-disorders (Accessed July 2, 2022).

234 Knol-de Vries, Grietje E., and Marco H. Blanker. "Prevalence of Co-existing Pelvic Floor Disorders: A Scoping Review in Males and Females." *Continence* 2 (2022): 100028.

235 "Roughly One Quarter of U.S. Women Affected by Pelvic Floor Disorders." *NIH* (September 27, 2015). http://www.nih.gov/news-events/news-releases/roughly-one-quarter-us-women-affected-pelvic-floor-disorders (Accessed July 2, 2022).

We create problems in the pelvic floor when we don't use the diaphragm to breathe. Other poor breathing habits can also impact the function of these muscles. The pelvic floor is intimately connected with the breath. Whenever there's pain, tightness, weakness, scar tissue, or bad habits in those muscles, dysfunction can occur. These bad habits include constantly sucking in the tummy. Or straining while going to the bathroom.[236] If you think about it, straining to poop usually manifests as a breath hold. Since the diaphragm and pelvic floor are linked, holding the breath effectively prevents the pelvic floor from relaxing, making it difficult to eliminate waste from the body.[237]

A PROFESSIONAL OPINION: DR. PAUL SLY ON THE PELVIC FLOOR

According to Dr. Paul Sly, OA™ Master Instructor and practising chiropractor, the pelvic floor has been ignored for years. Dr. Paul says that physiotherapists, chiropractors, gynaecologists, and obstetricians have only begun to pay attention to these muscles in the last five to ten years. We asked Dr. Paul to explain the connection between breathing and the pelvic floor, and to give some insight into how to strengthen those muscles.

Is it possible to strengthen a dysfunctional pelvic floor using yoga and breathing alone, or is professional intervention always required?

The role of the pelvic floor in breathing is critical. The diaphragm and the pelvic floor move in the same direction when we breathe.

---

236 McGeorge, Emma. "Pelvic Floor Basics Part Four--Breathing, You're Doing It Wrong." *The Pelvic Hub*. June 7, 2022. http://www.thepelvichub.com/post/pelvic-floor-basics-part-four-breathing-youre-doing-it-wrong (Accessed July 2, 2022).

237 "Don't Hold Your Breath! What You Do When You Poo." *Pelvic Pain Rehab*. (October 25, 2018). http://www.pelvicpainrehab.com/pelvic-floor-dysfunction/6013/dont-hold-your-breath-what-you-do-when-you-poo/ (Accessed July 2, 2022).

This allows for the movement of the organs in the abdomen and pelvis. When we inhale, the diaphragm contracts and moves down, while the pelvic floor relaxes and moves down. When we exhale, the opposite happens. Because of the connection between the diaphragm and the pelvic floor, optimal breathing can help maintain a healthy pelvic floor. If the diaphragm is not recruited, the pelvic floor is not recruited. Muscle weakness can come simply from the fact the muscles are not being used.

The numbers diagnosed with pelvic floor dysfunction tend to differ depending on which study you read. But, of those with dysfunction, about three-quarters are just not moving their pelvic floor.[238] Most have either a lack of mobility in the chest, thoracic spine, hips and pelvis, or dysfunctional breathing, or both. They are not using the diaphragm optimally, so they don't get the pelvic floor movement.

When you get into the idea of strengthening the pelvic floor to improve breathing, that's for the people who already have the basics right. The people who have good mobility and are breathing functionally. In these people, specific exercises to strengthen the pelvic floor can help, as long as they're done correctly. Unfortunately, Kegel exercises are not always done particularly well. What's more, when dysfunction in the pelvic floor is due to muscles that are too tight, traditional Kegel exercises can make matters worse.[239] As such, if you have pelvic floor dysfunction, it's always better to have professional guidance. This could be any physiotherapist, chiropractor, or osteopath who has some training in the pelvic floor. A trained professional will not only provide safety, but also help you get the most out of any exercises.

If you're self-assessing, the basics are really important. Learn functional breathing, so that you're getting the motion of the pelvic

238 "Roughly One Quarter of U.S. Women Affected by Pelvic Floor Disorders." NIH. (September 27, 2015). http://www.nih.gov/news-events/news-releases/roughly-one-quarter-us-women-affected-pelvic-floor-disorders (Accessed July 2, 2022).

239 McGeorge, Emma. "Pelvic Floor Basics Part Two--Pelvic Floor Dysfunction." *The Pelvic Hub.* (June 7, 2022). http://www.thepelvichub.com/post/pelvic-floor-basics-part-two-pelvic-floor-dysfunction (Accessed July 2, 2022).

floor with the breath. Practise that, so you can feel it. Make sure the mobility of the thoracic spine, thorax, pelvis, and hips is adequate. This may also require some professional input.

For the average person doing yoga, who doesn't have a diagnosed pelvic floor dysfunction, functional breathing exercises and combining the breathing with movement patterns will be sufficient to strengthen the pelvic floor.

How do you manage pelvic floor issues with clients?

If I have a client with pelvic floor issues, I start them with functional breathing. I work on any mobility issues they have in the thorax, hips, pelvis, and maybe elsewhere. Then, I may refer them out to a pelvic floor specialist if they need to get into some specific core strengthening. I'd recommend squatting, bridging, and some basic core exercises combined with functional breathing to strengthen the pelvic floor muscles. The basics are functional breathing to move the pelvic floor, and proper mobility of the thorax, thoracic spine, and pelvis/hips. Then and only then, you can work to strengthen the pelvic floor muscles if necessary. This should preferably be done under professional supervision. Some manual therapy may even be necessary from that professional.

The proper movement of the diaphragm and pelvic floor is an absolutely necessary precursor to strengthening. You can't strengthen dysfunction. A simple way to look at that is mobility trumps strength and stability. If a muscle is not moving correctly, strengthening exercises won't do any good. They can create more problems than they solve. This can include hypertonicity in the pelvic floor, a condition where muscles become too tight.

Whether there's a diagnosed pelvic floor dysfunction or not, the basics of learning functional breathing and getting the diaphragm to move is such a powerful thing, and it is too often overlooked.

How does posture impact the pelvic floor?

You can't separate posture, mobility, and functional breathing. They all go together. Studies have repeatedly shown that even the position of the feet and ankles impacts pelvic floor function.[240,241] *When the heels are up and the toes are down, as they are when you wear high-heeled shoes, the pelvis tilts, and activity in the pelvic floor decreases. The opposite happens when you rotate the ankles so that the toes point upward as they do in downward dog. The pelvis extends and activity in the pelvic floor muscles increases. If you spend all day walking or sitting in high heels, by default, the activity of your pelvic floor is reduced. This means you may not be able to use range of motion in the ankle to facilitate engagement in the pelvic floor.*

What Does This Mean for a Yoga Practice?

When you are new to yoga, you may have some difficulty activating individual muscles. As you practise the poses, you will become more attuned to your body. It becomes easier to locate and recruit different muscles and muscle groups. The same is true of the pelvic floor. In his book, Pelvic Power, the dancer and movement educator Eric Franklin explains it is difficult to activate individual pelvic floor muscles. To do so, you need clear perception training. Franklin states:

> "It is an illusion to believe that somebody can activate individual pelvic floor muscles without either excellent anatomical knowledge or else an almost magical body perception."[242]

240 Chen, Chia-Hsin, et al. "Relationship Between Ankle Position and Pelvic Floor Muscle Activity in Female Stress Urinary Incontinence." *Urology* 66.2 (2005): 288-292.

241 Lee, Kyeongjin. "Activation of Pelvic Floor Muscle During Ankle Posture Change on the Basis of a Three Dimensional Motion Analysis System." *Medical Science Monitor: International Medical Journal of Experimental and Clinical Research* 24 (2018): 7223.

242 Franklin, Eric N. *Pelvic Power: Mind/Body Exercises for Strength, Flexibility, Posture, and Balance for Men and Women.* Highstown, NJ: Elysian Editions, 2003.

This relates strongly to the root lock, mula bandha, which we know as a drawing up of the area around the perineum, mid-way between the genitals and anus. In other words, this bandha involves lifting the pelvic floor, but, even if you could execute the perfect mula bandha by activating the pelvic floor, it may not always have the desired results.[243] For a start, mula bandha is different for women and men. Women achieve this root lock by drawing in the areas around the vagina. This activates the same muscles that engage during female orgasm. According to Shiva Rea, author of *Tending the Heart Fire*, this can give women a potent sense of connection with the body and with their personal power.[244] Other teachers describe mula bandha as a practice designed by and for men. Colin Hall and Sarah Garden explain:

> "For one thing, you need a strong, dynamic pelvic floor to birth, not a short and tight pelvic floor. Hypertonicity in the pelvic floor can lead not only to pelvic pain and menstrual pain, but also to difficulties with natural childbirth. This is noteworthy because Mula bandha is a staple in so many prenatal yoga classes."[245]

To underline the advice given by Dr. Paul Sly, if in doubt, see a pelvic floor specialist. Despite common instruction to employ mula bandha, knowledge of the pelvic floor is outside the scope of most modern yoga teachers. A physiotherapist or osteopath will be better able to advise you about modifying your practice to support and improve symptoms.

As with other aspects of yoga, we need to let go of the idea of performing a perfect mula bandha and adjust to what our individual

243 Hall, Colin, and Sarah Garden. "Lost in Translation: Is Mulabandha Relevant for Modern Yogis?" *Yoga International*. (n.d.) https://yogainternational.com/article/view/lost-in-translation-is-mulabandha-relevant-for-modern-yogis (Accessed July 2, 2022).

244 "A Woman's Guide to Mula Bandha." *Yoga Journal*. (July 14, 2014). http://www.yogajournal.com/poses/lets-get-real-root-lock-shiva-reas-guide-mula-banda-women/ (Accessed July 2, 2022).

245 Hall, Colin, and Sarah Garden. "Lost in Translation: Is Mulabandha Relevant for Modern Yogis?" *Yoga International*. (n.d.) https://yogainternational.com/article/view/lost-in-translation-is-mulabandha-relevant-for-modern-yogis (Accessed July 2, 2022).

bodies need. For some of us, that will mean practising exercises that reduce tension in the pelvic floor muscles, realigning our posture, and releasing tension in the glutes, hips, and hamstrings.

A Note on Pelvic Tilt and Adjustments

In posterior pelvic tilt, the front of the pelvis lifts, the back of the pelvis drops, and the pelvis itself rotates upward. This movement is sometimes cued to increase mid-section engagement, but it is less effective for stabilising the spine than lower abdominal hollowing or abdominal bracing.[246] Pelvic tilt can therefore be considered more as a postural correction and less as a stabilisation of the mid-section.

Exercises to Strengthen the Pelvic Floor

The exercises most associated with pelvic floor strengthening are called Kegels. They are named after the gynaecologist, Dr. Arnold Kegel, who was one of the first doctors to develop research into pelvic floor strengthening. These exercises focus on tightening the muscles that control the flow of urine, but they are also effective for pelvic organ prolapse. They are suitable for both men and women.

Kegel Exercise:

- Sit upright in a straight-backed chair or in a comfortable seated posture on your mat. You may also practise the exercise standing, lying on your back, or crouching on all fours.
- Close your eyes and bring your attention to the muscles you would

246 Richardson, Carolyn, et al. 1992. "Techniques for Active Lumbar Stabilisation for Spinal Protection: A Pilot Study." *Australian Journal of Physiotherapy* 38.2 (1992): 105-112.

use to stop urine flow.

- Now tighten or squeeze those muscles as much as you can. You will feel the area around your pelvic floor lift.
- Hold the pose for 3-5 seconds.
- Release and rest for a few seconds.
- Repeat the exercise 10 times.

Bridge Pose:

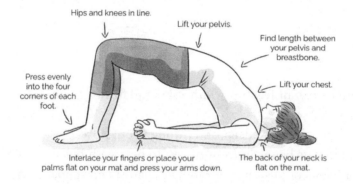

Hips and knees in line.

Lift your pelvis.

Find length between your pelvis and breastbone.

Press evenly into the four corners of each foot.

Lift your chest.

Interlace your fingers or place your palms flat on your mat and press your arms down.

The back of your neck is flat on the mat.

- Lie on your back and bend your knees. Place your feet on the floor, hip-width apart.
- Place your arms by your sides, with your palms facing down.
- Lift from your pelvis to raise your buttocks off the floor. At first, you may only be able to lift a few inches. Just do what you can.
- Hold for 5 breaths, in and out.
- Breathe light, slow, deep, and only through your nose.
- Repeat 10 times.
- Rest in between sets.

As your pelvic floor becomes stronger, you will be able to do more repetitions, stay in the pose longer, or get further into the pose. If your shoulders are flexible, you may then be able to interlace your fingers.

Squats:

- Stand with your feet hip-width apart and firmly grounded on your mat.
- Breathe Light, slow, deep, and through your nose.
- Extend your hands in front of you to help with balance. Clasping your hands or pushing your tongue against your upper front teeth can help.
- On an inhale, bend your knees to bring your buttocks toward the floor, as if you were sitting into a chair.
- Only go as low as is comfortable.
- Keep your back straight and lean forward slightly, keeping your knees in line with your toes.
- Exhale and return to a standing position, keeping your attention on the pelvic floor. See if you can squeeze the pelvic floor muscles as you stand.
- Repeat the exercise 10 times.
- You may then rest and perform more sets.

Dr. Paul Sly explains the benefit of combining breathing with squatting:

"When it comes to strengthening the pelvic floor, squatting is probably the most functional exercise we have. Doing it the way

Patrick teaches it, you inhale as you descend and exhale as you come back up. This corresponds with the movement of the pelvic floor, so it dynamically strengthens the pelvic floor muscles."

It is harder to engage the pelvic floor muscles during wide-leg, deep squats. Instead, practise narrow, shallow squats for optimal benefit to the pelvic floor.

Squeeze and Release:

This exercise is recommended by urologists. It speeds up the responsiveness of the pelvic floor muscles.

- Sit upright in a straight-backed chair or in a comfortable seated pose on your mat.
- Bring your attention to the pelvic floor, to those muscles you use to stop urine flow.
- Squeeze and release the muscles as quickly as you can. Do not try to hold the contraction.
- Rest for 3-5 seconds and repeat.
- Repeat the squeeze and release movement between 10 and 20 times.
- You can practise this exercise 3 times a day.[247]

According to Dr. Paul Sly, there are some other simple exercises that can be combined with breathing. These include Dead Bugs and Quadruped Diagonals. However, if you are experiencing pelvic floor dysfunction and are unsure of how to proceed, always seek the help of a specialist professional.

---

247 "Exercises to Strengthen Your Pelvic Floor—MIU." *Michigan Urology.* (n.d.) http://www.michiganurology.com/exercises-to-strengthen-your-pelvic-floor/ (Accessed July 2, 2022).

CHAPTER ELEVEN

THE DIAPHRAGM

Even people who have never given a second thought to their breathing and know nothing about functional breathing, will likely have heard the term 'diaphragmatic breathing'. It is so well known because it formulates the basis for functional breathing and is integral to the optimal functioning of several other body systems.

As we learned in Chapter One, there are three dimensions to functional breathing:

1. Biochemical
2. Biomechanical
3. Nervous System

BIOCHEMICAL BENEFITS

Diaphragm breathing facilitates a forward movement of the ribs. When the ribs move forward, the lower part of the lungs can inflate more. More air reaches deeper into the lung where gas exchange takes place. There is more blood supply in the lower parts of the lungs. This means more efficient transport of oxygen and carbon dioxide from the lower lungs to and from the bloodstream. Deeper breathing also slows the breath, so air stays in the lungs longer. This gives more time for the exchange of blood gases.

BIOMECHANICAL BENEFITS

From a biomechanical perspective, diaphragm breathing is beneficial in two ways. It alters abdominal pressure, and it massages the digestive organs in the abdominal region.

As the diaphragm contracts, it descends toward the pelvis. When this happens, pressure in the belly (intra-abdominal pressure or IAP) increases. The quality of IAP depends on our breathing pattern and the recruitment of the abdominal muscles. The descent of the diaphragm toward the pelvis applies increased pressure in the intestines. This promotes the natural movement of the gut that moves food through the digestive tract. It is therefore essential for digestive health.

NERVOUS SYSTEM

The diaphragm plays an important role in emotional regulation – a fact that is not surprising given its neurological and anatomical relationship with the heart. The function of the diaphragm directly impacts our emotional state. Indeed, the diaphragm is the organ that expresses physical and emotional pain. For this reason, diaphragm release is considered vital to emotional release.

When a child hurts him or herself, the diaphragm contracts in a sharp intake of breath. In the moments that follow, the child begins to cry, the wails interspersed by gasps. An article in the *Journal of Bodywork and Movement Therapies* explains it this way: "During the process of wailing or expressing the pain, the child is literally expressing, or exporting, the pain from the nervous system."[248] As adults, we take the same reflexive breath when we stub a toe or crack our head on a low door, but we rarely express our hurt beyond the occasional swear word. The article's authors ask, "Could it be that the diaphragm holds that tension within it?"

248 Wallden, Matt. "The Diaphragm--More Than an Inspired Design." *Journal of Bodywork and Movement Therapies* 21.2 (2017): 342-349.

It is undeniable that poor diaphragm function can alter our emotional experience.[249] It's also true that different emotional states have different metabolic requirements. According to the Rosen Method bodywork teacher, Ivy Green, "We need more oxygen for the fire of anger than for the glow of contentment." Green points out that our breathing patterns allow us to vocalise our emotions by laughing, crying, or sighing.[250]

From a nervous system perspective, diaphragm breathing slows the respiratory rate. A slower respiratory cycle and lengthened exhalation activates the 'rest and digest' parasympathetic nervous system (PNS).[251] At a rate of around six breaths per minute, nervous system balance is optimal.[252] During exhalation, the vagus nerve, the main driver of the PNS, secretes a chemical messenger (neurotransmitter) called acetylcholine. Acetylcholine slows the heart, calming the mind via a body-to-brain feedback loop. Breathing exercises that emphasise prolonged exhalation are often used for relaxation and are proven effective in dealing with stress.[253,254]

Psychological benefits of diaphragm breathing can also come by way of improved biochemistry. Studies into panic disorder have found that when breathing patterns are normalised to increase levels of blood CO_2, panic symptoms reduce.[255] This gives sufferers a greater sense of control over their panic attacks, which creates a positive feedback loop that further reduces symptoms.

249 Bordoni, Bruno, Fabiola Marelli, and Giovanni Bordoni. "A Review of Analgesic and Emotive Breathing: A Multidisciplinary Approach." *Journal of Multidisciplinary Healthcare* 9 (2016): 97.

250 Green, Ivy. "The Role of the Diaphragm in Self-Awareness and Transformation." *Rosen Method International Journal* 5 (2012): 5-29.

251 Omuluabi, Peter F. "Practical Steps in Learning Diaphragmatic Breathing: A First-Aid Technique for Sports Anxiety." *Ife Psychologia: An International Journal* 2.2 (1994): 129-135.

252 Russo, Marc A., Danielle M. Santarelli, and Dean O'Rourke. "The Physiological Effects of Slow Breathing in the Healthy Human." *Breathe* 13.4 (2017): 298-309.

253 Ma, Xiao, et al. "The Effect of Diaphragmatic Breathing on Attention, Negative Affect and Stress in Healthy Adults." *Frontiers in Psychology* 874 (2017).

254 Russell, Matthew Edward Brannon, et al. "Use of Controlled Diaphragmatic Breathing for the Management of Motion Sickness in a Virtual Reality Environment." *Applied Psychophysiology and Biofeedback* 39.3 (2014): 269-277.

255 Okuro, Renata T., et al. "Panic Disorder Respiratory Subtype: Psychpathology and Challenge Tests--An Update." *Brazilian Journal of Psychiatry* 42 (2020): 420-430.

WIDER BENEFITS OF DIAPHRAGM BREATHING

Beyond its obvious role in respiration, the diaphragm makes a critical contribution to several other body systems. These include:

- **Trunk stability:** The diaphragm forms the upper part of the core. Its proper function is essential for stability in the spine and pelvis.[256] The diaphragm's postural functions can be voluntarily controlled. This is useful during yoga postures and other physical activities that involve balance.
- **Spinal decompression:** Gravity, muscle tension, and other factors can cause the spine to compress, contributing to pain, disc disease, and trapped nerves. Diaphragm breathing activates the ribs, helping to create a top-down decompression in the spine.[257]
- **Fluid dynamics:** The diaphragm contributes to healthy movement of blood and other fluids around the body. It is important for lymphatic drainage and flow.[258]
- **Abdominal organ health:** The diaphragm also prevents acid reflux.[259]
- **Emotional regulation:** As noted above, a slower respiratory cycle and lengthened exhalation activates the 'rest and digest' response.

HOW TO BREATHE DIAPHRAGMATICALLY

Diaphragm breathing is healthy breathing, but many of us do not understand how to do it. There are two things to notice when breathing from the diaphragm:

256 Key, Josephine. "'The Core': Understanding it and Retraining Its Dysfunction." *Journal of Bodywork and Movement Therapies* 17.4 (2013): 541-559.
257 "Spinal Decompression Through Position and Breathing." *Azopt.* November 19, 2019. http://www.azopt.net/spinal-decompression/ (Accessed July 2, 2022).
258 Kocjan, Januz, et al. "Network of Breathing. Multifunctional Role of the Diaphragm: A Review." *Advances in Respiratory Medicine* 85.4 (2017): 224-232.
259 Habibulla, K. S. "The Diaphragm as an Anti-Reflux Barrier: A Manometric, Oesophagoscopic, and Transmucosal Potential Study." *Thorax* 27.6 (1972): 692-702.

1. **Your breath's flow rate:** Diaphragm recruitment increases when breathing is slower. This is why nasal breathing, which is slower than mouth breathing, increases diaphragm activation.

2. **The recruitment of secondary breathing muscles:** During diaphragm breathing, you want to feel the ribs move outward on the inhalation and inward on the exhalation. This is a subtle movement that will be most noticeable in the area around your lower ribs. The muscles in the upper back and chest will move a little. While the muscles in the neck should hardly move at all.

If you slow down your breath, breathe through your nose, and keep your shoulders down and relaxed, your diaphragm will engage. If you are new to a breath practice, work on diaphragm breathing before trying any other techniques. Try to gradually lengthen and soften each breath, while staying relaxed.

It's likely when you breathe this way that your belly will extend gently forward during each inhalation. This is where the term "belly breathing" comes from. Don't focus on the movement of the belly. Instead, concentrate on the slow filling of the lungs with air. If you find this difficult, you can bring your attention to your belly, but keep in mind that:

- Your belly muscles can move independent of your diaphragm.
- Your belly can even be pushed out during exhalation. This is called paradoxical breathing and is a type of dysfunctional breathing.
- There are situations in which you want to activate your diaphragm without allowing your belly to move out, such as in lateral breathing.

Exercises to Train Your Diaphragm

The diaphragm is a striated muscle,[260] just like the skeletal muscles. This logically means that it is possible to strengthen the diaphragm and improve its capacity for breathing and postural support. However, it is not as easy to work the diaphragm as it is to strengthen your leg or arm muscles. To strengthen any muscle, you must push it beyond its existing capacity, but physical exercise is only possible within the existing limits of the breathing muscles, so we need a creative approach if we want to strengthen those muscles.

There are five ways to challenge and improve the strength of the diaphragm:

1. Applying resistance to the abdomen or rib cage.
2. Practising breath holds.
3. Breathing through the nose.
4. Using "inspiration pressure threshold loading," which involves adding resistance to the inhalation using a device such as SportsMask.
5. Practising endurance breathing muscle training.

1. Applying Resistance to the Abdomen or Rib Cage

You can gently engage the diaphragm by applying light pressure to the abdomen. There are two versions of this practice:

a. Lie in a supine position (on your back). Rest a weight of between 0.5 and 3 kg on your abdomen.

260 Lewis, Philip, and Ken D. O'Halloran. "Diaphragm Muscle Adaptation to Sustained Hypoxia: Lessons From Animal Models With Relevance to High Altitude and Chronic Respiratory Diseases." *Frontiers in Physiology* 7 (2016): 623.

b. Lie in a prone position (on your front), balanced on your elbows. Place a pillow or yoga block beneath your abdominals.

In both postures, the movement of the abdominals is restricted. This restriction carries over to the diaphragm during every inhalation. A similar effect can be achieved by using a strap such as the Buteyko Belt (available on the website – **https://oxygenadvantage.com/**). The belt is worn around the lower part of the rib cage. It challenges the diaphragm by restricting the outward movement of the ribs.

As you breathe, a prop such as the Buteyko Belt will allow you to feel the outer rim of your diaphragm. During the inhalation, you will feel pressure against the belt as your ribs move outward. On the exhalation, you will feel the belt pushing against your ribs. Practise breathing against the expansion and contraction of the belt and notice how even or uneven the movement of your breathing is. You can wear the belt as you go about your day. It provides a useful reminder to check in with your breathing.

2. Breath holds

During voluntary breath holds, the diaphragm contracts independent of the pressure it receives from the abdominal cavity.[261] As you hold your breath, the respiratory centre in your brain signals to your diaphragm

---

261 Kolar, Pavel, et al. "Analysis of Diaphragm Movement During Tidal Breathing and During Its Activation While Breath Holding Using MRI Synchronized with Spirometry." *Physiological Research* 58.3 (2009).

to start breathing. The diaphragm begins to move, even as you maintain the breath hold. This means that you can give your diaphragm a workout by performing repeated maximal or submaximal breath holds.

3. Nose Breathing

Nasal breathing improves the function and strength of the diaphragm. The nose provides around 50% more resistance to airflow than the mouth – this help to maintain diaphragm muscle strength.[262]

4. Inspiration Pressure Threshold Loading

By applying resistance to breathing we can challenge the diaphragm (and other respiratory muscles) to work harder to fill the lungs. The easiest way to do this is by switching to nasal breathing as this automatically imposes a significant resistance to breathing. Breathing resistance can also be increased by using training devices, such as SportsMask (available at https://oxygenadvantage.com/), which have been shown to increase inspiratory muscle strength by as much as 45%.[263]

5. Endurance Breathing Muscle Training

You can use long sessions of heavy breathing to improve the endurance of your breathing muscles. Around 40 minutes of big, forceful breaths will work the diaphragm enough to strengthen it. However, it's important to avoid hypocapnia, so this hard breathing must be done without hyperventilating. This is not straightforward. To achieve it, you'll need to re-breathe a percentage of exhaled air to maintain CO_2 levels. This practice is known as voluntary isocapnic hyperventilation (VIH). It has

---

262 Ruth, Alan. "The Health Benefits of Nose Breathing." (2017).
263 McConnell, Alison. *Breathe Strong, Perform Better.* Human Kinetics, 2011.

been shown to improve the endurance of breathing muscles,[264] but it is time-consuming and challenging, and therefore not the most practical approach!

These techniques are used by respiratory physiologists. Having a variety of approaches can certainly be very useful as a complement to breath training, especially when there is illness and more complex work is not appropriate.

Patrick believes the techniques just described are beneficial and he has personally practised them for extended periods. However, he still favours incorporating breath training during physical practices such as yoga, Pilates, and sports. Yoga, itself, offers many versatile and unique ways to strengthen the diaphragm.

Patrick's approach to diaphragm strengthening:

- **For beginners:** Practise asanas that restrict the movement of the diaphragm or the supportive muscles of the respiratory tract.
- **For advanced practitioners:** Practise hypercapnic and/or hypoxic breathing exercises while holding the asanas.

HOW TO TRAIN YOUR DIAPHRAGM THROUGH ASANAS: ANASTASIS PERSPECTIVE

I only really made the connection between asanas and respiratory function in 2018. I was delivering day-long workshops on breathing. It was then that I started forming and testing the ideas expressed in this chapter. However, as often happens, when I look back, there were many earlier instances when I made use of the respiratory effects of asanas.

For example, November 2010 was an exceptionally stressful time for me. I remember coming off a phone call one Thursday afternoon

---

264 Verges, Samuel, Urs Boutellier, and Christina M. Spengler. "Effect of Respiratory Muscle Endurance Training on Respiratory Sensations, Respiratory Control and Exercise Performance: A 15-Year Experience." *Respiratory Physiology & Neurobiology* 161.1 (2008): 16-22.

with my blood boiling. The call had ended abruptly when the other person hung up. I was angry and it was not easy to think straight. Instinctively, I thought it would be a good idea to go into a headstand. I threw a pillow into the middle of the tiny studio flat I lived in, placed my head on it, and got into position. While in headstand, I followed an ujjayi breathing pattern with an inhalation-to-exhalation ratio of 1:5. I remember refusing to come down until I had to, in a similar way that a child would threaten his parents, "I'll hold my breath until I get what I want!" As I balanced in the headstand, my mental state began to change. By the time I came down, I was dizzy but much more level-headed. I checked my phone to see how long I'd remained in the pose. Nine minutes had passed.

Was a headstand necessary to calm me down? Probably not. Did it make me feel better? Yes. But why was it so helpful?

- I was balancing (and this is true whether you're upright or in an inversion), which meant I had to concentrate. It shifted my focus away from negative thoughts and brought me into the present.
- Balance is affected by the breath. The better your diaphragm functions, the less you will wobble.[265] The breath can also be used in different ways to assist with balance. For instance, you can establish a slow breathing pattern to optimise diaphragm recruitment. This will calm the nervous system.
- Inversions force the diaphragm to work against gravity, increasing diaphragm recruitment. This also calms the nervous system.

Which Asanas Strengthen the Diaphragm?

The asanas that challenge the movement of the diaphragm are those that involve spinal articulation and/or inversions.

---

265 Kocjan, Janusz, et al. "Impact of Diaphragm Function Parameters on Balance Maintenance." *PLoS* 13.12 (2018): e0208697.

The spine can be mobilised in six ways:

1. **Forward flexion:** For most people, this will impose the highest pressure in the diaphragm. In a forward bend, intra-abdominal pressure (IAP) increases, making it harder for the diaphragm to descend during inhalation.[266]
2. **Spine extension:** Backbends that lengthen the spine upward and backward.
3. **Lateral (sideways) flexion:** Poses like standing crescent pose.
4. **Rotation:** Any twist.
5. **Elongation:** This requires the use of gravity or manual manipulation.
6. **Compression:** We try to avoid this.

Of these six movements, the first four are necessary to challenge the diaphragm from all angles.

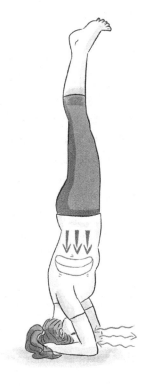

We can also use posture to challenge the diaphragm by using inversions. During inversions, the hips are above the shoulders. To inhale, your diaphragm must move against gravity. Therefore, inversions significantly amplify the workload of the diaphragm. The midsection now bears the load of the lower body, and IAP is higher. You can easily witness the impact of inversions on the breath just by observing the breath of a practitioner in a headstand.

As you move your spine in inversion, the diaphragm's movement is restricted from different angles. However, to adequately train the diaphragm, you must also

266 Liu, Tao, et al. "Numerical Investigation of Intra-Abdominal Pressure Effects on Spinal Loads and Load-Sharing in Forwar Flexion." *Frontiers in Bioengineering and Biotechnology* 7 (2019): 428.

consider how much it moves. The most mobile part of the diaphragm only descends about 1.5 cm during quiet breathing. When you breathe vigorously during sport, it moves between 6 and 10 cm.[267] This suggests that physical exertion is necessary to strengthen the diaphragm. Static poses alone will not do the job. A combination of dynamic sequences such as the Five Tibetan Rites or Ashtanga vinyasa and static poses such as those you might perform in Iyengar yoga can be helpful in strengthening this unique muscle. In most cases, a dynamic practice by itself is not enough, although this does depend on your individual constitution.

Ultimately, the diaphragm benefits from both static and dynamic strength work. This is because:

- Spine mobilisation (for most of us) is significantly greater when you move slowly. This allows you to target the diaphragm from different angles. Dynamic training will mobilise the spine less, but it demands a bigger range of movement from the diaphragm itself.
- Due to the link between the diaphragm, emotional states, and heart rate, a mix of static and dynamic training will teach you how to control your emotional states at different heart rates, using the breath.

Once you are familiar with the physical practices to release and strengthen the diaphragm, you can incorporate hypercapnic and/or hypoxic breath training into your practice (see Chapter Six for these practices).

---

267 Park, Hankyu, and Dongwook Han. "The Effect of the Correlation Between the Contraction of the Pelvic Floor Muscles and Diaphragmatic Motion During Breathing." *Journal of Physical Therapy Science* 27.7 (2015): 2113-2115.

Is It Possible to Stretch the Diaphragm?

Yes. As with any muscle, it's beneficial to stretch the diaphragm. The diaphragm is stretched when it ascends towards the throat during exhalation. Therefore, it's possible to stretch the diaphragm by lengthening your out-breath. When you perform prolonged, complete exhalations, such as you would in viloma (see page 270) or udgitha Prāṇāyāma (see page 288), you will feel your diaphragm stretch beyond the resting position it assumes in normal breathing.

One popular exercise to stretch the diaphragm is called "vacuum." In vacuum, you exhale as much air as possible through your mouth. After the full exhale, hold your breath. Keep your mouth closed, your belly in, and your diaphragm up. Hold your breath for your maximum duration. Repeat the breath hold thee to ten times.

Another way to stretch the diaphragm is using nauli, a cleansing technique (kriya) for the digestive tract. This technique requires the ascent of the diaphragm.

Physical manipulation can also be used to release tension in the diaphragm. The fingers are placed underneath the cartilage of the last ribs, massaging the muscle from beneath.

The Benefits of Diaphragm Manipulation

An innovative study from the University of Granada, published in the *Journal of Sport Rehabilitation*, shows that when the diaphragm is manipulated through a technique called "doming of the diaphragm," spinal flexion, extension, and lateral flexion all improve. So does hamstring flexibility.[268] The reason for this was not discussed in the paper, but the effect on the hamstrings is likely to be due to the stretch

268 Valenza, Marie Carmen, et al. "The Effects of Doming of the Diaphragm in Subjects With Short-Hamstring Syndrome: A Randomized Controlled Trial." *Journal of Sport Rehabilitation* 24.4 (2015): 342-348.

in the psoas affected by the doming of the diaphragm. Later studies have proven similar benefits from diaphragmatic stretching.[269,270]

The effects of breathing on the body's biochemistry have been well researched, but it is likely there are also significant and important effects on a biomechanical level. One study from scientists at Osaka Prefecture University shows such a result. Twenty-eight study participants were split into two groups. One group followed a basic asana-only practice, instructed by an Iyengar yoga teacher. The other practised asana with Prāṇāyāma – basic asanas with specific breathing instructions. After eight weeks, the asana/Prāṇāyāma group demonstrated greater improvement in flexibility in the lower limbs than the asana-only group.[271]

Diaphragmatic breathing has many positive effects on the body and mind. To train your diaphragm, switch to nasal breathing, try the exercises or incorporate the practices during your asanas and build up slowly over time, to optimize breathing.

269 Gonzalez-Alvarez, Francisco J, et al. "Effects of Diaphragm Stretching on Posterior Chain Muscle Kinematics and Rib Cage and Abdominal Excurion: A Randomized Controlled Trial." *Brazilian Journal of Physical Therapy* 20 (2016): 405-411.

270 Nair, Aishwarya, et al. "Comparison of Diaphragmatic Stretch Technique and Manual Diaphragm Release Technique on Diaphragmatic Excursion in Chronic Obstructive Pulmonary Disease: A Randomized Crossover Trial." *Pulmonary Medicine* (2019).

271 Yamamoto-Morimoto, Kuniko, et al. "Positive Effects of Yoga on Physical and Respiratory Functions in Healthy Inactive Middle-Aged People." *International Journal of Yoga* 12.1 (2019): 62.

CHAPTER TWELVE

THE TONGUE

Why devote an entire chapter to the tongue in a book about yoga and functional breathing? The tongue is one organ that is often overlooked when it comes to functional breathing and the relationships between breathing, sleep, movement, posture, and meditation. The tongue is a complex set of muscles, primarily associated with swallowing, taste, and speech. Some of us also realise, unhappily, that its placement is vital for restorative sleep because a flaccid, fatty tongue can encroach the airway contributing to snoring and sleep apnea. But there is even more to the tongue.

In yoga, the tongue is important for a number of reasons. A clear example of the interrelatedness between structure and function, it is considered a gateway between the gross and subtle bodies.[272] Daily tongue scraping is encouraged to support detoxification and stimulate the internal organs through energetic connections with the rest of the body. As in other Eastern philosophies, the health of the tongue is believed to reflect the wellbeing of the whole person.

Prāṇāyāma exercises such as Lion's Breath involve stretching or deliberately positioning the tongue. In khechari mudra, the tongue is rolled back to touch the most sensitive part of the soft palate, enabling the practitioner to move into a blissful state of infinite consciousness

---

272 "Milking the Tongue – An Ancient Cleansing Technique." *Ekhart Yoga.* (October 8, 2014). http://www.ekhartyoga.com/articles/practice/milking-the-tongue-an-ancient-cleansing-technique (Accessed July 2, 2022).

– a method used in several contemplative traditions and described by Osho in his *Book of Secrets*.[273] The tongue is also a vital part of the microcosmic loop portrayed in Taoism and Tibetan yoga – an energy circuit – that passes up the back of the body and down the front. You may have worked with that microcosmic loop during breathing practice where you are asked to imagine the breath flowing in a circuit around the body. Proper tongue position is considered vital to that flow of energy, Qi, or Prana. If the tongue is not placed in the upper palate, the energy circuit is broken.

From a scientific perspective, research demonstrates the resting position and muscular efficiency of the tongue are directly relevant to your breathing and to your asana practice. The physiologically healthy place for the tongue to sit is in a high resting position on the retro-incisal spot – the area of the hard upper palate, just behind the front teeth. If you try to breathe with your tongue resting high and then with your tongue resting low, you will notice the difference in the quality of breathing. According to scientists at the Universities of Rome and Sassari, Italy, "A low tongue position never guarantees the same breathing quality, especially when it's involved in oral breathing."[274]

The tongue muscles work to keep the airway open during normal breathing, whether you are awake or asleep.[275] However, when we look at any muscle or set of muscles, it's important to acknowledge that no muscle works independently. Everything in the body is connected, so the function of one muscle affects many systems and processes, even those that may seem unrelated. Research has shown that even distant muscles respond to changes in the fascia, even without active contraction of the muscle.[276]

273 Osho. *The Book of Secrets: 112 Meditations to Discover the Mystery Within: an Introduction to Meditation.* St. Martin's Press, 2010.

274 Bordoni, Bruno, et al. "The Anatomical Relationships of the Tongue with the Body System." *Cureus* 10.12 (2018).

275 Cheng, S., et al. "Movement of the Tongue During Normal Breathing in Awake Healthy Humans." *The Journal of Physiology* 586.17 (2008): 4283-4294.

276 Weisman, Martin H. S., et al. "Surface Electromyographic Recordings After Passive and Active Motion Along the Posterior Myofascial Kinematic Chain in Healthy Male Subjects." *Journal of Bodywork and Movement Therapies* 18.3 (2014): 452-461.

The tongue attaches to the diaphragm, the pelvic floor, lungs, quadratus lumborum, psoas major, knees, and even the feet, via a "pathway" of fascia known as the *deep front line* or *lingual chain* (the word *lingual* relates to the tongue or language).[277] The muscles of the throat and tongue are neurologically connected and coordinate with the movement of the diaphragm and the pelvic floor.[278] There are also intricate links with bones and with metabolism via the part of the nervous system responsible for digestion. One of these bones is a small U-shaped bone called the hyoid bone which sits at the base of the tongue in the front of the neck, between the lower jaw and the voice box. It functions as an attachment structure for the tongue and for other muscles on the floor of the mouth.[279]

When you swallow, the front of the tongue pushes up against the palate. The back of the tongue lifts, along with the hyoid bone. The hyoid bone is connected to the sternum of the rib cage and the shoulder girdle via muscles. As this small bone lifts, the rib cage and the organs in the chest also lift. The upward movement increases tension in the fascia around the voice box, ribcage, and thoracic organs. When the tongue relaxes, all these structures return to their resting positions. This relaxation is not caused by the downward pull of gravity. If gravity were involved, it would be impossible to swallow while you are lying down or in inversion.[280]

Because of these muscular and fascial connections, any constriction of the throat can cause the hyoid bone to lock, affecting the connected systems. For instance, if you grip or brace in your throat during ujjayi breathing, instead of creating a gentle resistance, you may experience a knock-on effect in your digestion.

277 Myers, Thomas W., and Susan K. Hillman. *Anatomy Trains*. Primal Pictures Limited, 2004.

278 Bordoni, Bruno, and Emiliano Zanier. "Anatomic Connections of the Diaphragm: Influence of Respiration on the Body System." *Journal of Multidisciplinary Healthcare* 6 (2013): 281.

279 "Hyoid Bone | Description, Anatomy, & Function." *Britannica*. (2019) http://www.britannica.com/science/hyoid-bone (Accessed July 2, 2022).

280 Lopez D. O., Daniel. "The Fascial Imbalance That Pulls the Tongue into the Airway." *Daniel Lopez, D. O.* (April 28, 2021). http://www.daniellopezdo.com/the-fascial-imbalance-that-pulls-the-tongue-into-the-airway/ (Accessed July 2, 2022).

From the simplest perspective, poor tongue posture can negatively affect neck position and stability because the muscles of the tongue are connected to the throat and jaw muscles. This affects balance, lower limb muscle strength, and full body posture.[281] This can lead to mouth breathing, which creates mechanical and chemical imbalances across all of the body's systems and leaves you more vulnerable to forward head thrust, neck and back pain, and injury.

THE IMPORTANCE OF THE TONGUE IN POSTURE AND MOVEMENT

When you are in a headstand or maintaining any challenging balance, you may have noticed that you instinctively pressed your tongue against your front teeth, engaging jihva bandha. In any pose where the muscles of the tubular core are active, the tongue will also engage. Try sticking your tongue out as you transition between poses. You will find it very difficult.

The position of the tongue is considered very important by professionals who work with posture and movement.[282] Several studies demonstrate unexpected connections to areas of the body as seemingly unrelated as the hamstrings. One 2014 study revealed that correct tongue position during strength training may increase an athlete's power in terms of knee flexion peak torque by up to 30%.[283]

Another, from 2020, showed that explosive power increases with different lower jaw postures. The increased airway space associated with correct tongue position changes the curvature of the cervical

281 Bordoni, Bruno, et al. "The Anatomical Relationships of the Tongue with the Body System." *Cureus* 10.12 (2018).
282 Russo, Luca, et al. "Can Tongue Position and Cervical ROM Affect Postural Oscillations? A Pilot and Preliminary Study." *Supplementary Issue: Spring Conferences of Sports Science.* 2020.
283 Di Vico, Rosa, et al. "The Acute Effect of the Tongue Position in the Mouth on Knee Isokinetic Test Performance: A Highly Surprising Pilot Study." *Muscles, Ligaments and Tendons Journal* 3.4 (2013): 318.

spine by reducing forward head thrust. When one part of any "muscle chain" works effectively, function and structure throughout the chain improves. The researchers suggest this could explain how lower jaw position affects muscles not directly connected to the lower jaw, such as the hamstring muscles.[284]

In the 2020 study, when the teeth were closed around a mouthguard and the athlete's bite was in a physiologically normal position, lower body power increased by 5.8%, upper body power by 10%, balance and stability by 4.8%, and hamstring flexibility by 14% compared with a "habitual bite" where teeth were clenched with no mouthguard. If you try, yourself, to clench your teeth, you will immediately find there is less room for your tongue, and it cannot sit in the correct resting spot.

Different types of mouthguards affect power too, with neuromuscular dentistry-designed mouthguards proving better for athletic performance and dynamic power than custom-fitted mouthguards.[285] The dentist-designed mouthguard aims to relax the jaw muscles, allowing a physiologically normal resting position for the jaws and tongue.

There is a common misconception that, to relax the jaw, you need to open your mouth. This is not the case. Clenching during the day or at night can be prevented by correct positioning and strengthening of the tongue.

Scientists have also explored how electrical stimulation of the tongue with biofeedback can improve postural control in the absence of visual cues.[286] The tongue influences posture due to its tactile sensitivity.[287]

284 Haughey, John Patrick, and Peter Fine. "Effects of the Lower Jaw Position on Athletic Performance of Elite Athletes." *BMJ Open Sport & Exercise Medicine* 6.1 (2020): e000886.

285 Arent, Shawn M., Jennifer McKenna, and Devon L. Golem. "Effects of a Neuromuscular Dentistry-Designed Mouthgard on Muscular Endurance and Anaerobic Power." *Comparative Exercise Physiology* 7.2 (2010): 73-79.

286 Vuillerme, Nicolas, et al. "Sensory Supplementation System Based on Elecrotactile Tongue Biofeedback of Head Position for Balance Control." *Neuroscience Letters* 431.3 (2008): 206-210.

287 Barnett-Cowan, Michael, Matin Soeizi, and Joseph F. X. DeSouza. "Visual Attention at the Tip of the Tongue." *i-Perception* 6.1 (2015): 1-4.

Research has found that electrical stimulation of the tongue improves balance, posture, and gait in people with postural impairments.[288,289]

Ultimately, tongue strength and endurance are important for airway health, and different types of exercise affect the strength and endurance of the tongue. It's well known that different types of physical exercise improve the strength and endurance of muscles that are directly targeted, but exercise boosts performance in non-targeted muscles too. This indirect muscle activation was previously only investigated in the skeletal system, but one study aimed to find out if tongue strength and endurance differed between runners and weightlifters.

In weightlifters, the front of the tongue was much stronger than the back part of the tongue. In runners, strength was comparable across the whole tongue. Although the front of the tongue in weightlifters was much stronger than it was in runners, tongue endurance was much greater in runners than in weightlifters.[290] No research yet exists to show how yoga affects the strength and function of the tongue, however, this study indicates that the type of exercise you do makes a difference.

THE TONGUE, POSTURE, TONGUE-TIE, AND SWALLOWING

The tongue also plays an essential role in balance. Proper tongue posture is more relevant for inversions and balancing postures than you might think. Even during mountain pose and simple standing postures, your tongue is important for balance. One study found that tongue position can modulate postural control mechanisms. When the

288 Wildenberg, Joseph C., et al. "Sustained Cortical and Subcortical Neuromodulation Induced by Electrical Tongue Stimulation." *Brain Imaging and Behavior* 4.3 (2010): 199-211.

289 Bordoni, Bruno, et al. "The Anatomical Relationships of the Tongue with the Body System." *Cureus* 10.12 (2018).

290 VanRavenhorst-Bell, Heidi A., et al. "A Comparative Study: Tongue Muscle Performance in Weightlifters and Runners." *Physiological Reports* 6.22 (2018): e13923.

tongue was positioned in the upper palate, against the back of the front teeth, subjects were better able to balance with their eyes closed on an uneven surface. The researchers suggest this discovery may be valuable for assessment and rehabilitation in people with dysfunctional postural control.[291]

Just as the posture of one part of the body can pull another part out of alignment, tongue function can be altered by problems in the lower limbs, the temporomandibular joint in the jaw, the breathing muscles, the pelvis, and the muscles of the airway.[292]

A detailed exploration of the relationship between the tongue and body posture was published by scientists in Italy in 2019. They describe the tongue as a diaphragmatic structure, akin to the diaphragm and the pelvis, explaining that it has a compensatory and balancing role in posture, especially in adulthood. The authors state:

"According to the classical principles of osteopathy, the various body diaphragms must be in balance and in harmony, in their mutual relationship, to ensure a good postural setting."

Like breathing, posture is affected by biomechanical, neurophysiological, and psycho-physiological factors. Muscles can become unbalanced for many reasons. For instance, a tight lingual frenulum or tongue-tie can create a domino effect of fascial and muscular dysfunction throughout the entire body.[293]

One pilot study assessed the benefits of laser tongue-tie release on body posture and on the movement of the shoulders. Twenty-four healthy people aged 10 to 26 years took part. All had a short lingual

---

291 Algahadir, Ahmad H., Hamayun Zafar, and Zaheen A. Iqbal. "Effect of Tongue Position on Postural Stability During Quiet Standing in Healthy Young Males." *Somatosensory & Motor Research* 32.3 (2015): 183-186.

292 Bordoni, Bruno, et al. "The Anatomical Relationships of the Tongue with the Body System." *Cureus* 10.12 (2018).

293 Scoppa, Fabio, and Alessio Pirino. "Is There a Relationship Between Body Posture and Tongue Posture? Glosso-postural Syndrome Between Myth and Reality." *Acta Medica Mediterranea* 35 (2019): 1897-1907.

frenulum – a condition where the band of tissue connecting the base of the tongue to the floor of the mouth is short or restrictive – and a corresponding low tongue and jaw posture. When the tongue ties were released, subjects saw immediate benefits. The body readjusted to within normal movement and postural parameters, improving flexion of the shoulder blades.[294] These results suggest a significant correlation between tongue position and body posture, a correlation that is found across the literature.

The researchers of the Italian review quote orthodontist and researcher, Dr. Gabriella Guaglio:

> "In the daily exercise of my profession, evaluating for years each patient from an orthodontic, gnathological, postural, functional point of view, I realised that in all cases of lingual (tongue) dysfunction, whatever the cause, by resuming the tongue [to] a more physiological position (pointing upwards in the direction of the retro-incisional papilla, and back of the tongue on the palate), an immediate change in the best was obtained of the whole postural attitude, starting from the head, down the vertebral column, up to the pelvis and feet."

Any dysfunction of the tongue can cause instability and compensatory development or muscle activation in the jaws. We swallow up to 1,200 times every day. Each time, the tongue pushes against the teeth and jaw bones – quite a feat of force every 24 hours. Swallowing also impacts your ability to keep your lips sealed. When the lips do not close effectively, it predisposes you to mouth breathing, airway irritation, and congested airways. "Those who swallow badly breathe worse," say the Italian research team. When swallowing is dysfunctional, your overall posture is affected too, due to those full-body fascial connections known as the *lingual chain*. "At the osteopathic level," they caution, "the tongue

---

294 Saccomanno, S., et al. "Does a Short Lingual Frenulum Affect Body Posture? Assessment of Posture in the Sagittal Plane Before and After Laser Frenulotomy: A Pilot Study." *Journal of Biological Regulators and Homeostatic Agents* 35: 30 (2021).

is a key organ." When the tongue is out of balance and swallowing is not functional, scoliotic-type postural imbalances can occur.[295]

Restricted swallowing is often the result of tongue tie, or short lingual frenulum, as described above in relation to posture. Tongue-tie is considered relatively harmless and can be easily corrected at birth, but it is also easily overlooked. Many paediatric doctors never check under the tongue, and there is no solid consensus on what constitutes a tongue tie. It is well-known that tongue-tie in newborns makes breastfeeding difficult, affecting the development of the face, teeth, jaws, and airways. However, scientists now acknowledge that untreated tongue tie can impact pelvic floor stability, toe walking, breathing, and posture. Indeed, for some people, this small band of tissue may be at the root of various dental and medical problems.[296]

Myofunctional therapists and many speech-language pathologists are trained to examine for tongue tie. Over the years, Patrick has been fortunate to attend talks given by myofunctional therapist Joy Moeller. Her life's work is helping children and adults with incorrect patterns of muscle functions used for swallowing, breathing, and chewing. If your baby has difficulty feeding, a consultation online or face-to-face with a MyoFunctional Therapist could be helpful. Visit *www.aomtinfo.org*

The continuous line of strong fascia that attaches to the tongue is anchored to the base of the skull. It attaches to the hyoid bone and continues down into the neck. It travels into the rib cage, lining its inner wall and enveloping the heart, blood vessels, and lungs. It connects to the diaphragm, the abdomen, continues to the pelvic floor, and right down to the toes. A tongue tie can disrupt the balance of tension in this chain. Anything that creates tension in one part of the fascia will affect the whole system. This can produce a forward head posture independent of mouth breathing, and it can contribute to

---

295 Scoppa, Fabio, and Alessio Pirino. "Is There a Relationship Between Body Posture and Tongue Posture? Glosso-postural Syndrome Between Myth and Reality." *Acta Medica Mediterranea* 35 (2019): 1897-1907.

296 "Tongue to Toes: The Whole body Connection." *Airway Matters.* (October 8, 2018). https://airwaymatters.blog/2018/10/08/tongue-to-toes-the-whole-body-connection/ (Accessed July 2, 2022).

dysfunctional swallowing and tongue thrust, because the tongue cannot rise easily.[297]

THE TONGUE-BRAIN CONNECTION

Compared to other body parts, the tongue is extensively connected to the motor and sensory parts of the brain.[298] It is also directly connected to the brain stem, the primitive brain responsible for regulating homeostatic, autonomic functions – those that occur pre-consciously. This means it essentially creates a shortcut to the same evolutionary parts of the brain we can access via breathing exercises. The tongue is innervated by the twelfth cranial nerve, a motor nerve known as the hypoglossal nerve. This controls the muscles we use to speak and to swallow.[299]

Research has shown that the neural network responsible for balance can be activated by sending electrical pulses through the tongue.[300] Speaking to Forbes in 2015, Dr. Jonathan Sackier, CMO at Helius Medical Technologies, explained:

> "We believe the tongue is a much more elegant and direct pathway for stimulating brain structures and inducing neuroplasticity. We are focused on investigating the tongue as a gateway to the brain to hopefully ease the disease of brain injury."[301]

297 Lopez D. O., Daniel. "The Fascial Imbalance That Pulls the Tongue Into the Airway." *Daniel Lopez D. O.* (April 28, 2021). http://www.daniellopezdo.com/the-fascial-imbalance-that-pulls-the-tongue-into-the-airway/ (Accessed July 2, 2022).

298 Barnett-Cowan, Michael, Matin Soeizi, and Joseph F. X. DeSouza. "Visual Attention at the Tip of the Tongue." *i-Perception* 6.1 (2015): 1-4.

299 "The Hypoglossal Nerve: The Brain Behind the Tongue. *Colgate.* (n.d.) http://www.colgate.com/en-us/oral-health/mouth-and-teeth-anatomy/the-hypoglossal-nerve-the-brain-behind-the-tongue (Accessed July 2, 2022).

300 Hsieh, Esther. "A Shock to the Tongue." Vers. 25.6. *Scientific American Mind.* (October 16, 2014). http://www. scientificamerican.com/article/tongue-shocks-hasten-healing/10.1038/scientificamericanmind1114-9 (Accessed July 2, 2022).

301 Roberts, Nicole F. "Is Your Tongue the Key to a Neuroscience Breakthrough?" *Forbes.* (November 02, 2015). http://www.forbes.com/sites/nicolefisher/2015/11/02/is-your-tongue-the-key-to-a-neuroscience-breakthrough/ (Accessed July 2, 2022).

The Tongue as a Key to Quiet the Monkey Mind

The tongue's connection with the brain can be used to access deeper states of consciousness, essentially acting like a dimmer switch for the constant chatter of the monkey mind. We experienced this during a workshop for Oxygen Advantage® instructors conducted by Dr. Mark Atkinson, a medical doctor, human potential teacher, and pioneer of the psychological fitness training system. Mark directed us to soften the eyes, open the mouth slightly as if we were about to speak, and allow the tongue to relax. When you do this, the thinking part of the brain quiets, producing a feeling synonymous with a meditative trance.

> OSHO explains this phenomenon with the simple statement: "The tongue has the centre of speech, and thought is speech." Thinking, at its root, is internal talking. Even when we are not talking to another person, we continue talking within our mind, and so the tongue is active. As you think about that, bring your awareness to your tongue. You will notice it is "vibrating" as if you were speaking. If you can bring your full awareness to the centre of your tongue and soften it, thinking simply stops.

OSHO also explains that when we practise silence in meditation, we must practice awareness of this inner chatter. If you simply stop talking for a long time without awareness of your thoughts, OSHO says the tongue can begin to vibrate violently because the energy is not released. Conversely, if you stop your tongue completely, it is impossible to think. The monkey mind becomes still.[302]

---

302 "Keep Your Mind in the Middle of Your Tongue." *OSHO.* (n.d.) http://www.osho.com/meditation/more-meditations/meditation-of-the-week/keep-your-mind-in-the-middle-of-your-tongue (Accessed July 2, 2022).

JIHVA BANDHA – TONGUE LOCK

Jihva bandha is the fourth bandha in yoga.[303] Each of the bandhas has a specific location in the body (see page 254), helping the mind connect with the inner experience and moderating and directing the flow of energy. Jihva bandha involves pressing the tongue against the root of the upper teeth. This supports the energy cycles so important in yoga, giving better control and concentration. It also increases space in the back of the nasal cavity, allowing for more efficient breathing and more room to breathe.

This resting position of the tongue, with the tip in the upper palate, lightly touching the base of the upper front teeth, is a vital component of both functional breathing and functional movement.

For the tongue to sit in its correct place, which is where it is held with light pressure during jihva bandha, you must breathe through the nose. This is consistent with the fact that yogis believe prana can only be absorbed through the sinuses, we can only assimilate this life force into the body via the nose.

We practise nose breathing during asanas, but, without attention to the tongue, nose breathing can contribute to tension in the jaw. Until we become accustomed to 24/7 nose breathing, we can find the practice difficult and restrictive. This can be exacerbated by forceful breathing, especially when our ujjayi breathing is too focused on producing sound. With the tongue engaged in jihva bandha, the airway is held open, and it's more difficult to brace the throat.

With this bandha in place, the effect is very soothing. The lower jaw drops away from the upper jaw, making it almost impossible to clench the teeth. The tongue relaxes and the airways open, optimising breathing.

---

303 "Jiva Bandha: Closing the Loop of the Soul." *Nicki Doane*. (May 31, 2016). http://www. nickidoane.com/blog/2018/1/11/jiva-bandha-closing-the-loop-of-the-soul (Accessed July 2, 2022).

Benefits of Jihva Bandha

We have explored many reasons why tongue position is important, but yogis claim that jihva bandha comes with many specific benefits of its own. These include:

- Better circulation in the neck muscles.[304]
- Better health in the nerves in the neck, larynx (voice box), pharynx, and thyroid and saliva glands.
- Relief from congestion in the throat and reduction of symptoms of tonsillitis.
- Toning of the face and throat muscles, shaping of the jaw, and reduction of double chins.
- Reduction of stammering.

In energetic terms as well as physical, the throat provides the connection between the head and the heart. The throat houses the fifth chakra, which is related to *satya* – your ability to speak your truth.[305] In jihva bandha, this area of communication opens and energy is free to flow around the body.

Exercise: How to Practise Jihva Bandha

1. Begin with your mouth closed and your lips gently sealed.
2. Bring your awareness to the tip of your tongue, and place it in the hard upper palate, just before your front upper teeth.
3. Place the tongue with a light pressure, without force.
4. Breathe through your nose in ujjayi prāṇāyāma.

304 "Jihva-Bandha." *Indian Net Zone.* http://www.indiannetzone.com/42/jihvahandha. htm (Accessed July 2, 2022).

305 "Tongue." *Prajna Yoga.* (July 19, 2011). http://www.prajnayoga.com/asana-anatomy-focus/tongue/ (Accessed July 2, 2022).

How to Find the Correct Tongue Position

We often ask students to practise tongue pops to determine where the tongue should be:

1. Press the tongue against the roof of the mouth to create suction.
2. Move your tongue from the roof of the mouth to create a "POP" sound.
3. The position that creates this "POP" sound is a good resting posture for the tongue.
4. Ideally three quarters of your tongue is resting on the roof of the mouth.

HOW TO CLEAN THE TONGUE

The practice of tongue cleaning and stretching recommended in yoga is called jihva dhauti or jihva shodhana. You can brush your tongue with a toothbrush or use a tongue scraper to remove the coating of gunk that appears on it. This is thought to promote lifelong good health and it can help prevent bad breath. In traditional Chinese medicine, different types of tongue coating are classified in terms of their relationship with disease. This connection has been confirmed in scientific research into the microbiome of the tongue. A thick, white tongue coating is associated with gastritis, while a thin yellow coating may indicate certain cancers.[306]

Yoga also suggests stretching the tongue. You can do this by gripping it with your fingers and gently tugging on it for a few minutes. In his book, *Prāṇāyāma, Beyond the Fundamentals,* Richard Rosen explains, "since our tongue is, after all, a muscle that for most of us gets a lot of use, it seems useful to stretch it occasionally." [307]

---

306 Chen, Hairong, et al. "Microbial Characteristics Across Different Tongue Coating Types in a Healthy Population." *Journal of Oral Microbiology* 13.1(2021): 1946316.
307 Rosen, Richard. *Prāṇāyāma Beyond the Fundamentals: An In-Depth Guide to Yogic Breathing.* Shambhala Publications, 2006.

Another yogic technique for tongue purification is called "milking." This involves rubbing the tongue with butter. It is thought to improve the function of the glands in the neck, including the thyroid and thymus.

PAYING ATTENTION TO YOUR TONGUE

Now that you understand that the tongue has many complex functions and connections outside of speech, taste, and swallowing, try bringing attention to your tongue placement during quiet breathing, breathing exercises, meditation, and asana practice. Notice your tongue position throughout the day.

Do you tend to hold your tongue low in your jaws, or is it correctly placed behind your upper front teeth? When you wake up in the morning, check where your tongue is. Is it on the roof of the mouth or resting low? Does your tongue activate during certain yoga poses? What happens when you relax your tongue to prepare for meditation? Where is your tongue when you focus on your breath? Can you sit with, and relax into, the unfamiliarity of that complete . . . inner . . . silence . . .? Can you stop your tongue?

CHAPTER THIRTEEN

BREATHING TO ACTIVATE THE CORE

How the core is defined depends on the source, and, so, there is considerable variation. One paper in the *Journal of Physical Therapy Science* describes the core as a box, with the diaphragm at the top, the abdominals at the front, the spinal and gluteal muscles at the back, and the hip and pelvic floor muscles at the bottom.[308]

The Core

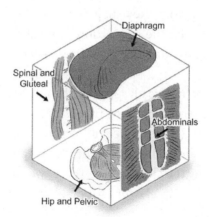

308 Cavaggioni, Luca, et al. "Effects of Different Core Exercises on Respiratory Parameters and Abdominal Strength." *Journal of Physical Therapy Science* 27.10 (2015): 3249-3253.

On the other hand, the neuro-musculoskeletal physiotherapist Josephine Key says that the common idea of the core as synonymous with the abs is a misunderstanding. The core, as she explains it, reaches from the sitting bones right up to the mid-thorax (chest), where the diaphragm and transversus abdominis attach. The rib cage, anterolateral (front and sides of the) abdominal wall, and the ring-shaped arches of the pelvis form a hoop-like framework that braces the spinal column. Key writes:

> "Transversus abdominis (TrA) has been singled out as *'the core muscle'* – transversus and *'core'* have become inextricably linked. This myth-conception is propagated as the panacea for just about everything from helping back pain, enhancing performance, to improving your shape. [But] Transversus abdominis dysfunction is only a part of the problem."

This idea of the TrA as a "powerhouse" indicates, Key says, a concept of core control that bypasses the "inner locus of control." The "hoop" of muscles she describes encloses an internal chamber, the volume of which changes through expansion and contraction as we breathe. The diaphragm divides this chamber into thoracic- abdominal-pelvic cavities. The lower cavities, Key suggests, form the core. [309] This view of the core suggests that the generation of intra-abdominal pressure is as important in core stability as the function of the various core muscles.

To appreciate how the breath supports the integrity of your core, it is useful to look at the structure of the trunk. The upper part of the trunk holds the respiratory (thoracic) cavity – containing your lungs. The lower half contains the abdominal cavity – containing your digestive organs surrounded by the abdominals. These two cavities are separated by the diaphragm. The Greek word for diaphragm, διάφραγμα, means *something that divides.*

---

309 Key, Josephine. "'The Core': Understanding It, and Retraining Its Dysfunction." *Journal of Bodywork and Movement Therapies* 17.4 (2013): 541-559.

There are several differences between the upper and lower cavities. The thoracic cavity has a slight negative pressure while pressure in the abdominal cavity is positive.[310] Another difference is that the volume of the thoracic cavity changes continually with the breath.

As we've previously noted, pressure in the thoracic cavity decreases during inhalation and increases during exhalation.[311,312] As your diaphragm descends during inhalation, pressure in the abdominal cavity increases too.

In a healthy adult, intra-abdominal pressure (IAP) is between 0 and 5 mmHg.[313] IAP is determined by the activation of the diaphragm and of the TrA and pelvic floor muscles.

THE LINK BETWEEN BACK PAIN AND BREATHING

Lower back pain and breathing patterns are related in several ways:

- Inadequate function of the diaphragm and abdominal muscles can cause instability to the spine and pelvis, postural imbalance, and overuse of the smaller muscles.
- Damage or tension in the thoracolumbar fascia around the lower spine can impact breathing. Any pain in the back, whatever its cause, can affect the breath and cause you to restrict diaphragm movement.
- An overly active sympathetic nervous system can contribute to pain, lowering pain tolerance, and perpetuating a dysfunctional breathing pattern.

---

310 De Backer, Daniel. "Abdominal Compartment Syndrome." *Critical Care* 3.6 (1999): 1-2.
311 Urmey, William F., et al. "Pleural Pressure Increases During Inspiration in the Zone of Apposition of Diaphragm to Rib Cage." *Journal of Applied Physiology* 65.5 (1988): 2207-2212.
312 De Troyer, Andre. "Effect of Hyperinflation on the Diaphragm." *European Respiratory Journal* 10.3 (1997): 708-713.
313 De Backer, Daniel. "Abdominal Compartment Syndrome." *Critical Care* 3.6 (1999): 1-2.

- 50% of people with lower back pain have faulty breathing patterns.[314] In many cases, it is unclear which comes first. Does lower back pain cause faulty breathing, or has dysfunctional breathing caused the pain?[315,316] It is highly likely there is a feedback loop between the two factors that contributes to and perpetuates symptoms.

One of the most important points to remember is that IAP is mediated by muscles that have both respiratory and postural responsibilities.[317] When these muscles are not properly activated, breathing and posture are both compromised. This leaves you susceptible to lower back pain, especially during exercise.[318] In one study, patients with lower back pain associated with the sacroiliac joint in the pelvis found that when breathing was faster, the pelvic floor was less active, and the amount of movement in the diaphragm decreased.[319]

Tension in the thoracolumbar fascia is related to both lower back pain and diaphragmatic function[320,321,322] independently. When

314 Whittaker, Jackie L. "Ultrasound Imaging of the Lateral Abdominal Wall Muscles in Individuals With Lumbopelvic Pain and Signs of Concurrent Hypocapnia." *Manual Therapy* 13.5 (2008): 404-410.

315 Kolar, Pavel, et al. "Postural Function of the Diaphragm in Persons With and Without Chronic Low Back Pain." *Journal of Orthopaedic & Sports Physical Therapy* 42.4 (2012): 352-362.

316 Smith, Michelle D., Russell, Anne, and Paul W. Hodges. "Disorders of Breathing and Continence Have a Stronger Association With Back Pain Than Obesity and Physical Activity." *Australian Journal of Physiotherapy* 52.1 (2006): 11-16.

317 Cresswell, A. G., H. Gundstrom, and Alf Thorestensson. "Observations on Intra-Abdominal Pressure and Patterns of Abdominal Intra-Muscular Activity in Man." *Acta Physiologica Scandinavica* 144.4 (1992): 409-418.

318 Ostwal, Priyanka P., and S. K. Wani. "Breathing Patterns in Patients With Low Back Pain." *International Journal of Physiotherapy and Research* 2.1 (2014): 347-53.

319 O'Sullivan, Peter B., et al. "Altered Motor Control Strategies in Subjects with Sacroliliac Joint Pain During the Active Straight-Leg-Raise Test." *Spine* 27.1 (2002): E1-E8.

320 Langevin, Helene M., et al. "Reduced Thoracolumbar Fascia Shear Strain in Human Chronic Low Back Pain." *BMC Musculoskeletal Disorders* 12.1 (2011): 1-11.

321 Taguchi, T., J. Tesarz, and S. Mense. *The Thoracolumbar Fascia as a Source of Low Back Pain.* Munich: Elsevier GmbH, 2009, 251.

322 Bordoni, Bruno, and Fabiola Marelli. "Failed Back Surgery Syndrome: Review and New Hypotheses." *Journal of Pain Research* 9 (2016): 17.

Anastasis experienced an injury to his thoracolumbar fascia, aside from the obvious limitations to movement, he also experienced restriction of his breathing. Full movement of his diaphragm caused pain. Part of his recovery involved breathing exercises that he performed while recruiting the affected muscles. He is a big advocate of this method.

The thoracolumbar fascia has a high concentration of sympathetic nerves.[323] This may explain why some people with lower back pain report more intense pain during mental stress when the sympathetic nervous system is activated.[324]

THE FOUR STAGES OF CORE ENGAGEMENT

Based on the fact that core activation depends primarily on intra-abdominal pressure, we suggest the following Progressive Core Activation Model: hypercapnia, lateral breathing, breath hold/ ADIM (abdominal drawing-in manoeuvre), and valsalva.

323 Hirsch, Carl, Bo-Eric Ingelmark, and Malcolme Miller. "The Anatomical Basis for Low Back Pain: Studies on the Presence of Sensory Nerve Endings in Ligamentous, Casular and Intervertebral Disc Structures in the Human Lumbar Spine." *Acta Orthopaedica Scandinavica* 33.1-4 (1963): 1-17.

324 Chou, Roger, and Paul Shekelle. "Will This Patient Develop Persistent Disabling Low Back Pain?" *Jama* 303.13 (2010): 1295-1302.

Hypercapnia

While we have the most leverage to increase IAP biomechanically, one innovative study showed that recruiting abdominal muscles, in particular the transversus abdominis, also depends on biochemistry. Scientists demonstrated that a gradual increase in CO_2 causes the recruitment of transversus abdominis muscles. What's more, this muscle recruitment is relative to the increased level of CO_2.[325] This means hypercapnia will increase IAP. While the increase may be small, the relationship of IAP to spinal and pelvic stability provides yet another reason to maintain nasal breathing during exercise.

The following breathing techniques aim to increase IAP further.

Lateral Breathing

The name lateral breathing is derived from the lateral expansion of the ribs that accompanies this technique. Regular breathing is maintained throughout.

This form of breathing is commonly found in Pilates. Its foundation is a hollowing of the abdomen where the lower abdomen is pulled in to maintain a neutral spine.[326] This results in the recruitment of the abdominal muscles (the transversus abdominis and internal and external obliques)[327] as well as the diaphragm.[328] This is the same movement as uddiyana bandha. The abdominal hollowing helps maintain a straight spine.

325 De Troyer, Andre, et al. "Transversus Abdominis Muscle Function in Humans." *Journal of Applied Physiology* 68.3 (1990): 1010-1016.

326 McGalliard, Michel K., et al. "Changes in Transversus Abdominis Thickness With Use of the Abdominal Drawing-In Maneuver During a Functional Task." *P M & R* 2.3 (2010): 187-194.

327 Richardson, Carolyn, et al. "Techniques for Active Lumbar Stabilisation for Spinal Protection: A Pilot Study." *Australian Journal of Physiotherapy* 38.2 (1992): 105-112.

328 Allison, Garry, et al. "The Role of the Diaphragm During Abdominal Hollowing Exercises." *Australian Journal of Physiotherapy* 44.2 (1998): 95-102.

The increase of IAP that accompanies abdominal hollowing has been shown in numerous studies to improve stability and reduce pain in the lower back.[329,330,331,332,333] This technique has been tested in side plank pose (vasisthasana), forearm plank,[334] bridge, and bird dog pose.[335] The simultaneous contraction of the pelvic floor muscles (mula bandha) during abdominal hollowing (uddiyana bandha) results in a greater recruitment of the transversus abdominis.[336]

How to Do Lateral Breathing

In this style of breathing, your focus is on the lower ribs and their movement out to the sides. Breathe into your mid-back, into the back of your lower ribs.

329 Richardson, Carolyn, et al. "Techniques for Active Lumbar Stabilisation for Spinal Protection: A Pilot Study." *Australian Journal of Physiotherapy* 38.2 (1992): 105-112.

330 Richarson, C. A., and G. A. Jull. "Muscle Control -- Pain Control. What Exercises Would You Prescribe?" *Manual Therapy* 1.1 (1995): 2-10.

331 O'Sullivan, Peter B., et al. "Evaluation of Specific Stabilizing Exercise in the Treatment of Chronic Low Back Pain With Radiologic Diagnosis of Spondylolysis or Spondylolisthesis." *Spine* 22.24 (1997): 2959-2967.

332 Kim, Minseock, et al. "The Effectiveness of Hollowing and Bracing Strategies With Lumbar Stabilization Exercise in Older Adult Women With Nonspecific Low Back Pain: A Quasi-Experimental Study on a Community-Based Rehabilitation." *Journal of Manipulative and Physiological Therapeutics* 41.1 (2018): 1-9.

333 Pulkovski, N., et al. "Ultrasound Assessment of Transversus Abdominis Muscle Contraction Ratio During Abdominal Hollowing: A Useful Tool to Distinguish Between Patients With Chronic Low Back Pain and Healthy Controls?" *European Spine Journal* 21.6 (2012): 750-759.

334 Garcia-Jaen, Miguel, et al. "Influence of Abdominal Hollowing Maneuver on the Core Musculature Activation During the Prone Plank Exercise." *International Journal of Environmental Research and Public Health* 17.20 (2020): 7410.

335 Oh, Youn-Jung, Sam-Ho Park, and Myung-Mo Lee. "Comparison of Effects of Abdominal Draw-In Lumbar Stabilization Exercises With and Without Respiratory Resistance on Women With Low Back Pain; A Randomized Controlled Trial." *Medical Science Monitor: International Medical Journal of Experimental and Clinical Research* 26 (2020): e921295-1.

336 Critchley, Duncan. "Instructing Pelvic Floor Contraction Facilitates Transversus Abdominis Thickness Increase During Low-Abdominal Hollowing." *Physiotherapy Research International* 7.2 (2002): 65-75.

Use these steps to get used to the feel of lateral breathing:

- Sit comfortably, cross-legged on your mat or on a block.
- Place your hands around your sides, at the level of your lower ribs.
- Breathe in through your nose, into the back and sides of your body. Remember your lungs sit inside your ribcage, and your ribs can expand with each inhalation.
- As you breathe in, feel your ribs move gently out.
- As you breathe out, feel your ribs move gently in.
- Breathe only through your nose.
- Now, pull your abdomen in toward your spine. Your spine should remain straight. In this exercise, as in uddiyana bandha, you may engage the abdomen right up to the ribs.
- Keep your abdomen contracted and feel the lateral movement of your ribs as you breathe in and out.

You should not feel any light headedness or dizziness when you practise lateral breathing. To avoid this, breathe softly and silently. If you do experience light headedness or dizziness, return to normal breathing.

Lateral Breathing

Sit comfortably, cross-legged on your mat or on a block.

Place your hands around your sides, at the level of your lower ribs.

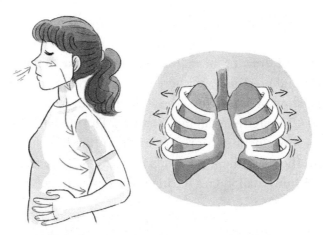

Breathe in through your nose, into the back and sides of your body. Remember your lungs sit inside your ribcage, and your ribs can expand with each inhalation.

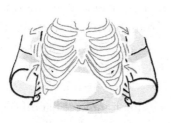

As you breathe in, feel your ribs move gently out.
As you breathe out, feel your ribs move gently in.

Breathe only through your nose.

Now, pull your abdomen in toward your spine. Your spine should remain straight. In this exercise, as in Uddiyana bandha, you may engage the abdomen right up to the ribs.

Keep your abdomen contracted and feel the lateral movement of your ribs as you breathe in and out.

Breath-Hold/Abdominal Drawing-In Maneuver

The abdominal drawing in manoeuvre involves a similar muscular action to lateral breathing, but here the breath can be held at the end of the inhalation or exhalation. The abdominal drawing in manoeuvre increases IAP more than lateral breathing. During lateral breathing, diaphragm movement is constant, but when the breath is held after inhalation, the diaphragm descends around 18.5% more (from 27.3 mm to 32.5 mm) than it does during normal breathing.[337]

How to do the abdominal drawing in maneuvre

To practise the abdominal drawing in manoeuvre, you first need to learn which muscles to activate. This practice strengthens the transversus abdominis, which is the deepest of your abdominal muscles. It's a safe, effective way to build core strength. It can be used during asana practice, but first, let's feel our way through the manoeuvre . . .

- Lie on your back, with your knees bent and feet flat on the floor.
- Now, find your belly button. The area below the belly button is your lower abdomen. This is where you will focus.
- Draw your lower abdomen in and down toward the floor. Hold for five seconds, breathing normally. Don't move your hips or your spine.
- Be sure not to push your belly out or hollow your entire abdomen right up to your rib cage. This is not like the uddiyana bandha where the whole abdomen hollows.

When we use this movement during practice, we will add a breath hold as the lower abdomen draws in.

---

337 Kolar, Pavel, et al. "Analysis of Diaphragm Movement During Tidal Breathing and During Its Activation While Breath Holding Using MRI Synchronized With Spirometry." *Physiological Research* 58.3 (2009).

The ADIM

Lie on your back, with your knees bent and feet flat on the floor.
Now, find your belly button. The area below the belly button
is your lower abdomen. This is where you will focus.

Draw your lower abdomen in and down towards the floor.
Hold for 5 seconds, breathing normally. Don't move your hips or your spine.

Be sure not to push your belly out, or to hollow your entire abdomen
right up to your rib cage. This is not the same as Uddiyana bandha
in which the whole abdomen hollows.

Valsalva Maneuver

The Valsalva Maneuver involves bracing (contraction or tightening) of the external abdominal muscles. This practice was first mentioned in medical literature by the Italian anatomist, Antonio Valsalva, in his 1704 work, *De Aure Humana Tractatus* (The Treatment of the Human Ear)[338]. As it is used today, the Valsalva Maneuver usually means an acute rise

338 Valsalva, Antonio Maria. "De Aure Humana Tractatus." *Typis Constantini Pisarii ad S. Michaelem Prope Archigymnasium,* 1704.

in intrathoracic and intra-abdominal pressure. This is facilitated by a contraction of the trunk muscles, right down to the pelvic floor. The contraction occurs against a lock at the glottis (jalandhara bandha) and the tongue. The Valsalva Maneuver happens automatically, if briefly, whenever we cough or sneeze, and for longer periods during functions such as defecation. It's used more consciously in various sports, during heavy lifting, and in the playing of wind instruments.[339] However, Valsalva first described this manoeuvre as a way to expel pus out of the middle ear by attempting to exhale forcibly against a closed airway.[340]

The Valsalva Maneuver is generally performed at the end of the inhalation, and the breath is held for the duration of the exercise. In contrast to abdominal hollowing, this practice recruits the rectus abdominis (your six-pack) at the front of the body and the erector spinae (a group of muscles that run the length of your spine) at the back of your body.[341] It also involves greater recruitment of the transversus abdominis, the internal and external obliques (your trunk rotation muscles), and the multifidus (the deep back muscles).[342] For this reason, the Valsalva Maneuver results in higher IAP than abdominal drawing in manoeuvre.[343,344,345]

339 Jellinek, E. H. "The Valsalva Manoeuvre and Antonio Valsalva (1666-1723)." *Journal of the Royal Society of Medicine*, (2006) 448-451.

340 Richard, N. "Valsalva Maneuver." *Very Well Health.* (July 20, 2011). http://www.verywellhealth.com/valsalva-maneuver-1746152 (Accessed July 2, 2022).

341 Bearn, J. G. "The Significance of the Activity of the Abdominal Muscles in Weight Lifting." *Cells Tissues Organs* 45.1-2 (1961): 83-89.

342 Muramoto, Yuki, and Hironobu Kuruma. "Comparison Between Bracing and Hollowing Trunk Exercise with a Focus on the Change in T2 Values Obtained by Magnetic Resonance Imaging." *Plos One* 15.10 (2020): e0240213.

343 Moghadam, Navid, et al. "Comparison of the Recruitment of Transverse Abdominis Through Drawing-In and Bracing in Different Core Stability Training Positions." *Journal of Exercise Rehabilitation* 15.6 (2019): 819.

344 Madokoro, Sachiko, Masami Yokogawa, and Hiroichi Miaki. "Effect of the Abdominal Draw-In Maneuver and Bracing on Abdominal Muscle Thickness and the Associated Subjective Difficulty in Healthy Individuals." *Healthcare* (MDPI) 8.4 (2020).

345 Koh, Hyung-Woo, Sung-Hyoun Cho, and Cheol-Yong Kim. "Caparison of the Effects of Hollowing and Bracing Exercises on Cross-Sectional Areas of Abdominal Muscles in Middle-Aged Women." *Journal of Physical Therapy Science* 26.2 (2014): 295-299.

How to Do the Valsalva Maneuver:

- Take a long, full inhalation through your nose.
- Pinch your nose to hold your breath.
- With your breath held, try to exhale as if you were blowing up a balloon.
- Bear down with your pelvic floor as you would during a bowel movement.
- Hold for 10-15 seconds.
- Breathe out through your nose.
- Resume normal breathing.

The Valsalva Maneuver

Take a long, full inhalation through your nose.

Pinch your nose to hold your breath.

With your breath held, try to exhale, as if you were blowing up a balloon.

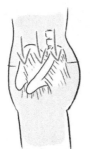

Bear down with your pelvic floor as you do during a bowel movement.

Hold for 10-15 seconds.

Breathe out through your nose. Resume normal breathing.

BREATHING IN A YOGA PRACTICE

CHAPTER FOURTEEN

BREATHING IN ASANAS

"The practice of asanas removes the obstructions which impede the flow of prana."

– B.K.S Iyengar[346]

The practice of physical postures requires discipline. In asana, the breath is extended, and the senses are withdrawn from the external environment.[347] Attention is drawn out of the mind and into the body as an important part of the practice.

While modern Western ideas of yoga focus on the physical, yogic philosophy still centres on the idea that the mind, body, and breath must work in unity and develop progressively, together.[348] A simple example of this can be found in the yoga tradition of Krishnamacharya, in which every movement in asana must be accompanied by the appropriate breathing phase: postures that open the chest are performed on inhalation, while those that compress the abdomen, such as forward bends and twists, are accompanied by exhalation.[349]

---

346 Iyengar, Bellur Krishnamukar Sundara. *BKS Iyengar Yoga: The Path to Holistic Health.* Penguin, 2007.
347 Mehta, Silva, Mira Mehta, and Shyam Mehta. *Yoga: The Iyengar Way.* Knopf, 1990.
348 Singh, Dr. Umesh Pal. *The Physiological Essentials of Yogic Relaxation: Body Mind Breath & Stress.* Partridge Publishing, India, 2015.
349 Pineault, D. "Breathing in Yoga: Role, Relevance and Technique." (n.d.)

Optimal breathing supports a safer, more effective asana practice, and controlling the breath impacts the external and subtle energies. When you practise asanas, as with any physical movement, your muscles work harder. This alters your metabolic needs. As you engage your muscles to achieve and maintain a pose, your body needs more energy, so it begins to use more O_2 and produce more CO_2.

As your cells generate energy, they release CO_2 into the bloodstream. This CO_2 is carried to the lungs, where the excess leaves the body in exhaled air.

This is a very efficient process. The more energy your muscles use during practice, the more O_2 your cells need. As you use more energy, CO_2 increases. When this happens, blood pH drops, which releases more O_2 from the haemoglobin in the red blood cells so that more O_2 is available to the cells that need it.

BREATHING AND MUSCLE OXYGENATION

Imagine you attend a vinyasa style class. During the opening sun salutations, the growing sensation of air hunger becomes uncomfortable. You want to open your mouth to take bigger breaths, but your teacher suggests you keep breathing softly through your nose, lengthening your exhalation.

Those slower exhalations calm your nervous system, slowing your heart rate and relieving some of the mental discomfort. The lower heart rate lowers your metabolism, slowing the production of CO_2. Yet, because you're exhaling less air, levels of CO_2 increase in your blood. This unlocks O_2 from haemoglobin, making it available to your working muscles. What's more, the plentiful supply of CO_2 keeps your blood vessels open. This supports your circulation, allowing your blood to efficiently carry the O_2 where it needs to go. Oxygenation is further aided by nasal NO, which is available because you are breathing through the nose. This NO redistributes blood and opens blood vessels throughout the lungs, allowing more efficient O_2 uptake by the blood.

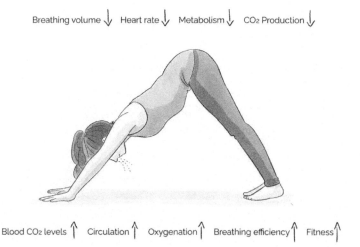

Breathing volume ↓   Heart rate ↓   Metabolism ↓   CO₂ Production ↓

Blood CO₂ levels ↑   Circulation ↑   Oxygenation ↑   Breathing efficiency ↑   Fitness ↑

If, instead, you had ignored your teacher's advice and succumbed to the urge to breathe through your mouth, you would have increased your breathing volume, losing more CO_2 from your blood with each exhale. The bond between O_2 and haemoglobin would have become stronger, tightening the red blood cell's grip on the O_2, making less O_2 available to your muscles.

Depending on your physical condition, your muscles may then have resorted to anaerobic respiration, which is less efficient and less sustainable. If that happens, you might feel less air hunger, but you are more likely to feel fatigue and muscle soreness after the class, due to lactic acid build-up. You would take longer to recover physically because O_2 is essential for muscle repair. What's more, longer-term, your respiratory capacity won't improve, so you are likely to continue to experience air hunger and breathlessness every time you repeat the sequence of sun salutations – no matter how committed you are to becoming more fit.

With this example, you can see why it is so important to use your yoga practice to improve your everyday breathing patterns for optimal blood flow and oxygenation, and why you should go beyond your current breath training practice to integrate functional breathing techniques into your asanas.

Breathing volume ↑   Injury risk ↑   Recovery time ↑

Blood CO₂ levels ↓   Oxygenation ↓   Breathing efficiency ↓   Fitness plateaus ↓

WORKING ON BREATHING MUSCLES AND POSTURE FOR BETTER BREATHING

People who have a sensitive constitution, tend to notice differences in their breathing very soon after exercises that address the supportive respiratory muscles. The fact is – good breathing patterns go hand in hand with a stable posture.[350]

Before we look at how to use asanas to address the muscles that support breathing, it's important to remember that muscles don't work in isolation. Each muscle tends to have more than one function. It is therefore important to assess the body as a whole and identify its patterns. This holistic approach gives us a better chance to resolve problems. For instance, when the shoulders are uneven, they apply uneven pressure on the lungs. Rather than just working on the shoulders, we also need to work out whether the hips or feet contribute to that unevenness. Everything in the body is connected, so your posture will improve when you address problems in muscles that support breathing.

350 Smith, Michelle D., Russell, Anne, and Paul W. Hodges. "Disorders of Breathing and Continence Have a Stronger Association with Back Pain Than Obesity and Physical Activity." *Australian Journal of Physiotherapy* 52.1 (2006): 11-16.

Likewise, by addressing poor posture, the function of your breathing muscles will improve.

FIVE POSES TO RELEASE THE DIAPHRAGM

Your ability to breathe efficiently is directly affected by your neck, back, shoulders, and abdominal muscles. The following five poses are designed to release pressure from the diaphragm and improve breathing. Most of us have only a vague idea of where the diaphragm is. The exercises in this chapter will help you to develop a feel for its position and movement. During each pose, bring your awareness to the area around your lower ribs, where your chest and abdomen meet. This is where your diaphragm sits. Notice the gentle expansion and contraction of the ribs as you breathe in and out.

1. Side-Lying Shoulder Horizontal Abduction Pose

Many of the day-to-day habits of modern life promote a constant forward-thrust of the neck that also affects the upper back. This causes the muscles in the front of the trunk to shorten. This exercise can help lengthen those muscles, restoring balance. It brings the shoulders back, allowing for the chest area to open, and it stretches the chest, shoulders, and armpits in preparation for breathing.

Application:

To get into the posture, lie on your front. Hold the pose for between 30 seconds and two minutes on each side. To begin with, practise two sets of 30 seconds per side.

Breathing:

Breathe only through your nose, light, slow, and deep.

Benefits:

This pose improves flexibility in the anterior deltoids (the shoulder muscle that helps move your arm forward) and pectoralis major (the largest muscle of the anterior chest wall).

Cautions:

The pose is entered by lying on your front. If you have tight shoulders, you may find that your spine twists. Extra caution needs to be applied for individuals with lower back problems. Pregnant women must not lie prone or perform spinal twists. However, horizontal mobilisation of the shoulders is safe for pregnant women who can perform this pose standing against the wall.

2. Uttanasana/ Standing Forward-Fold

Ut means intensity and *tan* means stretch. *Uttanasana* means intense stretch. In this pose, many muscles in the back of the body are stretched. Most important to breathing is the quadratus lumborum or QL, which is the deepest abdominal muscle and attaches to the rear of the diaphragm.

In this pose, it's common to feel a stretch in the hips, hamstrings, and calves without feeling much in the back muscles. When this happens, it is appropriate to bend the knees to get the most from the pose. As with all postures involving spine flexion, the diaphragm is under pressure and must work harder in the inhalation phase. Extra attention needs to be paid to keeping the breath soft.

Application:

Hold the pose for 30 seconds to five minutes. Start by holding the pose for three sets of 30 seconds.

Breathing:

Breathe only through your nose, light, slow, and deep.

Benefits:

This pose improves flexibility in the quadratus lumborum and the trapezius. The trapezius is a large muscle that starts at the base of your neck, crosses the shoulders, and extends to the middle of your back.

Cautions:

Due to the spinal flexion, this pose should not be practised during pregnancy. A modified variation with a straight spine will be appropriate for pregnant women. If you have high blood pressure, you should build up practice in this pose gradually.

3. Ashta Chandrasana/ Crescent Lunge

This variation on a lunge can be viewed as the single-leg counterpose of uttanasana. In this posture, many muscles in the front of the body are stretched. Most important to breathing is the psoas muscle in the lumbar spine and pelvis. It attaches to the rear part of the diaphragm. This pose is a good antidote to sitting down too much, especially if you perform a lot of forward-reaching tasks like typing.

Application:

Hold this pose for one to five minutes per side. Start by holding the pose for two sets of one minute per side.

Breathing:

Breathe only through your nose, light, slow, and deep.

Benefits:

This pose improves flexibility in the psoas and anterior deltoids, while strengthening muscles in the upper back. The psoas is considered a fear reflex muscle. In evolutionary terms, we would engage the psoas to prepare to run from danger. We tend to unconsciously tighten the psoas when stressed or sitting for long periods. For this reason, you may feel a deep sense of release after this asana.

Cautions:

None. However, if you have a sensitive lower back, you should be extra careful to maintain good form in the posture.

If your hamstrings are tight and you feel pinching in your lower back, you may bend your back knee to maintain a neutral pelvis or place the back knee on the floor to reduce intensity.

4. Parsva Urdhva Hastasana/ Upward Salute Side-Bend Pose/ Standing Half-Moon

Standing half-moon pose will improve flexibility in the muscles on the side of the body (primarily the trunk).

Application:

Hold this pose for 15 seconds to one minute per side. Start by holding the pose for three sets of 15 seconds, alternating from side to side.

Breathing:

Breathe only through your nose, light, slow, and deep.

Benefits:

Improves flexibility in psoas and quadratus lumborum.

Cautions:

None.

5. Sarvangasana/Shoulder Stand

Sarva means entire, *anga* means body part, and *asana* means pose. *Sarvangasana* means all body parts pose. Here, the body is inverted, so the diaphragm moves against gravity during inhalation. The weight of the lower body will provide an additional challenge during the diaphragm's active phase (the inhalation).

Application:

Hold this pose for 20 seconds to five minutes. Start by holding the pose for 30 seconds if you can.

Breathing:

Breathe only through your nose, light, slow, and deep.

Benefits:

This pose improves flexibility in the muscles of the upper back and strengthens the abdominals.

Cautions:

If you have high blood pressure, you should only practise this pose if you maintain regular soft breathing while holding it.

If you are pregnant, you may need to refrain from this pose unless you can maintain a straight back and flex only from the neck. If this is not possible for you, rest your hips on a pillow, and put your legs up the wall instead.

How These Five Poses Will Help Your Breathing

To the extent you practise these poses regularly, they will make your breathing easier. At the same time, you are likely to notice improvements in your posture.

Moving Better Means Breathing Better

We'd like to share another story, again with permission, to illustrate the impact functional breathing can have. In her late 30s, Alison launched a wellness company offering one-to-one yoga and Pilates classes. She was slim, and her flexibility was above average. Alison was a Pilates instructor; she was very keen on meditation and enjoyed running. However, due to the demands of her fast-paced start-up company, she rarely had time to do much else in the way of self-care.

Alison confessed that her body often felt tight. Her mind was always busy, so she found it difficult to fall asleep. She often caught herself feeling out of breath. Working for over two years on bodywork that can enhance breathing and mental capacity, Alison was very aware of her body and easily able to detect changes in it. While she had minimal experience with breath training, she had practised meditation a lot before (mainly through a guided meditation app called *Headspace*). This experience meant that Alison was able to give immediate feedback on the exercises. Straight after performing stretches to release the diaphragm, she often said, "I can breathe better now," or "I was not aware how shallow my breath was. I now feel my diaphragm moving."

The way you move and the way you breathe are interrelated. If someone asked you to jump into the air or sprint, you'd automatically adjust your breathing before you started. But habit doesn't always produce the best results. Although the body intrinsically knows what to do, when you start from a place of dysfunction and imbalance, the body's responses are dulled, often as a result of compounding stresses.

What's more, when your breathing is dysfunctional, you may normalise it. For example, Anastasis recalls students with paradoxical breathing who'd argue for more than ten minutes over whether the belly should move in or out during the inhale. Paradoxical breathing is a breathing pattern disorder in which the abdomen moves in during inhalation and out during exhalation – the precise opposite of what should happen. These students were so accustomed to their own breathing pattern that they believed it was correct. Fortunately, with a solid understanding, the breath can be trained. Even when bad habits have crept in, they can be replaced with good ones.

How to Breathe During Asana Practice

Those who have practised different styles of yoga soon notice that different asana practices have a significant effect on their breathing patterns. With that in mind, you probably want to know how to adjust your breathing to support your asana. Movement and breath can have a synergistic effect.

In general, you want to ensure soft, nasal breathing at all times. This is important for both metabolic efficiency and safety. You may be able to maintain nasal breathing throughout a class but find that the amplitude (volume) of your breath fluctuates. As your practice evolves, you should aim to maintain low breathing volume throughout practice. An inhalation to exhalation ratio of 1:2 or an ujjayi breath can also be beneficial.[351] Breathing nose and low helps to establish a slow breathing rhythm that can prevent respiratory muscle fatigue.[352]

It is also important to maintain nasal breathing as you go about your day once you step off your mat. Restoring full-time nasal breathing is a huge step towards functional everyday breathing.

Once your practice has progressed to the point where the steadiness of your breath is constant, you can prioritise different aspects of

---

351 Singh, Virendra, et al. "Effect of Yoga Breathing Exercises (Prāṇāyāma) on Airway Reactivity in Subjects With Asthma." *The Lancet* 335.8702 (1990): 1381-1383.

352 Burtch, Alex R., et al. "Controlled Frequency Breathing Reduces Inspiratory Muscle Fatigue." *The Journal of Strength & Conditioning Research* 31.5 (2017): 1273-1281.

your breath depending on the focus of your practice. It's important, however, always to take into consideration your own metabolic and anatomical needs. The same goes when working with students. Each of us is different. The BOLT score may give a good starting point for this work so long as students are not competitive about taking that score.

Breathing in Vinyasa-Style Classes (Including Ashtanga)

In Sanskrit, *Vinyasa* means *transition* or *secondary action*. Vinyasa-style classes include many transitions between asanas. These transitions often form set sequences, like sun salutations, which are repeated throughout the class.

Compared to other styles of yoga, Vinyasa classes are likely to impose higher demands on the cardiovascular system. In vinyasa-style classes (much of which is inspired by Ashtanga Vinyasa), it is often suggested for the breath to match the movement. If the pace is fast and no attention is given to the volume of air inhaled and exhaled, there is a risk of hyperventilation. During any fast-paced class, whether Vinyasa, Five Tibetan Rites, or any other, you want to ensure an adequate supply of oxygen to your brain and working muscles. For this, it is crucial to maintain soft, nasal breathing.

In these yoga classes there is limited time to settle into a position, yet the demands on core stability can be high. The Abdominal Drawing-In Maneuver, or ADIM (see page 216) can be useful. It can be held as you practise lateral breathing (page 212).

Breathing in Yin or Restorative Classes

In classes that focus on relaxation, the breath can complement the physical postures. Slow your heart rate and activate the parasympathetic nervous system by elongating your breathing cycle and increasing the ratio of exhalation to inhalation.

Breathing in Flexibility Work

The breath can be used to enhance physical flexibility. The pH of your blood is likely to contribute to your flexibility or lack of it. When the blood is too alkaline (CO_2 levels are low), the smooth muscle cells constrict.[353] Smooth muscle is actively involved in fascial contraction[354] – which leads me to believe it is possible to control tension within the body by using the breath to regulate blood biochemistry. If you simply breathe through the nose in a light and slow manner, it will help you sustain moderate to elevated levels of CO_2 and also activate the vagus nerve. This will help muscles to relax and will enhance flexibility.[355]

Breathing in Balance Work

Balancing poses provide a series of challenges to the body, some of which relate to the breath. A healthier, stronger, better-functioning diaphragm (as assessed by diaphragm thickness, diaphragm thickness fraction, and diaphragm range of movement during quiet, deep breathing[356]) supports greater equilibrium in balancing poses.[357] Fatigue of the inspiratory muscles can compromise balance. Therefore, you can positively impact your ability to balance by strengthening your diaphragm.[358]

Core stability is important in balancing too. Lateral breathing with

353 Restini, Carolina A., and Lusiane M. Bendhack. "Involvement of Non-Selective Ca2+ Channels in the Contraction Induced by Alkalinization of Rat Anococcygeus Muscle Cells." *European Journal of Pharmacology* 553.1-3 (2006): 288-296.

354 Schleip, Robert. "Fascial Plasticity -- A New Neurobiological Explanation: Part 1." *Journal of Bodywork and Movement Therapies* 7.1 (2003): 11-19.

355 Singh, U. P. "Evidence-Based Role of Hypercapnia and Exhalation Phase in Vagus Nerve Stimulation: Insights into Hypercapnic Yoga Breathing Exercises." *Journal of Yoga & Physical Therapy* 7.3 (2017): 1000270-1000276.

356 Summerhill, Eleanor M., et al. "Monitoring Recovery from Diaphragm Paralysis with Ultrasound." *Chest* 133.3 (2008): 737-743.

357 Kocjan, Janusz, et al. "Impact of Diaphragm Function Parameters on Balance Maintenance." *PLoS* 13.12 (2018): e0208697.

358 Janssens, Lotte, et al. "The Effect of Inspiratory Muscles Fatigue on Postural Control in People with and Without Recurrent Low Back Pain." *Spine* 35.10 (2010): 1088-1094.

the use of the ADIM is by far the most efficient way to increase spinal stability in balance poses.

Attention also matters. The four phases of breathing have been linked with mental readiness.[359] Mental abilities including attention[360] and pattern recognition[361] are better during inhalation. Scientists have shown we tend to initiate most voluntary physical movements during the transition from exhalation to inhalation.[362] With this in mind, it is worth initiating balance after exhaling.

It's important to note that the effects described here are diminished during mouth breathing.[363]

Breathing in Hot Yoga

In a heated environment, the bond between O_2 and haemoglobin weakens. The reduced affinity of O_2 for haemoglobin means that practising in a heated room can result in easier oxygenation of the muscles. This may make physical practice feel easier.

However, when you exercise in a heated environment, breathing speed can become up to three times faster.[364,365,366] Breathing adjusts

359 Boyadzhieva, Asena, and Ezgi Kayhan. "Keeping the Breath in Mind: Respiration, Neural Oscillations, and the Free Energy Principle." *Frontiers in Neuroscience* 742 (2021).

360 Mather, Mara, et al. "Norepinephrine Ignites Local Hotspots of Neuronal Excitation: How Arousal Amplifies Selectivity in Perception and Memory." *Behavioral and Brain Sciences* 39 (2016).

361 Zelano, Christina, et al. "Nasal Respiration Entrains Human Limbic Oscillations and Modulates Cognitive Function." *Journal of Neuroscience* 36.49 (2016): 12448-12467.

362 Park, Hyeong-Dong, et al. "Breathing Is Coupled with Voluntary Action and the Cortical Readiness Potential." *Nature Communications* 11.1 (2020): 1-8.

363 Zelano, Christina, et al. "Nasal Respiration Entrains Human Limbic Oscillations and Modulates Cognitive Function." *Journal Of Neuroscience* 36.49 (2016): 12448-12467.

364 Boden, A. G., M. C. Harris, and M. J. Parkes. "A Respiratory Drive in Addition to the Increase in CO2 Production at Raised Body Temperature in Rats." *Experimental Physiology* 85.3 (2000): 309-319.

365 Hayashi, Keiji, et al. "Effect of CO2 on the Ventilatory Sensitivity to Rising Body Temperature During Exercise." *Journal of Applied Physiology* 110.5 (2011): 1334-1341.

366 Tsuji, Bun, et al. "Comparison of Hyperthermic Hyperventilation During Passive Heating and Prolonged Light and Moderate Exercise in the Heat." *Journal of Applied Physiology* 113.9 (2012): 1388-1397.

to keep body temperature at 37°C (98.6°F), regardless of room temperature. If you allow your breathing rate to get significantly faster during practice, it is likely you will hyperventilate. This will reduce CO_2 in your blood, which will end up depriving your working muscles of O_2.

Some yoga styles practised in a hot studio, such as Bikram yoga, begin with sitali prāṇāyāma (see page 290). Mouth breathing in sitali cools the body, but it also promotes dehydration and compromises CO_2 levels. Hydration is important for temperature regulation,[367] and low CO_2 will reduce oxygenation, just when the body needs more O_2 to sustain the physical practice.

Practising in a heated room may *feel* easier, but it is more important than ever to breathe through your nose in a controlled way.

PHYSICAL LIMITATIONS THAT AFFECT BREATHING IN YOGA

In yoga classes where the focus is on asana, breathing can, and should, still play a critical role. At the same time, biomechanical limitations are likely to interfere with the breath.

Injuries can affect breathing patterns. The limitation created by an injury may be as obvious as a fracture in the nose or as subtle and invisible as a muscle strain. The pain from a pulled or tender muscle can cause involuntary breath holds. Injuries such as hernias in the inner unit of the abdomen, especially in the TrA, are also a common factor limiting efficient breathing.

Asana-specific requirements can increase the workload of certain muscles, compromising the movement of the diaphragm and intra-abdominal muscles. This usually happens when muscles (for instance in the trunk) are stiff or weak. For example, you may find that your superficial abdominal muscles engage before your deep abdominals.

---

367 Hertzman, A. R. "Failure in Temperature Regulation During Progressive Dehydration." *Journal of Occupational and Environmental Medicine* 2.1 (1960): 55.

BREATH-FOCUSED ASANA PRACTICES

Sun Salutation (in Three Breathing Styles)

This sun salutation sequence can be practised in three different ways – accompanied by three different breathing techniques.

The first (option A) is likely to be familiar if you take Vinyasa-style classes. Instructions for Lateral Breathing, the ADIM, and the Valsalva Maneuver can be found on page 217.

Breathing Style: Option A

Maintain soft, nasal breathing throughout.

1. **Mountain Pose/Tadasana** – Light breathing, relaxed abdomen
2. **Upward Salute** – Inhale, light breathing
3. **Standing Forward Fold** – Exhale, light breathing
4. **Half Standing Forward Fold** – Inhale, light breathing
5. **Jump or Step Back** – Exhale
6. **Plank** – Inhale, Valsalva Manoeuvre
7. **Lower Down to the Floor** – Exhale
8. **Upward Facing Dog** – Inhale, light breathing
9. **Downward Dog** – Exhale, 5 breaths, light breathing
10. **Half Standing Forward Fold** – Inhale, light breathing
11. **Upward Salute** – Inhale, light breathing
12. **Mountain Pose/Tadasana** – Exhale, light breathing, relaxed abdomen.

Breathing Style: Option B

This practice will slightly increase levels of CO_2. Maintain soft nasal breathing throughout, except during the breath holds.

1. **Mountain Pose/Tadasana** – Lateral breathing
2. **Upward Salute** – Inhale, hold + ADIM
3. **Standing Forward Fold** – Exhale, light breathing
4. **Half Standing Forward Fold** – Inhale, light breathing
5. **Jump or Step Back** – Exhale, hold + ADIM
6. **Plank** – Inhale, Valsalva Manoeuvre
7. **Lower Down to the Floor** – Exhale
8. **Upward Facing Dog** – Inhale, lateral breathing
9. **Downward Dog** – Exhale, five breaths, lateral breathing
10. **Half Standing Forward Fold** – Inhale, hold + ADIM
11. **Upward Salute** – Inhale, lateral breathing
12. **Mountain Pose/Tadasana** – Exhale, lateral breathing

Breathing Style: Option C

This practice will markedly increase CO_2, and, if performed sequentially, it will also induce strong hypoxia. You can read more about hypoxia in Chapter Six. Maintain soft, nasal breathing throughout, except during the breath holds.

1. ***Mountain Pose/Tadasana*** – Lateral breathing
2. ***Upward Salute*** – Inhale, exhale, use the ADIM and hold your breath
3. ***Standing Forward Fold*** – Continue to hold the breath from pose 2 through pose 11
4. ***Half Standing Forward Fold***
5. ***Jump or Step Back***
6. ***Plank***
7. ***Lower Down to the Floor***
8. ***Upward Facing Dog***
9. ***Downward Dog***
10. ***Half Standing Forward Fold***
11. ***Upward Salute***
12. ***Mountain Pose/Tadasana*** – Inhale, lateral breathing

Sequence for Concentration and Balance

This sequence is designed to improve concentration and balance. Aim to hold each pose for two full breath cycles or 10 seconds. The way you breathe in the transitions will depend on how challenging this sequence is for you – and on how challenging you want to make it. If the practice is easy, maintain soft, regular nasal breathing. If the practice is challenging, you can include ADIM or breath holds during the transitions between each pose.

Always return to soft nasal breathing as soon as possible.

Notice how many times you lose your balance and concentration during the practice.

Mountain pose
(Tadasana)

Warrior III
(Virabhadrasana III)

Tree pose
(Vrksasana)

Warrior III

Tree pose

Mountain pose,
heels elevated

Squat (Malasana),
heels elevated

Thunderbolt pose
(Vajrasana), toes
tucked under

Transition

Squat, heels
elevated

Mountain pose,
heels elevated

Transition

Wide-legged standing
forward bend (Prasarita
Padottanasana A)

Wide-legged standing
forward-bend, lean to
the left

Wide-legged standing
forward-bend, lean to
the right

Horse stance
(Vatayanasana),
heels elevated

Wide-legged standing
forward-bend twist

Wide-legged standing
forward-bend twist

Mountain pose

Breath in Transitions

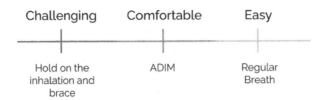

Challenging   Comfortable   Easy

Hold on the   ADIM   Regular
inhalation and   Breath
brace

Yin Sequence

This Yin (restorative) sequence is geared to help relax your nervous system and mobilise your primary and secondary respiratory muscles.

The first time you practise this sequence, hold each pose for three minutes. The poses that feature one side should be repeated on the other side. Hold the pose for three minutes on each side.

You can gradually increase the time you hold the pose up to as much as 20 minutes for each pose. On days when you feel extra tense, you should reduce the initial holding time to one minute, come out of the position, and go back in to hold it for longer.

Your breath should be soft and almost unnoticeable during this sequence. If your BOLT score is 15 seconds or more, you can practise the **Breathe Light** exercise during the poses. You will find this on page 69. Everyone may also practise kevali prāṇāyāma (page 272) or maintain soft, nasal breathing.

Yin Sequence

CHAPTER FIFTEEN

INTRODUCING TRADITIONAL BREATHING PRACTICES – PRĀṆĀYĀMA

With the emphasis on functional breathing across different yogic traditions, it should be no surprise that the very first prāṇāyāma exercises described in the literature involve restoring healthy breathing. As with any skill, we cannot master the more advanced techniques until the basics are in place. It's important to find your authentic breath before moving to the more formal prāṇāyāma practices. In the Oxygen Advantage® method, the ability to hold the breath for longer comes from increased tolerance for carbon dioxide, not through willpower and forcing. The same principles apply in yoga and yogic breathing.

In the preparatory stages, *Yoga, The Iyengar Way* introduces normal breathing as a breathing practice. Savasana (lying on the back) can be far more than just relaxation and assimilation at the end of practice. It can be the preliminary pose for prāṇāyāma (as an alternative to sitting). Normal breathing can be practised first lying, then sitting:

Each breath smooth, soft and rhythmic, and of similar volume. Feel both sides of the rib cage moving evenly out and in. Do not go to sleep.[368]

368 Mehta, Silva, Mira Mehta, and Shyam Mehta. *Yoga: The Iyengar Way*. Knopf, 1990.

Similarly, according to Swami Rama's book, prāṇāyāma begins with connecting to the diaphragm.[369] Slow, soft diaphragm breathing is practised, first on the back in savasana, then lying on the front. Next, while in savasana, a sandbag is placed on the abdomen, deepening awareness, and adding a load to strengthen the diaphragm. The practitioner simply observes the bag as it moves up on the inhale and down on the exhale. You can practise the same exercise by placing a book, or anything with a little weight, on your abdomen.

369   Rama, Swami, Rudolph Ballentine, and Alan Hymes. *Science of Breath: A Practical Guide.* Himalayan Institute Press, 1998.

These initial prāṇāyāmas are about the process of the breath. The object is to train the lungs without strain. For most of us, our everyday breathing is not always easy and smooth. It can be tense, erratic, and even strained. Once breathing becomes steady in a supine position, the techniques can be practised sitting and walking, whilst you go about normal daily activities. Prāṇāyāma depends on a strong foundation – a steady seat – and this requires practice. Prāṇāyāma is usually practised in a sitting position with the spine erect. Most yogis will practise in a seated pose. Depending on the purpose of the practice and the type of prāṇāyāma, many of the breathing techniques can also be done while lying down, standing, or walking. We see no reason why beginners cannot practise simple prāṇāyāma without any knowledge of asanas, providing the practice is not goal or ego oriented.

PRĀṆĀYĀMA AND KUNDALINI

The more advanced prāṇāyāmas focus on the characteristics of the breath. However, the objective has nothing to do with lung capacity, nervous system balance, or radiant health – *it's enlightenment* – clearing away the clouds of thinking to leave a state of unconditional love for all beings. In this context, prāṇāyāma is one structural piece in the process of Kundalini awakening. In Hindu Tantric literature, Kundalini awakening is considered essential for enlightenment.

In contrast, much of Western yoga has developed into a form of fitness training or entertainment according to Andrey Lappa. For many of us, it's enough to enjoy a toned body, calmer relationships, and a growing Instagram fanbase, but these benefits have nothing to do with the true purpose of practice. In modern interpretations, we tend to take a glimpse, a single facet, and think it represents the whole of yoga. We are missing the point.

In Sanskrit, the word *kundalini* means *circular* or *coiled*. In yogic literature, it is depicted as a coiled serpent at the base of the spine. This idea of a coiled snake represents the divine feminine energy, which is present in people of all genders. From a psychological perspective, kundalini can be seen as an unconscious source of psychic, creative, or sexual energy. The goal in kundalini awakening is to cause this energy to rise through the central channel, the sushumna, which runs up the spine to the crown of the head, transfiguring consciousness and transcending the ego. No small feat.

Kundalini is described in the literature with three different manifestations: universal energy (para-kundalini), energising the mind and body (prana-kundalini), and energising the consciousness (shakti-kundalini). The concept of prana-kundalini is equivalent to the idea of prana. The concepts of kundalini as a cosmic energy or in relation to consciousness are also synonymous with prana. However, Tibetan yogis consider the activation of prana to be a prerequisite for kundalini awakening.

Kurt Keuzer, a computer scientist at the University of California, Berkeley, describes his own experience of kundalini awakening as the difference between "simply having pleasant sensations in the spine and the much more powerful experience of having a freight-train-like full kundalini experience."[370] In the Western world, we are keen to experience the full, freight-train-like version of everything. We constantly look for mechanisms by which we can change or charge our energy and our consciousness, from ice baths to hyperventilation techniques. These are often quick, sometimes temporary fixes that don't create the necessary

---

370 "Kundalini FAQ." *Berkeley.* (n.d.) http://people.eecs.berkeley.edu/~keutzer/kundalini/kundalini-faq.html#13 (Accessed July 2, 2022).

conditions for the defined yogic path to enlightenment. They can also be dangerous, if approached without the proper guidance. And they can serve to cement the ego instead of providing liberation from it.

THE OXYGEN ADVANTAGE® APPROACH TO PRĀṆĀYĀMA

Prāṇāyāmas can be grouped in many ways, but it's always useful to learn them based on the outcome you want to achieve. These outcomes fall into four primary categories:

1. Controlling the autonomic nervous system, such as body temperature, heart rate, and balancing stress and relaxation responses.
2. Improving unconscious breathing.
3. Enhancing breathing during a specific activity.
4. Entering meditation.

When you practise any breathing exercise, it is important to know why you're doing it – which dimension of breathing the exercise targets, the effect it has on your body, and what your goal is. This is especially true if you plan to teach breathing. Try not to fall into the trap of passing on information just because a guru told you to do something a certain way. This approach risks perpetuating misunderstandings and superstitions.

In the Oxygen Advantage®, we look at the biochemistry and biomechanics of breathing, and the impact on the nervous system. In this system, all breathing exercises can be analysed in this way. Here's a quick reminder of the three dimensions of breathing:

Biochemistry of breathing

Exercises that target the biochemistry of breathing involve manipulating the levels of carbon dioxide in the blood.

Many of us habitually over-breathe and this is exacerbated during yoga and other physical activities. When you breathe more air, either through an increased respiratory rate or volume of breath, you lower your CO_2 levels. This can happen inadvertently when you take full, deep, audible breaths during practice. Even if you breathe through your nose, breathing this way will still cause too large a volume of air. It can also happen if you extend the breath during prāṇāyāma without paying attention to breathing volume.

Functional breathing from a biochemical perspective includes reducing the volume of air you breathe in to create a slight air hunger. This can be done with light, nasal breathing, by softening and slowing the breath, and also by holding the breath. The air hunger these practices create, occurs because when you breathe less, CO_2 levels increase in the lungs and blood, and CO_2 is the primary driver to breathe. Air hunger is thus a good sign because it signifies higher CO_2 levels.

Regular practice of reduced volume breathing lowers your ventilatory response to CO_2, creating steadiness of breath, which is a primary goal of traditional yoga practice. It also reduces sensitivity to air hunger and chemosensitivity to CO_2. Plus, it reduces the respiratory rate, dilates the blood vessels, and increases blood flow, oxygen uptake, and the delivery of oxygen to the tissues and organs. Moreover, it directs attention to the brain and can improve blood flow to the brain by as much as 10%; and it stimulates the vagus nerve shifting your body into the rest and digest response.

Biomechanics of breathing

Biomechanics encompasses the functioning of the breathing muscles including the diaphragm. Poor biomechanical breathing usually manifests as fast, hard, upper chest breathing. Biomechanical exercises focus on light and low breathing, and lateral expansion and contraction of the lower ribs. Wearing a Buteyko Belt or SportsMask or activating the diaphragm with a sandbag or book are also methods for optimising the biomechanics of breathing. Breathing exercises that target the biomechanics of breathing result in greater diaphragm recruitment and better functioning of the breathing muscles. This results in better breathing efficiency and helps to calm the mind, stimulate the vagus nerve, activate the parasympathetic relaxation response, and improve sleep quality.

Nervous System and breathing

Breathing exercises can be used to either up-regulate or down-regulate the autonomic nervous system.

Up-regulation involves activating the sympathetic stress response. You can do this with fast and hard breathing, fast exhalations and strong breath holds. Any exercise that involves deliberate hyperventilation followed by a strong breath hold is a stressor that will activate the sympathetic nervous system.

Conversely, down-regulating the nervous system involves activating the parasympathetic relaxation response. You can do this by practising light breathing, slow, prolonged exhalations and slow, diaphragmatic breathing at a rate of 4.5 to 6.5 breaths per minute. This slower breath has been found to increase heart rate variability (HRV). HRV is the measure of the change in timing between successive heartbeats. It is an indicator of heart health, cardiovascular fitness, and a measure of physical and emotional resilience.[371] Increasing HRV can have the following effects:

- **dampening the stress response** – shifting instead into the rest and digest response.
- **increasing sensitivity to baroreceptors** – for better blood pressure control.
- **improving vagal nerve tone** – vagal tone is a measure of how well the vagus nerve is working.
- **promoting sympathovagal balance** – the term "sympathovagal" refers to the interaction between the SNS and the vagus nerve. It reflects the autonomic state resulting from the sympathetic and parasympathetic influences[372,373,374].

You can also use light breathing to generate a tolerable air hunger. Traditional counting methods for these types of exercises include mantras, which can be recited silently to measure different phases of the breath. However, it can be helpful not to always focus on counting. Instead, sometimes simply concentrate on soft, steady breathing.

Again, in slowing the respiratory rate, you must be careful not to disproportionately increase the volume of air. On the other hand,

---

371 Lehrer, P. M., and R. Gevirtz. "Heart Rate Variability Biofeedback: How and Why Does It Work?" *Frontiers in Psychology* 756 (2014).

372 Goldberger, J J. "Sympathovagal balance: how should we measure it?." *The American journal of physiology* vol. 276,4 (1999): H1273-80. doi:10.1152/ajpheart.1999.276.4.H1273

373 Zaccaro, Andrea et al. "How Breath-Control Can Change Your Life: A Systematic Review on Psycho-Physiological Correlates of Slow Breathing." *Frontiers in human neuroscience* vol. 12 353. 7 Sep. 2018.

374 Pal, Gopal Krushna et al. "Slow yogic breathing through right and left nostril influences sympathovagal balance, heart rate variability, and cardiovascular risks in young adults." *North American journal of medical sciences* vol. 6,3 (2014): 145-51.

breathing too little air in prolonging the breath phase can create a strong feeling of air hunger. Either occurrence can tip the nervous system into stress, increasing respiratory rate and heart rate immediately after the exercise, which cancels out the benefit of practice. This is especially true for those students with a perfectionist nature who are strongly attracted to achievement. Just like in Goldilocks and the three bears, one must manage the speed and volume of breathing so that the resultant air hunger is not too strong or too little, but just right.

Learning to control prana should be approached gradually and cautiously. Sometimes we think of breathing as a simple and therefore harmless practice, but it is incredibly powerful and must be approached with care. We must never experiment with our students, so it is important to go gently and to understand the science.

THE BANDHAS

Prāṇāyāmas are practised in combination with bandhas, or energy locks. On a physical level, there are three main bandhas, and these are activated through muscular contraction and body position. These are the root lock, naval lock, and chin lock.

Mula Bandha,
Root Lock

Uddiyana Bandha,
Naval Lock

Jalandhara
Bandha,
Chin Lock

Mula Bandha (Root Lock)

Mula bandha is activated by drawing the pelvic floor, the area between the anus and the perineum, up and in. The exact location may be different depending on your gender, but you will find it at the end of a complete exhalation. It helps stabilise the pelvis, gives a strong foundation to the body, and directs prana upward. It corresponds to the first (or root) chakra, Muladhara.

Uddiyana Bandha (Naval Lock)

Uddiyana bandha is practised by drawing the naval up and in. It helps activate the transversus abdominis muscle (TrA), which extends between the ribs and the pelvis, wrapping around the trunk from front to back. Uddiyana bandha is easiest to locate from the downward dog pose and can also be found via the sensations at the end of a full exhalation. It corresponds to the third (or solar) chakra, Manipura, and is directly related to diaphragm function and to the workings of the ribs and intercostal muscles.

Jalandhara Bandha (Chin Lock)

Jalandhara bandha is activated by pulling the chin in toward the spine and gently pressing downward to constrict the windpipe. This can be spontaneously activated using *dristi* or gazing point. It helps with breath retention and the stimulation of the thyroid and parathyroid glands. It corresponds to the fifth (or throat) chakra, Vishuddha.

CHAPTER SIXTEEN

PRĀṆĀYĀMAS TO ALTER THE LENGTH OF THE BREATHING CYCLE

In this and the following chapter, prāṇāyāma exercises will be presented according to the groupings Andrey Lappa uses in his *Universal Yoga System:*[375]

1. Exercises that manipulate the length of the four stages of the breathing cycle, and
2. Exercises that produce a specific outcome.

The prāṇāyāmas that manipulate the length of the breathing cycle and its four stages are:

- Kumbhaka (retention of breath/breath hold)
- Ujjayi
- Sama/Visama Vritti
- Anuloma/Pratiloma
- Viloma/Anuloma

375 https://www.andreylappa.com/universal-yoga

- Kevali I and Kevali II
- Bhastrika
- Kapalabhati
- Sahita

In all except bhastrika and kapalabhati, the breathing cycle can be prolonged as your practice progresses. By manipulating the length of the breathing phases, we slowly begin to change our relationship with time and therefore with our thoughts. As Lappa puts it – "Time is the root of breath. Breath is the root of thinking."

The Prāṇāyāmas that produce a specific outcome are:

- Surya/Chandra Bhedana
- Nadi Shodhana
- Bhramari
- Sitali
- Sitakari
- Murccha
- Plavini

We will explain how these exercises work, but, with respect for the many opinions that you cannot safely learn prāṇāyāma from a book, we will refrain from describing their complex methods in detail. That has already been done in the existing literature by people with more expertise (much of which is referenced here).

1. KUMBHAKA (PAUSING AFTER INHALING OR EXHALING)

A healthy breathing cycle includes slight natural pauses at the end of each inhalation and exhalation. Either (or both) can be prolonged by holding the breath. In Sanskrit, this pause is called *kumbhaka*. The pause holds a place of importance in yoga.

According to Swami Rama:

"Actually, prāṇāyāma in practice means *pause* . . . all the breathing exercises are meant to control, eliminate and expand that pause."

The *Bhagavad-Gita* 4, 29 states:

"When both air currents are completely stopped, one is said to be in kumbhaka yoga . . . By practice of kumbhaka yoga, the yogis increase the duration of life by many, many years."[376]

Advanced practitioners can extend this pause for many minutes.

Kumbhaka can be performed while seated, lying down, or during asanas. It is the first breathing exercise a student should get comfortable with after soft breathing. This exercise supports functional breathing in all three dimensions. It manipulates the biochemistry of breathing and can be used to achieve hypoxia[377] (below-normal level of O_2 in the blood) and/or hypercapnia (raised levels of CO_2 in the blood). It alters the biomechanics of breathing and is a component of many other exercises. And it is also an extremely effective way to shift mental states via the autonomic nervous system.

Humans (like most land mammals) cannot live for more than a few minutes without breathing. When you hold your breath, a sort of primordial "fire alarm" is triggered, activating a series of pathways in the body that stimulate your blood pressure receptors (baroreceptors) to slow your heart rate and metabolism and jolt you out of conscious thinking.

When oxygen supply is disrupted, no matter what was bothering you a few seconds earlier, your brain will focus on restoring breathing. Sympathetic activity in the muscles increases, constricting the peripheral blood vessels, preserving blood flow and oxygen supply to your vital organs. This response, which can be induced through the use

---

376 Prabhupada, Swami A. C. Bhaktivedanta, and Swami Bhaktivedanta. *Bhagavad-Gita as It Is.* Los Angeles: Bhaktivedanta Book Trust, 1972.
377 Malshe, Prakash Chintamani. "Nisshesha Rechaka Prāṇāyāma Offers Benefits Through Brief Intermittent Hypoxia." *Ayu* 32.4 (2011): 451.

of breath holds, is called the *diving reflex*. Whether the diving reflex is the result of diving or induced through breath holds, it has nearly identical effects.[378,379]

Kumbhaka offers the benefits associated with hypoxic training. Long breath holds cause the spleen to contract. The spleen is the body's blood bank, and the blood in the spleen is of incredibly good quality. It contains a high concentration of red blood cells. When the spleen contracts and

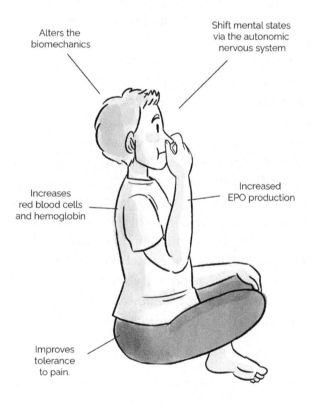

Alters the
biomechanics

Shift mental states
via the autonomic
nervous system

Increases
red blood cells
and hemoglobin

Increased
EPO production

Improves
tolerance
to pain.

Kumbhaka

378 Foster, G. E., and A. W. Sheel. "The Human Diving Response, Its Function, and Its Control." *Scandinavian Journal of Medicine & Science in Sports* 15.1 (2005): 3-12.

379 Schagatay, Erika, Johan Andersson, and Bodil Nielsen. "Hematological Response and Diving Response During Apnea and Apnea with Face Immersion." *European Journal of Applied Physiology* 101.1 (2007): 125-132.

releases this blood, the proportion of red blood cells in circulation and the amount of haemoglobin available to carry oxygen increase.[380]

Maximal breath holds also stimulate the production of the hormone erythropoietin (EPO),[381] which is important for maturing new red blood cells. The result of splenic contraction and increased EPO production is that the oxygen-carrying capacity of the blood increases both short and long term. This improves speed, endurance, exercise recovery, and repeated-sprint ability. It is also believed to have health benefits. It is why top athletes train at high altitudes where atmospheric oxygen pressure is low.

Traditionally, kumbhaka is most often performed as a breath retention at the end of the inhale, called *puraka kumbhaka* or *antara kumbhaka*, but it can also be performed as a breath suspension after the exhale, called *rechaka kumbhaka* or *bahya kumbhaka*.

The balance of blood gases changes during breath holds. When the breath is held for a period of time after exhaling, oxygen levels drop, bringing the body into hypoxia. This typically occurs when the breath is held for 50 seconds or more – though some people will experience lowering of blood oxygen saturation sooner than this. During the breath hold, carbon dioxide increases which improves blood circulation to the brain.[382] Nitric oxide builds up in the nasal passages (most of the NO in exhaled air is produced in the upper airways, not in the alveoli)[383], and the longer you hold your breath, the more NO accumulates.[384] After the breath hold/suspension, the accumulated NO is inhaled.

380 Schagatay, Erika, et al. "Selected Contribution: Role of Spleen Emptying in Prolonging Apneas in Humans." *Journal of Applied Physiology* 90.4 (2001): 1623-1629.

381 De Bruijn, R., M. Richardson, and E. Schagatay. "Increased Erythropoietin Concentration After Repeated Apneas in Humans." *European Journal of Applied Physiology* 102 (5) (2008): 609-613.

382 Nivethitha, L., et al. "Cerebrovascular Hemodynamics During Prāṇāyāma Techniques." *Journal of Neurosciences in Rural Practice* 8.01 (2017): 60-63.

383 Brynes, C. A., et al. "Is Nitric Oxide in Exhaled Air Produced at Airway or Alveolar Level?" *European Respiratory Journal* 10.5 (1997): 1021-1025.

384 Kimberly, Brent, et al. "Nasal Contribution to Exhaled Nitric Oxide at Rest and During Breathholding in Humans." *American Journal of Respiratory and Critical Care Medicine* 153.2 (1996): 829-836.

It is important to consider the role of the diaphragm in this exercise. When you hold the breath after inhaling, the diaphragm descends, increasing pressure in the abdomen (called intra-abdominal pressure or IAP). As well as manipulating blood gases and activating the diaphragm, breath holds after inhaling can also improve tolerance to pain. In one study, breath holds after a seven-second inhalation and followed by a seven-second exhalation were shown to reduce pain perception when compared to slow breathing.[385] It is our belief that other exercises, such as ujjayi, which have a similar effect on the nervous system, can also be used to relieve pain.

How to Practise Kumbhaka

Once you are comfortable with the exercise, you can practise it standing, walking, or during asanas. At first, practise it seated or lying down. Make sure your body is relaxed and your heart rate is reduced.

Directions:

- Take a normal breath in and out through your nose. Exhaling to functional residual capacity (the volume remaining in the lungs after a normal, passive exhalation) before holding your breath helps to ensure a comfortable breath hold.
- After you exhale, pinch your nose to hold your breath. If you don't have a hand free or feel self-conscious holding your nose, you may simply stop breathing. At first, however, we suggest that you do pinch your nose to ensure you don't inhale any air. When you are new to breathing exercises, it is quite easy to breathe in without realising.
- Keep your mouth closed.
- Hold your breath until you reach about 80% of your maximum breath hold.

---

385 Reyes del Paso, Gustavo A., Cristina Munoz Ladron De Guevara, and Casandra I. Montoro. "Breathholding During Exhalation as a Simple Manipulation to Reduce Pain Perception." *Pain Medicine* 16.9 (2015): 1835-1841.

- Now, let go of your nose and take a soft breath in through it. Avoid the urge to open your mouth.
- Recover your breath by breathing softly. Initially, this may feel challenging but, over time, it will get easier.

Variations:

There are three ways to practise kumbhaka:

1. Hold your breath after exhaling.
2. Hold your breath after inhaling.
3. Hold your breath after both inhaling and exhaling.

Most people will find these versions progressively more challenging. Stéphanie Blanche Legros, who is an Oxygen Advantage® instructor based in Paris, France, explains it like this:

> "At their root, Oxygen Advantage® exercises were developed for people in dis-ease, and that's why we measure the BOLT score after exhalation. Yoga systems have breath holds after inhalation and exhalation. They are almost equal according to their physiological effect. But breath holding after exhalation is advantageous at the outset. When we exhale, we are able to completely relax during the breath hold. We return the rib cage to its resting position. On the other hand, when the breath is paused after inhalation, we're much more likely to experience tension as we try to stop ourselves from breathing. The key to these exercises is the ability to relax during them."

Also, be aware that, while retention after inhaling can sometimes feel more familiar, it can increase pressure on the heart.[386] Therefore, breath

---

386 Rothenberg, Robin L. *Restoring Prana: A Therapeutic Guide to Prāṇāyāma and Healing Through the Breath for Yoga Therapists, Yoga Teachers, and Healthcare Practitioners.* Singing Dragon, 2019.

suspension after exhaling is safer. When you hold the breath after exhaling, your brain's CO_2 monitor will prevent you from holding your breath for longer than is safe. Start with the variation you are currently comfortable with. As your breath hold time increases, you will find all three variations easier.

During the breath hold, it is important to stay relaxed. There are several things you can do to help:

- Maintain a comfortable (upright if you are seated) posture. You may have to correct your posture during the exercise. Try moving slowly and avoid too many adjustments.
- Keep your muscles soft and monitor any tension throughout the breath hold. It's likely that about halfway through the breath hold, your body will tense up somewhere.
- It's common to tense the jaw. Keep your mouth closed but relax your jaw. If you notice yourself clenching, soften your face. Adjust your tongue position so the tip of your tongue sits behind your front upper teeth and the teeth do not meet.
- At the end of the practice, stay still for between one and three minutes. Scan your brain and body, noticing any changes you may experience.

Kumbhaka can be practised as a recovery exercise when you have lost control of your breathing. If your breathing symptoms are due to a panic or asthma attack, many small breath holds can be used. You will find this exercise (Breathing Recovery) on page 67.

Contraindications:

Strong breath holding exercises are only suitable if you are in good health. If you have any concerns, consult your medical doctor before practising. You must never practise breath holds if you are in or near water or if you are pregnant. Do not practise strong breath holds if you have high blood pressure, epilepsy, diabetes, schizophrenia, uncontrolled hyperthyroidism, chest pains, heart problems, sickle cell anaemia, cancer, an arterial aneurysm, kidney disease, panic disorder and/or anxiety, sleep apnea, cardiovascular issues, or long COVID.

2. UJJAYI BREATHING (THROAT CONSTRICTION)

Ujjayi, or Victorious Breath, is achieved by constricting the back of the throat while exhaling to create a deep, sibilant sound. Air is drawn in and out through the nose, with the noise originating in the throat.

When air is drawn in from the back of the throat, its flow can be regulated by the muscles around the glottis. This friction creates a noise not unlike gentle waves lapping on a beach or wind in the trees. The inhale makes a sound rather like *sa*, and the exhale like *ha*. As Timothy McCall says in his book, *Yoga as Medicine*, the subtle constriction can be generated by pretending to fog your glasses.[387]

Take notice of the subtlety: it's important that, during the practice, your glottis is tensed but remains open. You will feel the airflow on the roof of your palate. Despite the fact you will breathe through your nose, you must not sniff. By sniffing or closing the glottis, you will effectively block your breath. This stops the flow of energy and limits the amount of oxygen getting to your muscles. If you find yourself sniffing, you can dilate your nostrils using your fingers or a nasal dilator to correct the air flow. If you notice yourself grunting at the end of the inhalation or exhalation, it is likely your glottis has closed.[388]

Ujjayi is one of the first breathing exercises taught in yoga, and for a good reason. The light constriction of the throat encourages the breath to slow down and warms the air before it enters the lungs. It teaches practitioners to extend their breath. However, it is important not to strain, to keep the face and jaw relaxed. You should also apply

---

387 McCall, Timothy. *Yoga as Medicine: The Yogic Prescription for Health & Healing: A Yoga Journal Book.* Bantam, 2007.
388 Scott, John. *Ashtanga Yoga: The Essential Step-by-Step Guide to Dynamic Yoga.* Gaia, 2018.

the bandhas correctly during practice. In his book, *Ashtanga Yoga, The Definitive Step-By-Step Guide to Dynamic Yoga*, John Scott explains:

> "The development of bandha control cultivates and increases prana, and it is from the integration of ujjayi and bandha that an internal alchemy is achieved."[389]

The three bandhas described in the previous chapter are all integral to ujjayi breathing. Swami Rama describes a slight contraction of the abdominal muscles during ujjayi inhalation and says that, during exhalation, "abdominal pressure is exerted until the breath is completely expelled."[390] Again, the bandhas are held with subtlety, in the same way you approach the breath. Nothing should ever be forced.

When you first start out, you may find it easier to produce quite a loud sound during ujjayi, but the sound itself is not the point. Over time, as you learn to stretch and metre the breath and to synchronise it comfortably with movement, the sound can become so gentle it is almost imperceptible. You may block your ears with foam earplugs to allow you

Ujjayi Breathing

Good For:

Hyperventilation, Poor Circulation, Hypothyroidism

Result:

Increase body temperature,
Establish a breathing pattern (during yoga practice)

389 Scott, John. *Ashtanga Yoga: The Essential Step-by-Step Guide to Dynamic Yoga*. Gaia, 2018.

390 Rama, Swami, Rudolph Ballentine, and Alan Hymes. *Science of Breath: A Practical Guide*. Himalayan Institute Press, 1998.

to better follow the nuances of the breath. This is a useful practice during any subtle breathing exercise.

Physiological Effects of Ujjayi

Scientists compared ujjayi breathing to normal healthy breathing at six breaths per minute among yoga practitioners. Both techniques were found to have similar effects. These were:

- Increased activation of the vagus nerve, indicating a calming of the nervous system.
- Increased baroreflex sensitivity, for better blood pressure control.
- Decreased dead space, reflecting better respiratory efficiency – more air reaching the deep parts of the lungs where gas exchange takes place.
- Decreased chemoreflex sensitivity – less sensitivity to CO_2.
- Lower blood pressure.[391]

When it is slow enough, ujjayi breath leads to hypercapnia. It also has a reputation for increasing body temperature. When Anastasis was undergoing cold exposure training in Poland, most of his fellow participants practised ujjayi breathing. During exposure to cold water and while walking topless in the mountain, even those with no prior exposure to yoga used the technique. The breathing was not part of the training, and many of them were acting intuitively to keep warm. One common explanation for this warmth is that the friction of air in the throat generates internal heat. But there's more to it than that.

Scientists have discovered that regular ujjayi practice over three months significantly reduces the breathing rate, pulse rate, and hyper-reactivity of the cardiovascular system in response to cold.

---

391   Mason, Heather, et al. "Cardiovascular and Respiratory Effect of Yogic Slow Breathing in the Yoga Beginner: What Is the Best Approach?" *Evidence-Based Complementary and Alternative Medicine* (2013).

All 60 participants in a 2016 study reduced their reactivity to cold stress through regular ujjayi practice. The researchers concluded that ujjayi breathing balances the autonomic nervous system toward the parasympathetic relaxation branch, regulating the stress response in the blood vessels of the skeletal muscles and causing peripheral blood vessels to dilate.[392]

Ujjayi can be combined with kumbhaka after inhalation and/or exhalation. This will increase hypercapnia, and, during short breath holds, it will cause more oxygen to offload to the muscles. A study examining the effects of ujjayi prāṇāyāma combined with either short or prolonged kumbhaka observed an increase in oxygen consumption during short breath holds and a reduction during prolonged breath holds.[393]

3. SAMA VRITTI/VISAMA VRITTI (EQUAL/ UNEQUAL)

Sama vritti and visama vritti manipulate the balance between the four stages of a breathing cycle. *Sama* means identical or equal. *Vritti* means action, movement, or course of conduct. In sama vritti, you work to make the inhale, retention, exhale, and suspension equal. If, for example, the inhale and exhale are five seconds, the retention and suspension will be the same.

This pattern is often referred to as Box Breathing, an exercise commonly depicted as a square box where the equal sides represent the inhale, retention, exhale, and suspension. In Box Breathing, you inhale for four seconds, hold for four seconds, exhale for four seconds and hold for four seconds, repeating the pattern for several minutes. In

---

392 Mahour, Jitendra, and Pratibha Verma. "Effect of Ujjayi Prāṇāyāma on Cardiovascular Autonomic Function Tests." *National Journal of Physiology, Pharmacy and Pharmacology* 7.4 (2017): 391.

393 Telles, Shirley, and T. Desiraju. "Oxygen Consumption During Pranayamic Type of Very Slow-Rate Breathing." *The Indian Journal of Medical Research* 94 (1991): 357-63.

sama vritti prāṇāyāma, each phase of the breath can be extended much longer than it is in Box Breathing.

Visama has many meanings, including irregular, immoral, and bad. In visama vritti the four stages of the breathing cycle are practised with unequal ratios. In *Light on Prāṇāyāma*, B.K.S. Iyengar cautions that this irregular pattern can cause "great difficulty and danger for the pupil unless he is gifted with strong nerves and good lungs." The different ratios, he warns, tax the respiratory, cardiovascular, and nervous systems. They may cause tension in the brain, high blood pressure, and mental irritation.[394] It is worth mentioning that we don't know why Iyengar (and his teacher Krishnamacharya) discouraged the use of unequal ratios. The most common breath ratio taught historically by yogis was 1:4:2, and this unequal ratio dates back to at least to 1000 CE.

Sama Vritti
(Equal action, Box breathing)

Good For:

Hyperventilation, Anxiety

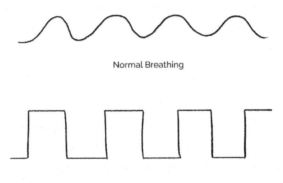

Normal Breathing

Box Breathing

Result:

Balance the four stages of breath, Introduction to breath holds, Slow down breathing cycle, Introduction to hypercapnia

394 Iyengar, Belur Krishnamacharya Sundaraja. *Light on Prāṇāyāma : The Yogic Art of Breathing.* Crossroad, 1981.

4. ANULOMA, VILOMA, AND PRATILOMA

Anuloma, viloma, and pratiloma change the balance between inhalation and exhalation. *Loma* means hair, or in the natural order. *Anu* means in orderly succession. *Vi* denotes privation, so *viloma* means against the natural order, or against the grain. *Pratiloma* also means against the hair or grain.

Keep in mind that the specifics of these exercises are described somewhat differently in different texts.

For example, in *Light on Prāṇāyāma*, Iyengar explains anuloma as ujjayi inhalation through both nostrils with exhalation through alternate nostrils. In viloma, exhaling and inhaling are not continuous. The lungs are filled and emptied gradually. Each part of the inhale or exhale is interrupted by several pauses. Pratiloma involves alternate nostril inhales, controlled with the fingers, then exhaling through open nostrils.[395]

However, in *Restoring Prana*, anuloma involves inhaling with ujjayi breath and exhaling through alternate nostrils. Viloma is practised using alternate nostril inhalation and ujjayi exhalation. Pratiloma is a combination of the two with the following pattern: inhale ujjayi, exhale left nostril, inhale left, exhale ujjayi, inhale ujjayi, exhale right nostril, inhale right, exhale ujjayi.[396]

Whichever method you agree with, the upshot of the practice is that, in anuloma, exhaling is emphasised. This produces longer exhalations which have a calming effect on the nervous system. In viloma and pratiloma, inhaling is emphasised. This will excite or enliven the nervous system. The names given to these techniques seem to suggest that a prolonged exhalation is more in line with the natural order, while a prolonged inhalation is against it.

---

395 Iyengar, Belur Krishnamacharya Sundaraja. *Light on Prāṇāyāma: The Yogic Art of Breathing.* Crossroad, 1981.

396 Rothenberg, Robin L. *Restoring Prana: A Therapeutic Guide to Prāṇāyāma and Healing Through the Breath for Yoga Therapists, Yoga Teachers, and Healthcare Practitioners.* Singing Dragon, 2019.

The main benefit of these prāṇāyāmas is to establish a rhythm in the breathing cycle in order to have an effect on the nervous system. All five of the above techniques, if adjusted appropriately, can also impact the body's biochemistry, leading to hypoxia or to hypercapnia.

Anuloma
(Natural order, prolonged exhalation)

Good For:

Pregnancy, Hyperventilation, Anxiety, Hypertension

Result:

Slow down breathing cycle, Reduce minute ventilation

Practising Viloma

In viloma prāṇāyāma, inhaling and/or exhaling are interrupted by several pauses. You can approach this exercise progressively as follows:

- Perform the pauses while inhaling, then exhale slowly.
- Inhale slowly, then perform the pauses while exhaling.
- Perform pauses during both inhalation and exhalation.

Start by taking two or three pauses during each breath cycle and gradually increase the number. To make this easier, at first, just take small sips of air in or out. The less air you take in during each part of the inhale, the easier it will be to pause as you fill your lungs. Similarly, if you expel air gradually on the exhale, you will be able to pause more as you gradually empty your lungs.

Viloma prāṇāyāma is useful for significantly slowing down the breath. It requires diaphragm control to perform without tension and so it strengthens the diaphragm. When the pause at the end of the inhalation and/or exhalation is extended, you will experience the biochemical effects of hypercapnia and/or hypoxia. Viloma is also a great exercise to help with breathing recovery during hyperventilation.

Viloma
(Against the naturalised order)

Good For:

Hyperventilation

Result:

Slow down breathing cycle

5. KEVALI (I AND II)

Kevali or kevala is the state in which the breath stops naturally. It cannot be practised as such because it is the result of mastering light, subtle breathing and breath holds and is not consciously controlled. You may have experienced natural stopping of your breath during deep, relaxed concentration known as flow state. Complete temporary breath suspension is a feature of some types of meditation.[397]

Kevala means *pure*[398]. It is related to *kaivalya*, which means alone. By untying this cord, it is considered possible to prolong life and extend consciousness to infinity. Thus, kevala prāṇāyāma could be understood as *prāṇāyāma of the soul*. The advanced yogi who achieves this state was known as a *kevalin*. When kevala prāṇāyāma is mastered, it leads to kevala kumbhaka, a natural state in which breath is suspended. This is explained in the *Hatha Yoga Pradipika*, 2,73-74, and is the goal of all serious yogis. As Yogananda explained it, "Breathlessness is deathlessness."[399] This statement may be a little over the top as one who practises prāṇāyāma will not become immortal.

Andrey Lappa describes kevali I as a slow breath that has become automatic. Many of us can achieve very slow breathing during guided practice. Sometimes students stay in this state for five or even ten minutes, but this is not kevali. Kevali is unconscious, a state where reduced volume breathing becomes constant, when you breathe minimally all the time.

In kevali II, minimal inhalation and exhalation take place. Andrey Lappa told me:

"Kevali II breathing leads you straight to samadhi, as it generates zero fluctuations in the mind."

397 Farrow, John T., and Russell J. Hebert. "Breath Suspension During the Transcendental Meditation Technique." *Psychosomatic Medicine* 44.2 (1982): 133-53.

398 Mallinson & Singleton 2017, Roots of Yoga, p. 131

399 "Kriya Yoga in the Ancient Scriptures." *Yogananda Harmony*. (n.d.) http://www.yoganandaharmony.com/kriya-yoga-in-the-ancient-scriptures (Accessed July 2, 2022).

Or as Swami Sri Yukteshvar Giri ji Maharaj says in his commentary on the *Bhagavad-Gita*, 4, 29:

"By this, the movement of prana and apana stops naturally and on its own, stilling the mind and all prana, manifesting eternal happiness and illuminating the lamp of Knowledge. When the mind and prana are still in this way, the inhalation and exhalation of the physical airs, speech, body, sight – all of these things – also become still."

Kevali
(Liberation)

Good For:

Agitated Mind, Pregnancy

Result:

Meditation

6. BHASTRIKA & KAPALABHATI (VOLUNTARY HYPERVENTILATION)

In bhastrika or bellows breath, air is forcibly drawn in and out of the body as if using a pair of bellows. The exhalation sets the pace.

Kapalabhati is a cleansing practice that is a milder version of the same exercise. *Kapala* means skull or forehead, and *bhati* light or shining, and so *kapalabhati* means shining forehead. In this exercise, inhalation is slow and exhalation vigorous. There is a split-second retention at the end of the exhale. The inhale tends to be slightly longer than the exhale, which is generated by a vigorous contraction of the lower abdominal muscle. The abdominal exhale is forceful and the inhale is almost passive – the reverse of normal diaphragm breathing, where the exhale is passive.[400]

In agnisara, or fire breath, another cleansing practice, as with kapalabhati, the focus is on the out breath. *Agni* means fire and *sara* means essence. In this exercise, inhalation takes place through the nose (one or both nostrils) and exhalation from the mouth with the tongue stretched down towards the chin. The pace is much slower than in kapalabhati and bhastrika, making this exercise more accessible and safer for those starting out. The effects are similar.

Although you will often find them listed as breathing exercises, kapalabhati and agnisara are kriyas. This information is usually missed when prāṇāyāmas like bhastrika are demonstrated for the purpose of YouTube follows. A kriya is a cleansing rite. It should be practised on an empty stomach. What's more, kriyas must be approached with care and not practised as a quick fix. B.K.S. Iyengar dismissed popular use of kapalabhati as a short-cut to yoga,[401] and it is worth bearing in mind that such exercises can be dangerous. It is important to remember that kapalabhati and bhastrika are forms of hyperventilation.

400 Rosen, Richard. *Prāṇāyāma Beyond the Fundamentals: An In-Depth Guide to Yogic Breathing*. Shambhala Publications, 2006.

401 Jayaraman, Gayatri. "Is Kapalbhati Killing You?" *Livemint*. (June 23, 2011). http://www.livemint.com/Leisure/154E5M51xPpBsjV1109W7M/Is-Kapalhbhati-killing-you.html (accessed July 7, 2022).

There have, for instance, been reports of heart attacks while practising kapalabhati.[402] In 2008, the Asian Heart Institute in Mumbai linked the incorrect or unsupervised practice of kapalabhati to 31 heart attack cases. The exercise can lead to vertigo, hernia, high blood pressure, epilepsy, and related brain problems.[403] Kriyas should not be practised if you have a hiatus hernia or are menstruating or pregnant. Agnisara may cause irritation in women with an intrauterine contraceptive device.

Bhastrika and Kapalabhati

Good For:

Lethargy, Depression

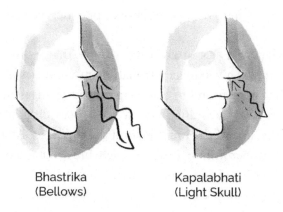

Bhastrika
(Bellows)

Kapalabhati
(Light Skull)

Result:

Decrease vagal tone. Improve attention.
Reduce supply of oxygen to the brain.

402 Gupta, Rajeev. "Acute Effect of Kapalbhati Yoga on Cardiac Autonomic Control Using Heart Rate Variability Analysis in Healthy Male Individuals." *Journal of Human Physiology* 2.1 (2020).

403 Jayaraman, Gayatri. "Is Kapalbhati Killing You?" *Livemint.* (June 23, 2011). http://www.livemint.com/Leisure/154E5M51xPpBsjV1109W7M/Is-Kapalhbhati-killing-you.html (Accessed July 7, 2022).

If you do want to practise these, do so mindfully. If you feel lightheaded or irritable, stop immediately.

In the book *Behavioral and Psychological Approaches to Breathing Disorders*, the researchers Timmons and Ley explain that prāṇāyāma exercises are likely to be beneficial to anyone suffering with hyperventilation, anxiety disorders, asthma, and other conditions. Bhastrika, they say, "may help mild depressives and asthmatics, and perhaps assist in evacuation of excess liquid and semi liquid material from the lungs in chronic obstructive pulmonary disease and bronchiectasis." But they too are quick to point out that patients with these conditions should only be referred to a yoga teacher once a medical diagnosis has been made and that it is essential the teacher understands the condition. They emphasise that care must be taken not to teach the wrong exercise at the wrong time. For instance, bhastrika, "should not be taught to hyperventilators, epileptics, or cases of angina pectoris."[404]

With all that said, it's interesting to note that, while the name *shining forehead* was given to kapalabhati many centuries ago, recently, kapalabhati has been found to cause significant changes in the brain. Specifically, in healthy individuals, it influences circulation in the frontal lobe, the area of the brain behind the forehead. At a breathing rate of 60 breaths per minute (one complete breath phase per second), kapalabhati can cause frontal lobe activity to reduce.[405] At 120 breaths per minute (two complete breath phases per second), it can cause activity to increase.[406]

Kapalabhati has also been shown to reduce vagal activity in the nervous system, both during and following the practice. Any stressor

404 Ley, Ronald, and Beverly H. Timmons. *Behavioral and Psychological Approaches to Breathing Disorders*. Springer Science & Business Media, 1994.
405 Telles, Shirley, et al. "A Functional Near-Infrared Spectroscopy Study of High-Frequency Yoga Breathing Compared to Breath Awareness." *Medical Science Monitor Basic Research* 22 (2016): 58.
406 Bhargav, Hemant, et al. "Frontal Hemodynamic Responses to High Frequency Yoga Breathing in Schizophrenia: A Functional Near-Infrared Spectroscopy Study." *Frontiers in Psychiatry* 5 (2014): 29.

exercise should be practised with awareness, and *only* once your BOLT score is 25 seconds or more. We always recommend balancing these exercises with a few minutes of reduced volume breathing (Breathe Light) to down-regulate the nervous system.

In both bhastrika and kapalabhati, as breathing rate increases, the depth of each breath decreases. These methods, which qualify as voluntary hyperventilation techniques, will result in changes to the blood biochemistry. You may experience some very noticeable physical symptoms such as a change in body temperature, tingling, or spasms in your hands.

CHAPTER SEVENTEEN

PRĀṆĀYĀMAS WITH SPECIFIC OUTCOMES

This second group of prāṇāyāmas are ones that produce specific outcomes. These outcomes are grouped into prāṇāyāmas that:

1. Activate each side of the body separately
2. Manipulate the (subtle) body (producing a humming or Aum sound)
3. Cool the body
4. Calm the mind
5. Enable floating in the water

1. PRĀṆĀYĀMAS THAT ACTIVATE ONE SIDE OF THE BODY/BRAIN

These first exercises allow us to manipulate which part of the body (left or right) is more activated. Many associate the right/left sides of the body with the masculine/feminine sides respectively of an individual's personality. When we breathe through one nostril (by partly or fully obstructing airflow in the opposite nostril), the sympathetic activity in the side of the body with the open nostril increases. The parasympathetic activity in the opposite side of the body also increases. Since cerebral circulation diminishes during increased sympathetic activity, breathing through one nostril (e. g. the right nostril) will correlate with increased metabolic activity in the contralateral hemisphere (e.g. the left hemisphere)[407].

Digital Breathing

In digital breathing, the fingers (the digits) are used to partly or fully block the nostrils. This can be done in various combinations. One nostril may be fully blocked while the other is fully open. One may be partially blocked while the other is fully blocked. Both may be open. Or you may fully or partially block alternate nostrils.

Blocking the nostrils is achieved with a special hand mudra, mrigi mudra (deer seal), that allows you to easily control the flow of air through both nostrils at the same time. In mrigi mudra, the first and second fingers are folded into the palm. The little finger extends outward, with the third/ring finger sitting on top of it. The pad of the ring finger overlaps the little finger, sitting on its fingernail. The thumb extends outward. The thumb and the third/fourth finger in combination actively control the airflow through each nostril.

Breathing through the nose always produces about 50% more resistance to airflow than the mouth, and this improves oxygen uptake by 10-20%.[408,409] Any full or partial blockage of the nostrils will increase that resistance to breathing through the nose. The extra resistance created by digital breathing causes lung volume to improve and can lead to hypercapnia – raised levels of CO_2 in the blood.

Depending on the way the nostril(s) are blocked, a variety of effects can occur. You will find that, when you block one nostril, either partly

---

407 Werntz, D. A., Bickford R. G., Bloom F. E., and D. S. Shannahoff-Khalsa. "Alternating Cerebral Hemispheric Activity and the Lateralization of Autonomic Nervous Function." *Human Neurobiology* 2.1 (1983): 39-43.

408 Cottle, M. H. "The Work, Ways, Positions and Patterns of Nasal Breathing (Relevance in Heart and Lung Illness)." *Proceedings of the American Rhinologic Society.* (1972) 377-385.

409 Gilbert, Chris, Leon Chaitow, and Dinah Bradley. *Recognizing and Treating Breathing Disorders.* Elsevier Health Sciences, 2014.

or fully, the free nostril will decongest. Blood flow will increase to the opposite side of the body and brain. Single nostril breathing through either nostril will reduce heart rate[410] and has been found to improve spatial and verbal skills.[411] Right nostril breathing significantly increases both systolic and diastolic blood pressure,[412] while left nostril breathing decreases it. Alternate nostril breathing is known to improve both systolic and diastolic blood pressure, and to improve performance in the digit vigilance test (DVT).[413] The DVT is a test of selectivity and mental capacity, in which participants are asked to identify and cross out all the sixes and nines on two pages containing 59 lines of single-digit numbers.[414]

The cognitive effects from single-nostril breathing are relatively minor, and we believe this is due to the more significant impact of increased CO_2. There is more detailed information about the physiological and cognitive impact of single nostril breathing in Chapter Twenty-one.

Surya/Chandra Bhedana

Surya means sun. *Chandra* means moon. *Bhedana* means to pierce or pass through. Surya bhedana is typically practised with the inhale through the right nostril and the exhale through the left. In chandra

410 Malhotra, Varun, Prashant Kumar Jain, and Akanksha Deswal. *Right Nostril Breathing Calms the Restless Mind and Heart* (n.d.).

411 Sharma, Sakshi, L. Nivethitha, and A. Mooventhan. "Effect of Moola Bandha (Perineum Contraction), A Yogic Lock on Cognitive Functions of College Students: An Exploratory Study." *Journal of Religion and Health* 59.3 (2020): 1388-1397.

412 Raghuraj, Puthige, and Shirley Telles. "Immediate Effect of Specific Nostril Manipulating Yoga Breathing Practices on Autonomic and Respiratory Variables." *Applied Psychophysiology and Biofeedback* 33.2 (2008): 65-75.

413 Telles, Shirley, et al. "Alternate-Nostril Yoga Breathing Reduced Blood Pressure While Increasing Performance in a Vigilance Test." *Medical Science Monitor Basic Research* 23 (2017): 392.

414 "PAR | DVT | Digit Vigilance Test." *Par Inc.* (n.d.) http://www.parinc.com/Products/Pkey/94 (Accessed July 7, 2022).

bhedana, this is reversed: the inhale is through the left nostril and the exhale through the right. When the inhalation is initiated through the right nostril, the sympathetic nervous system activates.

Surya/Chandra Bhedana
(Piercing of the sun/moon)

Good For:

Congested nose, Foggy brain, Feeling unbalanced

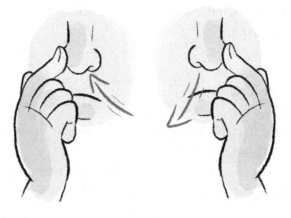

Result:

Increased blood flow in the opposite side of the body and brain, Increase lung volume, Decrease heart rate

How to Block Your Nostrils

There is no right or wrong way to close your nostrils. However, the process outlined below is the most comfortable option, especially if you are practising for long periods.

- Decide which hand you want to use. Traditionally, the right hand is used, but this is not essential.
- Place your index and middle fingers in the centre of your forehead,

just above your eyebrows. This takes the weight off your arm muscles, in particular the deltoid muscle in your shoulder.
- Use your thumb to close one nostril and your ring finger to close the other.

This hand shape is called *nasika mudra*. Alternatively, you can use *vishnu mudra*, in which the index and middle fingers are placed toward the base of your palm while the thumb and ring finger are used to block the nostrils. This option requires a certain independence in finger movement that not all of us have. *Mudra* means seal, mark, or gesture. Mudras are sacred or symbolic gestures used during practice. Many of them involve the hands.

Surya Bhedana (Sun)

- Assume a comfortable seated position on a chair or on your mat.
- Exhale fully through both nostrils.
- Block your left nostril, and inhale through the right one.
- At the top of your inhalation, pause briefly and close your right nostril.
- Exhale through your left nostril.
- Continue, inhaling slowly through your right nostril.
- Exhale slowly through your left nostril.
- Continue for between 10 rounds and 10 minutes, depending on your level of experience.

This is an ideal exercise before asana practice if you're feeling tired or cold.

Chandra Bhedana (Moon)

- Exhale fully through both nostrils.
- Block your right nostril, and inhale through the left one.

- At the top of your inhalation, pause briefly and close your left nostril.
- Exhale through your right nostril.
- Continue, inhaling slowly through your left nostril.
- Exhale slowly through your right nostril.
- Continue for between 10 rounds and 10 minutes, depending on your level of experience.

This is an ideal exercise before asana practice if you're feeling tense or hot.

Nadi Shodhana (Alternate Nostril Breathing)

Nadi means tubular organ for the passage of prana. The sun (surya) nadi ends in the right nostril, while the moon (chandra) nadi ends in the left nostril. *Shodhana* means purifying. In nadi shodhana, the inhalation and exhalation of each breathing cycle takes place via alternate nostrils. The direction reverses at the end of each cycle. If you start from the right side, you will breathe in from the right nostril, exhale from the left, breathe in from the left, exhale from the right, and so on. This is a symmetrical Prāṇāyāma, which means it doesn't need to be reversed to bring balance. This contrasts with digital breathing and surya or chandra bhedana, both of which focus on one-sided breathing.

Alternate nostril breathing increases heart rate variability (HRV).[415] HRV is a valuable marker of physical and mental health and nervous system balance. Alternate nostril breathing also improves sustained mental attention, motor activity, and hand-eye coordination.[416]

---

415 Telles, Shirley, Sachin Kumar Sharma, and Acharya Balkrishna. "Blood Pressure and Heart Rate Variability During Yoga-Based Alternate Nostril Breathing Practice and Breath Awareness." *Medical Science Monitor Basic Research* 20 (2014): 184.
416 Telles, Shirley, et al. "Alternate-Nostril Yoga Breathing Reduced Blood Pressure While Increasing Performance in a Vigilance Test." *Medical Science Monitor Basic Research* 23 (2017): 392.

Nadi Shodhana
(Purifying the passage of prana/
Alternate nostril breathing)

Good For:

Congested nose, Foggy brain, Agitated mind

Result:

Increase lung volume. Increase vigilance. Increase HRV

2. PRĀṆĀYĀMAS THAT GENERATE SOUND

Bhramari (Bee Breath/Humming)

Bhramari prāṇāyāma is often called "bee breath," from the word *bhramara*, which means large black bumble bee. It involves inhaling through both nostrils and exhaling through the nose, during which you hum to produce a sound like a large, satiated bee. The mouth remains closed throughout. You can use your fingers to close your ears. This increases your focus on the sound.

Humming slows the exhalation, making it much longer than the inhalation. By following the humming sound with your attention, it is possible to prolong the exhalations further.

The humming action also stimulates production of nasal nitric oxide in the paranasal sinuses (sinuses around your nose). This has attracted a lot of scientific interest and this prāṇāyāma is relatively well-researched. Nitric oxide (NO) production during this prāṇāyāma is not constant. When you practise consecutive exhalations with humming, NO production decreases with every subsequent breathing cycle. The frequency or pitch at which you hum also has an impact on NO levels. Humming at a higher pitch reduces the amount of NO produced, while humming at a lower pitch increases it. [417]

Research has provided some profound examples of the therapeutic effect of humming. Nitric oxide has antifungal properties. In one study, strong humming for one hour per day over four days cleared symptoms of chronic rhinosinusitis. [418]

Bhramari prāṇāyāma has also been shown to:

- Improve tolerance to cold exposure.[419]
- Alleviate symptoms of tinnitus.[420]
- Increase theta wave activity in the brain – theta waves are related to intuition, creativity, and daydreaming, and are connected to memories and emotions. They are strong during meditation, spiritual awareness, prayer, and reflection. In one study, the increase in theta waves during bhramari was described by participants as creating a blissful state of mental stillness, which yogis know as

417 Maniscalco, M., et al. "Assessment of Nasal and Sinus Nitric Oxide Output Using Single-Breath Humming Exhalations." *European Respiratory Journal* 22.2 (2003): 323-329.

418 Eby, George A. "Strong Humming for One Hour Daily to Terminate Chronic Rhinosinusitis in Four Days: A Case Report and Hypothesis for Action by Stimulation of Endogenous Nasal Nitric Oxide Production." *Medical Hypotheses* 66.4 (2006): 851-854.

419 Jain, Gaurav, and Sanjeev Rampalliwar. "Effect of Bhramari Prāṇāyāma on Volunteers Having Cardiovascular Hyper-Reactivity to Cold Pressor Test." *Journal of Yoga & Physical Therapy* 1.1 (2011): 1-4.

420 Pandey, Sidheshwar, Niladri Kumar Mahato, and Ravishankar Navale. "Role of Self-Induced Sound Therapy: Bhramari Prāṇāyāma in Tinnitus." *Audiological Medicine* 8.3 (2010): 137-141.

samahdi. In the same study, increased gamma wave activity was noted. Gamma waves indicate peak concentration states.[421]

- Improve voice production in healthy adults.[422] This has positive implications for those with vocal disorders.

Bhramari
(Humming)

Good For:

Blocked nose, Agitated mind

Result:

Increased Nitric Oxide

421 Vialatte, Francois, B., et al. "EEG Paroxysmal Gamma Waves During Bhramari Prāṇāyāma : A Yoga Breathing Technique." *Consciousness and Cognition* 18.4 (2009): 977-988.

422 Manjunatha, Usha, et al. "Effect of Bhramari Prāṇāyāma on the Acoustic and Aerodynamic Parameters of Voice in Normophonic Females." *Evidence-Based Complementary and Alternative Medicine* (2018).

How to Practise Bee Breath the Oxygen Advantage® Way

Stéphanie Blanche Legros, our Parisian instructor, has adapted the practice of bhramari prāṇāyāma in line with Oxygen Advantage® methods. This exercise is suitable once your BOLT score is above 15 seconds.

- Sit upright in a straight-backed chair or in a comfortable seated posture on your mat.
- Breathe in through your nose, engaging your diaphragm.
- You will feel your lower ribs move outwards.
- Breathe in for 5 seconds.
- Exhale for 15 seconds, breathing out through your nose and humming as you exhale. Richard Rosen describes the hum as an "eee" sound, like the noise a bee would make as it buzzes around a flower.[423]
- Keep the sound as steady as you can, but keep your lips and face relaxed.
- Repeat the pattern, breathing in for 5 seconds and exhaling with a humming sound for 15 seconds.
- Continue the exercise for 5 minutes.

As you hum, focus on the sound at the centre of your skull, right at the very top of your spine. Allow the sound to radiate out from this point, as if you had a speaker at the nape of your neck. Feel the humming sound travel down your spine and spread through your whole body. Soon every cell will be buzzing with the sound of the bee.

As you become more advanced with the exercise, you may like to perform a breath hold after each full exhalation. By holding the breath in this phase for as long as you can, you will increase CO_2, dilating the blood vessels and revitalising your body and brain. Stay relaxed during the breath hold.

---

423 Rosen, Richard. Prāṇāyāma Beyond the Fundamentals: An In-Depth Guide to Yogic Breathing. Shambhala Publications, 2006.

Udgitha Prāṇāyāma (Om)

This practice involves rhythmic chanting of the sound *Om* with conscious control of the breath. The word *udgitha* means deep and rhythmic chant. In one study, prāṇāyāma with Om chanting was practised alongside bhramari prāṇāyāma. Significant reductions in weight and body mass index were recorded in the study group, as well as improvements in lung function.[424] Ten minutes of udgitha prāṇāyāma has also been found to improve mood and social cognition.[425]

Udgitha

Reduced weight and BMI

Improved lung function

Improved mood

Improved social function

424 Mooventhan, A., and Vitthal Khode. "Effect of Bhramari Prāṇāyāma and OM Chanting on Pulmonary Function in Healthy Individuals: A Prospective Randomized Control Trial." *International Journal of Yoga* 7.2 (2014): 104.

425 Perry, Gemma, Vince Polito, and William Forde Thompson. "Chanting Meditation Improves Mood and Social Cohesion." *International Conference on Music Perception and Cognition.* San Francisco: The Society for Music Perception and Cognition (SMPC), 2016.

How to Practise Udgitha Prāṇāyāma

- Sit upright on your mat, or on a chair, with your spine straight. If you are seated on the floor, you can use a block or folded blanket under your hips for support. If you're on a chair, place both feet on the floor.
- Close your eyes or relax your gaze.
- Take a slow, deep breath in through your nose. Let your body relax and bring your awareness to your breath.
- Exhale slowly and chant the sound *Aum* as you breathe out.

Although you must open your mouth to begin the first part of the sound *Aum* (a-u), the humming sound completes (m) with exhaling through the nose. Be mindful not to precede the sound *Aum* by opening your mouth on the inhale, as this will lead to mouth breathing.

- Keep your face, neck, and shoulders relaxed.
- Work to extend your exhale for as long as you can without strain. The breath should create the sound.
- As you chant, bring your attention to the feeling of vibration. Experiment with keeping the sound just loud enough to focus your attention.
- Repeat the prāṇāyāma for between 2 and 10 minutes, ending with a moment of silence to integrate the practice.

You can practise this prāṇāyāma once or twice a day.

GREATER DIAPHRAGM ACTIVATION

In both udgitha and bhramari prāṇāyāmas, the focus on producing sound results in a fuller-than-normal exhalation. You will feel your diaphragm return to its domed resting position. When you inhale, you will feel it flatten down into your abdomen in quite an exaggerated way. The diaphragm is a striated muscle, the same kind of muscle as those that move your joints. Any exercise that encourages greater diaphragm oscillations will strengthen and thicken that muscle.

When your skeletal muscles are tense, it is likely your organs are constricted too. The diaphragm breathing in these exercises massages the stomach, small intestine, liver, and pancreas. The diaphragm is connected via the fascia to your heart, so these exercises will massage your heart. Diaphragm breathing, therefore, improves metabolism and circulation. It boosts efficiency and drainage in the heart. And, because it's impossible to perform these exercises if you are slumping, it enhances posture.

3. COOLING THE BODY: SITALI AND SITAKARI

While most breathing exercises exclusively use nasal breathing, these next two involve the mouth. The emphasis on nasal breathing is important, but it is perfectly okay to practise conscious mouth breathing during a breathing exercise that specifically calls for it, especially once your BOLT score is 25 seconds or more.

In sitali and sitakari prāṇāyāmas, inhaling is performed with the mouth partly open. Exhaling is through the nose.

In sitali, the tongue is rolled into a tight U shape and placed between the open lips. The breath is drawn in through the tongue on inhalation, as if drinking through a straw. At the end of the inhale, close your mouth and exhale slowly through the nose. You may like to perform a short breath hold at the top of the inhalation.

If you are one of the 20-40% of the population for whom tongue-rolling is not an option, the exercise is done by making an O shape with the lips.

In sitakari, or hissing breath, the upper and lower teeth press gently against each other. The lips are open, so the teeth are exposed to the air. The tongue either curls to touch the upper palette or the tongue-tip is placed against the back of the upper teeth. The inhale is drawn in through the teeth with a hissing noise. Then the lips are closed. Again, you can hold your breath for a few seconds after inhaling if you choose. Exhaling is through the nose.

In both exercises, inhaling through the mouth means air is not heated as it enters the body. For this reason, these techniques are used for cooling the body.

Sitali

Good For:

Feeling over heated

Result:
Cool down the body

CHAPTER EIGHTEEN

COMPARING PRĀṆĀYĀMA TO OXYGEN ADVANTAGE® EXERCISES

While prāṇāyāma exercises are an integral part of yoga, not every Western yogi is attracted to them, partly due to a misconception that we cannot progress to the later stages of yoga while living a normal, modern life. Nevertheless, to some extent, elements of these breathing techniques are practised in most yoga classes. In some cases, practitioners will attribute the benefits to their asana practice when breathing should really get the credit.

We've already explored some of the benefits of prāṇāyāma as they relate to specific exercises. Most of the exercises we've discussed so far promote breathing that is soft, nasal, rhythmic, diaphragmatic, and silent. These are the same qualities you are aiming for during automatic everyday functional breathing as taught in the Oxygen Advantage®.

One of the most important benefits of prāṇāyāma generally is the improvement of breathing capacity. When breathing capacity improves, it's easier to achieve functional breathing. However, prāṇāyāma breathing exercises have many other benefits. For instance, as we've seen, they can alter blood pressure and autonomic balance. They can improve digestion. They can alter body temperature and cold tolerance. And they can cleanse and detoxify the system. All these benefits are interesting, but they tend to be indirect. They are also perhaps of less importance in the context of this book than the impact of prāṇāyāma practice on breathing.

The benefits of prāṇāyāma also depend on your goals and the reasons you practise yoga in the first place. This "why" factor will determine the role prāṇāyāma plays in your practice. Most Western students use yoga as a vehicle to improve flexibility and coordination, increase vitality, and develop self-awareness. To achieve these goals, the way you breathe is crucial.

However, these are not the only benefits yoga can offer. Indeed, as we have previously discussed, they are not even really the point of yoga. You can also achieve two types of enlightenment with prāṇāyāma: mind control through awareness and kundalini awakening.

The Oxygen Advantage® exercises, on the other hand, serve a clear purpose – restoring functional breathing and improving oxygenation of the tissues. They alter the temperature in the hands and feet by means of improved circulation. Oxygen Advantage® exercises also support detoxification since many toxins leave the body via the lungs. Plus, they can help create the mental stillness familiar to yoga practitioners.

While we may never know why each prāṇāyāma technique was developed, we can see that most are in line with the findings of scientific research into respiratory training and Oxygen Advantage®. The following table shows how prāṇāyāma exercises work to affect the biochemistry (hypoxia and hypercapnia), cadence (slow rhythm), and functional qualities of breathing. These elements are all integral to the Oxygen Advantage® method. Oxygen Advantage® breathing exercises are always explained in terms of their impact on the biochemistry and biomechanics of breathing and on the nervous system. Prāṇāyāma can benefit from similar analysis.

To achieve a state of hypercapnia and/or hypoxia with these techniques, a lot of practice is required and, ideally, the guidance of an experienced practitioner as well.

The symbols shown in the table below represent the following:

✓   This quality is always present in this prāṇāyāma
~   This quality can occur in this prāṇāyāma
≠   This prāṇāyāma is likely to achieve the opposite quality (i.e., hyperoxia/high blood oxygen instead of hypoxia/low blood oxygen)
•   Can be used to achieve Kundalini awakening
✗   Involves control of the mind with awareness

	Slow	Rhythmic	Nasal	Hyper-capnia	Hypoxia	Enlighten-ment
Sama Vritti	✓	✓	✓	~	~	✗
Visama Vritti	✓	✓	✓	~	~	✗
Viloma	✓	✓	✓	~	~	✗
Bhramari	✓	~	✓			•
Digital	✓	✓	✓			✗
Bhastrika		~	✓	≠		•
Kapalabhati		~	✓	≠		•
Sitali	~	~		≠		•
Anuloma	✓	✓	✓	~	~	•
Pratiloma	✓	✓	✓	~	~	•
Nadi Shodhana	✓	✓	✓	~	~	•
Kevali	✓	✓	✓	~	~	✗

Prāṇāyāma and Enlightenment

The potential for spiritual growth through prāṇāyāma and breathing practices is widely explored in the yogic literature. While the potential of attaining enlightenment is a valuable window into what prāṇāyāma can offer, most of us do not have such aspirations.

PRĀṆĀYĀMA & BREATHING EXERCISES IN REAL LIFE

We all have responsibilities in life and many of us have families and jobs. Bring the benefits of breath training into our everyday life can allow us to be better, happier, healthier humans.

Regular practice is the only way to experience real benefit from any breathing technique. In India, even the yogis who are raising a family are assigned six hours of prāṇāyāma practice a day by their teachers. But you don't have to practise six hours a day to see benefits. It is possible to fit your practice into your schedule and manage between 4 to 20 sessions of 5 to 15 minutes each week and see a lot of benefit. The Oxygen Advantage® method encourages you to integrate the breathing exercises into your daily routine – to practise them in the shower, while driving, or out walking. When you are familiar enough with the exercises to work them into your day, it is easy to maintain progress.

Why Breathing Exercises Don't Have the Same Effect on Everyone

When breathing exercises are cued to predetermined time patterns, they don't address breathing volume or individual tolerance to CO_2.

To illustrate, let's consider two hypothetical students, Paul and Emma. Emma has a good tolerance to CO_2. She takes about 10 breaths per minute at 550 ml of air per breath. Paul takes around 16 breaths per minute at 700 ml per breath. Some rudimentary math would alert you to the fact Paul's minute volume is much higher. He breathes about 11 litres of air each minute to Emma's 5.5 litres. As a result of Paul's low CO_2 tolerance, his minute volume is higher.

Now imagine that Paul and Emma are both asked to perform the Oxygen Advantage® exercise, **Breathe slow**, at six breaths per minute. They inhale for five seconds and exhale for five seconds, continuing the exercise for several minutes. For someone with functional breathing, six breaths per minute is the optimal breathing rate to activate the rest and digest relaxation response. However, the exercise would not be as calming for Paul as it is for Emma. Paul will feel air hunger and may disproportionately increase his breathing volume to compensate. Instead of reducing his respiratory at near normal rate, while maintaining breathing volume, he will hyperventilate. Paul may also activate his stress response instead of bringing his body and mind into relaxation.

This example shows why it is so important to assess your breathing pattern and the breathing patterns of your students – and to adjust practices accordingly. Without such assessment, an exercise can produce a result that is opposite to what is desired or expected.

Best Poses for Practising Breathing Exercises

Traditionally, prāṇāyāma is practised in seated postures. The standard positions are siddhasana, padmasana, sukhasana, and vajrasana.

To execute the first three of these poses comfortably, you need a certain degree of flexibility in the external rotation of the hips. For vajrasana, you need flexibility in the plantar flexion of the ankle. For most people, this flexibility can be achieved with regular practice. To progress toward these postures, allocate some time to opening your hips.

Being unable to sit comfortably in these poses should not put you off practising breath training. Your nose, after all, is not in your hips!

Padmasana or Ardha Padma sana (Lotus or Half Lotus)

One or both legs are crossed. The feet are placed on the crease of the opposite hip. Ideally, the heels should be underneath the naval and the soles of the feet facing up to the ceiling.

Vajrasana (Thunderbolt Pose)

In a kneeling position, the hips rest on the heels. The top of the foot is against the floor.

Siddhasana (Accomplished Pose)

One foot is positioned at the perineum, with the other foot over the first. The knees should be below the level of the naval, preferably resting on the floor. If this is not possible, the practitioner can sit on blocks and support his/her knees with blocks or bolsters.

Sukhasana (Comfortable Pose)

This is a regular cross-legged position.

Padmasana

Vajrasana

Siddhasana

Sukhasan

As you practise sitting, you can also practise "witnessing." You will notice there is a continuous interplay between your body and your breath. As you surrender to the pose, your posture will adjust. Your body will subtly respond to your breath, creating more space for your breathing muscles.

Ultimately, breath training can be practised in different positions. Once you are able to comfortably hold the physical poses while maintaining regular breathing, you can practise most breathing exercises during asanas.

HOW THE BREATH AFFECTS DIFFERENT SITUATIONS

CHAPTER NINETEEN

BREATHING, THE BRAIN, IDENTITY, & EMOTIONS

THE EGO, YOGA, & BREATHING

Would it be possible to publish a book on yoga without talking about the ego? Probably not. The journey of ego and non-attachment is a topic that fascinates yogis – trying to rid ourselves of something so integral to our human experience while detaching from the outcome is something many of us face throughout our practice. After all, when we step onto our mat, we invariably come face-to-face with ourselves. As breathing and yoga teachers, we are often on some sort of mission to overcome our ego and to guide students to do the same. This is a paradoxical quest since the thing we focus on or try to avoid generally becomes stronger. It is only by transcending the ego gradually, in stages, that we progress toward enlightenment.

And what possible relationship could breathing have with our ego or sense of self? While breathing is not commonly discussed in yoga practices in terms of its significance for the ego, as we will see, our breath is a powerful means to achieving a healthier relationship with our ego.

Just What Is the Ego?

Although we often equate the word "ego" with selfishness, arrogance, or egoism, the Latin word "ego" simply means "I." According to Buddhist scholars, the ego is nothing more than a mental construct that we need to navigate the world.[426] In Sigmund Freud's psychoanalytic theory, it is the part of our personality that we experience as the self. Freud splits the personality into three parts, the ego, the id, and the super-ego. The id is our primitive, instinct-driven mind. The super-ego is our moral conscience. The ego is the realistic part, mediating between our animalistic desires (id) and our ethics or values (super-ego), providing our interface with the world.

How Can We Soften the Ego?

When we practise bringing our attention into the body, into the present moment, through asanas and breathing practices, we spend time away from our stories. We stop reinforcing the story of who we are. The story dissolves a little, allowing our true selves to emerge. The more we practise outside of thought, without focusing on an outcome, the more we are able to step away from the ego for brief periods. Yes, we may want to feel better, get more fit, or reduce stress, but the focus needs to be on the practice more than the results.

This ego journey is specific to us as humans. Animals have a sense of self that exists in the moment, but no animal lives its life according to an ego story. Can you imagine your dog saying to himself how beautiful he looks, what a great coat of fur he has, what a lovely face he has? He doesn't have a story like this. He lives in the present.

---

426 Brzosko, Marta. "Why You Should Hold on to Your Ego, According to Buddhist Scholars." *Self Awareness.* (February 3, 2020). http://www.selfawareness.blog/dont-let-go-of-your-ego/ (Accessed July 14, 2022).

Our ego stories can form an inner dialogue and inform the way we speak to ourselves. Common ego stories, like "I am not good enough," get tangled up with our in-the-moment experience. We affirm them to ourselves over and over, perpetuating our ego's notion of separateness. The quest to eradicate the ego often comes from a subtle sense of self-loathing. The "I" we want to transcend is not good enough, so we struggle to become enlightened. To rise above the "others" and achieve perfection.

Ego feeds into the way we bring up our children. Or is fed by the way we were brought up. When children are constantly praised, they grow full of confidence, ready to take on anything. But, if we teach them that their value depends on their achievements, what happens when they "fail"? Perfectionism based on the need for approval from others is increasing among young people. It is causing rising levels of anxiety and neurosis and a sense of social disconnection.[427] Research has linked depression and suicidal ideation with this "socially prescribed

427 Curran, Thomas, and Andrew P. Hill. "Perfectionism Is Increasing Over Time: A Meta-Analysis of Birth Cohort Differences From 1989 to 2016." *Psycholoical Bulletin* 145.4 (2019): 410.

perfectionism."[428] Depression is commonly thought of as anger turned against the self.[429]

Breathing and a Healthy Ego

What if we could be less attached to the ego stories that make us angry with ourselves in the first place? What if we could teach the next generation to soften their ego evaluations of themselves and others? Studies have shown that mindfulness practice reduces depression and anxiety.[430] By learning to step outside of thought, by bringing our attention into the present moment, we can relieve the torturous repetitive thought that keeps us stuck. Learning to breathe in a healthy functional way can be a simple path toward having a more healthy and functional ego.

Buddhist teachings suggest that a functional ego is important, and that, rather than trying to dissolve our identity, we must instead work to reclaim our true selves within a framework of humility. Humility is a tough concept to grasp. In essence, it simply involves becoming "right sized." This idea is congruent with many spiritual paths and the realisation of your true nature.

Osho, the Indian mystic, points out that the ego itself can become a barrier to connecting with our breath. "Breathing is so natural," he says, "that ego cannot proclaim itself the doer; hence it is none of its interest." He also explains the danger of becoming good at anything, whether

---

428 Sandoiu, Ana. "The Effects of Perfectionism on Mental and Physical Health." *Medical News Today.* (October 12, 2018). http://www.medicalnewstoday.com/articles/323323#How-perfectionism-affects-our-overall-health (Accessed July 14, 2022).

429 "The Perplexing Notion of Depression as 'Anger Turned Inward.'" *Psychology Today.* http://www.psychologytoday.com/gb/blog/intense-emotions-and-strong-feelings/201906/the-perplexing-notion-depression-anger-turned (Accessed July 14, 2022).

430 Parmetier, Fabrice B. R., et al. "Mindfulness and Symptoms of Depression and Anxiety in the General Population: the Mediating Roles of Worry, Rumination, Reappraisal and Suppression." *Frontiers in Psychology* 10 (2019): 506.

that's yoga or any other challenging pursuit. A breathing practice may well be the antidote to this danger:

> "The people who became concerned about breathing were the people who became aware of a certain truth – that if you go on doing difficult things, ego is never going to leave you, because each difficult step taken becomes a strengthening to the ego, and the stronger the ego is, the farther away you are from yourself."[431]

This explains why certain difficult asanas are so very attractive to our ego. It also implies that, by the simpler attention to the breath, we can reduce the attraction of achievement and become closer to ourselves. More connected.

It could be said that ego *is* thought, or, as Eckhart Tolle explains,

> "Becoming free of Ego means becoming free of thought, identification with thought. That's the end of the Ego."[432]

431 "Ego—Breath—Yoga?" *OSHO Online Library.* http://www.osho.com/osho-online-library/osho-talks/ego-breath-yoga-4416cfc8-3de?p=763a538486f3ce1e49aed3908d 2071e9 (Accessed July 14, 2022).

432 "Are Thoughts the Source of Ego?" *YouTube.* (n.d.) http://www.youtube.com/watch?v=hbj4nLOPN8o&t=446s (Accessed July 14, 2022).

Is it that simple? Does the ego dissolve when we stop thinking? Perhaps. But only briefly. If we do momentarily transcend the ego, who is there left to notice it has happened? As soon as we are aware of our new spiritual state, we are back in the ego story! In a sense then, the whole spiritual process is a paradox. We need our ego to navigate the world. But we also need space from it to evolve into our true selves. The ego, like everything else, must be held lightly. Too much of anything can be destructive.

The question to ask is this: are you living life according to your true self? Or are you always acting out the story that's in your head?

One way to begin, is to improve your breathing and learn the tools to get out of your own head. This can be a challenge in today's world, but physical yoga practice, combined with breathing techniques, provides an excellent pathway. Used together, breathing and yoga can break the patterns of your thinking mind and allow you to stand outside of thought – just long enough to gain a little more perspective.

Writing in the *Journal of Humanistic Psychology* in 1977, the American psychoanalyst, Michael Eigen, said:

> "It is surprising to think what little role the experience of breathing has played in Western accounts of personality, considering the importance of breathing in Eastern systems of personality change and the age-old association of breath with psyche, spirit, or soul." [433]

WHERE IS THE EGO? MEDITATION, THE BRAIN, AND THE DEFAULT MODE NETWORK

Scientists have tried to find out where the ego is located in the brain. Their research has been driven, in part, by studies into the effects of psychedelics on patients with addiction, end-of-life anxiety, and

---

433 Eigen, Michael. "On Breathing and Identity." *Journal of Humanistic Psychology*. (1977).

depression.[434,435] Studies so far have concluded that the ego sits in an area of the brain known as the *default mode network*. The default mode network is a relatively recent and still slightly controversial concept. It refers to an interconnected group of structures in the brain that are active when we're not engaged in any specific mental task. These regions seem to be less active when we are focused on what we're doing but become more active in those moments when we find ourselves 'just thinking.'[436]

In her book, *Why Meditate*, Jillian Lavender says, "A thought is an excitation of consciousness."[437] When we're stressed or distracted, we may experience a constant stream of running thoughts without even being aware of it. This significantly contributes to our unhappiness. As research has shown, a mind that wanders is likely to be unhappy.[438]

And that stream of thoughts appears through the filter of our own perceptions. Or, as the philosopher Jiddu Krishnamurti explains it, "The observer is the observed." Krishnamurti once famously surprised his audience by asking, "Do you want to know my secret?" Many of his followers had been coming to hear him speak for years and had not fully grasped the essence of his teaching. They were attentive, waiting for the key to this understanding. Krishnamurti said – "This is my secret. I don't mind what happens." He did not explain further.

Like anything worth doing, meditation takes practice. When we are trapped in thought, we may spend our meditation consciously thinking about meditating. If our meditation focuses on breathing, we find we

434 Smigielski, Lukasz, et al. "Psilocybin-Assisted Mindfulness Training Modulates Self-Consciousness and Brain Default Mode Network Connectivity with Lasting Effects." *NeuroImage* 196 (2019): 207-215.

435 Vollenweider, Franz X., and Michael Kometer. "The Neurobiology of Psychedelic Drugs: Implications for the Treatment of Mood Disorders." *Nature Reviews Neuroscience* 11.9 (2010): 642-651.

436 "Know Your Brain: Default Mode Network." *Neuroscientifically Challenged.* (n.d.) http://www.neuroscientificallychallenged.com/posts/know-your-brain-default-mode-network (Accessed July 14, 2022).

437 Lavender, Jillian. *Why Meditate? Because It Works.* Hodder & Stoughton, 2022.

438 Killingsworth, Matthew A., and Daniel T. Gilbert. "A Wandering Mind Is an Unhappy Mind." *Science* 330.6006 (2010): 932.

are observing the breath but also thinking about the breath – we are still in the mind. Even experienced meditators have days when meditation is twitchy, anxious, and busy with thought. The key is, as Krishnamurti explained, to not "mind" what happens. To remain detached from the outcome. To not make meditation another channel for perfectionism. To go easy on yourself and practise anyway.

Meditations with repeated mantras can help you subtly train your brain to hold attention. Rather than actively trying to clear your mind of thought, you are asked to gently return to the meditation mantra, a meaningless vibrational sound. This is more an "allowing" than a forced type of concentration. As soon as you realise your mind has strayed from the mantra, you have already returned to the task at hand. There is no more to do. You can bring this conscious way of being to everything you do. How many times, for instance, have you eaten a meal without really tasting anything on your plate? Satu Chantal, one of our OA™ instructors in Finland explains it like this:

> "In meditation, you are releasing thoughts and sensations when they pop up in your mind, so you're gently emptying the mind. Meditation exercises are about returning to the silence and stillness as soon as you notice a thought or sensation comes up. Your brain is built so that the activity is always there, so there will always be thoughts popping up. Sometimes in meditation we use mantras to help detach the mind. This eases the journey to quieting the mind. The Sanskrit word mantra actually means *mind vehicle*."

Now, let's circle back to the default mode network, where unconscious thinking happens in our brain. The identification of the ego within the default mode network was brought to our attention partway through writing this book, when Anastasis hosted Miguel Toribio-Mateas in his final podcast for 2021. Miguel is a certified yoga teacher and clinical neuroscientist. While discussing the benefits of yoga, he said:

> "Psychedelics have been shown to bring the body into a state where the sense of self is lost. A similar state, possibly at a moderate level,

at least in novice practitioners, can be experienced through yoga. During that state the default mode network is temporarily shut down."

He went on to say that psychedelic compounds, such as psilocybin and ayahuasca, have been found to benefit patients with anxiety and depression, both emotionally and cognitively. He explained:

"Healthy individuals go about their day focusing on only a few of the stimuli they receive at any given moment. At the same time, they ignore a lot of input from the environment. Focusing on a specific stimulus is the equivalent of walking across a field by following the path. The brain filters out most "irrelevant" information. People with anxiety and depression lack the ability to ignore most of the environmental stimuli and end up getting inundated by all the possibilities and distractions. They are unable to see the path across the field."

Knowing how much breathing affects people with depression and anxiety, we did some digging to see if we could find out how much the breath affects the default mode network. We found that low blood oxygen (hypoxia) reduces the activity of the default mode network.[439] The longer you are exposed to hypoxia, the less activity occurs in those brain areas.[440] This makes sense, since the brain needs oxygen to think. Chronic hypoxia is also associated with hallucinations.[441, 442]

This may be why breath suspension, especially natural suspension of the breath during meditation, plays a role in kundalini awakening.[443] It may also explain the loss of self commonly experienced when you practise breathing methods that involve hyperventilation followed by breath holding. (However, it should be noted that kundalini yoga experts say that the Breath of Fire prāṇāyāma used in their practice is purely through the nose and does not involve hyperventilation.[444] This prāṇāyāma is also called Tummo breathing. Note that, while many believe that Wim Hof breathing is the same as Tummo, Hof has clarified that the techniques, while comparable, are different.)[445]

Default mode network activity is not only lower when blood oxygen is lower (hypoxia), but also reduced in the following circumstances:

- During rapid-eye-movement (REM) sleep,[446] the stage of sleep in which we dream

439 Rossetti, Gabriella M. K., et al. 2021. "Reversal of Neurovascular Coupling in the Default Mode Network: Evidence from Hypoxia." *Journal of Cerebral Blood Flow & Metabolism* 41.4 (2021): 805-818.

440 Lawley, Justin S., et al. "Unexpected Reductions in Regional Cerebral Perfusion During Prolonged Hypoxia." *The Journal of Physiology* 595.3 (2017): 935-947.

441 Windsor, Jeremy S. "Voices in the Air." *BMJ* 337, 2008.

442 Wilson, Jo Ellen, et al. "Delirium." *Nature Reviews Disease Primers* 6.1 (2020): 1-26.

443 "AYP Lesson 378—How Does Prāṇāyāma Awaken Kundalini?" *AYP Site.* (n.d.) http://www.aypsite.com/378.html (Accessed July 14, 2022).

444 "Breath of Fire (BOF)." *Spirit Rising Yoga.* (n.d.) http://www.spiritrisingyoga.org/kundalini-info/breath-of-fire (Accessed July 14, 2022).

445 "Tummo Meditation | Your Inner Fire and the Wim Hof Method." *Wim Hof Method.* (n.d.) http://wimhofmethod.com/tummo-meditation (Accessed July 14, 2022).

446 Kiviniemi, Vesa J., et al. "Mapping Transient Hyperventilation Induced Alterations with Estimates of the Multi-Scale Dynamics of BOLD Signal." *Frontiers in Neuroinformatics* 18 (2009).

- In experienced meditators[447]
- In novice meditators, after six days of mindfulness meditation[448]
- During focused attention meditation, which includes breathing meditations
- During meditation in a "non-directive" style

Non-directive meditation, during which there is less default mode network activity and thus less egoic thought, is meditation that uses a relaxed focus on a mantra or short series of syllables but allows thoughts to emerge. Attention is neither directed toward nor away from new or recurring thoughts. Vedic Meditation, Transcendental Meditation, and Acem Meditation are all forms of non-directive meditation.

In research, transcendental meditation has been shown to result in reduced breathing. In one substantial study of a single advanced meditation practitioner, experiences of pure consciousness, which are synonymous with the stopping of thought, were linked with significantly lower breathing rates, minute ventilation, heart rate, and metabolic rate. Results showed "statistically consistent" changes in EEG – a reduction in brain activity.[449]

Another study examined 16 meditators alongside 16 non-meditators. During meditation, breathing decreased with a lower tidal volume that was due to shorter inhalations. Meditation was linked with a decreased response to hypercapnia (raised CO_2 levels).[450]

---

447 Trova, Sara, et al. "Decrease of Functional Connectivity Within the Default Mode Network by a Brief Training of Focused Attention on the Breath in Novices." *bioRxiv.* (2021).

448 Trova, Sara, et al. "Decrease of Functional Connectivity Within the Default Mode Network by a Brief Training of Focused Attention on the Breath in Novices." *bioRxiv.* (2021).

449 Wolkove, Norman, et al. "Effect of Transcendental Meditation on Breathing and Respiratory Control." *Journal of Applied Physiology* 56.3 (1984): 607-612.

450 Trova, Sara, et al. "Decrease of Functional Connectivity Within the Default Mode Network by a Brief Training of Focused Attention on the Breath in Novices." *bioRxiv.* (2021).

However, not all meditation techniques are the same. For instance, during the practice of open monitoring meditation techniques, default mode network activity increases.[451] In open monitoring meditation, there is no focus on any specific stimulus or object. Instead, the practitioner remains open and attentive to whatever comes up in his experience, moment-to-moment.[452] This involves more interaction between the practitioner, his thoughts, and his environment. The goal is to effortlessly maintain awareness without explicit selection.

EMOTIONS, THE BREATH, AND THE BRAIN

In recent years, scientists have confirmed that breathing has functions beyond the life-supporting exchange of oxygen and CO_2. Breathing links fundamental states of body and mind that go beyond identity and ego.[453] Advances in brain imaging techniques have allowed scientists to identify which parts of the brain control breathing and which relate to different emotional states.

The three main areas of the brain controlling breathing are:

- **The brain stem**
  The lower part of the brain. It is connected to the spinal cord and is part of the central nervous system. It regulates many automatic functions including breathing and works to maintain a stable homeostasis within the body.[454]

451 Xu, Jian, et al. "Nondirective Meditation Activates Default Mode Network and Areas Associated with Memory Retrieval and Emotional Processing." *Frontiers in Human Neuroscience* 86 (2014).

452 *Positive Psychology.* (Accessed July 14, 2022).

453 Heck, Detlef H., et al. "Breathing as a Fundamental Rhythm of Brain Function." *Frontiers in Neural Circuits* 10 (2017): 115.

454 Yackle, Kevin, et al. "Breathing Control Center Neurons That Promote Arousal in Mice." *Science* 355.6332 (2017): 1411-1415.

- **The limbic system**

  A group of structures involved in behaviour and emotional processing and response.[455] It includes the amygdala, a primitive part of the brain often called the "lizard brain," which is associated with survival fight-flight-freeze responses.

- **The cerebral cortex**

  Commonly referred to as "grey matter." This neural tissue is important for sensory, motor, and information-processing tasks, and it controls intention.[456]

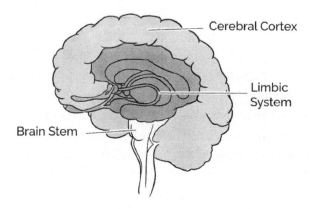

Most studies into the connection between breathing and emotions measure respiratory rate and depth of breath. Some examine chest vs. abdominal breathing, inhale-to-exhale ratio, and breathing regularity. While a lot of laboratory time has been dedicated to research on anxiety and panic attacks, other emotional states have received less attention.

455 Bordoni, Bruno, Fabiola Marelli, and Giovanni Bordoni. "A Review of Analgesic and Emotive Breathing: A Multidisciplinary Approach." *Journal of Multidisciplinary Healthcare* 9 (2016): 97.

456 Masaoka, Yuri, Masahiko Izumizaki, and Ikuo Homma. "Where Is the Rhythm Generator for Emotional Breathing?" *Progress in Brain Research* 209 (2014): 367-377.

ANASTASIS ON THE BREATH AND MENTAL STATE

It was a regular Wednesday afternoon at the yoga studio in the Near Bank station in the City of London. The teaching spaces were busy with students, and the therapy rooms were bursting with clients. I had just finished work and was sitting in the lobby, checking my emails before I headed home. Petra, a homoeopath I had known for a few years, was sitting opposite me, waiting to start her shift. She was clearly unhappy. I asked her what was wrong, and she told me that in the last three days, a series of minor yet unfortunate events had occurred, causing her to feel distressed. Every 20 seconds or so, she would let out a big sigh.

It had been a long time since I offered to give advice to someone who hadn't explicitly requested it, but I thought of Petra as a friend. I asked her if she had considered using her breathing to help her mental state. She replied that was what she was doing – it was why she kept sighing. She had read an article by a popular celebrity recommending the technique. I asked her if the exercise was having a positive effect.

"I think so," she said. "The sighs feel like a relief."

"But you have been sighing non-stop for the last 20 minutes," I replied. "If it were really changing your mental state, you wouldn't need to keep doing it."

Petra shrugged. "It's the only thing I know how to do."

I offered to guide my friend through a breathing exercise. The exercise aimed to establish the four phases of breathing (inhale, retention, exhale, suspension), progressively lengthening the breath hold after inhaling. Within three minutes, Petra felt calm enough to stop sighing.

While I know she found some of the initial breath holds uncomfortable, the exercise created a more permanent shift in her mental state. The sighing provided respite, but it was a relief similar to the fix you get when you give in to your sugar cravings and take a bite of chocolate. It was only fleeting.

Physiological Sighing

Petra was practising a technique called *physiological sighing*, popularised in recent years by Dr. Andrew Huberman, Professor of Neurobiology and Ophthalmology at Stanford University.[457]

A sigh involves two inhalations followed by a long exhalation. It's normally involuntary, and it happens every few minutes when we cry and during sleep. The double inhalation inflates the alveoli, increasing the surface area of the lungs in contact with the air. This facilitates better gas exchange. The long exhalation activates the vagus nerve, slowing the heart rate.

The practice of physiological sighing involves two consecutive inhales followed by a long exhale, between one and three times. This "mindful sighing" is believed to reduce stress within a few seconds. It should not be practised non-stop for 20 minutes, as Petra was doing. Neither will it be very helpful in the long run if your sensitivity to carbon dioxide is high. If breathing is already dysfunctional, conscious

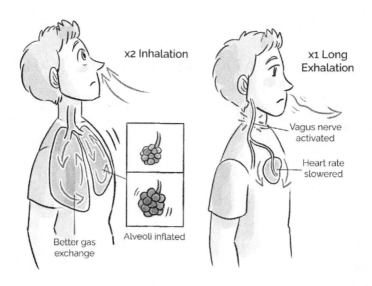

457 "Is a Sigh Just a Sigh? – Government Science and Engineering." *Government Science and Engineering.* (November 26, 2021). http://www.governmentscienceandengineering. blog.gov.uk/2021/11/26/is-a-sigh-just-a-sigh/ (Accessed July 14, 2022).

sighing can keep your biochemistry stuck. You won't experience any real change in your nervous system. Your anxiety won't reduce long-term either.

Frequent sighing is itself a symptom of dysfunctional breathing and is common in people with panic disorder. Sighing is defined by a breathing volume during one breath that's three times greater than normal. It often overlaps with hyperventilation.

When your biochemistry is out of balance, it is common to sigh frequently to relieve feelings of air hunger or suffocation. Someone with dysfunctional breathing and feelings of breathlessness may sigh as many as 15 times in 15 minutes.[458] This breathlessness should be a key signal for yoga instructors and in your own practice. Often, those students who need the most help with breathing will find that slow breathing is too challenging and that sighing keeps them anxious. This is where the BOLT score can be used to tailor exercises to each person.

Instead of sighing, consider practising **Breathe Light** or many small breath holds (see Chapter Four) to gently increase levels of CO_2 in the blood. This will more reliably bring the body and mind into a state of relaxation.

BREATHING IN VARIOUS EMOTIONAL STATES

One study mapped breathing patterns across the following different emotions:

- Tenderness
- Erotic love
- Anger
- Fear
- Joy
- Sadness

---

458 Boulding, Richard, et al. "Dysfunctional Breathing: A Review of the Literature and Proposal for Classification." *European Respiratory Review* 25.141 (2016):287-291.

Pleasant or positive emotions were found to be associated with similar breathing characteristics. In the following table, those six emotions are ranked according to the different breathing parameters as described in the study.[459] You can clearly see patterns emerging.

	Size of Breaths	Breath Cycles Per Minute	Pause After Exhalation	Inhale to Exhale Ratio
High	Fear	Anger	Tenderness	Fear
	Anger	Erotic love	Sadness/ crying	Sadness/ crying
	Joy/ laughter	Tenderness	Joy/laughter	Erotic love
	Sadness/ crying	Sadness/ crying	Erotic love	Anger
	Erotic love	Joy/laughter	Anger*	Tenderness
Low	Tenderness	Fear	Fear *	Joy/laughter

* Zero time

In his book, *The Psychophysiology of Self-Awareness*, Professor Emeritus of Psychology and Rosen method practitioner, Alan Fogel, describes the emotion-to-breath relationship in detail:

- In tenderness and joy, breathing is regularly spaced. Breaths are slow with longer exhales than inhales, and a long pause after the out-breath. Muscles are relaxed.
- In erotic love, breaths are deep and fast, interspersed with slow, short breaths. Muscles may be relaxed, or breathing may be effortful.
- Laughter and crying have their own distinct breathing patterns.
- Anger, fear, and anxiety all have fast breathing patterns, though

459   Bloch, Susana, Madeleine Lemeignan, and Nancy Aguilera-T. "Specific Respiratory Patterns Distinguish Among Human Basic Emotions." *International Journal of Psychophysiology* 11.2 (1991): 141-154.

breaths during anger have little variability whereas during anxiety breathing is highly variable. Anxious breathing involves incomplete exhalations with no pause after the exhale. Breathing is effortful.

Interestingly, in this research, the number of breaths per minute did not reliably indicate emotional state. These patterns may differ depending on your BOLT score, that is, on your tolerance for CO_2.

Scientists at Amsterdam University's Department of Experimental Psychology examined breathing during positive and negative emotions.[460] Findings are summarised in the following table:

	Negative Emotions	Positive Emotions
Respiratory rate and depth (speed and volume of breathing)	High	Low
Inhale/exhale ratio	High	Low
Abdominal (diaphragmatic) or Thoracic (chest)	Thoracic	Abdominal
Breathing irregularity	High	

This study also grouped emotions according to respiratory rate and depth, providing further insights:

Speed vs. Volume of breath	Deep	Shallow
Fast	Excitement	Effortful, stressful mental tasks
Slow	Relaxed resting state	Passive grief, calm, happiness

460 Boiten, Frans A., Nico H. Frijda, and Cornelis J. E. Wientjes. "Emotions and Respiratory Patterns: Review and Critical Analysis." *International Journal of Psychophysiology* 17.2 (1994): 103-128.

It is worth noting that the word "shallow" here does not differentiate between breathing volume and mechanics, and it does not specify whether breathing is into the upper chest or from the diaphragm. A state of calm happiness would suggest light breathing from the diaphragm, whereas passive grief is more likely to involve chest breathing.

Breath and the Brain: Metabolic and Hormonal Links

The breath and the brain are linked in many ways. As we've described, one is the metabolic link: your breathing pattern is responsible for the supply of oxygen and glucose that fuels the brain.

The way you breathe also affects the release of hormones, many of which act as neurotransmitters. A neurotransmitter is a chemical substance secreted by a neuron to affect another cell. The brain is an organ with high energy demands. It also regulates metabolism and the use of energy for the rest of the body via the hormones released by the pituitary and thyroid glands. To produce the required energy, the body needs oxygen and glucose, and breathing can affect the availability of both. When blood vessels become constricted due to low blood CO_2, glucose is not able to circulate freely. Glucose circulation also decreases when O_2 levels are low.

The following table provides a quick overview of the various relationships between different hormones and the breath. Note: here, dopamine is identified as a hormone. Although it is technically a neurotransmitter, it is sometimes called a neurohormone and is commonly referred to as a "happy hormone".

Hormone	Role in the body	Effect on the breath
Adenosine	One of the four building blocks of DNA (your genetic "code") and RNA (a messenger that carries "instructions" from DNA to make the proteins that form new cells). Protects the neurons. Upregulated during ketosis (when blood glucose is low). [461]	Excitatory[462]
Dopamine	Activates the reward pathways in the brain. Has an important role in enabling normal movement.[463]	Reduces ventilation[464]
Insulin	Regulates blood glucose levels.[465]	Increases ventilation
Noradrenaline	Mobilises the body and brain for action	Causes hyperventilation[466]

461 Masino, S. A., et al. "Adenosine, Ketogenic Diet and Epilepsy: the Emerging Therapeutic Relationship Between Metabolism and Brain Activity." *Current Neuropharmacology* 7.3 (2009): 257-268.

462 Zhang, Min, Cathy Vollmer, and Colin A. Nurse. "Adenosine and Dopamine Oppositely Modulate a Hyperpolarization-Activated Current Ih in Chemosensory Neurons of the Rat Carotid Body in Co-Culture." *The Journal of Physiology* 596.15 (2018): 3101-3117.

463 Gepshtein, Sergei, et al. "Dopamine Function and the Efficiency of Human Movement." *Journal of Cognitive Neuroscience*. 26.3 (2014): 645-657.

464 Van De Borne, Philippe, Ron Oren, and Virend K. Somers. 1998. "Dopamine Depresses Minute Ventilation in Patients with Heart Failure." *Circulation* 98.2 (1998): 126-131.

465 Barbosa, Thales C., et al. 2018. "Insulin Increases Ventilation During Euglycemia in Humans." *American Journal of Physiology-Regulatory, Integrative and Comparative Physiology* 315.1 (2018): R84-R89.

466 Heistad, Donald D., et al. 1972. "Effects of Adrenergic Stimulation on Ventilation in Man." *The Journal of Clinical Investigation* 51.6 (1972): 1469-1475.

Progesterone	Plays an important role in the menstrual cycle and in early pregnancy. May protect against lung disease and sleep-disordered breathing (along with oestrogen). Important for testosterone production in men.[467]	Increases ventilation[468]
Testosterone	Regulates sex drive and factors including fat distribution, muscle mass, and strength in men.[469] In women, it supports the growth and repair of reproductive tissues and bone mass[470] Plays a role in human behaviours	Predisposes to sleep-disordered breathing.
Thyroxine (secreted by the thyroid)	Important for brain development, digestion, muscle and heart function, and maintenance of bones[471]	Increases respiration

467 "Progesterone and Progestin: What Are They, Medication, for Men." *Medical News Today.* (n.d.) http://www.medicalnewstoday.com/articles/277737#progesterone-in-men (Accessed July 14, 2022).

468 Slatkovska, Lubomira, et al. "Phasic Menstrual Cycle Effects on the Control of Breathing in Healthy Women." *Respiratory Physiology & Neurobiology* 154.3 (2006): 379-388.

469 Wein, Harrison. "Understanding How Testosterone Affects Men." *NIH.* (April 25, 2016). http://www.nih.gov/news-events/nih-research-matters/understanding-how-testosterone-affects-men (Accessed July 14, 2022).

470 Anthony, Kiara. "High Testosterone Levels in Women." *Healthline Media.* (October 13, 2017). http://www.healthline.com/health/high-testosterone-in-women (Accessed July 14, 2022).

471 "Thyroxine | You and Your Hormones from the Society for Endocrinology." *Your Hormones.* Society for Endocrinology. (2018). http://www.yourhormones.info/hormones/thyroxine/ (Accessed July 14, 2022).

CHAPTER TWENTY

BREATH TRAINING FOR STRESS, ANXIETY, PANIC, & PAIN

Chronic stress, anxiety, and anxiety disorders such as panic disorder are more common than ever. Left untreated, they can greatly affect mental and physical health, reduce quality of life, productivity, and ability to function, and impact the sufferer and society at large.[472] So what does this have to do with yoga and breathing? Research suggests yoga can effectively reduce stress and anxiety and it may be a viable complementary therapy for people with anxiety and other mental health concerns.[473,474] While the research for yoga as an anti-anxiety tool is still preliminary,[475] there is ample and indisputable evidence for the use of breathing practises to effectively manage stress, anxiety, and

472 Siegfried Kasper. "Anxiety disorders: under-diagnosed and insufficiently treated." *International Journal of Psychiatry in Clinical practise.* 2006;10 Suppl 1:3-9

473 Crystal L. Park, et al. "Yoga as an Integrative Therapy for Mental Health Concerns: An Overview of Current Research Evidence." *Psychiatry International.* 2021, 2(4), 386-401.

474 Masoumeh Shohani, et al. "The Effect of Yoga on Stress, Anxiety, and Depression in Women" *International Journal of Preventive Medicine.* 2018; 9: 21.

475 G Kirkwood. "Yoga for anxiety: a systematic review of the research evidence." *British Journal of Sports Medicine.* 2005 Dec; 39(12): 884–891.

panic attacks.[476,477,478] Therefore, learning how to harness the breath, both on and off the yoga mat, should be considered a key element for any yogi struggling with these conditions. What's more, doing so may allow for a synergistic effect, maximising the benefits of both.

Studies show that many people with stress and anxiety disorders have dysfunctional breathing and there is a direct link between hyperventilation, anxiety, and panic attacks.[479,480] In fact, most of the damaging physical impacts of these conditions stem from the chronic hyperventilation (over-breathing) that they perpetuate. Harder and faster breathing is a perfectly normal response to temporary stress as rises in heart rate and breathing rate are necessary to prepare the body to fight or flee. But this natural response becomes abnormal when stress is sustained long term and breathing volume does not have an opportunity to normalise, leading to chronic hyperventilation.

As a reminder from Chapter Six, chronic hyperventilation is not quite what most of us think. Chronic hyperventilation happens subtly, without paper bags or the obvious chaotic breathing that you see with panic attacks. It's often so subtle that it is unnoticeable by others, and it is habitual – it involves breathing too much air on a constant and long-term basis. This over-breathing creates a state of heightened alertness and sensory perception. Your muscles become tense, and your reflexes quicken. Lights appear brighter and sounds seem louder.

These evolutionary stress responses are useful when you are in immediate danger, but they are largely inappropriate for the sort of

476 Andrea Zaccaro, et al. "How Breath-Control Can Change Your Life: A Systematic Review on Psycho-Physiological Correlates of Slow Breathing." *Frontiers in Human Neuroscience.* 2018; 12: 353.

477 Teresa M. Leyro, et al. "Respiratory therapy for the treatment of anxiety: meta-analytic review and regression." *Clinical Psychology Review.* Published on 2021, Jan 24.

478 Volker Busch, MD, et al. "The Effect of Deep and Slow Breathing on Pain Perception, Autonomic Activity, and Mood Processing—An Experimental Study." *Pain Medicine.* Volume 13, Issue 2, February 2012, Pages 215–228.

479 Guy William Fincham, et al. "Effect of breathwork on stress and mental health: A meta-analysis of randomised-controlled trials." *Sci Rep.* 13, 432 (2023).

480 Teresa M. Leyro, et al. "Respiratory therapy for the treatment of anxiety: meta-analytic review and regression." *Clinical Psychology Review.* Published on 2021, Jan 24.

stress most of us face in day-to-day modern life. They can also lead to internal conflict arising from the instinctive desire to run from a stressor. Imagine you're in a difficult meeting or presentation at work. You may be sitting still, but, internally, you're running as fast as you can. Your brain is designed to protect your body, and it's screaming at you to get out of the room. This creates a mismatch between your evolutionary response and the thing you need to do in real life – stay in the meeting and act normal! To cope, you stuff your stress down rather than dealing with it. You're likely to feel like you have a short fuse and that the smallest challenge may tip you over the edge. The reasoning part of your brain will switch off, making it harder for you to make decisions.

Unfortunately, when hyperventilation becomes habitual, the evolutionary stress response can become jammed in the "always on" position. This leads to a continual state of arousal and hypervigilance. This is exhausting and feeds back to cause greater anxiety. In this case, over-breathing can itself become the cause of anxiety. When you are already chronically stressed and your breathing is dysfunctional and you sleep badly, your stress will flare up many times a day, and it will hit you more quickly and more strongly every time you encounter any new challenge.

THE SCIENCE BEHIND THE BREATH-ANXIETY CONNECTION

To understand how hyperventilation can trigger stress and anxiety states, we must first recap the effects of breathing on carbon dioxide (CO_2) levels in the blood. When a person breathes too rapidly from their upper chest it leads to a greater volume of air being taken in than the body requires. This, in turn, causes levels of CO_2 in the blood to lower. The drop in blood CO_2 and oxygen delivery that occurs from hyperventilation triggers a fight or flight response which in turn perpetuates hyperventilation. Studies show that in people who are susceptible to panic attacks, the feeling of suffocation provokes a very strong fear response and sends them into a state of panic, deep air hunger, and more hyperventilation, which further fuels panic.[481,482]

Compounding this negative snowball effect is the fact that emotions such as fear which accompany anxiety cause an increase in adrenaline and noradrenaline. This makes the body around 30% more sensitive to CO_2 – and CO_2 operates as the stimulus to breathe. Because of this, when you are more sensitive to CO_2 you tend to breathe more, and this fuels hyperventilation and worsens anxiety symptoms.[483] This creates another feedback loop in which shallow, fast, upper-chest breathing (hyperventilation), increases CO_2 sensitivity and feelings of anxiety, and increased anxiety leads to more hyperventilation. This is not a hypothesis, countless studies have confirmed anxious people are more sensitive to changes in CO_2, and higher CO_2 sensitivity increases both the rate of breathing and symptoms of anxiety.[484]

Perhaps not surprisingly, given the above, it's estimated that up to 75% of people with panic disorder have dysfunctional breathing.[485,486] Studies also show people with panic disorder have lower than normal CO_2 levels and deep breathing can exacerbate this. Conversely, when CO_2 is normalised using light and slow, diaphragm breathing, panic symptoms lessen. In fact, a clinical study found light, slow breathing

481 J Bras Pneumol. Respiratory manifestations of Panic Disorder: causes, consequences and therapeutic implications. 2009 Jul;35(7):698-708.

482 Nardi AE, Freire RC, Zin WA. Panic disorder and control of breathing. Respir Physiol Neurobiol. 2009 May 30;167(1):133-43.

483 Heistad, Donald D., Robert C. Wheeler, Allyn L. Mark, Phillip G. Schmid, and Francois M. Abboud. "Effects of adrenergic stimulation on ventilation in man." The Journal of clinical investigation 51, no. 6 (1972): 1469-1475.

484 Pine, Daniel S., Rachel G. Klein, Jeremy D. Coplan, Laszlo A. Papp, Christina W. Hoven, Jose Martinez, Pavel Kovalenko et al. "Differential carbon dioxide sensitivity in childhood Anxiety Disorders and nonill comparison group." Archives of General Psychiatry 57, no. 10 (2000): 960-967.

485 Courtney, Rosalba. "Multi-dimensional model of dysfunctional breathing and integrative breathing therapy–commentary on the functions of breathing and its dysfunctions and their relationship to breathing therapy." J Yoga Phys Ther 6.4 (2016): 257.

486 Leyro, Teresa M., et al. "Respiratory therapy for the treatment of anxiety: Meta-analytic review and regression." Clinical psychology review 84 (2021): 101980.

exercises to be equally as effective at reducing the severity of panic symptoms as treatment with Cognitive Behavioral Therapy (CBT).[487]

Worth noting here is that while mindful breathing exercises are appealing because of their simplicity, they don't achieve the manipulation of blood gases that is so beneficial for the body. Scientists compared the effects of nadi shodhana (alternate nostril breathing) and mindful breathing in people with anxiety. When mindful breath was practised for ten minutes, two days in a row, anxiety symptoms reduced by 8%. In contrast, when subjects practised nadi shodhana for the same period, symptoms reduced by 25%. While both types of exercise serve a purpose, mindful breathing is most useful when breathing and sleep are already optimal, whereas breath training practises, including prāṇāyāma, are effective tools to help you achieve optimal breathing and sleep.

DEEP, SLOW BREATHING, PAIN PERCEPTION, AND MOOD

Slow, diaphragmatic, reduced-volume breathing can decrease anxiety and other sympathetic responses (fight or flight) even during dangerous and painful situations. When a person is in pain, it is the sympathetic nerves of the brain that are activated, which increases stress levels, activates pain pathways, and increases breathing rate and blood pressure. The pain caused by the increased sympathetic activity can be reduced by learning to control a physical sympathetic response such as breathing. So, could being in a relaxed state make deep and slow breathing more effective in relieving pain?

A study was designed to "disentangle the effects of relaxation" from the effects of breathing. In it, 16 healthy subjects practised two different deep and slow breathing techniques at the same depth and respiration

---

487 Meuret, Alicia E., et al. "Respiratory and Cognitive Mediators of Treatment Change in Panic Disorder: Evidence for Intervention Specificity." *Journal of Consulting and Clinical Psychology* 78.5 (2010): 691.

rate. One was a deep and slow breathing intervention where the subjects focused on a task requiring a high degree of concentration and constant attention. The others practised deep and slow breathing while they relaxed.[488] This experiment was designed to compare the effect of the two deep and slow breathing techniques on the depth of pain perception and mood. Before, during, and after the breathing exercise, the subjects' skin conductance, pain threshold for hot and cold stimuli, and mood profile were measured. Skin conductance was measured as an indicator of the level of sympathetic activity and, therefore, the body's level of relaxation.

The mean pain threshold for the deep and slow breathing subjects who were relaxed increased significantly. They had a higher threshold for pain and were more able to withstand it than those who were not relaxed. The skin conductance results showed a significant decrease in sympathetic activity during the relaxed deep and slow breathing intervention, while no change was recorded for the attentive subjects. Both attentive and relaxed deep and slow breathing interventions showed a decrease in hostile, negative emotions such as anger and depression. The subjects felt calmer and were generally in better moods just from the deep and slow breathing.

While deep and slow breathing is helpful overall, a relaxed person will benefit more from it than a person who is not relaxed. Next time you wonder why your pain persists or you are still pretty worked up after taking several deep and slow breaths, ask yourself, "Am I calm and relaxed enough to benefit?" The results of the study suggest that you should be as relaxed and comfortable as possible when doing deep and slow breathing exercises to reduce pain or relieve stress. Combining breathing exercises with yoga relaxation techniques can provide an effective combination for reducing sympathetic responses.

---

488   Busch, V., et al. "The Effect of Deep and Slow Breathing on Pain Perception, Autonomic Activity, and Mood Processing -- An Experimental Study." *Pain Medicine* 13.2 (2012): 215-228.

The Excitable Brain & Anxiety Connection

Fluctuations of the breath are not only reflected in our emotions and pain thresholds, they also shape our cognitive function. The brain and the breath are intimately linked, as are thoughts and emotions. The moment you change your thinking, your breathing pattern will alter, and vice versa.

To begin to understand the influence of the breath on the functioning of the brain, it is important to remember that respiration is all about the body and brain's access to and use of energy (see Chapter Two). While the brain accounts for only about 2% of your body's weight, it uses a hugely disproportionate amount of energy. In a resting state, it is responsible for around 20% of your entire oxygen and calorie consumption.[489,490]

The human brain has about one hundred billion nerve cells (or neurons). Neurons are specialised cells that conduct nerve impulses, the electrical signals that communicate between cells. These neurons generate electrical impulses in the brain in response to stimuli as a product of neuronal excitability.[491]

We generally identify with the brain's idiosyncrasies as part of our identity because its function is so tied to our behaviour, experience, and responses. We identify with the chemical patterns in our brains with statements like, "I am an anxious person," or "I tend to overthink things." This connects the breath, the brain, and the ego in a way that doesn't necessarily reflect reality.

Some people have highly excitable neurons while others have much calmer brains. Higher excitability means neurons fire more frequently,

489 Attwell, David, and Simon B. Laughlin. "An Energy Budget for Signaling in the Grey Matter of the Brain." *Journal of Cerebral Blood Flow & Metabolism* 21.10 (2001): 1133-1145.

490 Raichle, Marcus E., and Debra A. Gusnard. "Appraising the Brain's Energy Budget." *Proceedings of the National Academy of Sciences* 99.16 (2002): 10237-10239.

491 Vecchio, Fabrizio, Francesca Miraglia, and Paolo Maria Rossini. 2019. "Tracking Neuronal Connectivity from Electric Brain Signals to Predict Performance." *The Neuroscientist* 25.1 (2019): 86-93.

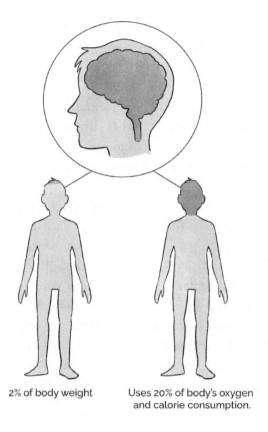

2% of body weight   Uses 20% of body's oxygen
                         and calorie consumption.

producing more electrical impulses.[492] A 2021 paper that examines neuronal excitability in relation to the diagnosis and treatment of mental illness explains that those with the lowest levels of neuronal excitability are the least likely to develop psychiatric symptoms. Their nervous systems, when disrupted by stress, react slowly, and recover quickly. At the other extreme, those people with the highest levels of neuronal excitability have nervous systems that are highly reactive to stress, and they recover slowly from it. They are likely to experience psychiatric symptoms constantly. The paper's author, Michael Raymond Binder, a psychiatrist at Northshore University, explains that this neuronal

492 Xie, Rou-Gang, et al. "Characterization of Different Types of Excitability in Large Somatosensory Neurons and Its Plastic Changes in Pathological Pain States." *International Journal of Molecular Sciences* 19.1 (2018): 161.

hyperexcitability can be elusive because it involves microcircuitry in the brain rather than specific areas of the brain.[493]

How does this relate to our experience and our susceptibility to anxiety, panic, and chronic stress? Binder says – "When the neurons are hyperexcitable, the mind replays thoughts like a broken record. It causes the mind to keep rethinking things, holding on to anger, ruminating about the past, and second-guessing oneself. Anticipating the next emotionally traumatic experience, the mind maintains an overly defensive posture."[494]

There are a variety of factors that can affect the level of neuron excitability. For example, the excitability of your brain's nerve cells changes when you're in pain.[495] There is a bidirectional link between anxiety and stress and high neuronal excitability.[496] Depression is also associated with hyperexcitable neurons, and those born with hyperexcitable neurons are more vulnerable to depression.[497]

Binder's paper explains that neuronal hyperexcitability drives a subtle but noticeable increase in resting respiratory and heart rates.[498] It has been suggested that a resting respiratory rate faster than 15 breaths per minute indicates a predisposition to neuronal hyperexcitability.

493 Binder, Michael Raymond. "The Neuronal Excitability Spectrum: A New Paradigm in the Diagnosis, Treatment, and Prevention of Mental Illness and Its Relation to Chronic Disease." *American Journal of Clinical and Experimental Medicine* 9.6 (2021): 187-203.

494 Binder, Michael Raymond. "The Neuronal Excitability Spectrum: A New Paradigm in the Diagnosis, Treatment, and Prevention of Mental Illness and Its Relation to Chronic Disease." *American Journal of Clinical and Experimental Medicine* 9.6 (2021): 187-203.

495 Xie, Rou-Gang, et al. "Characterization of Different Types of Excitability in Large Somatosensory Neurons and Its Plastic Changes in Pathological Pain States." *International Journal of Molecular Sciences* 19.1 (2018): 161.

496 "Anxiety and Amygdalar Hyperexcitability. The Chicken Or the Egg?" *Austin Publishing Group.* (n.d.) http://www.austinpublishinggroup.com/depression-anxiety/fulltest/depression-v2-id1038.php (Accessed July 14, 2022).

497 "6 Depression and Neuronal Excitability." *YouTube.* (n.d.) http://www.youtube.com/watch?v=Hm1DICMciMk (Accessed July 2022).

498 Binder, Michael Raymond. "The Neuronal Excitability Spectrum: A New Paradigm in the Diagnosis, Treatment, and Prevention of Mental Illness and Its Relation to Chronic Disease." *American Journal of Clinical and Experimental Medicine* 9.6 (2021): 187-203.

On the flip side, hyperventilation can cause hypocapnia (low blood CO_2), which may heighten neuronal excitability. This causes metabolic demands to increase in the brain, which means that the brain consumes more oxygen and glucose to have the energy it needs to meet those metabolic demands.[499] According to Dr. Artour Rakhimov, when oxygen supply to the brain is reduced due to over-breathing, vasoconstriction, and suppression of the Bohr effect, brain cells become more acidic. This is the result of brain cells switching to anaerobic respiration to make energy, increasing the production of lactic acid. That acidity will further intensify abnormal electrical activity.[500]

People who live longer have fewer active genes related to neural excitation according to recent Harvard research on the ageing process.[501,502] However, of the 20-25,000 genes in the human genome,[503]

499   Zhang, Zhong, Quilian Guo, and E. Wang. "Hyperventilation in Neurological Patients: From Physiology to Outcome Evidence." *Current Opinion in Anaesthesiology* 32.5 (2019): 568.

500   Rakhimov, Arthur. *Breathing and Epilepsy.* (n.d.)

501   "Damping Down Brain Cell Activity May Help Us to Live Longer." *New Scientist.* (n.d.) http://www.newscientist.com/article/2220138-damping-down-brain-cell-activity-may-help-us-to-live-longer/ (Accessed July 14, 2022).

502   Zullo, Joseph M., et al. "Regulation of Lifespan by Neural Excitation and REST." *Nature* 574.7778 (2019): 359-364.

503   "What Is a Gene?: MedlinePlus Genetics." *Medline Plus.* (September 17, 2020). http://www.medlineplus.gov/genetics/understanding/basics/gene/ (Accessed July 14, 2022).

only a fraction are "switched on" at any given time.[504] Amazingly, this means that we may be able to choose which genes are active using simple stress-reducing techniques like breath training and meditation.

There's an interesting connection here. Traditional yogic ideas suggest that the breath is the root of thought, and that when a yogi learns to breathe less, he or she will enjoy a longer life. The Harvard study raises the possibility that meditation (and perhaps breathing exercises) could increase longevity precisely because they reduce neuronal excitability and the kind of repetitive, negative thoughts described by Binder. This is not to say you should bulldoze through life without thinking. More accurately, it is that you must work to refine the quality, direction, and purpose of your thoughts and develop the ability to quieten your mind when you need to.

Brain Waves & the Breath

The electrical activity the brain generates in response to what happens within the body, and in the external environment, is rhythmic. These brain waves occur in different areas of the brain. Depending on which circuits are lighting up, different brain functions are enhanced or inhibited.

The breath has long been linked with the generation of those brain waves. In 1912, William James wrote in his *Essays in Radical Empiricism*:

> "The 'I think' which Kant said must be able to accompany all my objects, is the 'I breathe' which actually does accompany them. Breath is the essence out of which philosophers have constructed the entity known to them as consciousness."[505]

---

504 "Can Genes Be Turned On and Off in Cells?: MedlinePlus Genetics." *Medline Plus*. (n.d.) http://www.medlineplus.gov/genetics/understanding/howgeneswork/geneonoff/ (Accessed July 14, 2022).

505 James, William, Fredson Bowers, and Ignas K. Skrupskelis. *Essays in Radical Empiricism*. Vol. 3. Harvard University Press, 1976.

More recently, research in 2020 demonstrated that the rhythm of the breath, as maintained by the breathing muscles, interacts with brain waves in a bi-directional manner. That is, the breath affects the rhythm of neural oscillations, and the rhythms in the brain affect the breath.[506] What's more, brain activity differs depending on whether or not breathing is consciously controlled. Various studies suggest that controlled breathing plays a special role in mediating organisation in the brain, enhancing movement patterns[507] and synchrony in the areas of the brain responsible for movement.[508] The brain's processing of sensory signals can also be strongly influenced by the breath, as in the case of pain perception.[509]

There are five basic types of brain waves that range from very slow to very fast.

Delta	Drowsiness, trance, deeply relaxed
Theta	Drifting, trance-like state
Alpha	Relaxation, inner awareness, balance
Beta	Focus, relaxed alertness, mental activities, high beta waves associated with anxiety.
Gamma	Information-rich task processing, thinking

A systematic review of EEG studies exploring the impact of mindfulness meditation on brainwaves revealed that this meditative practice was most commonly associated with enhanced alpha and theta power when compared to an eyes-closed resting state.

506 Kluger, Daniel S., and Gross Joachim. "Depth and Phase of Respiration Modulate Cortico-Muscular Communication." *Neuroimage* 222 (2020): 117272.

507 Boyadzhieva, Asena, and Ezgi Kayhan. "Keeping the Breath in Mind: Respiration, Neural Oscillations, and the Free Energy Principle." *Frontiers in Neuroscience* (2021) 742.

508 Herrero, Jose L., et al. "Breathing Above the BrainStem: Volitional Control and Attentional Modulation in Humans." *Journal of Neurophysiology.* (2018).

509 Boyadzhieva, Asena, and Ezgi Kayhan. "Keeping the Breath in Mind: Respiration, Neural Oscillations, and the Free Energy Principle." *Frontiers in Neuroscience* (2021) 742.

- **Alpha brain waves** are produced when a person is not focusing too hard on anything in particular and is likely feeling relatively calm and relaxed.
- **Theta brain waves** are produced when a person is in a light sleep or extremely relaxed.

The authors proposed this co-presence of elevated alpha and theta may signify a state of relaxed alertness, due to increased inwardly directed attention, that is, to the self-regulated act of breathing.[510]

Similarly, in 2009, Lagopoulos and colleagues used EEGs to monitor changes during 20 minutes of non-directive meditation. They found that theta power was greater throughout the brain but particularly in the front and temporal–central areas compared to the rear regions of the brain. Also, alpha power was greater across all brain regions but especially in the back compared to the front of the brain. This indicated a shift away from frontal lobe activity such as thinking and attention.[511] This accords with non-directive meditation that allows for spontaneous thoughts, images, scenes, sensations, etc., as opposed to directive meditation, where your mind is directed to focus on something particular or a task such as breathing where frontal lobe activity is likely to increase.[512]

While increased alpha power is a consistent finding across these reviews and studies, other changes in brainwaves are not always consistent and may depend on the type of meditation or breathing exercise.

510   Lomas, T., I. Ivtzan, and C. H. Fu. "A Systematic Review of the Neurophysiology of Mindfulness on EEG Oscillations." *Neuroscience & Biobehavioral Reviews* 57 (2015): 401-410.

511   Lagopoulos, J., et al. "Increased Theta and Alpha EEG Activity During Non-Directive Meditation." *Journal of Alternative and Complementary Medicine* 15.11 (2009): 1187-1192.

512   Xu, Jian, et al. "Nondirective Meditation Activates Default Mode Network and Areas Associated with Memory Retrieval and Emotional Processing." *Frontiers in Human Neuroscience* 86 (2014).

BREATH TRAINING FOR DISSOLVING STRESS, ANXIETY, & PANIC

Whether or not you have a diagnosable anxiety disorder, you undoubt-edly experience stress, as it's unavoidable in our modern world. Therefore, the breath training guidelines below are beneficial for every-one. When high-stress or anxiety-triggering situations happen, you might not be in a position to focus on your breathing straight away, but, when you incorporate breath training into your daily life, you cul-tivate breath awareness. This breath awareness in combination with an understanding of the link between breathing and stress, will make you more likely to bring your attention back to your breath after just a few minutes. This, in turn, will help you respond better to the situation and to recover more quickly from the negative effects of stress.

If you do suffer with chronic stress, panic disorder, or any other anxiety disorder, by addressing the biochemical triggers, it is possible to reduce neuronal excitability, reliably take control over your symptoms, and shift into a calmer state both short and long-term. You don't need expensive capnography training to do this. Simply breathing through the nose and into the diaphragm will calm the nervous system and increase resilience. So too will practising small breath holds, or softening, slowing, and reducing your breathing volume to the point where you feel a light air hunger. This signifies that CO_2 has increased in the blood. If you would like a specific breath exercise to practise daily, we recommend the OA™ Exercise: Breathing Recovery, Sitting, outlined on page 67. This is your emergency exercise for when the mind and breath are agitated.

An additional beneficial method for down-regulating the nervous system is simply lengthening your exhalation. This can be done both in moments of stress and frequently throughout the day. For a greater effect, practise the below exercise 'Increase the Out:In Ratio' for five to ten minutes, three times daily. This is a simple, efficient exercise to calm your body and mind, and relieve anxiety. It involves longer exhalations to activate your vagus nerve. The vagus nerve is the main driver of the parasympathetic 'rest and digest' nervous system. It is stimulated during the out-breath, triggering the relaxation response. It does this by secreting the chemical messenger acetylcholine, which slows your heart.

Increase the Out: In Ratio (An Exercise for Anxiety)

This exercise can be practised seated or lying down. It is a version of anuloma prāṇāyāma, which can be found in Chapter Sixteen.

- Begin by following your breath. As you do this, your breathing may naturally become slower.
- Follow your breath for 5 rounds, silently in and out through the nose.
- Now, in your head, begin to count the length of your inhale and exhale.
- Depending on your starting point, you can proceed to lengthen the exhalation in one of the following ways:

  1. If your inhale is longer than your exhale, try to equalise the breaths so the in and out phases have a 1:1 ratio.
  2. If your inhale and exhale are equal, work to make the exhalation twice as long. You can achieve this either by shortening the inhalation and/or by prolonging the exhalation.
  3. If your inhale is already shorter than your exhale, work to lengthen the out-breath even more. You can bring your breathing ratio to 1:3 or 1:4 and so on.

- Make sure you stay relaxed. Don't change the breathing ratios too much or too quickly. The exercise should be free from strain. You can continue the practise for 5 to 10 minutes.

Numerous studies have shown that the inhale/exhale ratio can affect our responses to both predictable and unexpected stress. In one study, scientists compared different patterns of breathing. A rate of six breaths per minute with a two-second inhalation and an eight-second exhalation

Follow your breath.
It may become slower.

Silently breathe in and out
through your nose for 5 breaths.

Begin to count the length of your inhale and exhale.

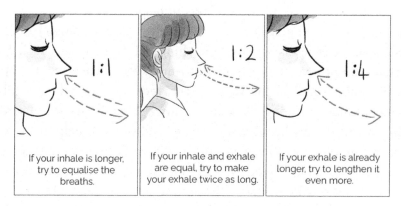

If your inhale is longer,
try to equalise the
breaths.

If your inhale and exhale
are equal, try to make
your exhale twice as long.

If your exhale is already
longer, try to lengthen it
even more.

Stay relaxed. You can continue the practise for 5 to 10 minutes.

was found to help deal with stress triggered by a small electric shock.[513] Another study compared this 2:8 ratio with Tactical Breathing, a stress-management technique taught to Navy SEALS. The 2:8 breathing was found to be more effective.[514]

513 Cappo, Bruce M., et al. "The Utility of Prolonged Respiratory Exhalation for Reducing Physiological and Psychological Arousal in Non-Threatening and Threatening Situations." *Journal of Psychosomatic Research* 28.4 (1984): 265-273.

514 Rottger, Stefan, et al. "The Effectiveness of Combat Tactical Breathing as Compared With Prolonged Exhalation." *Applied Psychophysiology and Biofeedback* 46.1 (2021): 19-28.

Those people who are most stressed will find slow breathing most difficult. Not everyone will be able to achieve an eight-second exhalation. Remember, up to 75% of people with anxiety already have dysfunctional breathing.[515,516,517,518] This is why it is vital to tailor exercises based on the BOLT score. For someone with a very low breath hold time, it is better to slow the breathing using a three-second inhalation and a three-second exhalation. You can also use small breath holds to stimulate the vagus nerve. Either option is better than pushing someone to achieve very slow breathing before they are ready.

Benefits of Breath Retraining for Anxiety

As you practise the above methods to help improve breathing from a biochemical dimension, you will reduce your sensitivity to CO_2, normalise CO_2 levels, and your breathing will naturally become lighter. This will improve blood circulation and oxygen delivery to the body and brain, stimulate the vagus nerve, reduce neuronal excitability, and produce a calming effect on the mind. If you have panic disorder, biochemical breath exercises can be additionally helpful because when you purposefully create small, tailored doses of air hunger, you desensitise yourself to the fear of suffocation that perpetuates panic.

Another notable benefit of breath training for stress and anxiety is it empowers you to take control over your nervous system, as well as

515 Kiesel, Kyle et al. "Development of a Screening Protocol to Identify Individuals with Dysfunctional Breathing." International journal of sports physical therapy vol. 12,5 (2017): 774-786.

516 Hibbert, George, and David Pilsbury. "Hyperventilation in panic attacks: Ambulant monitoring of transcutaneous carbon dioxide." *The British Journal of Psychiatry* 153.1 (1988): 76-80.

517 Spinhoven, Ph, et al. "Hyperventilation and panic attacks in general hospital patients." *General hospital psychiatry* 15.3 (1993): 148-154.

518 Courtney, Rosalba. "Multi-dimensional model of dysfunctional breathing and integrative breathing therapy–commentary on the functions of breathing and its dysfunctions and their relationship to breathing therapy." *J Yoga Phys Ther* 6.4 (2016): 257.

your emotional and physical state. A new study by Stanford University School of Medicine and published in the journal *Science* helps to shed some light on how this happens. The scientists found there are a handful of nerve cells in the brainstem that connect breathing to states of mind. In other words, part of the brain is spying on your breathing and when you breathe a little harder and faster, the brain goes into sympathetic stress mode to protect the body. Conversely, by utilising the breathing patterns outlined above, you will activate the relaxation response, calm down the nervous system, and dramatically reduce anxiety and panic attacks.

CHAPTER TWENTY-ONE

THE NASAL CYCLE & UNI-NOSTRIL BREATHING

In this chapter, we will explore the nasal cycle and the impact of one-sided or "uni-nostril" breathing on the brain and body, from both yogic and scientific points of view. We will also describe ways you can engage the potential of the nasal cycle by incorporating certain practices in your yoga or meditation practice, or indeed daily life.

As already stated, given the pace of modern life, many of us find ourselves feeling overwhelmed, stressed, or anxious more often than we would like. With that in mind, we will explore in more detail how you may use your breath to switch into calmer, more relaxed states.

Before we jump in, it's important to remember the importance of nasal breathing in general, and to understand why it is superior to mouth breathing.

NASAL BREATHING & BRAIN EXCITABILITY

There are significant differences in your brain and nervous system functions depending on whether you breathe through your nose or your mouth. Nasal breathing enhances brain functions,[519] whereas faster and

---

519 Jung, Ju-Yeon, and Chang-Ki Kang. "Investigation on the Effect of Oral Breathing on Cognitive Activity Using Functional Brain Imaging." *Healthcare*. Vol. 9. No. 6. MDPI, 2021.

harder breathing through the mouth can result in neurons in the limbic system firing in a disorganised way.[520] The limbic system is the part of the brain involved in behavioural and emotional responses. The nose is closely linked with the limbic system, mediating emotion, memory, and behaviour.[521] The brain, by regulating breathing, controls its own excitability.[522] When neurons fire chaotically in this area of the brain you will likely feel "all over the place." This is one reason why meditative traditions promote the practice of *nasal breathing* for brain health. Not surprisingly, nasal breathing improves emotional judgement and recognition memory[523] (the ability to recognize previously encountered people, objects, or events).

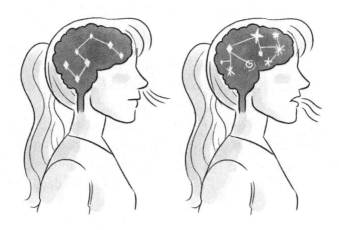

520   Zelano, Christina, et al. "Nasal respiration entrains human limbic oscillations and modulates cognitive function." *Journal of Neuroscience* 36.49 (2016): 12448-12467.

521   Zelano, Christina, et al. "Nasal respiration entrains human limbic oscillations and modulates cognitive function." *Journal of Neuroscience* 36.49 (2016): 12448-12467.

522   Balestrino M, Somjen GG. Concentration of carbon dioxide, interstitial pH and synaptic transmission in hippocampal formation of the rat. J Physiol. 1988 Feb;396:247-66

523   Zelano, Christina, et al. "Nasal respiration entrains human limbic oscillations and modulates cognitive function." *Journal of Neuroscience* 36.49 (2016): 12448-12467.

THE LEFT/RIGHT NASAL CYCLE

Throughout the 24-hour day, your nostrils go through cycles of congestion and decongestion. During each phase of the cycle, one nostril will block as the other becomes more open.[524] The dominant nostril switches from right to left and vice versa every 1.5 to 5 hours, as the erectile tissue within the nose expands and contracts.[525,526] This one-sided congestion and decongestion was first noted in 1895, by the German physician Richard Kayser. This process has since been called the *nasal cycle*.[527] Although the physical mechanisms of the nasal cycle have been identified, the physiological mechanisms that drive it are not as well understood.[528,529]

This nasal cycle is present in 70-80% of all healthy adults. It is controlled by the autonomic nervous system and thought to be regulated by a small area in the brain called the hypothalamus. The nasal cycle may exist to allow nasal mucus to rehydrate, maintaining the humidifying effects of nasal breathing on inhaled air. It is thought to allow for better accumulation of nitric oxide. And it may reflect the dynamic balance in the autonomic nervous system.[530]

The nasal cycle also influences the levels and activities of hormones and neurotransmitters in the body. For example, conscious unilateral nostril breathing changes the rate of involuntary blinking, which is directly related to the activity of the neurotransmitter dopamine [531].

524 Pendolino, Alfonso Luca, et al. "The Nasal Cycle: A Comprehensive Review." *Rhinology Online* 1.1 (2018): 67-76.

525 Ley, Ronald, and Beverly H. Timmons. *Behavioral and Psychological Approaches to Breathing Disorders.* Springer Science & Business Media, 1994.

526 Atanasov, A. "Length of Periods in the Nasal Cycle During 24-Hours Registration." *Open Journal of Biophysics* 4 (2014): 93-96.

527 Eccles, R. "Nasal Airflow in Health and Disease." *Acta Otolaryngol* 120 (2000): 580-595.

528 White, D. E., J. Bartley, and R. J. Nates. "Model Demonstrates Functional Purpose of the Nasal Cycle." *Biomedical Engineering Online* 14.38 (2015): 1-11.

529 Price, A., and R. Eccles. "Nasal Airflow and Brain Activity: Is There a Link?" *The Journal of Laryngology and Otology* 130.9 (2016): 794-799. doi:10.1017/S0022215116008537.

530 Pendolino, Alfonso Luca, et al. "The Nasal Cycle: A Comprehensive Review." *Rhinology Online* 1.1 (2018): 67-76.

531 Kumaran, Elangovan Muthu. "Alteration in Nasal Cycle Rhythm as an Index of the Diseased Condition." in *Pathophysiology: Altered Physiological States*, edited by David C. Gaze, 23-34. London: InTech, 2018.

Yogis have described the nasal cycle for hundreds of years. Yogic theory consistently highlights important links between the nostrils and the psyche.[532] Nostril dominance has been associated with greater activity in opposite sides of the brain. When airflow is freer through the right nostril, the left brain is more active. When the left nostril is open, activity increases in the right brain. This relationship has been analysed using conscious single-nostril breathing.[533]

The synchronisation of brain waves with the nasal cycle also occurs during sleep.[534] Throughout the night, the nasal cycle commonly reverses when you shift position and during rapid eye movement (REM) sleep (a stage of sleep associated with dreaming and memory consolidation). When you lie on your side, although your nasal cycle will persist, nasal resistance will increase in the nostril nearest the pillow.[535]

A 2018 study of 21 healthy, right-handed men found differences in sleep quality during right and left nostril dominance. The researchers manipulated nostril dominance by observing the men for three nights. On the first night, they breathed naturally with no nasal obstruction. On the second night, the right nostril was blocked, and, on the third night, the left was blocked. When breathing was through the right nostril, sleep duration and deep sleep (non-REM stage 3 sleep) duration were greater. During left nostril dominance, sleep apnea symptoms (number of apneas, oxygen desaturation, and limb movements) were more severe.[536]

---

532 Ley, Ronald, and Beverly H. Timmons. *Behavioral and Psychological Approaches to Breathing Disorders.* Springer Science & Business Media, 1994.

533 Werntz, D. A., Bickford R. G., Bloom F. E., and D. S. Shannahoff-Khalsa. "Alternating Cerebral Hemispheric Activity and the Lateralization of Autonomic Nervous Function." *Human Neurobiology* 2.1 (1983): 39-43.

534 Werntz, D. A., Bickford R. G., Bloom F. E., and D. S. Shannahoff-Khalsa. "Alternating Cerebral Hemispheric Activity and the Lateralization of Autonomic Nervous Function." *Human Neurobiology* 2.1 (1983): 39-43.

535 Cole, Philip, and James S. J. Haight. "Posture and the Nasal Cycle." *Annals of Otology, Rhinology & Laryngology* 95.3 (1986): 233-237.

536 Ozturk, Deniz, et al. "The Effect of Unilateral Forced Nostril Breathing on Sleep in Healthy Right-Handed Men: A Preliminary Report." *Sleep and Breathing* 22.3 (2018): 769 772.

The nasal cycle does not occur during slow wave sleep (the deep sleep stage during which the mind and body rebuild and recover). It is also likely that if you have obstructive sleep apnea (OSA), your nasal cycle will not function during the night. One study suggests this may be because people with OSA have altered physiology in the nasal cavities, but it's equally likely the nasal cycle is compromised because people with sleep-disordered breathing tend to breathe through an open mouth.[537] Please see Chapter Twenty-two *Breathing, Sleep and Yoga* for further information.

YOGIC THEORY & THE BREATH

To understand the influence of the nasal cycle on your body, we need to revisit a branch of the autonomic nervous system called the *parasympathetic nervous system* (PNS), which controls relaxation and rest and digest functions. Remember, the ANS is responsible for maintaining balance (homeostasis) in the body's internal environment. This balance is mediated by the vagus nerve.

As noted above, in yogic theory, the ANS is affected by which nostril is dominant. When inhalation is through the right nostril and the left hemisphere of the brain is active, the sympathetic nervous system activates. This is excitatory and enlivening. During left nostril dominance, when the right side of the brain is stimulated, the body is in a more parasympathetic "rest and digest" state. This has a calm, stabilising effect.[538] A balance between the two branches of the autonomic nervous system makes us best able to deal with the challenges of daily life. This, in itself, provides one explanation for the existence of the nasal cycle.[539]

537 Li, Yun, et al. "0437 Differences of Electroencephalogram Activity During Nonrapid Eye Movement Sleep Between Objective and Subjective Daytime Sleepiness in Sleep Apnea Patients." *Sleep* 42.Supplement 1 (2019): A176-A177.

538 Pendolino, Alfonso Luca, et al. "The Nasal Cycle: A Comprehensive Review." *Rhinology Online* 1.1 (2018): 67-76.

539 Ley, Ronald, and Beverly H. Timmons. *Behavioral and Psychological Approaches to Breathing Disorders.* Springer Science & Business Media, 1994.

This balance between the sympathetic and parasympathetic nervous systems reflects the ancient yogic concept of nadis, energy channels within the body. The nostrils represent the end points of two of the most important nadis, the *ida* and *pingala nadis*. Both begin at the base of the spine and run up the central axis of the body, crossing over each other at each major chakra. Ida nadi ends at the left nostril, and pingala nadi at the right.

These two nadis are considered to have the same sun/moon significance of masculine and feminine energy that pervades many yogic ideas. Ida nadi (left nostril) is related to the moon, to feminine energy and right brain dominance. This corresponds with parasympathetic activation. Pingala nadi (right nostril) is associated with the masculine sun, and left-brain dominance. This is consistent with sympathetic activation. The third main nadi, sushumna nadi, ends in the centre of the face, where the septum meets the upper lip. When this nadi is activated,

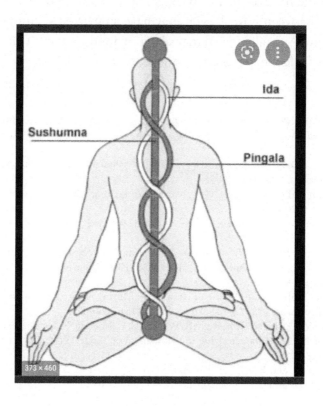

nostril dominance is equal, and the brain comes into balance.[540] This represents balance in the autonomic nervous system. The benefits of alternate nostril breathing/nadi shodhana on cardiopulmonary, autonomic and cognitive functioning are well established.[541]

ALTERING NASAL DOMINANCE

The ideal nasal cycle would involve an identical balance between nostrils with total nasal airflow remaining constant. This "perfect" nasal cycle is rarely found, for a number of reasons.[542] First, both the amplitude and frequency of the nasal cycle decrease with age.[543,544] Second, a deviated nasal septum can compromise the nasal cycle.[545] After exercise, spontaneous changes in the nasal cycle also increase in amplitude.

Fortunately, you don't generally notice your nasal cycle as total nasal airflow remains relatively constant.[546] If you notice your breath switching between nostrils, you may have a deviated septum or nasal obstruction. A single nostril may also remain dominant if you have a respiratory infection or allergic rhinitis.[547]

540 "What Are Nadis? Here's Your In-Depth Guide to These Energy Channels." *Yogi Approved.* (August 2 2020). http://www.yogiapproved.com/nadis-101/ (Accessed July 14, 2022).

541 Ghiya, S. (2017). Alternate nostril breathing: a systematic review of clinical trials. *Int J Res Med Sci*, 5(8), 3273-3286.

542 Pendolino, Alfonso Luca, et al. "The Nasal Cycle: A Comprehensive Review." *Rhinology Online* 1.1 (2018): 67-76.

543 Hasegawa, M., and E. B. Kern. "The Human Nasal Cycle." *Mayo Clinic Proceedings*, 1977.

544 Hasegawa, M., and E. B. Kern. "Variations in Nasal Resistance in Man: A Rhinomanometric Study of the Nasal Cycle in 50 Human Subjects." *Rhinology* 16.1 (1978): 19-29.

545 Kimura, Akihiro, et al. "Phase of Nasal Cycle During Sleep Tends to be Associated With Sleep Stage." *The Laryngoscope* 123.8 (2013): 2050-2055.

546 Kahana-Zweig, R., M. Geva-Sagiv, A. Weissbrod, L. Secundo, N. Soroker, and N. Sobel. "Measuring and Characterizing the Human Nasal Cycle." *PLoS One* 11.10 (2016): e0162918.

547 Ley, Ronald, and Beverly H. Timmons. *Behavioral and Psychological Approaches to Breathing Disorders.* Springer Science & Business Media, 1994.

You can check which nostril is dominant by doing the "fogging" test. Hold your smartphone under your nose, with the screen upward. Breathe normally through your nose onto the screen, then look at the size of the halo under each nostril. This will show you immediately which nostril is freer. It is useful to practise this before and after breath-holding exercises to see the difference in your breathing.

Traditionally, alternate nostril breathing exercises such as nadi shodhana are used to purify the nadis and open each nostril. Practising prāṇāyāma can alter the dominance of nasal airflow by allowing the practitioner to develop voluntary control of which nostril is active.[548] Part of this voluntary control is the ability to open the nose. There are three proven ways to open the nose:

- Breath holding
- Physical exercise with the mouth closed
- Sex

There are many breath holding exercises in Oxygen Advantage®. Box Breathing (Sama vritti) may also open the nose through its consecutive breath holds after inhalation and exhalation. The activation of each branch of the nervous system on the inhale and exhale, along with the breath holds, may bring a balance to the brain by opening both nostrils. This may be why Box Breathing creates a calm alertness.

THE AUTONOMIC NERVOUS SYSTEM & UNI-NOSTRIL BREATHING

The correlation of uninostril breathing and other bodily systems, notably the parasympathetic nervous system, has been of interest to yoga and meditation practitioners for centuries. In more recent years, this phenomenon has attracted scientific attention too. To elucidate

---

548 Ley, Ronald, and Beverly H. Timmons. 1994. *Behavioral and Psychological Approaches to Breathing Disorders.* Springer Science & Business Media.

this relationship, researchers have monitored cardio-respiratory measures such as heart rate, blood pressure, and respiratory rate. Heart rate variability (HRV), vagal tone, and baroreceptor sensitivity have also been studied. Please see Chapter Nine if you would like revisit the nervous system and its interconnection with the breath in more detail.

As a reminder, HRV is an indicator of heart health and cardiovascular fitness. It is the measure of the change in timing between successive heartbeats and is affected by the sympathetic and parasympathetic nervous systems. People are more resilient, physically and emotionally, when HRV is higher and more complex.[549] HRV is considered a reliable measure of vagal tone (which indicates how well the vagus nerve is working). Vagal tone, itself, is frequently used to assess heart function and is also useful in assessing emotional regulation and other processes that alter, or are altered by, changes in parasympathetic activity.

Baroreceptor sensitivity is also an important cardio-respiratory indicator. The baroreflex is a homeostatic function that helps maintain blood pressure at healthy, near-constant levels. All major blood vessels contain pressure baroreceptors. When blood pressure rises, the baroreflex immediately causes the blood vessels to dilate and the heart rate to drop. Conversely, when blood pressure falls, the baroreflex ensures the blood vessels constrict and heart rate increases.[550]

In a 2022 study of left uninostril yogic breathing (chandra anuloma viloma prāṇāyāma), participants demonstrated a significantly reduced respiratory rate, pulse rate, systolic blood pressure, and diastolic blood pressure, as well as a significant increase in vital capacity and peak expiratory flow rate. The study involved 106 healthy young individuals who performed two weeks of left nostril breathing exercise for 45 minutes daily (from 9:00 am to 9:45 am). The authors note that the breathing practice may increase vagal tone and improve baroreceptor

549 Lehrer, P. M., and R. Gevirtz. "Heart Rate Variability Biofeedback: How and Why Does It Work?" *Frontiers in Psychology* 756 (2014).

550 Lehrer, P. M., and R. Gevirtz. "Heart Rate Variability Biofeedback: How and Why Does It Work?" *Frontiers in Psychology* 756 (2014).

Left Nostril Breathing

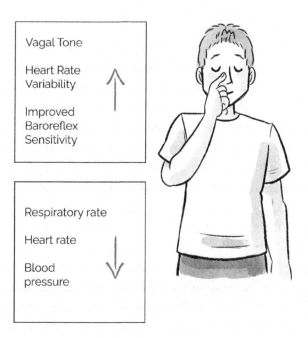

sensitivity, to which they attribute the changes in the cardiovascular markers.[551]

These findings are consistent with an earlier study carried out by Krushna Pal and colleagues in 2014. A total of 85 volunteers were divided into three groups (the unilateral left-nostril breathing had 30 participants). Each group practised for one hour every day for six weeks. The study aimed to understand the effects of right nostril breathing and left nostril breathing on autonomic functions, which they assessed via heart rate variability and cardiovascular parameters (basal heart rate, systolic and diastolic blood pressure, mean arterial pressure and rate-pressure product).

The study found that the short-term practice of left nostril breathing improved vagal tone, increased heart rate variability, and promoted the

551 Bargal, S., V. Nalgirkar, A. Patil, and D. Langade. "Evaluation of the Effect of Left Nostril Breathing on Cardiorespiratory Parameters and Reaction Time in Young Healthy Individuals." *Cureus* 14.2 (2022): e22351.

cardiovascular health of the study participants. Conversely, the practice of right nostril breathing increased sympathetic activity, blood pressure, and mean arterial pressure.[552]

A smaller study of 22 patients with high blood pressure had similar findings. They were taught to perform unilateral left nostril breathing by a qualified yoga instructor with a regularity of six breaths per minute for 27 rounds.[553] The researchers concluded that left uninostril breathing reduces heart rate and systolic blood pressure in hypertensive patients on regular standard medical management. They proposed that this may be due to normalising autonomic cardiovascular rhythms with increased vagal modulation and/or decreased sympathetic activity along with improved baroreflex sensitivity.

Breathing through the left nostril has also been shown to correspond with a reduced sympathetic outflow to certain sweat glands compared to breathing through the right nostril. In a study by Telles and colleagues, 48 participants were randomly assigned to different groups. Each group was asked to practise one of three prāṇāyāmas (right nostril breathing, left nostril breathing, or alternate nostril breathing). These practices were carried out as 27 respiratory cycles, repeated four times a day for one month. The left nostril prāṇāyāma group showed an increase in volar galvanic skin resistance, interpreted as a reduction in sympathetic nervous system activity supplying the sweat glands. The authors concluded that left uninostril breathing had a relaxing effect on the sympathetic nervous system, bringing about parasympathetic dominance.[554]

These studies show that left uni-nostril breathing can have considerable physiological effects, down-regulating the autonomic nervous

552 Pal, Gopal Krushna, et al. "Slow Yogic Breathing Through Right and Left Nostril Influences Sympathovagal Balance, Heart Rate Variability, and Cardiovascular Risks in Young Adults." *North American Journal of Medical Sciences* 6.3 (2014): 145.

553 Bhavanani, A. B., and S. Z. Madanmohan. "Immediate Effect of Chandra Nadi Prāṇāyāma (Left Unilateral Forced Nostril Breathing) on Cardiovascular Parameters in Hypertensive Patients." *International Journal of Yoga* 5 (2012): 108-111.

554 Telles, S., R. Nagarathna, and H. R. Nagendra. "Breathing Through a Particular Nostril Can Alter Metabolism and Autonomic Activities." *Indian Journal of Physiology and Pharmacology* 38.2 (1994): 133-137.

system. It's worth noting, however, that the type, frequency, and duration of breathing protocols employed in the studies above varied. Further research is required to determine precisely how long the practice should be maintained to achieve benefits, and how long the benefits remain.

THE BRAIN & UNI-NOSTRIL BREATHING

New technologies have enabled researchers to map changes in brain activity during uni-nostril breathing practice. This emerging field of study has yielded some interesting results. Before describing the research, we will begin with a brief overview of relevant brain structures and functions.

The brain has three main regions, the forebrain, the midbrain, and the hindbrain (at the rear of the brain).

The forebrain is the largest, containing the outer layer of the brain, the wrinkly cerebral cortex, which is divided into the left and right cerebral hemispheres. These hemispheres are often referred to in yogic theory of the breath. The forebrain is also home to the limbic system. This important system sits just under the cerebral cortex and is responsible for emotional and behavioural responses. Parts of the limbic system also have a key role in ensuring balance in the body – regulating blood pressure, body temperature, hormone production, and sleep[555].

Each cerebral hemisphere controls movement on the opposite side of the body. The right hemisphere controls movement for the left side of the body, while its left counterpart controls movement for the right side of the body.[556] Although specific areas of the brain are more active than others during certain tasks, the two hemispheres of the brain generally work together and are interdependent.[557]

A few small studies have identified a relationship between nostril dominance during the nasal cycle and activation of the opposite cerebral hemisphere – as proposed by yogic texts. A study by Werntz

---

555 The forebrain – Queensland Brain Institute – University of Queensland (uq.edu.au)
556 Ju, W. *Neuroscience.* 2nd Canadian Edition, 2020.
557 Kaczmarek, B. L. J. "The Life of the Brain." *ACTA Neuropsychologica* 1.1 (2003): 12-21.

in 1983 showed that relatively greater EEG activity in one hemisphere correlates with predominant airflow in the opposite nostril.[558] A small number of other studies have also reported this.[559,560,561] Although these findings are widely quoted in yoga journals, the studies are few, with small numbers of participants.

Scientific investigation of the physiological effects of breathing on the brain has particularly focused on the frontal lobes of the forebrain. The frontal lobes are responsible for *higher executive functions* such as planning, attention, reasoning, and problem solving, along with motor and speech functions.[562]

Executive functions have been described as "the management system of the brain." That's because the skills involved allow us to set goals, plan, organise, manage time, and get things done. These skills

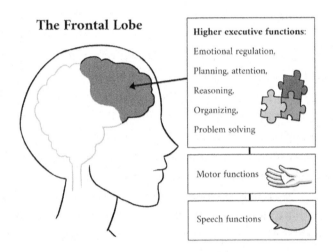

The Frontal Lobe

Higher executive functions:
Emotional regulation,
Planning, attention,
Reasoning,
Organizing,
Problem solving

Motor functions

Speech functions

558 Werntz, D. A., et al. "Alternating Cerebral Hemispheric Activity and the Lateralization of Autonomic Nervous Function." *Human Neurobiology* 2.1 (1983): 39-43.

559 Telles, S., et al. "Yoga Breathing Through a Particular Nostril Is Associated With Contralateral Event-Related Potential Changes." *International Journal of Yoga* 5 (2012): 102-107.

560 Price, A., and R. Eccles. "Nasal Airflow and Brain Activity: Is There a Link?" *The Journal of Laryngology and Otology* 130.9 (2016): 794-799. doi:10.1017/S0022215116008537.

561 Singh, K., et al. "Effect of Uninostril Yoga Breathing on Brain Hemodynamics: A Functional Near-Infrared Spectroscopy Study." *International Journal of Yoga* 9.1 (2016): 12-19.

562 Ju, W. *Neuroscience.* 2nd Canadian Edition, 2020.

are of course essential for daily life, but in modern life, with its many stressors, we can feel stuck in the thinking mind and unable to "switch off." Breathing practices can allow you to shift states, either away from "thinking" functions and into a calmer state of mind, or vice versa.

In 2016, Singh and colleagues sought to measure the effect of unilateral nostril yoga breathing on the frontal lobes of the brain. The study involved 32 right-handed healthy male participants, who each practised right nostril yoga breathing, left nostril yoga breathing, or breath awareness (acting as a control group), for 10 minutes at the same time of the day for three consecutive days, respectively. All the participants had substantial experience in practising the three yoga breathing techniques.

In the study, blood flow in the frontal lobe of the brain was measured for changes in oxygen concentration and blood volume before and during the breathing practices, using a neuroimaging technique called functional near-infrared system. The study found a significant reduction in oxyhaemoglobin (indicating changes in blood flow) in the right prefrontal cortex during left-nostril-breathing and breath awareness. Conversely, right-nostril-breathing led to significant increases in the levels of oxyhaemoglobin and total haemoglobin in the left prefrontal cortex. The authors suggest this change in blood flow and oxygenation in the opposite side of the brain likely reflects the deactivating or relaxing effect of left nostril breathing on the right prefrontal cortex.

In essence, Singh et al. found that the right prefrontal cortex was less active during left-uninostril breathing. They noted that, while the exact mechanism through which uninostril breathing influences brain blood flow is not known, two neurotransmitter systems, serotonin and noradrenaline, were implicated. Serotonin and noradrenaline are known to modulate the function of the prefrontal cortex and may play a role by altering the release of stress hormones (corticotropin releasing hormone and cortisol).[563] Corticotropin-releasing hormone is the primary driver of the body's response to stress. It is also present in

563 Singh, K., H. Bhargav, and T. M. Srinivasan. "Effect of Uninostril Yoga Breathing on Brain Hemodynamics: A Functional Near-Infrared Spectroscopy Study." *International Journal of Yoga* 9.1 (2016): 12-19.

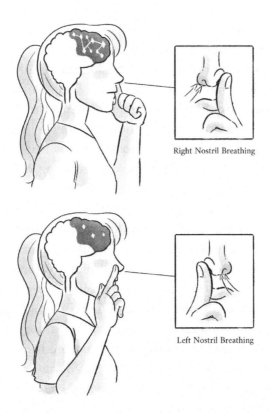

Right Nostril Breathing

Left Nostril Breathing

diseases that cause inflammation. Too much or too little corticotropin-releasing hormone can have a range of negative effects.

It is worth noting that the reduction in oxyhaemoglobin observed in the Singh study could also be seen as an indicator of an increased demand for oxygen in this region of the brain. Whilst the study reported the right prefrontal area of the brain was *less* active during left nostril breathing, other studies have found the opposite – with unilateral or dominant nostril breathing causing *increased* activity in the opposite side of the cerebral hemisphere.[564,565]

564 Werntz, D. A., Bickford R. G., Bloom F. E., and D. S. Shannahoff-Khalsa. "Alternating Cerebral Hemispheric Activity and the Lateralization of Autonomic Nervous Function." *Human Neurobiology* 2.1 (2012): 39-43.

565 Telles, S., M Joshi, and P. Somvanshi. "Yoga Breathing Through a Particular Nostril Is Associated With Contralateral Event-Related Potential Changes." *International Journal of Yoga* 5 (2012): 102-107.

Research carried out by Niazi et al. in 2022, supports the idea that unilateral nostril breathing patterns and nostril dominance influence brain activity. The study involved 30 participants and used EEG to monitor changes in cortical brain activity. Left uni-nostril and non-dominant nostril breathing (usually the left nostril) caused more activity in the rear areas of the brain (on both the left and right sides of the brain) and less activity in the front and central areas of the brain. According to the researchers, activity in the posterior part of the brain is associated with relaxation, restoration, and what they call "eyes-closed conditions."[566]

The Niazi study also found that right uni-nostril or dominant nostril breathing (usually the right) elicited higher activity in the left frontal and left mid regions of the brain. As already noted, the frontal areas of the brain are associated with planning, attention, reasoning, and problem-solving. The regions responsible for these executive functions were found to be more active during right uni-nostril breathing and less active during left nostril breathing.

SCIENTIFIC STUDIES & ANCIENT YOGIC WISDOM

Although scientific attempts to validate what yogis intuitively knew about the breath are intriguing, scientific endeavour in this area of study is fairly new. The available brain imaging studies are often based on a small number of participants and results aren't always consistent. Additional neuroscientific studies will help us better understand brain activation patterns and their relationship with the breath during uni-nostril breathing.

Since ancient times, yogis have understood and appreciated the value of the breath. We still benefit from that intuitive wisdom today. We see it interwoven and adapted in more modern-day approaches to

566 Niazi, Imran Khan, et al. "EEG Signatures Change During Unilateral Yogi Nasal Breathing." *Scientific Reports* 12.1 (2022): 1-13.

breath training or breathing practices. The scientific studies outlined in this chapter largely echo yogic theory.

Your breath is a freely available means to influence your nervous system, allowing you to change states or bring about balance, as desired. In particular, left uni-nostril breathing, or nadi shodhana, has unique potential to calm, still and relax the brain and body and is a wonderful tool to help us manage the pace and demands of modern life.

PRACTISING LEFT UNI-NOSTRIL BREATHING

When your mind is racing, or you feel a little stressed, anxious or overwhelmed, switching to left nostril breathing for even a few minutes may yield many benefits and help you to down-regulate into a calmer, more relaxed mental and bodily state.

The easiest way to breathe only through the left nostril is to block your right nostril with a finger or a small piece of skin-friendly tape to concentrate air flow through the left side of the nose. If your left nostril feels quite congested, practise nose unblocking strategies (see page 65) to decongest the nose. Remember – a deviated septum may also restrict airflow through one side or the other of the nose.

With your right nostril gently taped, you can walk or do chores or work on your computer and get the benefits of a more relaxed state of mind without having to think about your breathing. You may practise your asanas with your right nostril blocked. This has the added benefit of increasing carbon dioxide – thus helping to improve your breathing from a biochemical point of view.

Left uninostril breathing can be especially helpful for those who have difficulty focusing on their breathing. It is normal for some people to get anxious when they bring their attention to their breathing. Instead, they can simply place a small piece of skin-friendly tape across their right nostril and spend some time breathing through the left side of the nose while engaged in everyday activities such as yoga, walking, gardening, watching TV, and working on the computer.

CHAPTER TWENTY-TWO

BREATHING, SLEEP & YOGA

Sleep, like breathing, is something we do throughout our lives. It has its own yogic tradition – Yoga Nidra. Still, how much do you know in general about sleep, sleep health, or how it relates to breathing?

Sleep is an integral part of health, and if quantity or quality is not ideal, day-to-day mood, attention span, wellbeing and even your appearance suffers. There is no better feeling than waking up bright and totally refreshed . . . but many don't have such a great start to their day, as they lift their head from the pillow in a daze, with a groggy feeling akin to a hangover.

So, what constitutes a good night's sleep? Sleep health has been defined as "a multidimensional pattern of sleep-wakefulness, adapted to individual, social, and environmental demands, that promotes physical and mental well-being. Good sleep health is characterized by subjective satisfaction, appropriate timing, adequate duration, high efficiency, and sustained alertness during waking hours."[567] Sustained alertness during waking hours? Isn't that why we drink coffee?!

---

567 Buysse, Daniel J. "Sleep Health: Can We Define It? Does It Matter?" *Sleep* 37.1 (2014): 9-17.

Sleep, breathing & mood

There is a strong interrelationship between sleep, breathing and mood. Understanding this interrelationship is key to learning how to improve our sleep health. It's probably not surprising that happiness research has shown we're more likely to feel satisfied with our lives when the quality of our sleep is good. Scientists suggest that the relationship between happiness and sleep may be bi-directional: if you're generally satisfied with your lot, your sleep is likely to be better, while, conversely, a good night's sleep tends to make you feel more positive.[568]

Likewise, there is a two-way relationship between breathing and emotions. When your breathing is dysfunctional, you're more likely to experience anxiety, chronic stress, and negative, repetitive thoughts. Conversely, when you're stressed, anxious, and ruminating, your breathing is likely to become dysfunctional.

Finally, there's also a two-way relationship between breathing and sleep. When your breathing is a little faster, harder, into the upper chest or through an open mouth, your sleep will suffer, while a bad night's

568 Shin, Ji-eun, and Jung Ki Kim. "How a Good Sleep Predicts Life Satisfaction: The Role of Zero-Sum Beliefs About Happiness." *Frontiers in Psychology* 9 (2018): 1589.

sleep will leave you anxious, stressed, and dehydrated[569] – all states that perpetuate dysfunctional breathing.

Yogis, already appreciative of the importance of the breath, are ideally placed to integrate optimal breathing into daily routines. Integrating light, slow, deep breathing into your yoga practice and everyday habits can be transformative for yoga teachers and students alike.

In this chapter, we will consider the factors that contribute to poor sleep, the impact on mind and body, and the potential for Oxygen Advantage® breathing exercises and yoga to help you achieve a restful night's sleep and awaken feeling refreshed, energized, and ready for whatever the new day brings.

POOR SLEEP & SLEEP DISORDERS

Although what counts as a good night's sleep varies from person to person, many of us simply do not get enough restful sleep. According to a review of the scientific literature by the US National Sleep

---

569 Rosinger, Asher Y., et al. "Short Sleep Duration Is Associated with Inadequate Hydration: Cross-Cultural Evidence from US and Chinese Adults," *Sleep* 42.2 (2019): zsy210.

Foundation, most adults need about seven to nine hours of restful sleep each night.[570] Of course, it's common to have difficulty getting to sleep, or staying asleep from time to time. But if sleep issues occur frequently and begin to impact your day-to-day life, this could indicate a sleep disorder.

Sleep disorders are a group of conditions that affect quality, timing, and amount of sleep on a regular basis. There are different types of sleep disorders, including insomnia, obstructive sleep apnea, parasomnias, narcolepsy, and restless leg syndrome.[571] Unfortunately, in this modern age, sleep disorders are becoming more common. Every year, problems with falling asleep or daytime sleepiness affect approximately 35 to 40% of the U.S. adult population and are a significant cause of illness and death.[572] They have a negative impact on energy, mood, concentration, memory, and overall health. Sleep disorders often occur along with medical conditions or other mental health conditions, such as depression, anxiety, or cognitive disorders.

Unsurprisingly, sleep disorders were amplified by the COVID-19 pandemic. Since the pandemic began, researchers around the world have documented a surge in sleep disorders, with two out of three Americans reporting that they are sleeping either more or less than desired.[573] The first studies of COVID-19-associated sleep disorders were reported in China. Huang and Zhao surveyed 7,236 volunteers (mean age 35.3 years). About a third were health-care workers. About 35% reported symptoms of general anxiety, 20% depression, and 18% poor sleep quality.[574] Upended routines, increased screen time, higher alcohol consumption, and dissolving boundaries between work and private life are just a few of the factors contributing to problems with sleep.

570 https://www.sleepfoundation.org/physical-health. Accessed February 26, 2023.

571 https://www.psychiatry.org/patients-families/sleep-disorders/what-are-sleep-disorders. Accessed February 26, 2023.

572 Hossain, Jamil L., and Colin M. Shapiro. "The prevalence, cost implications, and management of sleep disorders: an overview." *Sleep and Breathing* 6.02 (2002): 085-102.

573 www.apa.org One year later, a new wave of pandemic health concerns. Accessed June 6, 2023.

574 Buysse, Daniel J. "Sleep Health: Can We Define It? Does It Matter?" *Sleep* 37.1 (2014): 9-17.

Many sleep disorders are characterized by abnormal breathing patterns. Breathing too intensely, often through the mouth, can result in many sleep-disordered breathing symptoms, including:

- Snoring
- Sleep apnea
- Disrupted sleep
- Night time asthma symptoms (3-5am)
- Needing to use the bathroom during the night

- Fatigue first thing in the morning
- Dry mouth
- Symptoms upon waking, such as wheezing, coughing, breathlessness or a blocked nose.

How many of these do you experience?

The relationship between nasal obstruction, mouth breathing, snoring and sleep apnea is well documented.[575,576,577] Oxygen Advantage®

575 Kim EJ, et al. "The impacts of open-mouth breathing on upper airway space in obstructive sleep apnea: 3-D MDCT analysis." *Eur Arch Otorhinolaryngol.* 2010 Oct 19.
576 Ohki M, et al. "Relationship between oral breathing and nasal obstruction in patients with obstructive sleep apnea." *Acta Otolaryngol Suppl.* 1996; 523: 228-30.
577 Kreivi HR, et al. "Frequency of upper airway symptoms before and during continuous positive airway pressure treatment in patients with obstructive sleep apnea syndrome." *Respiration.* 2010; 80(6): 488-94.

breathing practices have been successfully implemented to help control these conditions and to activate the bodies rest and digest state – helping ensure a restorative sleep. For a deeper dive of the science, please see the book titled *The Breathing Cure* by Patrick McKeown.

MODERN DAY TECHNOLOGY & OVERSTIMULATED MINDS

It is evident that problems with sleep are significant, widespread, and can have many causes or contributing factors. I can't help but wonder – *did our ancestors have such problems sleeping?* Advances in technology like computers, tablets and smart phones have brought many benefits, allowing us to connect and access information 24/7. For many, they have become indispensable . . . but at what cost?

I would like to explore the topic of over stimulation of the mind, precisely because it is endemic, exacerbates chronic stress and disrupts sleep patterns. Experiment by going to bed with phone in hand and scroll for an hour or so before you drift off. You are likely to wake up feeling tired, even if you have slept for long enough.

It seems like modern day technology, particularly smart phones, have stolen our attention-span and our time, often to the detriment of our wellbeing. The major multinational online platforms continue to invest millions of dollars to devise ways to capture our attention in their quest to make profit.

Phone-use triggers the release of dopamine – a chemical in the brain that makes us feel rewarded. This reinforces the compulsion to continue scrolling. In her book *Dopamine Nation*, psychiatrist Dr Anna Lembke describes the smartphone as "the modern-day hypodermic needle, delivering digital dopamine 24/7 for a wired generation. As such we've all become vulnerable to compulsive overconsumption."[578] Online platforms and advertisers are counting on that drive to keep you compulsively checking your phone and scrolling.

In recent years, the pace of research into sleep health has accelerated: between 2005 and 2018, the number of peer-reviewed sleep journals more than tripled. But even with this increasing positive attention on sleep, according to Dr. David Dinges, Professor of Sleep Studies at Pennsylvania's Perelman School of Medicine, this growth in research has been pushing against a "shoreline of indifference."[579]

Today's culture brings many barriers to attaining a restful night's sleep. The modern workday has increased time pressures. There's more shift work. Supermarkets, airports, and many other workplaces operate 24/7. Western society has embraced the idea that sleep is a waste of time. The need to sleep is almost viewed a sign of weakness.

Those of you who are my vintage are likely to remember feeling bored or switched off while waiting in a queue at the bank (when banks did exist), the post office or for the bus. As I made my way to and from school each day, the bus journey was spent looking out the window daydreaming, bored and in a state of semi rest.

Roll on 35 years, and students taking that same journey are likely to have their faces immersed in phones, fingers flitting from one screen to the other. With all that information screaming for attention, the mind can be no other than over stimulated and exhausted. The feeling of being wired and tired at the same time. The opportunity to have a still mind and enjoy quiet time, maybe even experience boredom, is in short supply in the modern age.

For most people, accessing their phone is the first and last thing they do in their day. Already, it is an ingrained habit, and the data supports this. In 2019, 69% of mobile users reported that they looked at their

---

578 Lembke, Anna. *Dopamine nation: Finding balance in the age of indulgence*. Penguin, 2021.

579 Dr Dinges is quoted in: Worley, Susan L. "The Extraordinary Importance of Sleep: The Detrimental Effects of Inadequate Sleep on Health and Public Safety Drive an Explosion of Sleep Research." *Pharmacy and Therapeutics* 43.12 (2018): 758.

phone in the first five minutes of waking, with a cumulative three hours and 23 minutes spent on the device each day.[580] So, when people say that they don't have enough time for physical or breathing exercise, one could question – *where has all the time gone?*

Digital legacy of the pandemic

The pandemic prompted a surge in internet usage, further cementing reliance on phones. In the UK, once lockdown began to bite, average duration of phone use stretched out to almost 4 hours per day.[581] Online platforms became a lifeline for many during pandemic lockdowns, as people sought out new ways to keep connected, informed, entertained, and fit.

With yoga studios closed, many pivoted to offering classes via on zoom or YouTube. Already popular sites and apps such as YouTube, Snapchat, Instagram, TikTok and Video calling services surged in usage. Remember Zoom quizzes?! Understandably, the pandemic radically changed the way we live, work, and communicate online. Although our lives have largely returned to normal, this has undoubtedly left a digital legacy.

This topic came up the other day during a meeting with four breathing nerds, myself included. One of those present spoke about her young niece staying up to 4am peering into a screen. What hope does the next generation have if this is what they are reducing their life to?

That same day, I had a podcast with Caroline McKenna from the Insta handle *@acountydownunder*. A young woman of 31 years, she is acutely aware of the effects of mobile phone use and how it impacted her sleep. Her strategy to acquire decent shut eye is to put her phone out of reach, locked into a timed safe box so that she doesn't have access to it. I couldn't help but think of how addictive these devices can be

580 Levratto, Valeria, et al. "Smartphones: reading habits and overuse. A qualitative study in Denmark, Lithuania and Spain." *Educación XX1* 24.2 (2021): 167-188.
581 OFCOM Online Nation 2022 Report. June 2022. Accessed February 14, 2023.

to younger people. Out of curiosity, I searched "timed phone boxes" on Amazon, and yes, they exist in plentiful. Imagine – jails for mobile phones!

Impact on attention span

With information overload and limited attention spans, brains are trained to skim the surface, to cherry pick information that interests them but to read nothing at any great depth. People read so differently now and deep reading that we practised for centuries is now replaced by shallow forms of reading.[582] Reading for the fun of it is at an all-time low. In 2018, it was reported that the share of Americans who read for pleasure on a given day has fallen by more than 30% with total reading times averaging 17 minutes per day. Furthermore, data from the Pew Research Center and Gallup have shown that the share of adults not reading any book in a given year nearly tripled between 1978 and 2014.[583]

I believe the demise of the paperback is due to screens. Five decades ago, the television screen was to blame for stealing our attention. Nowadays, mobile phones are accessible during all waking hours, regardless of location or time. Unfortunately, this accessibility can come at the expense of our attention span.

Of course, sustained phone or computer use isn't always a purely recreational activity. For many running their own businesses, social media and online platforms are necessary to promote their services. They are valuable tools to connect with people globally as well as in your own community. Many people use their phones to access apps, audio books, podcasts, and other tools to enhance their health and wellbeing.

582 Mangen, Anne, and Adriaan Van der Weel. "The evolution of reading in the age of digitisation: an integrative framework for reading research."*Literacy* 50.3 (2016): 116-124.
583 https://www.washingtonpost.com/news/wonk/wp/2018/06/29/leisure-reading-in-the-u-s-is-at-an-all-time-low/. Accessed February 13, 2023.

But there are downsides to excessive phone use and moderation is important – particularly before bedtime, as we will discuss in the *Sleep Hygiene* section of this chapter.

CHRONIC STRESS AND MENTAL HEALTH ISSUES

In tandem with technological advances and overstimulated minds, the accelerated pace of modern life has caused many to live in a chronically elevated sympathetic "fight-or-flight" state.[584] It's not surprising then, that chronic stress and mental health issues are all too common in today's world. These conditions are often interrelated and accompanied by poor sleep.

Most of us feel stressed at times – it is our body's natural reaction to a specific event or stressor. However, this parasympathetic response system was developed by evolutionary mechanisms for short-term stress response. When the body experiences stressors with such frequency or intensity that *chronic* stress occurs, the autonomic nervous system does not have an adequate chance to activate the parasympathetic "rest and digest" response on a regular basis.[585] As a result, the fight-or-flight response stays turned on and the body remains in a constant state of physiological arousal.

Long-term activation of the stress response results in overexposure to cortisol and other stress hormones, affecting virtually every system in the body, either directly or indirectly. Stress makes it hard for us to relax and can come with a range of emotions, including anxiety and irritability. When stressed, we may find it difficult to concentrate. We may experience headaches or other body pains, an upset stomach or trouble sleeping. We may find we lose our appetite or eat more than usual.[586]

584 Jerath, Ravinder, Connor Beveridge, and Vernon A. Barnes. "Self-regulation of breathing as an adjunctive treatment of insomnia." *Frontiers in psychiatry* (2019): 780.
585 https://www.verywellmind.com/chronic-stress-3145104. Accessed March 08, 2023.
586 https://www.who.int/news-room/questions-and-answers/item/stress. Accessed March 13, 2023.

According to a poll carried out by the American Psychological Association in 2022, about 55% of adults in the United States said they had experienced stress during "a lot of the day" prior. Around a third of adults in the poll (34%) reported that stress is completely overwhelming most days.[587] These figures are certainly concerning. The cited causes of stress included: living conditions, the political climate, the news, financial insecurity, discrimination and work issues.[588]

When symptoms of stress become persistent and affect daily functioning, it can have a detrimental impact on your health and well-being. Chronic stress can worsen pre-existing health problems such as heart disease, hypertension, diabetes and irritable bowel syndrome,[589] and may result in increased use of alcohol, tobacco and other substances.[590]

Stress has also been shown to induce inflammation in the body, both peripherally and centrally.[591] Chronic inflammatory diseases have been recognized as the most significant cause of death in the world today, with more than 50% of all deaths being attributable to inflammation-related diseases such as ischemic heart disease, stroke, cancer, diabetes mellitus, chronic kidney disease, and autoimmune and neurodegenerative conditions.[592]

Prolonged stress can also cause or exacerbate mental health conditions, most commonly anxiety and depression.[593] As many as 20% of

587 https://www.apa.org/news/press/releases/stress. Accessed March 13, 2023.

588 https://www.apa.org/news/press/releases/stress/2022/concerned-future-inflation. Accessed March 13, 2023.

589 https://www.verywellmind.com Chronic Stress: Definition, Symptoms, Traits, Causes, Treatment. Accessed March 13, 2023.

590 https://www.who.int/news-room/questions-and-answers/item/stress. Accessed March 13, 2023.

591 Liu, Y. Z., Y. X. Wang, and C. L. Jiang. "Inflammation: the common pathway of stressrelated diseases. Front Hum Neurosci. 2017; 11." (2017).

592 Roth, Gregory A., et al. "Global, regional, and national age-sex-specific mortality for 282 causes of death in 195 countries and territories, 1980–2017: a systematic analysis for the Global Burden of Disease Study 2017." The Lancet 392.10159 (2018): 1736-1788.

593 https://www.who.int/news-room/questions-and-answers/item/stress. Accessed March 13, 2023.

adults in the United States are affected by anxiety disorders each year.[594] Global incidence of anxiety disorders increased about 25% during the COVID-19 pandemic.[595]

These conditions are very difficult to manage and address if sleep quality is poor. Think of how you feel when you have experienced sleep disruption. Individuals with high anxiety and chronic stress tend to have dysfunctional breathing – where breathing is fast, shallow and into the upper chest. It's easy to see why those with anxiety or chronic stress can have difficulty falling asleep and/or staying asleep. Please see Chapter Nine for more detail on breathing and anxiety along with other emotional states.

We live in a world where long-term activation of the sympathetic nervous system (where the fight-or-flight reaction stays turned on) has become the norm. We are distracted, tired, busy, stressed, and overwhelmed. No wonder our sleep suffers!

Unfortunately, disrupted sleep, regardless of the cause, has serious adverse short- and long-term health consequences, because sleep plays such a vital role in brain function and many body systems.[596]

IMPACT OF POOR SLEEP

While many people think of sleep simply for its rejuvenating power, there's much more to how good sleep contributes to your overall health and wellbeing than you may realize.

594 www.hopkinsmedicine.org/health/wellness-and-prevention/mental-health-disorder-statistics. Accessed March 08, 2023.

595 World Health Organization. Mental Health and COVID-19: Early evidence of the pandemic's impact: Scientific brief, 2 March 2022. https://www.who.int/publications/i/item/WHO-2019-nCoV-Sci_Brief-Mental_health-2022. Accessed March 08, 2023.

596 Worley, Susan L. "The Extraordinary Importance of Sleep: The Detrimental Effects of Inadequate Sleep on Health and Public Safety Drive an Explosion of Sleep Research." *Pharmacy and Therapeutics* 43.12 (2018): 758.

Poor sleep & appearance

Researchers have found that sleep deprived people appear less healthy, less attractive, and more tired compared with when they are well rested. A Swedish study photographed 23 healthy adults between 18 and 31 after a regular night's 8 hours of sleep and after 31 hours of wakefulness. The pictures were submitted to untrained observers to rate. Sleep-deprived persons were rated as less attractive, with unattractiveness ratings increasing with tiredness.[597]

Sleep deprivation causes people to look tired, strained and less happy. They may have dark circles under their eyes, red or swollen eyes, drooping eyelids, hanging corners of the mouth.[598] Collagen production is impacted, causing increased wrinkles and frown lines.[599] Poor sleep also contributes to inflammation, a major cause of skin issues such as acne and eczema, and significantly affects your body's ability to repair itself.[600]

Poor sleep & brain health

Aside from your appearance, sleep is of huge importance to many body functions and processes. Sleep (like the breath) has a powerfully positive, restorative effect on the brain. Just like our body has a lymphatic system that helps remove waste products from our tissues, our brain has a similar system called the glymphatic system.

A 2015 study found that if we sleep well throughout the night, the "garbage" that accumulates in our brain during the day is thoroughly

---

597 Axelsson, John et al. "Beauty sleep: experimental study on the perceived health and attractiveness of sleep deprived people." BMJ (Clinical research ed.) vol. 341 c6614. 14 Dec. 2010.

598 https://www.sleepfoundation.org/physical-health/beauty-sleep. Accessed February 26, 2023.

599 Jang SI, Lee M, Han J, et al. A study of skin characteristics with long-term sleep restriction in Korean women in their 40s. Skin Res Technol. 2020; 26(2): 193-199.

600 https://www.webmd.com/beauty/ss/slideshow-beauty-sleep. Accessed April 15, 2023.

removed. Cellular waste by-products build up in and around the brain cells. The researchers concluded that the primary purpose of sleep is as a sort of "garbage disposal for the brain." Essentially, they say sleeping acts as a garbage collector that comes during the night and  removes the waste product left by the brain. This allows the brain to function normally the next day when one wakes up.[601]

The *glymphatic system* works by using a network of specialized cells called astrocytes that act as a plumbing system. These cells surround the blood vessels in the brain, forming a network of tunnels that allow cerebrospinal fluid to flow freely around the brain tissue. This cerebrospinal fluid is then able to flush out the waste and toxins that have accumulated during the day.

When sleep is deprived, the active process of the glymphatic system does not have time to perform that function, so potentially neurotoxic waste products, such as amyloid beta (that is known to accumulate in conditions like Alzheimer's Disease), can build up. Short-term these effects will become apparent in cognitive abilities, behavior, and judgment, but it has suggested that longer term, sleep deprivation could have more serious, negative consequences on brain health.[602]

A recent study by Min et al., in 2023 found that a simple biofeedback practice (incorporating a breathing exercise), reduced levels of Alzheimer's-associated amyloid beta peptides. As we know, the way we breathe affects our heart rate, which in turn affects our nervous system. The study's findings suggest that the sympathetic and parasympathetic

601   Eugene, Andy R, and Jolanta Masiak. "The Neuroprotective Aspects of Sleep." MEDtube science vol. 3,1 (2015): 35-40.

602   Vinje, Vegard et al. "Respiratory influence on cerebrospinal fluid flow – a computational study based on long-term intracranial pressure measurements." Scientific reports vol. 9,1 9732. 5 Jul. 2019,

systems influence the production and clearance of Alzheimer's related peptides and proteins.

The breathing exercise used in the study involved inhaling for a count of five, then exhaling for a count of five, for 20 minutes, twice a day, for four weeks. This was accompanied by a biofeedback exercise, whereby participants paced their breathing in rhythm with a pacer on a laptop screen. They also monitored their heart rates, with the goal of increasing the breathing-induced oscillations in their heart rate.

As noted above, accumulation of amyloid beta in the brain due to increased production and/or decreased clearance is believed to trigger the Alzheimer's disease process. The study found that after four weeks of biofeedback training, participants' blood plasma levels of amyloid beta peptides decreased.[603] This promising finding appears to be the first evidence of a behavioral intervention that reduces amyloid beta levels compared to a randomized control group.

Short term impact: memory & emotional wellbeing

In otherwise healthy adults, in the short-term, sleep disruption causes increased stress response, somatic pain (pain in muscles, skin or bone), reduced quality of life, emotional distress and mood disorders, and cognitive, memory, and performance deficits. With a lack of sleep, neurons do not have a chance to create long-term memory, and this manifests as various clinical symptoms of behavioral, personality, cognitive, and physical complaints.[604] In adolescents, disturbed sleep affects psychosocial health, school performance, and risk-taking behaviors. In children, disrupted sleep affects cognitive function and behaviour.[605]

---

603 Min, Jungwon, et al. "Modulating heart rate oscillation affects plasma amyloid beta and tau levels in younger and older adults." *Scientific Reports* 13.1 (2023): 3967.
604 Eugene, Andy R, and Jolanta Masiak. "The Neuroprotective Aspects of Sleep." *MEDtube science* vol. 3,1 (2015): 35-40.
605 Medic, Goran et al. "Short- and long-term health consequences of sleep disruption." *Nature and science of sleep* vol. 9 151-161. 19 May. 2017

Increased stress

Somatic pain

Reduced quality of life

Emotional distress

Cognitive memory performance deficiencies

Researchers from Tel Aviv University headed by the late Dr. Avi Sadeh, a pioneer in the field of paediatric sleep, found that disrupted sleep may be just as damaging as no sleep at all. Students volunteered to have their sleep monitored as they slept at home using wristwatch-like devices that detected when they were asleep and when they were awake.[606]

On one night, they had their usual normal sleep. On another night, they were wakened four times by a phone call in order to complete a short computer task lasting no more than 15 minutes before going back to asleep. I can only imagine the student's enthusiasm for this task! It comes as no surprise that the student's attention and mood were affected after only one night of frequent interruptions. According to Dr. Sadeh, these effects accumulate and if one is awakened three to ten times a night for months on end, the disturbance to sleep is enormous.[607]

606 Kahn, Michal, et al. "Effects of one night of induced night-wakings versus sleep restriction on sustained attention and mood: a pilot study." Sleep medicine 15.7 (2014): 825-832.

607 https://www.universityherald.com/articles/10300/20140708/interrupted-sleep-may-be-as-detrimental-as-no-sleep.htm. Accessed February 10, 2023.

Long term impact: cardiovascular disease and mortality

In the long-term, sleep disruption can cause high blood pressure, high cholesterol, cardiovascular disease, weight-related problems, metabolic syndrome, diabetes, and colorectal cancer in otherwise healthy people. Disrupted sleep may reduce the quality of life of children and adolescents who have underlying medical conditions and may make common gastrointestinal disorders more severe.[608]

It is estimated that mortality rates double in those with sleep disorder – the estimated mortality rate for those having a sleep disorder is 9.3% compared to 5.2% in those without a sleep disorder.[609] This is concerning, as symptoms of one particular sleep disorder – *sleep apnea* – are difficult to observe, so the condition often goes undiagnosed. It is proposed that approximately 93% of women and 82% of men that have at least moderate sleep apnea are undiagnosed.[610]

Several studies have shown an association between sleep apena and increased cardiovascular risk, along with other significant complications.[611] As the consequences of disturbed sleep can be so serious, and difficult to diagnose, I would encourage health care professionals to look for ways to screen, manage and treat underlying sleep disorders.

The following section explores the importance of nasal breathing, the circadian rhythm, and sleep hygiene in more detail.

608 Medic, Goran et al. "Short- and long-term health consequences of sleep disruption." *Nature and science of sleep* vol. 9 151-161. 19 May. 2017,

609 Huyett, Phillip, Noah Siegel, and Neil Bhattacharyya. "Prevalence of sleep disorders and association with mortality: results from the NHANES 2009–2010." The Laryngoscope 131.3 (2021): 686-689.

610 www.snoozeuniversity.com 27 Sleep Apnea Statistics and Trends (2023) Accessed March 13, 2023.

611 https://www.hopkinsmedicine.org/health/wellness-and-prevention/the-dangers-of-uncontrolled-sleep-apnea. Accessed March 13, 2023.

NASAL BREATHING

By now, you will be well aware of the benefits of nasal breathing – but how does this apply to sleep? You may not be aware of it, but many of us spend at least part of the night breathing through an open mouth.[612] Do you ever waken up with a dry mouth? Perhaps a partner has mentioned that you snore. Perhaps you suffer from allergies or asthma. If so, you may well be breathing orally during sleep and this can have a range of negative consequences.

Mouth breathing can be drying, leading to bad breath, dental caries and gum disease. It can alter craniofacial development, causing crowed teeth and narrow mouths.[613] Mouth breathing and sleep disordered breathing has also been shown to impact cognitive development in children, leading to difficulty concentrating, poor academic performance and a tendency towards hyperactivity and behavioural difficulties.[614]

As a reminder – breathing through the nose is the normal healthy mode for healthy adults, both waking and sleeping, because the nasal air passages are especially suited for filtering and conditioning inhaled air. During wakefulness, the narrow nasal air passages slow down the respiratory rate, help to maintain diaphragm strength and provide more time for oxygen transfer to take place from the lungs to the blood.[615] As the diaphragm breathing muscle is mechanically linked to the muscles in the throat which serve to keep the airway open, the upper airway is stiffer and less likely to collapse during sleep.

Mouth breathing during sleep leads to a larger breathing volume as too much air is drawn into the lungs. Not only does the negative

---

612 Madronio, M. R., et al. "Older individuals have increased oro-nasal breathing during sleep." European Respiratory Journal 24.1 (2004): 71-77.

613 https://www.healthline.com/health/mouth-breathing#complications. Accessed March 14, 2023.

614 Bonuck, Karen, et al. "Sleep-disordered breathing in a population-based cohort: behavioral outcomes at 4 and 7 years." Pediatrics 129.4 (2012): e857-e865.

615 T. Metin Önerci. Nasal physiology and pathophysiology of nasal disorders. Chapter by Bartley and Wong. August 17, 2013.

pressure on the upper airways increase, but over-breathing also causes the airways to cool and dry out, leading to inflammation and further narrowing of the airways. Anyone who has ever had a little too much alcohol to drink of an evening will know how it feels to wake the following morning with your throat raw, hoarse, and inflamed. The same thing happens to your airways when you breathe through your mouth at night, inflaming and narrowing the airways.

Whilst mouth breathing, your body also expends energy to condition incoming air within the upper airways condition before it is drawn to the lungs. The effort involved with breathing through your mouth during sleep is two and a half times more as compared to breathing through your nose.[616] Breathing through the mouth causes the tongue to drop from the roof of your mouth to a lower resting posture (the roof of the mouth is the ideal resting tongue placement). The lower jaw hinges downwards to further narrow the airway. The combination of larger breathing volume and narrower airways caused by mouth breathing predisposes the body to a greater risk of sleep disordered breathing.

Several research studies have shown how nasal breathing offers a distinct advantage during sleep, resulting in fewer incidences of obstructive sleep apnea than when a patient breathes through the mouth.[617,618] Using mouth tape during sleep, such as Myotape, brings the lips together gently and safely, encouraging nasal breathing during sleep, has been found to reduce snoring and sleep apnea.

How we breathe during wakefulness influences how we breathe during sleep. If breathing during the day is a little faster, harder, upper chest or through an open mouth, breathing during sleep will be similar. In my co-authored article with Ear Nose and Throat Dr Carlos

---

616 Fitzpatrick et al. Effect of nasal or oral breathing route on upper airway resistance during sleep. European Respiratory Journal. Volume 22, Issue 5. December 2003.

617 Fitzpatrick et al. Effect of nasal or oral breathing route on upper airway resistance during sleep. European Respiratory Journal. Volume 22, Issue 5. December 2003.

618 Olsen, Kerry D., Eugene B. Kern, and Philip R. Westbrook. "Sleep and breathing disturbance secondary to nasal obstruction." Otolaryngology--Head and Neck Surgery 89.5 (1981): 804-810.

O'Connor and Dr Guillermo Plaza, we reviewed how breathing during wakefulness can help with reducing the risk of sleep problems.[619]

Improving breathing from a biochemical dimension helps to normalise the volume of air drawn into the body during wakefulness and sleep. With a lighter breathing pattern, there is less turbulence as air moves to and from the lungs. Breathing slowly helps to balance the autonomic nervous system to bring a quietness to the mind and allow one to drift off to sleep more easily. Breathing deeply with optimal recruitment of the diaphragm stiffens the throat to reduce the risk of collapse (as happens during sleep apnea).

PATRICK'S THOUGHTS ON SLEEP:

Many of us don't have enough understanding of sleep – and the role light, nasal breathing can play in our ability to fall and stay asleep. It is not just about quantity of sleep. One can sleep for ten hours and still wake up feeling lousy. We have become a population sadly missing out on the restorative benefits of sleep. As a result, many are dependent on caffeinated products to help daytime functioning and perhaps even prescription sleep medicine to help get some nighttime rest. A vicious cycle that it is incredibly difficult to disengage from.

Poor sleep can have a huge and wide-ranging impact on your quality of life. All this might sound quite concerning, but don't worry! A better understanding of sleep and some simple, effective, freely available tools and techniques will make it easier to sleep soundly throughout the night and wake up well-rested. Light and calm breathing reduces both snoring and obstructive sleep apnea as well as activating the body's relaxation mode, leading to deeper and better-quality sleep.

If you want to sleep better and wake up feeling energised and refreshed, breathe through your nose and breathe light by applying the

619 McKeown, Patrick, Carlos O'Connor-Reina, and Guillermo Plaza. "Breathing re-education and phenotypes of sleep apnea: a review." *Journal of Clinical Medicine* 10.3 (2021): 471.

Oxygen Advantage® exercises included at the end of this chapter and freely available on the Oxygen Advantage® App.

Don't forget – breathing off the yoga mat is as important if not more important as breathing on the mat. Please also be kind to your mind and limit phone use, particularly before bedtime, along with other sleep hygiene practices.

CIRCADIAN RHYTHMS

Disrupted sleep is associated with increased activity of the sympathetic nervous system and changes in the circadian rhythm. The circadian rhythm is a powerful force that affects the natural processes of all living things – animals, plants, and even microbes. The term circadian comes from the Latin words "circa" and "dies". "Circa" in English means approximately, which implies approaching a role or state. "Dies" means day.

One of the most familiar examples of a circadian rhythm is the sleep-wake cycle: we sleep at night and are awake during the day. But the circadian rhythm is much more than just a sleep schedule, it's often referred to as the "internal body clock" that regulates the 24-hour cycle of biological processes in all kinds of living things.

Have you ever thought about how your body will react when you travel to a country with a different time zone? For example, if you travel from New York City to Canberra, Australia which has a 16-hour time difference, do you think you would feel energetic during the day? Well, the answer is "no". Your body will take time to adapt to the new system – approximately one day for each hour of time zone changes. This delay period is a common experience for travelers who visit countries with different daytime variations.[620]

When we travel to a new place or work in shifts, we often experience changes in our sleep patterns. This adjustment process is because of the circadian rhythm. It's not just about sleep; our body, mind, and behavior

---

620 https://www.betterhealth.vic.gov.au/health/healthyliving/jet-lag. Accessed March 02, 2023.

also follow a 24-hour cycle. This includes all the internal processes that regulate our sleep-wake cycle. So, when we talk about the circadian rhythm, we mean the way our body responds to the natural rhythm of day and night, affecting everything from our mood and energy levels to our digestion and metabolism.

This is not only important if we travel or work night shifts. Many of us stay up a little later than usual at the weekend, catching up on sleep by sleeping-in later the next day. The dreaded *Monday morning feeling* can be partly due to going to bed later and lying in the following day, at the weekend. The change in sleep-wake times can bring you out of sync with your body's circadian rhythms. Come Sunday night, the hormonal and physical signals that encourage sleep aren't yet at their peak at the time you're getting into bed, leading to difficulty in getting to sleep.[621] To compound this, the signals to wake up are also be delayed and this can produce that groggy Monday morning feeling when your alarm clock unkindly jolts you into your usual weekday sleep schedule.

The circadian rhythm is a natural process that originates within the body. While this rhythm is internal, external factors such as light and temperature help adjust it to the local environment. Hormones such as melatonin, ghrelin, and cortisol are produced by the body to regulate this rhythm, but the rate at which they are produced is influenced by the environment in which the person lives. This means that although the circadian rhythm is controlled internally, it is shaped by the individual's surroundings. In essence, the environment plays a crucial role in maintaining a healthy circadian rhythm.

You may have guessed that light exposure negatively affects sleep quality . . . but how? Exposure to light prevents the production of the hormone melatonin which causes the body to sleep. That's why exposure to natural light early in the day is recommended. At night on the other hand, the body senses the absence of light and therefore produces melatonin which causes the body to sleep. The presence of light from electronic devices at night can confuse our biological clocks.

621 https://www.sleepstation.org.uk/articles/sleep-science/weekend-lie-ins/. Accessed March 14, 2023.

Breathing during sleep is complex and there are many factors that can disrupt the natural sleep rhythm. It's not ideal to go to sleep at 10pm and either awake fully or partially from deep sleep several times during the night. Faster and harder breathing during sleep can shift sleep from deep to light. Increased breathing commonly occurs in persons with asthma and those with poor breathing patterns.

Breathing during sleep can also speed up when the temperature of the bedroom is too warm. In a study of the effects of air temperature on the sleep quality of elderly subjects, it was found that even a small increase in temperature caused an increased stress to the body and mind which reduced sleep quality. An increase in room temperature of 3 degrees decreased Rapid Eye Movement (REM) sleep by 26.3 minutes, and increased the time awake by 27 minutes. REM sleep is a stage of sleep associated with dreaming and memory consolidation, during which, your eyes move rapidly behind your closed eyes, your heart rate speeds up, and your breathing becomes irregular.[622] The general consensus is that bedroom temperature should be approximately 65 degrees Fahrenheit (18.3 degrees Celsius).

Ultimately, the importance of the circadian rhythm cannot be underestimated as it has big impact on the entire person psychologically, physiologically, emotionally, and mentally. The circadian rhythm cannot be perfectly controlled, but there are healthy sleep tips that can better regulate your 24-hour sleep cycle.

SLEEP HYGEINE++

You may be familiar with the recommendations for good sleep hygiene, but it is worth reminding ourselves of the basics. Sleep hygiene is a catchall term for practices and behaviors that influence sleep quality and duration. It can include bedtime and wake-up routines, as well as your diet, physical activity, and other aspects of daily life.[623]

---

622   REM Sleep: What It Is and Why It Matters | Sleep Foundation. Accessed July 15, 2003.
623   https://www.sleepfoundation.org/physical-health. Accessed February 26, 2023.

The core components of good sleep hygiene include:

 Early natural light: Exposure to natural light, especially early in the day, helps strengthen the circadian rhythms, regulating the sleep-wake cycle.

 Keep regular sleep hours: Make a habit of going to bed and getting up at roughly the same times each day. Try to avoid napping where possible.

 Create a restful environment: Dark, quiet and cool environments generally make it easier to fall asleep and stay asleep.

 Move more, sleep better: Regular exercise is good for your physical health and your mind too – and being active during the day can help you sleep better.

 Healthy Habits: Caffeine and alcohol can stop you falling asleep and prevent deep sleep. Try to cut down on alcohol and avoid caffeine close to bedtime. Dining late in the evening can negatively impact sleep as well.

 Confront sleeplessness: If you are lying awake unable to sleep, do not force it. Get up and do something relaxing for a bit and return to bed when you feel sleepier. Alternatively, listen to the 20 minute guided breathing and relaxation for insomnia, spoken by Patrick and available on YouTube and Spotify. Google: "patrick mckeown guided insomnia". It works and you are likely to be asleep by the end of the track.

 Limit screentime before bed: Exposure to artificial light at night can hinder the production of melatonin and disrupt your circadian rhythm. Experts recommend dimming the lights before bed and keeping electronic devices out of your bedroom.[624]

624 https://www.nhs.uk/every-mind-matters/mental-health-issues/sleep/. Accessed March 13, 2023.

I suggest a couple of further, crucial components to the above recommendations – hence the title "sleep hygiene**++**".

Pre-sleep breathing practice: adopting a routine breathing practice before sleep helps you down-regulate from the day's activity, shifting your nervous system into rest & digest. Many practices are suggested at the end of this chapter.

Nasal breathing during sleep: applying a simple piece of microcopore tape or Myotape to your lips at night can encourage nasal breathing during the night, which has many benefits.

Sleep hygiene practices can be tailored to suit your needs and preferences. Following a relaxing pre-bed routine and building healthy habits during the day can all contribute to an ideal night's sleep. It has been proposed that modulation of the autonomic nervous system, via slow breathing techniques along with relaxation techniques and sleep hygiene may be a more powerful tool in combating insomnia than the prevailing method of using hypnotics and other pharmaceutical interventions.[625]

MENOPAUSE & SLEEP

Women approaching perimenopause or indeed menopause often find their sleep is disrupted. Night-time waking can be caused by hot flashes, night sweats, restless legs, or the increased anxiety levels that can accompany menopause.

As breathing is influenced by hormones, women can become dysfunctional breathers during menopause, and this too impacts sleep. As women reach their late 40s to early 50s, approximately 40% experience sleep complaints.[626] The advent of menopause marks the beginning of

---

625 Jerath, Ravinder, Connor Beveridge, and Vernon A. Barnes. "Self-regulation of breathing as an adjunctive treatment of insomnia." *Frontiers in psychiatry* (2019): 780.

626 https://www.sleepfoundation.org/women-sleep/menopause-and-sleep. Accessed March 13, 2023.

an increased risk for sleep apnea for women, due to waning levels of estrogen and progesterone – hormones that maintain the airway's muscle tone and keep it from collapsing.[627] Once perimenopause begins, a woman's risk of developing sleep apnea increases four percent with each year.[628]

Although menopausal symptoms that can disrupt sleep such as hot flashes may be relieved by pharmaceutical means such as hormone replacement therapy or antidepressants, these options are not suitable or desirable to everyone. A review of research on "mind-body" interventions for menopause found that breathing and relaxation techniques, as well as Cognitive Behaviour Therapy, can be beneficial for alleviating vasomotor symptoms such as hot flashes and night sweats.[629]

Paced breathing has been found to reduce hot flash frequency and severity in a small number of studies.[630] Paced breathing involves slowing your breath down intentionally while focusing on its length and breadth to help calm the mind and the body. Such practices may be used instead of, or as an adjunct to pharmaceutical interventions. For paced breathing exercises, download the free Oxygen Advantage® app.

Please see Chapter Twenty-three for a deeper exploration of hormones, menopause and dysfunctional breathing.

627 https://www.verywellhealth.com/menopause-and-the-risk-of-sleep-apnea-in-women-3014736. Accessed March 13, 2023.

628 Mirer, A. G., Young, T., Palta, M., Benca, R. M., Rasmuson, A., & Peppard, P. E. (2017). Sleep-disordered breathing and the menopausal transition among participants in the Sleep in Midlife Women Study. *Menopause (New York, N.Y.), 24*(2), 157–162.

629 Stefanopoulou, E., & Grunfeld, E. A. (2017). Mind-body interventions for vasomotor symptoms in healthy menopausal women and breast cancer survivors. A systematic review. *Journal of psychosomatic obstetrics and gynaecology,38*(3), 210–225.

630 Freedman, R. R., & Woodward, S. (1992). Behavioral treatment of menopausal hot flushes: evaluation by ambulatory monitoring. *American journal of obstetrics and gynecology,167*(2), 436-439.

YOGA AND SLEEP

Given the importance of sleep for health and happiness, are there ways that yoga can improve sleep? It is easy to understand that yoga postures involve stretching and relaxing of muscles, and enhanced mental activity leads to better sleep quality. Other specific mechanisms for the way yoga improves sleep quality have also been proposed. Studies have shown increased vagal tone and decreased sympathetic activity after yoga practice.[631] All of these things may improve sleep.

A study of medical trainees showed that those who attended yoga classes had significantly more total sleep (425.14 minutes) than those who did not (357.33 minutes). Yoga improved trainee sleep by approximately 60 minutes. The study concluded by encouraging medical training programs to provide access to yoga and mindfulness programs to improve sleep and, therefore, potentially, trainee's clinical performance.[632]

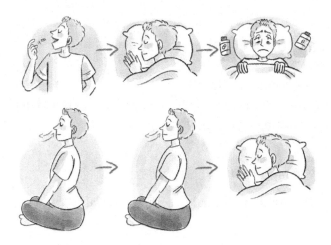

631 Panjwani, Usha, Sharmila Dudani, and Meetu Wadhwa. "Sleep, Cognition, and Yoga." *International Journal of Yoga* 14.2 (2021): 100.

632 Babbar, Shilpa, Karen B. Williams, and An-Lin Cheng. "Sleep Among Obstetrics and Gynecology Trainees: Results from a Yoga-Based Wellness Initiative." *American Journal of Perinatology.* (2021).

Yoga teachers who understand the connection between everyday breathing and sleep quality and duration will be uniquely positioned to help their students. Without sounding too repetitive, it is worth mentioning that light, slow and low breathing through the nose improves sleep quality. If the yoga student continues to mouth breathe, faster and harder during wakefulness and sleep, both sleep and stillness of the mind is sacrificed. Yoga could be the gateway to spread awareness of the importance and utility of functional breathing for sleep and wellbeing.

EXERCISES TO IMPROVE SLEEP

You can support healthy, restorative sleep by consciously making time to practice Oxygen Advantage® and yoga breathing exercises during the day, as well as before sleeping, or if awakened during the night. Breathing exercises to unblock the nose prior to sleep are also beneficial. The Oxygen Advantage® app is freely available and can guide you through many exercises.

Before bed

Breathe Light, Anuloma, Kevali
Samavritti*, Bhramari, Surya followed by Chandra Bhredana
(* Each cycle lasting < your BOLT score)

If woken up in the middle of the night:

Breathe Light, Anuloma (Inhale < Exhale), Kevali

In the morning:

3-5 max breath-holds, Nadi Sodhana (Alternate Nostril Breathing), Samavritti** (Box Breathing)
(** Each cycle lasting > your BOLT score)
Pratiloma, Bhastrika, Kapalabhati, Lion's breath, Bhramari

When feeling uncentered or having a blocked nose:

Nadi Sodhana, short breath holds after exhalation (seated or while walking)

For the above breathing exercises to have the desired effect, you need to practice them over a period of time.

Yoga Nidra (Yogic Sleep)

While yoga exercises and meditations and Oxygen Advantage® breathing exercises will certainly help to improve the quality and quantity of sleep a person gets, there is also a further state of "conscious" sleep in the yogic tradition, a state known as yoga nidra, a state both affecting and affected by breathing.

While the term *yoganidra* has a diverse and ancient history and its specific meaning depends on its historical context, yoga nidra is, in essence, a fourth state . . . beyond the usual three states of waking, dreaming and deep sleep, a state where normal mental activity ceases, a state of aware consciousness during a psychic sleep.

In modern terms, yoga nidra has also come to be understood as a specific practice of guided meditation that allows a practitioner to enter that unique state of conscious sleep. In other words, yoga nidra can be understood in two different ways, both as "a state of meditation" to be achieved and as the name for unique systemizations of "various yoga techniques from different religious traditions."[633]

---

633 Birch, Jason, and Jacqueline Hargreaves. "Yoganidra: An Understanding of the History and Context." *The Luminescent.* (January 2015). https://www.theluminescent. org/2015/01/yoganidra.html (Accessed October 1, 2022).

Yoga Nidra Guided Meditation

Yoga nidra has been popularized by various practitioners as a specific type of guided meditation performed in a supine position. In particular, Swami Satyananda Saraswati, of the Bihar School of Yoga, describes a seven-step practice in his book, *Yoga Nidra:*[634]

1. *Preparation*

The person lays prone in savasana.

2. *Resolve*

The practitioner formulates "a personal 'Sankalpa', which is described as a short, positive, clear statement such as 'I will awaken my spiritual potential', 'I will be successful in all that I undertake', etc." This type of intentional or directed thought is related to "the practice of auto-suggestion," which can be traced back to 19th-century Western relaxation therapies.

3. *Rotation of Consciousness*

This type of body scan meditation involves moving the mind from one part of the body to another in a definite sequence.

4. *Awareness of Breath*

The breath is passively observed in the nostrils, chest or the passage between the navel and throat without forcing or changing it in order to achieve a deeper relaxation.

---

634 Birch, Jason, and Jacqueline Hargreaves. "Yoganidra: An Understanding of the History and Context." *The Luminescent.* (January 2015). https://www.theluminescent. org/2015/01/yoganidra.html (Accessed October 1, 2022).

5. Feelings and Sensations

Opposite feelings and sensations, such as heat and cold, heaviness and lightness, pain and pleasure, are paired in order to harmonize the opposite hemispheres of the brain.

6. Visualisation

Images, such as landscapes, oceans, mountains, temples, saints, flowers, are visualized to lead to a state in which distractions cease.

7. Ending the practice

The sankalpa is repeated and the practitioner gradually returns to a waking state.

For an even more in-depth exploration of this topic, please see the book titled *The Breathing Cure,* or check out some of the breathing exercises and information on our website **https://oxygenadvantage. com** and social media channels.

CHAPTER TWENTY-THREE

YOGA AND THE FEMALE BREATH

Throughout the lifespan, there are differences in the way women and men breathe. These differences are due to the way hormones affect the breath, physical differences and the hormonal and anatomical features of pregnancy and menopause. These differences are also relevant for people taking synthetic sex hormones, including the oral contraceptive pill, hormone replacement therapy, and transgender hormone therapy. There is a difference even in infancy. At four weeks, male babies breathe faster than female babies, suggesting the male respiratory system matures more slowly.[635]

It has been known since the early twentieth century that biological female sex hormones impact breathing. In 1904, pioneering research found that pregnant women hyperventilate.[636] In 1912, it was discovered that the concentration of CO_2 in the lungs decreases during pregnancy.[637] The symptoms of premenstrual syndrome (PMS) are almost identical

---

635 Carroll, John L., and David F. Donnelly. "Respiratory Physiology and Pathophysiology During Sleep." in *Principles and Practice of Pediatric Sleep Medicine*, 179-194. Philadelphia: Elsevier, 2014.

636 Gargaglioni, Luciane H., Danusia A. Marques, and Luis Gustavo A. Patrone. "Sex Differences in Breathing." *Comparative Biochemistry and Physiology Part A: Molecular & Integrative Physiology* 238 (2019): 110543.

637 Hasselbalch, Karl Albert. "Ein Beitrag zur Respirationsphysiologie der Graviditat 1." *Skandinavisches Archiv fur Physiologie* 27.2 (1912): 1-12.

to those of hyperventilation.[638] Contraceptives, HRT, and even the ages at which menstruation or menopause begins can contribute to changes in breathing. Breathing pattern disorders are almost twice as common in females,[639] and sleep-disordered breathing increases after menopause and in other situations that disrupt hormonal balance.[640,641]

Stress has a significant impact on the menstrual cycle too.[642] In a year-long study of 738 female students, it was found that 39% of the participants had high levels of perceived stress, and 91% reported some type of menstrual problem, including irregular or painful periods, abnormal bleeding, and PMS.[643] The stresses these women were experiencing were deemed to be the type of day-to-day pressure most of us face.

These "normal" stresses have been exacerbated during the pandemic, adding to the burden of stress-related symptoms for people of all genders. In 2020, due to government-imposed lockdowns, many people found themselves isolated from family members and loved ones.

For example, Amy was living in London at the time while her partner and family all lived overseas. She found social distancing very stressful, and her mental wellbeing suffered. As often happens when the mind suffers, the body struggles too. Anastasis met Amy through yoga. She regularly attended his twice-weekly breath training class. She often messaged to say she found the class helpful for her mental

638 Ott, Helmut W., et al. "Symptoms of Premenstrual Syndrome May Be Caused by Hyperventilation." *Fertility and Sterility* 86.4 (2006): 1001-e17.

639 Gilbert, Chris, Leon Chaitow, and Dinah Bradley. *Recognizing and Treating Breathing Disorders*. Elsevier Health Sciences, 2014.

640 Jehan S, Auguste E, Zizi F, Pandi-Perumal SR, Gupta R, Attarian H, Jean-Louis G, McFarlane SI. Obstructive Sleep Apnea: Women's Perspective. J Sleep Med Disord. 2016;3(6):1064. Epub 2016 Aug 25. PMID: 28239685; PMCID: PMC5323064.

641 https://www.hopkinsmedicine.org/health/wellness-and-prevention/how-does-menopause-affect-my-sleep. Accessed June 24, 2023.

642 Suess, William M., et al. "The Effects of Psychological Stress on Respiration: A Preliminary Study of Anxiety and Hyperventilation." *Psychophysiology* 17.6 (1980): 535-540.

643 Rafique, Nazish, and Mona Al-Sheikh. "Prevalence of Menstral Problems and Their Association With Psychological Stress in Young Female Students Studying Health Sciences." *Saudi Medical Journal* 39.1 (2018): 67.

health but, three months into her practice, she asked whether there was a connection between breathing and the menstrual cycle. She had just had her period for the first time in nearly a year. The only thing she had been doing differently was attending the breathing classes. She credits the breath practice for her menstrual cycle's return.

Anatomical & mechanical differences

In addition to the hormonal differences, there are anatomical and mechanical differences between the genders that are evident throughout the breathing systems. In females, compared with males:

- The lungs are smaller, meaning lung volume is lower.
- There are fewer respiratory bronchioles, the passages that branch off in the lungs to deliver air to the alveoli.
- The rib cage is smaller, even though the rib cage volume is approximately equal. Rib cage volume to lung-size ratio is greater in females. A pregnant woman's rib cage must accommodate volume changes in the lungs and abdomen. The greater rib cage volume to lung ratio accommodates a growing foetus during pregnancy while minimising its effect on lung function.
- The ribs are inclined, whereas in men they are more horizontal.
- Rib cage movement is predominantly "pump handle," while a "bucket handle" movement is more common in men.
- The diaphragm is around 9% shorter and more dome-shaped.[644]
- Women have about 12% less haemoglobin in the blood, but similar levels of circulating erythropoietin (EPO), a hormone important for maturing new red blood cells.[645]

644 LoMauro, Antonella, and Andrea Aliverti. "Sex Differences in Respiratory Function." *Breathe* 14.2 (2018): 131-140.
645 Murphy, William G. "The Sex Difference in Haemoglobin Levels in Adults—Mechanisms, Causes, and Consequences." *Blood Reviews* 28.2 (2014): 47.

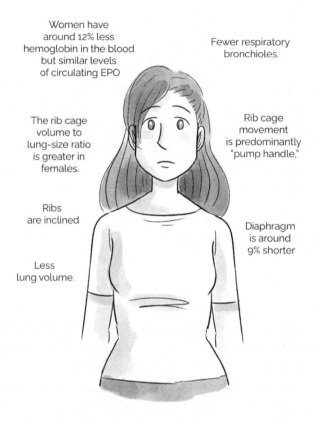

Women have around 12% less hemoglobin in the blood but similar levels of circulating EPO

Fewer respiratory bronchioles.

The rib cage volume to lung-size ratio is greater in females.

Rib cage movement is predominantly "pump handle."

Ribs are inclined

Diaphragm is around 9% shorter

Less lung volume.

Differences in airway size, from the nose right down to the lungs, have implications for the way females breathe during physical exercise. During physical yoga practice, the female respiratory system demands more energy. Intensive exercise increases turbulence in the airway, meaning females must work harder to breathe.[646]

Females are also more susceptible to the adverse effects of hypoxemia – low levels of arterial oxygen.[647] It is therefore likely that they can benefit more from breath training than males when it comes to physical

646 Granger, Emily A., et al. "Reducing Turbulent Airflow Lowers Healthy Females Work of Breathing During Exercise to a Level Similar to Males." *The FASEB Journal* 34.S1 (2020): 1-1.

647 LoMauro, Antonella, and Andrea Aliverti. "Sex Differences in Respiratory Function." *Breathe* 14.2 (2018): 131-140.

performance. Given this high energy cost of breathing during exercise, females can benefit from a breathing program that involves:

- Long-term training targeted to the metabolic and biomechanical demands of their sport – for yoga, this would include exercises to release the breathing muscles and strengthen posture.
- Recovery breathing techniques.
- Strengthening of the secondary (smaller) respiratory muscles.
- A gradual approach to hypoxic training.

THE MENSTRUAL CYCLE

Oestrogen, Progesterone, and the Breath

Hormonal differences are relevant to most women of fertile age in terms of the menstrual cycle. Different types of hormonal contraceptives can also impact breathing. While there is limited research in some of these areas, female hormones can affect the breath after menopause, during pregnancy, and following miscarriage or hysterectomy.

During different phases of the menstrual cycle, levels of oestrogen and progesterone fluctuate. As this happens, breathing changes cyclically. Hyperventilation is common during the luteal phase of the menstrual cycle. Cyclical respiratory fluctuations stop after menopause.[648]

Many women are not particularly familiar with the phases of their menstrual cycle, but, with the rise in popularity of wearable devices that can track cyclical changes, this is now an easy problem to solve. The phases of the menstrual cycle are as follows:

- **Menstruation:** During the period, the lining of the uterus sheds, causing bleeding. Levels of both oestrogen and progesterone are low.

---

648 Gargaglioni, Luciane H., Danuzia A. Marques, and Luis Gustavo A. Patrone. "Sex Differences in Breathing." *Comparative Biochemistry and Physiology Part A: Molecular & Integrative Physiology* 238 (2019): 110543.

- **The follicular phase:** Between menstruation and ovulation, oestrogen rises as the body prepares to release an egg.
- **Ovulation:** Oestrogen levels peak just before the egg is released and drop again shortly after.
- **The luteal phase:** After ovulation and before the period, progesterone peaks as the body prepares for a potential pregnancy.

The hormone progesterone is present in both males and females, but in females, it is important because of its significance in the menstrual cycle, pregnancy, and menopause. Scientists have examined the role of progesterone in breathing and found it acts as a respiratory stimulant. It increases chemoreceptor sensitivity to both hypercapnia and hypoxia and improves upper airway muscle tone.[649] It is the stimulatory effect of progesterone that predisposes women to hyperventilate during the luteal phase of their menstrual cycle[650] and during the early stages of pregnancy.[651]

Serotonin, a hormone/neurotransmitter responsible for mood regulation, sleep, appetite, learning ability, memory, and digestion, fluctuates throughout the menstrual cycle.[652] These fluctuations may be responsible for the mood swings, food cravings, and greater difficulty in concentrating during the run-up to the period that some women experience.

649 Wimms, Alison, et al. "Obstructive Sleep Apnea in Women: Specific Issues and Interventions." *BioMed Research International* 2016.

650 Slatkovska, Lubomira, et al. "Phasic Menstrual Cycle Effects on the Control of Breathing in Healthy Women." *Respiratory Physiology & Neurobiology* 154.3 (2006): 379-388.

651 Jensen, Dennis, et al. "Effects of Human Pregnancy on the Ventilatory Chemoreflex Response to Carbon Dioxide." *American Journal of Physiology -- Regulatory, Integrative and Comparative Physiology* 288.5 (2005): R1369-R1375.

652 Warren, D. E., W. H. Tedford Jr., and W. E. Flynn. "Behavioral Effects of Cyclic Changes in Serotonin During the Human Menstrual Cycle." *Medical Hypotheses* 5.3 (1979): 359-364.

Menstruation and Asana Practice

The menstrual cycle is one of the most important biological cycles affecting the human body. This is acknowledged and ingrained in many traditions. Unfortunately, advice in yoga on how to practise during menstruation is often contradictory. In the Ashtanga yoga tradition, women are encouraged to take a break from physical practice altogether for the first three days of menstruation.[653] It is common for teachers to advise against inversions such as head and shoulder stand (and sometimes other poses that invert the uterus including downward dog and standing forward bend) during menstruation, although there is no consensus on this. Some yoga schools, including Iyengar yoga, offer specific sequences to be practised during menstruation.

The common advice against inversions is based on the notion that they may cause certain physical problems. For instance, there was a concern that retrograde menstruation (backward flow of menstrual blood and uterine tissue into the abdomen) could lead to endometriosis, but it is now known that this is not the case. According to Boston yoga teacher Barbara Benagh, writing for Yoga Journal, the most valid argument against inversions is that they are high-energy poses, and, for some women, energy is low during menstruation. However, Benagh argues, this is not the case for every woman. [654]

From a philosophical perspective, the energy of menstruation has a downward flow. According to one system of understanding the organisation of prana in the body (there are various systems), our life force, prana, divides into five vayus (or "winds"), each governing different functions, systems, and aspects of being.

---

653 Oates, Jennifer. "The Effect of Yoga on Menstrual Disorders: A Systematic Review." *The Journal of Alternative and Complementary Medicine* 23.6 (2017): 407-417.

654 "Why Avoid Inversions During Menstruation?" *Yoga Journal.* (August 28, 2007). http://www.yogajournal.com/practice/yoga-sequences/inversions-and-menstruation/ (Accessed July 6, 2022).

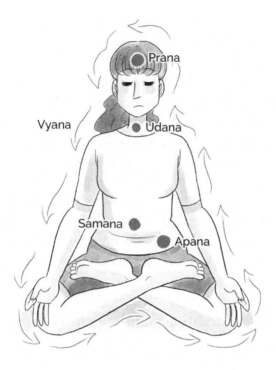

- **Prana** governs the head and chest and controls inspiration and forward movement.
- **Apana** sits in the pelvis and regulates downward/outward movement and elimination.
- **Samana** is at the navel and is responsible for assimilation.
- **Udana** sits at the throat and governs speech, self-expression, and upward movement.
- **Vyana** covers the whole body and controls circulation and expansiveness.[655]

From this energetic perspective, menstruation is *apana* – downward moving energy. Any hindrance to the flow of apana vayu is thought to result in unpleasant physical symptoms. According to Nithin Sridar, an expert in Indian history, the advice against yoga practice and religious

---

655 "The 5 Prana Vayus Chart." *Yoga International.* (n.d.) http://www.yogainternational.com/article/view/the-5-prana-vayus-chart (Accessed July 6, 2022).

activities during menstruation must be understood in relation to the flow of apana vayu.[656] For instance, the restriction on religious activities reflects the idea that spiritual upliftment causes apana vayu to move upwards, interfering with the downward flow of menstruation.[657]

In modern yoga, inversions are often avoided during menstruation. In some traditions, however, inversions are considered therapeutic because they help remove excess apana. For instance, Iyengar suggests inversions to relieve menstrual problems such as irregular and heavy periods.[658]

No research currently exists to define whether inverted poses should be avoided during menstruation. A 2017 review of the literature reports that what research there is into the benefits of yoga for menstrual disorders is inconclusive and lacks enough consistency to give clear guidance.

Attitudes to Menstruation and the Female Yogic Tradition

The modern narrative around menstruation often centres on negative experiences and physical and psychological symptoms. The menstrual cycle is viewed almost as an inconvenience. Advertisements for period products cement this perspective, suggesting women should barely acknowledge, let alone accommodate, their monthly cycle. Conversely, ancient Hindu and Tantric traditions promote a positive attitude to menstruation, viewing it as sacred and important. Menstruation in yoga is a complex topic, which you can explore in more detail by following the various references cited in this chapter. It's worth looking at the

---

656   Sridhar, Nithin. "Hindu View of Menstruation-IV: Menstruation from Yogic Perspective." *India Facts.* (July 12, 2016). http://www.indiafacts.org/hindu-view-menstruation-iv-menstruation-yogic-perspective/ (Accessed July 6, 2022).

657   Sridhar, Nithin. "Hindu View of Menstruation – VI: Menstruation Restrictions and Attitudes." *India Facts.* (August 10, 2016). http://www.indiafacts.org/hindu-view-menstruation-vi-menstruation-restrictions-attitudes/#1 (Accessed July 6, 2022).

658   Iyengar, Bellur Krishnamukar Sundara. *BKS Iyengar Yoga: The Path to Holistic Health.* Penguin, 2007.

physical aspect of menstruation with some understanding of the yogic attitude towards it.

One interesting aspect here is that some historians argue yoga was invented by women, and that early yogic rituals were practised by women long before the emergence of the Vedic tradition. It is commonly accepted that an artefact discovered in the Indus Valley depicting a man seated in lotus pose is the first historical record of yoga. But the healer and historian, Vicki Noble, highlights the depiction of female Buddhas, priestesses, and shamans, prominent from around 6,000 BCE.[659] As the yoga therapist and scholar, Uma Dinsmore-Tuli writes in her book, *Yoni Shakti*, "The fact that most of the figurines unearthed in the Indus Valley were female is the Indian link from the matriarchal Palaeolithic civilizations to the prehistory of yoga."[660]

Hinduism associates menstruation with sacred celebration, purification, and rest.[661] However, menstruation in modern Indian culture, much like modern Western culture, is largely taboo. Menstruating women are excluded from places of worship and not allowed to prepare food, and menstruation is seen as polluting, unclean, and impure. This view can be traced back to the Rig Vedas (the oldest of the sacred Hindu texts) and linked with the myth of Indra's slaying of Vritras.[662,663] However, author and researcher, Janet Chawla argues that traditional interpretations of the Rig Vedas overlook the idea of the female physiology as the "locus of power." When we speak of female physiology, she explains –

659 Olson, Danielle Prohom. "Did Women Invent Yoga?" *Body Divine*. (February 25, 2011). http://www.bodydivine.wordpress.com/2011/02/25/did-women-invent-yoga/ (Accessed July 6, 2022).

660 Dinsmore-Tuli, Uma, and Nirlipta Tuli. *Yoni Shakti: A Woman's Guide to Power and Freedom Through Yoga and Tantra*. Pinter & Martin Limited, 2015.

661 Sridhar, Nithin. "Hindu View of Menstruation-IV: Menstruation from Yogic Perspective." *India Facts*. (July 12, 2016). http://www.indiafacts.org/hindu-view-menstruation-iv-menstruation-yogic-perspective/ (Accessed July 6, 2022).

662 Garg, Suneela, and Tanu Anand. "Menstruation Related Myths in India: Strategies for Combating It." *Journal of Family Medicine and Primary Care* 4.2 (2015): 184.

663 Chawla, Janet. "The Mythic Origins of the Menstrual Taboo in the Rig Veda." *Economic and Political Weekly* 29.43 (1994): 2817-2827.

"We do so in a gynocentric sense of the total range of female bodily processes; menstruation, female capacity for sexual pleasure, as well as potential for pregnancy, childbirth and lactation. Such a holistic, woman centred – and biologically accurate – definition of female physiology implicitly questions the patriarchal assumption of woman's value as "the mother of sons."

She suggests that the Rig Vedas not only marginalised but also demonised women and their biological processes. Chawla points out that the women in servitude at the time were likely captured, enslaved, and subjugated by the conquering Aryans and thus disappeared from history.[664]

However, the idea of menstrual blood as pure and sacred persists in the Tantric tradition. This is highlighted by the practice of yoni puja, in which the female genitals are considered symbolic of the cosmic energy from which the entire universe emerged. Women are celebrated as facets of Shakti, the divine feminine energy.[665] Shakti is often depicted as a goddess and represents creativity, power, and universal energy.

The Devipuram temple in Andhra Pradesh is an important centre of Devi worship in the tantric tradition of Srividya. In his book, *Menstruation Across Cultures: A Historical Perspective,* Nithin Sridhar explains that most of the priests at Devipuram are women. They are all free to remain in the temple during menstruation. According to the temple's founder, Sri Amritananda Natha Saraswati:

"What is pure, we don't touch. And what we don't touch, we call it a Taboo. She (the menstruating woman) was so pure, that she was worshipped as a Goddess."[666]

664 Chawla, Janet. "The Mythic Origins of the Menstrual Taboo in the Rig Veda." *Economic and Political Weekly* 29.43 (1994): 2817-2827.

665 Hridaya. "Tantric Rituals: Yoni Puja." *Hridaya Yoga.* (May 29, 2017). http://hridaya-yoga.com/blog/tantric-rituals-yoni-puja/ (Accessed July 6, 2022).

666 Sridhar, Nithin. "Menstruation Across Cultures: The Sabarimala Confusion: A Historical Perspective." in *Menstruation Across Cultures*, 2021, 1-362.

This suggests an alternative to the idea of menstruating women as unclean, rather that her power during menstruation would unbalance the energy in the temple.

In Hinduism too, the idea of the sacred feminine is central, but this has become lost or clouded. Writing for *India Facts*, in a series of articles about menstruation in the yogic traditions, Nithin Sridhar explains:

> "It is an irony that this positive sacred view of menstruation that honours the sacred feminine energies gets dubbed as "misogynistic" by a modernity that mocks and trivialises this sacred process as "women on the rag" . . . This is the ultimate triumph of patriarchy."[667]

The yogic rituals around menstruation involve the process of honouring and protecting the woman's body, ensuring good health for her and any children she may conceive. To this end, the Ayurvedic tradition provides a strict protocol to be followed during menstruation.

So, Should You Practise Yoga During Menstruation?

As with every practice, the best answer is to listen to your body. If your energy is very low during menstruation, you may benefit from restorative poses and *yoga nidra*, yogic sleep, which is typically induced using a guided meditation. You could also replace your asana practice with gentle breath training until you feel more energised.[668] Whenever your body is challenged, you should be thinking about recovery.

667 Sridhar, Nithin. "Hindu View of Menstruation – VI: Menstruation Restrictions and Attitudes." *India Facts.* (August 10, 2016). http://www.indiafacts.org/hindu-view-menstruation-vi-menstruation-restrictions-attitudes/#1 (Accessed July 6, 2022).
668 Oates, Jennifer. "The Effect of Yoga on Menstrual Disorders: A Systematic Review." *The Journal of Alternative and Complementary Medicine* 23.6 (2017): 407-417.

PREGNANCY

Breath Training to Prepare for Pregnancy

It is common for doctors to advise women who want to get pregnant to follow similar protocols to those adopted during pregnancy. Extra caution is needed at this time as, in the first days or weeks of conception, a woman may not be aware of this new phase her body has entered.

Any breathing exercises that put the body under stress must be avoided, while exercises that cause the body to relax are beneficial. It is worth noting that an exercise that is calming for one person may be stressful for another, depending on the respiratory capacity and BOLT score of the individual.

Hormones both affect and are affected by breathing. This includes prolactin, a key hormone for conception. When prolactin levels are lower[669] or much higher than normal,[670] a miscarriage can occur. Hypercapnia, when practised for four minutes, has been shown to cause a modest increase in prolactin of around 16% that lasts for about ten minutes after the exercise.[671,672] Hyperventilation has no effect on prolactin. Prolactin was found to increase after Sudarshan Kriya Yoga (SKY) controlled breathing practice. SKY has four distinct components:

1. Ujjayi breathing at between two and four breaths per minute.
2. Bhastrika/Bellows Breath.
3. Om, chanted three times with a very long exhalation.

669 Li, W., et al. "The Relationship Between Serum Prolactin Concentration and Pregnancy Outcome in Women with Unexplained Recurrent Miscarriage." *Journal of Obstretrics and Gynacology* 33.3 (2013): 285-288.

670 Hirahara, Fumiki, et al. "Hyperprolactinemic Recurrent Miscarriage and Results of Randomized Bromocirptine Treatment Trials." *Fertility and Sterily* 70.2 (1998): 246-252.

671 Vega, S. Rojas, H. K. Studer, and W. Hollmann. "Plasma Prolactic Concentration Increases After Hypercapnia Acidosis." *Hormone and Metabolic Research* 35.10 (2003): 598-602.

672 Hirahara, Fumiki, et al. "Hyperprolactinemic Recurrent Miscarriage and Results of Randomized Bromocirptine Treatment Trials." *Fertility and Sterily* 70.2 (1998): 246-252.

4. Sudarshan Kriya – a cleansing rite that involves cyclical, rhythmic breathing with slow, medium, and fast cycles.[673]

What to Practise During Pregnancy

Pregnancy is an interesting period when it comes to breathing physiology. During the nine months in which the foetus develops, the body's acid-base balance is affected. The pressure of CO_2 in the blood vessels decreases to a low of 31.3mmHg, which is 21.75% lower than the 40 mmHg found in healthy adults.[674] For the fetus to develop with healthy CO_2 levels, the mother's physiology must compromise.[675] During pregnancy, the body becomes more sensitive to CO_2 due to fluctuations in progesterone and oestrogen. Progesterone increases sixfold between week 6 and 37 of gestation. Oestrogen levels rise too,[676] enhancing the number and sensitivity of progesterone receptors in the brain, which amplifies the effect of circulating progesterone.[677]

It almost goes without saying that pregnancy is a period during which extra caution is required. This applies to breath training too.

The utmost care should be taken during the first trimester. During this time, do not practise any form of breath training involving reduced volume breathing or breath holds. However, many women need stress management and emotional support during pregnancy, and breath training is a valuable tool for this. You may find gentle, slow breathing, such as the guided breathing meditation available from OxygenAdvantage. com, to be calming. Google: "patrick mckeown guided breathing".

673 Zope, Sameer A., and Rakesh A. Zope. "Sudarshan Kriya Yoga: Breathing for Health." *International Journal of Yoga* 6.1 (2013): 4.
674 Omo-Aghoja, L. "Maternal and Fetal Acid-Base Chemistry: A Major Determinant of Perinatal Outcome." *Annals of Medical and Health Sciences Research* 4.1 (2014): 8-17.
675 Blechner, Jack N. 1993. "Maternal—Fetal Acid—Base Physiology." *Clinical Obstetrics and Gynecology* 36.1 (1993): 3-12.
676 LoMauro, Antonella, and Andrea Aliverti. "Sex Differences in Respiratory Function." *Breathe* 14.2 (2018): 131-140.
677 LoMauro, Antonella, and Andrea Aliverti. "Respiratory Physiology of Pregnancy: Physiology Masterclass." *Breathe* 11.4 (2015): 297-301.

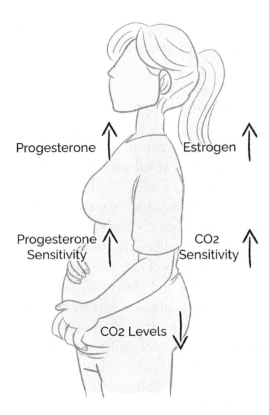

Progesterone ↑

Estrogen ↑

Progesterone Sensitivity ↑

CO2 Sensitivity ↑

CO2 Levels ↓

While research involving pregnant women is limited, alternate nostril breathing can help with anxiety.[678] You can read much more about the connection between breathing and pregnancy in *The Breathing Cure*, including advice about sleep apnea. Pregnancy increases the risk of sleep apnea by around 8%,[679] and this can have a harmful effect on the developing baby.

678 Styles, Amanda, et al. "Prenatal Yoga for Young Women a Mixed Methods Study of Acceptability and Benefits." BMC Pregnancy and Childbirth 19.1 (2019): 1-12.

679 Wimms, Alison, et al. "Obstructive Sleep Apnea in Women: Specific Issues and Interventions." *BioMed Research International* 2016, (2016).

Smell and Mating Partner Selection

If you had any doubt about the importance of your nose, olfaction, and how you breathe – or about the interrelatedness of every system and the importance of the substances you bring into your body, consider the following interesting and thought-provoking research.

According to research studies, a woman's selection of mating partner is influenced by male scent. Breathing through the nose provides a woman with genetically valuable information (especially around the time of ovulation) that "tells" her that the male has a dissimilar MHC. MHC is the Major Histocompatibility Complex (MHC), also known as the Human Leukocyte Antigen. The MHC is a set of genes concerned with immune response. MHC produces chemosensory signals in human bodily secretions. These signals can then be picked up by smell. Mating with a partner with genetically dissimilar MHC not only avoids inbreeding and improves genetic diversity, it also helps produce a genetic profile with broader immunity and greater fitness to ensure survival.[680]

Once a woman is pregnant, studies suggest that her preference shifts to the smells of males with more similar MHC (higher possibility of being genetically related), suggesting a preference for kinship relationships that can assist with child-rearing.[681]

While studies are not conclusive, there is also a suggestion that oral contraceptives can alter a woman's preference. Since most oral contraceptives mimic the hormonal state of pregnancy, a woman's preference shifts to similar MHC profiles. Notably, this preference for

---

680 "The Nose Knows: MHC-Dependent Mate Selection in Humans Through Odor Preference." *Lake Forest.* (February 18, 2017). https://www.lakeforest.edu/news/the-nose-knows-mhc-dependent-mate-selection-in-humans-through-odor-preference (Accessed October 1, 2022).

681 "The Nose Knows: MHC-Dependent Mate Selection in Humans Through Odor Preference." *Lake Forest.* (February 18, 2017). https://www.lakeforest.edu/news/the-nose-knows-mhc-dependent-mate-selection-in-humans-through-odor-preference (Accessed October 1, 2022).

greater similarity may have a negative influence on relationship stability and even the viability of pregnancies.[682]

In other words, medications, hormones, and other behaviours can affect the way women respond to the very important chemical signals that they inhale.

The lesson here: don't underestimate the importance of functional nasal breathing – it could even affect your choice of mate, viability of pregnancies, and the future health of your children. And finally, don't underestimate how many common everyday activities (such as smoking) could impair the subtler functions of your breathing and nose. Breathing in through your nose can literally change your life and the lives of those around you!

PACED BREATHING FOR MENOPAUSE & HOT FLASHES

There are many changes that occur as a result of menopause that are affected by or that affect breathing. After menopause, women are much more susceptible to sleep-disordered breathing including sleep apnea. Changes in body-fat distribution and the permanent reduction in progesterone both contribute. Menopausal symptoms such as hot flashes and panic disorder can also be attributed to changes in sex hormone levels and to imbalances in the autonomic nervous system.

There is even a connection between osteoporosis and breathing pattern disorders. Women with bone loss disorders display disturbances in blood exchange and altered breathing patterns. There is detailed information about these links in *The Breathing Cure*. Suffice to say, breathing exercises to normalise blood gas exchange,

---

682 Roberts, S. C., L. M., Carter, V. Gosling, and M. Petrie. "MHC-Correlated Odour Preferences in Humans and the Use of Oral Contraceptives." *Proceedings. Biogical Sciences* 275(2008): 2715-2722.

CO_2 levels, and nervous system balance will only be beneficial. However, as always, listen to your body and begin your practice very gently.

Paced breathing involves slowing your breath down intentionally while focusing on its length and breadth to help calm the mind and the body. If you have ever observed a monk in real life or in a film, you may have seen that they breathe in and out in a deliberate manner when they meditate. Sitting quietly with legs folded in and backs straight, they quietly inhale air, hold their breath for some time, usually longer than normal, and then exhale. This enhances the focus and clarity of attention needed for meditation.

Yoga practitioners also perform this paced breathing exercise. Paced breathing is known to help relieve stress and reduce aches from exercises that may have hurt or stressed the muscles. Experienced musicians master paced breathing to help when musical notes require air to be exhaled more slowly than usual. Some athletes also practise paced breathing as they have a limited volume of oxygen available, especially for intense exercises, such as running. Concentrating on their breathing and slowing it also helps athletes control their heart rate and prevent quick burnout. Overall, it boosts endurance and general well-being.

One of the most common and disagreeable features of menopause is hot flashes. Hot flashes are sudden feelings of warmth in a person's body, usually intense and over the neck, chest, and face. They are usually accompanied by profuse sweating. While common in women during menopause, other common causes of hot flashes are embarrassment, eating spicy food and drinks, underlying health conditions, and adrenal triggers from dangerous situations. Hot flashes are caused by increased sympathetic activity in the brain, causing blood to rush to the face and neck, hence the warm feeling.

Changing our breathing pattern influences our body in ways that can ultimately affect how we feel and think. Paced breathing reduces the fight or flight sympathetic responses in the central nervous system, facilitating relaxation. Paced breathing also stimulates the vagus nerve and increases parasympathetic activities in the body, causing relaxation and reducing stress. When we pace our breathing, our responses to fear, anger, and anxiety are reduced significantly.[683]

Scientific evidence has shown that paced breathing helps the body relax, relieves insomnia, and alleviates symptoms of anxiety and depression. It helps to regulate blood pressure and helps people manage pain, even chronic pain such as that caused by arthritis.[684] Paced breathing can provide benefits for everyone, including women suffering from the many unpleasant effects of menopause, many of which can be impacted by breathing patterns.[685,686,687, 688]

OTHER HORMONAL CONSIDERATIONS THAT MAY AFFECT BREATHING

Yoga instructors regularly ask their students if they have any physical injury or other issue, so the physical practice can be adjusted accordingly. The same goes for breathing. Instructors should be aware of any issues that may be causing their student's difficulty. The impact of sex hormones on the breath should not be underestimated, and this includes the use of synthetic hormones, such as oral contraceptives, HRT, and hormone therapy. This affects a broad group of people.

683 Sood, R., A. Sood, S. L. Wolf, B. M. Linquist, H. Liu, J. A. Sloan, D. V. Satele, C. L. Loprinzi, and D. L. Barton. 2013. "Paced Breathing Compared With Usual Breathing for Hot Flashes." *Menopause* 20.2 (2013): 179-184. (Accessed October 1, 2022).

684 Larsen KL, Brilla LR, McLaughlin WL, Li Y. Effect of Deep Slow Breathing on Pain-Related Variables in Osteoarthritis. Pain Res Manag. 2019 Jun 3;2019:5487050.

685 Jacqueline Brenner, Suzanne LeBlang, Michelle Lizotte-Waniewski, Barbara Schmidt, Patricio S. Espinosa, David L. DeMets, Andrew Newberg, Charles H. Hennekens. Mindfulness with paced breathing reduces blood pressure. *Medical Hypotheses*, 2020; 142.

686 Freedman RR, Woodward S. Behavioral treatment of menopausal hot flushes: evaluation by ambulatory monitoring. Am J Obstet Gynecol. 1992;167(2):436-439. 11.

687 Freedman RR, Woodward S, Brown B, Javiad JI, Pandey GN. Biochemical and thermoregulatory effects of behavioral treatment for menopausal hot fl ashes. Menopause. 1995;2(4):211-218

688 https://www.menopause.org/docs/professional/tfppaced0712.pdf (accessed June 24, 2020).

Around 65% of women aged between 15 and 49 in the United States take an oral contraceptive.

After menopause, approximately 44% of women take hormone replacement therapies (HRT). HRT and other hormone therapies are also widely used by women after hysterectomy and by the transgender community. There is currently little research into the impact of hormone therapies on breathing, but one recent case series reports an increase in sleep-disordered breathing in transgender men (assigned female at birth). This may be due to the adding of testosterone or to the suppressing of oestrogen and/or progesterone. Hormone treatments are also used by women with breast cancer who have been treated with medications that lower oestrogen and by men with prostate cancer who have been treated surgically and/or anti-androgen medications.[689]

These are obviously sensitive, personal matters and need to be treated with the utmost discretion – like any other personal or medical information. However, it's worth knowing that these matters may be relevant to any breathing difficulties. This is where the BOLT score can provide a gentle, objective assessment. By measuring the BOLT, an instructor can get a simple perspective on where a student's breathing is today, without having to ask personal questions. This alone allows the teacher to tailor breathing exercises and physical postures. However, between the class intake form and the fact yoga students often confide in their teacher about personal and health issues, more information may be available to help guide the student's breathing. Awareness of the link between breathing and hormones can certainly be helpful.

689 Robertson, Brian D., et al. "The Effects of Transgender Hormone Therapy on Sleep and Breathing: A Case Series." *Journal of Clinical Sleep Medicine* 15.10 (2019): 1529-1533.

CONCLUSION

Our intention with this book was to provide a thorough, accessible and practical guide on the topic of breathing for yoga, viewing breathing and ancient yogic wisdom through a modern scientific lens. In doing so, we have produced a rather weighty tome. If you have made it this far – well done!

It is not easy to accept ideas and practices that may be counter to what you have taught, and have been taught, for years. I put this to Robin Rothenberg, breath expert and yoga therapist, during our interview. According to Robin:

> It would be skirting the issue not to acknowledge that there is some resistance in the yoga world to the ideas in the Oxygen Advantage® and Buteyko Methods. Yoga has its own breathing traditions, and yogis are understandably keen not to muddy the waters. But, as you have been exploring throughout this book, these approaches have more in common than a first glance might suggest. Indeed, modern scientific understanding helps us get closer to prāṇāyāma as it was originally intended.

Magdalena Kraler, an academic specialising in the history of modern prāṇāyāma, has offered some reflective commentary to close the book:

> Modern prāṇāyāma is a blended product of various influences. That profound ingenuity and creativity has led to many approaches to the practice. There is no reason why it should not be extended by the added knowledge of breathing mechanics, biochemistry, and functional breathing that Oxygen Advantage® offers.
>
> Given that people are now living in high-stress environments, knowing how to regulate breathing during the day can be beneficial.

It makes sense that everyday breathing can be improved by techniques that support breathing off the mat. Since many practitioners do not have experienced teachers by their side, Oxygen Advantage® helps to carefully guide attention to one's breathing habits and to gradually change them. For example, as soon as one becomes aware of situations where one tends to breathe through the mouth, this pattern will change, helping to clear the nostrils, which will, in turn, benefit prāṇāyāma practice.

It has been shown extensively that there are overlaps between prāṇāyāma and the Oxygen Advantage® idea of breathing light, slow, and low, most notably in Patanjali's concept that the breath should be made "long and subtle." The hygienic influence in modern yoga as well as premodern examples make it clear that prāṇāyāma acts on the body, improving health and its overall functions. At the same time, prāṇāyāma and related techniques can have profound effects on the mind and induce spiritual states.

In the end, the path that leads toward deep experiences with one's breath, body and mind is highly individual. B.K.S. Iyengar held that, in the art of prāṇāyāma, there are indeed an "infinite number of permutations and combinations possible." So, he says, even the inexperienced practitioner can practise independently without fear of ill effects. In this highly subjective practice with movements infinitely subtle, one has to learn to guide oneself and develop a refined sense of self. This, in turn, will bring "peace in body, poise in mind, and tranquillity in the self," as experienced yogis promise.[690]

SOME FINAL WORDS FROM PATRICK

Breathing is vital to life, from our first gasp of air to our last. Yet for many, the innate, subtle art of healthy breathing gets lost along the way. The impact can be profound, permeating many domains of life, from health and wellbeing to work and relationships.

690 Iyengar, B. K. S. *Light on Prāṇāyāma: Prāṇāyāma Dīpikā*. With an Introduction by Yehudi Menuhin, London: Unwin Paperbacks, 1983, p. xxi.

My goal is simply this: to help more people breathe optimally. Through personal experience and that of my clients over the past twenty-plus years, I have observed how learning to breathe functionally can enhance health, wellbeing, and performance. But don't just take my word for it! Throughout this book, we have woven-in the abundance of research now available to back this up. Case in point, this book has around 700 scientific and yogic references. I can only apologize that our drive to be thorough has come at the expense of brevity.

I hope you have already begun to integrate the Oxygen Advantage® approach into your regular practice and are experiencing the benefits of functional everyday breathing for yourself. I also hope you will continue to use this book as a resource to guide and enrich your practice going forward.

Yoga has enormous potential to generate a better understanding of prāṇāyāma and the causes and effects of different breathing practices during asanas. Yoga teachers are ideally placed to share these messages to benefit an extensive audience. Equipped with an understanding of functional breathing from a multidimensional perspective, I can foresee a time when yoga teachers provide the BOLT score as feedback on everyday breathing and tailor breathing exercises according to the state of health, breathing, and age of each student. Those with asthma, panic disorder, and anxiety often find the asanas challenging due to the resulting air hunger. This may put them off yoga and deprive them of the benefits of a yoga practice, or cause them to hyperventilate, and aggravate their symptoms. But it doesn't have to be that way!

If the ancient appreciation for subtle, silent, nasal, diaphragmatic breathing is restored to the practice, yoga can become accessible and beneficial to nearly everyone. The need for the benefits we can get from meditation, yoga, and breath training has never been greater. Yoga originated thousands of years ago, at a time when life was fundamentally less complex and there was a greater sense of connection. Nowadays, life is very different.

The late Irish poet and philosopher John O'Donohue, a fellow native of Connemara here in County Galway, wrote:

These times are riven with anxiety and uncertainty, given the current global crisis. In the hearts of people, some natural ease has been broken. It is astounding how this has reached deep into the heart. Our trust in the future has lost innocence.[691]

Whilst John wrote those words following the financial crisis that started in 2007, as we find ourselves in the wake of the COVID-19 pandemic, they are more apt than ever today.

Modern life now could be regarded as a system based on commercial values and pressures. Our roles are to be productive, pay our taxes, and contribute to society – with little regard for the chronic stress that this forces on us. It's no surprise that rates of chronic stress and autoimmune illnesses are rampant. The disquiet evident in today's society is a manifestation of the inner turmoil of the human being.

If we as a human race are to leave a legacy of life to our children, we need to quell the pace and overwhelm of everyday living. The first step is to look at ourselves, not to be too critical, but to be compassionate and have a sense of self-awareness. This is a lot easier when our physiology is in a state of balance, when we have optimal sleep and a calm and clear state of mind. We can't rely on society to give us the tools to deal with stress and anxiety – and fortunately, we don't have to. We can be self-reliant. Healthy and functional breathing empowers us to take control of our nervous systems, and ultimately, our health.

I'd like to leave you with a final thought. I introduced this book by reflecting that my journey with breath training began with the **Breathe Light** exercise. That was the hook for me. It changed my life. Twenty-plus years later, it's still my go-to breathing exercise. Recently, in a high-pressure situation where I was interviewed by five high-flying candidates, I used my breath to self-regulate and stay focused. All I did was simply take a soft inhalation through my nose and a relaxed and slow exhalation. Even during the interview, when there were breaks between questions, I focused on my breath. Just an example of the

691 O'Donohue, John. *Divine beauty: The invisible embrace.* Random House, 2010.

application of breathing in one's everyday life. That's what it is all about. There is no spectacle with the exercise. There is nothing to see, but it's incredibly effective.

That's the power of breathing.

APPENDICES

YOGA & BREATHING – A HISTORICAL PERSPECTIVE ON THE SYNTHESIS OF OXYGEN ADVANTAGE® & PRĀṆĀYĀMA

By Magdalena Kraler

Magdalena is an academic specialising in the history of modern prāṇ āyāma (PhD 2022, University of Vienna, Religious Studies). Currently living in Austria, she works as a music and dance teacher. Over the past 20 years, she has explored different forms of body and breath work.

Various cultures, East and West, have developed breathing exercises that help improve one's health, wellbeing, and overall quality of life. Yoga is certainly one of the most prominent with a focus on breath practices to improve a person's health and alter their mindset. And, by which, many texts claim, even superpowers may be attained.

Most people, when they think of yoga, first think of postures that are combined with controlled breathing. Indeed, controlled breathing is a central part of yoga. While the focus on posture (asana) in yoga is a rather recent development, breath control (prāṇāyāma) can be traced back to the Vedic period (ca. 1500–500 BCE). It was first related to the practice of chanting mantras in which one had to be able to manage long phases of controlled outbreathing. Early breath practices that arise in the context of Hindu asceticism mainly focused on rigorous breath holding. Even Gautama Buddha practised these but found that they were too painful and intense and that they did not lead to final liberation, at least for him. Hindu ascetics stuck to the practices (including severe and somewhat easier ones), and Patanjali's *Yogasutra* describes prāṇāyāma in five rather cryptic sutras. Within Hatha yoga, prāṇāyāma played a paramount role, and we will look into those premodern practices and their goals below.

However, what we practise as prāṇāyāma today in yoga studios is not necessarily directly derived from Patanjali or the Hatha yogis. Many influences shaped the large variety of practices now subsumed under the umbrella of prāṇāyāma. My dissertation at the University of Vienna,[692] was a historical study tracing various lineages of today's prāṇāyāma teachings. I analysed a huge amount of historical material – including Hatha yoga texts and their translations from the late nineteenth-century and a myriad of prāṇāyāma-related texts from between 1850 and 1945. The main strands of practices and ideas that I found are derived from:

1. The yoga traditions (including the yoga of Patanjali and Hatha yoga)
2. Nineteenth-century hygienic culture, which tried to revive ancient Greek Galenic medicine, and
3. Esoteric and occult societies which were active in both India and the West.

---

692 Kraler, Magdalena. *Yoga Breath: The Reinvention of Prāṇa and Prāṇāyāma in Early Modern Yoga.* University of Vienna, 2022. https://utheses.univie.ac.at/detail/63089/.

In other words, in today's prāṇāyāma, we see a mix of influences which explains the contradictory practices and ideas one may encounter in the yoga studio. I think it is helpful to be aware of these various influences so that each practitioner can decide which strands, lineages, and practices work best for them.

I won't go into much detail regarding the esoteric and occult influences because they are less relevant to this book. Instead, I am highlighting the influences of the yoga traditions and hygienic culture for two main reasons. First, it helps to know more about practices from the yoga traditions and what their original goals were. While some aspects of premodern techniques are still to be uncovered by experts of Indology, we can at least delineate some important features of these traditions that are (in part) still relevant for today's prāṇāyāma. Second, hygienic contexts were important for health-oriented prāṇāyāma, and these contexts were also the major drivers for new interpretations of prāṇ āyāma. For example, hygienic and medical contexts in the nineteenth century promoted deep breathing – which included practices of filling one's lungs to the fullest and taking as much air in as possible in order to "oxygenate the blood." On the other hand, there were also overlaps between the yoga traditions and hygienic culture: nasal breathing was promoted in hygienic culture as early as the 1860s,[693] and, in most prāṇāyāma practices (except sitali and sitkari), one breathes through the nose, not the mouth.

A Few Examples from the Yoga Traditions

Patanjali's *Yogasutra* (written some time between 325 and 425 CE) describes four types of prāṇāyāma in *Yogasutra* 2.49–53. According to Patanjali, a prerequisite for practising prāṇāyāma is having established a firm seat (asana) and adhering to moral standards and acquiring personal integrity (yama and niyama). The first two types of prāṇāyāma can

---

693 Catlin, George. *The Breath of Life*, Trubner, London, 1862. (Also published under the title *Shut Your Mouth and Save Your Live*).

be interpreted either as a retention after inhalation and after exhalation or as simply prolonging and refining the inhalation and exhalation.[694] The third type is usually interpreted as a *deliberate* suspension of the breath with a "sudden effort." The fourth type is a *spontaneous* or effortless breath retention that is likely an outcome of the first three practices. It may occur at any stage during any phase of breathing.[695]

We do not know exactly what Patanjali's prāṇāyāma looked like (the cryptic nature of the sutras and Vyasa's commentary are difficult to interpret and leave much space for speculation), but there are some ideas regarding the outcomes of prāṇāyāma that are quite clear. Patanjali states that prāṇāyāma uncovers the light enabling one to proceed to higher yogic practices like dharana and samadhi. According to Swami Hariharananda, a modern interpreter of Patanjali, the veil is caused by the accumulation of one's actions based on ignorance (karma). Once prāṇāyāma thins this blanket of karmic ignorance, one can see one's inner light of discriminative knowledge more clearly, and it will start to shine through.[696] *Yogasutra* 2.50 further notes that the breath becomes "long and subtle" (*dirgha-suksma*) by prāṇāyāma. Although this may not be a direct prāṇāyāma instruction, this signals to the practitioner that they are on the right track. When the breath becomes so subtle that it is hardly perceptible, this is the fourth state of Patanjali's prāṇāyāma and what is later called kevala kumbhaka in Hatha yoga. A literal translation of this term is "pure retention."

In Hatha yoga, which is documented from the eleventh century CE onward, there are eight varieties of prāṇāyāma (also called the

---

694 In this interpretation of the four types of Patanjali's Prāṇāyāma , I follow Karambelkar, P.V. "Patanjala Yoga Sutras: Sanskrit Sutra with Transliteration, Translation & Commentary." *Yoga Mimansa* 24.4 (1986): 257–296, p. 284, 295. (Note: Patanjali's *Prāṇāyāma* is highly under-researched and there is as yet no definite answer as to what the practices exactly looked like. There are a myriad of interpretations, which may or may not be close to the original practices.)

695 Mallinson, James & Mark Singleton. *Roots of Yoga*, 2017, p. 141. This also follows Karambelkar, P. V. "Patanjala Yoga Sutras: Sanskrit Sutra with Transliteration, Translation & Commentary. Continued." *Yoga Mimansa* 25.1-2 (1986): 297-432, p. 304.

696 Cf. "The Yoga Sadhakas." *Prāṇāyāma Made Easy*. Santa Cruz, Bombay: The Yoga Institute, 1981, p. 15.

eight kumbhakas which translates as the "eight retentions"). As a set of techniques, they are also mentioned in the fifteenth century *Hathapradipika*. All of them involve breath retention. While each is distinctive in its ways of inhaling and exhaling, the technique of breath retention itself remains the same.

The following table provides an overview of the practices:[697]

Suryabhedana (the "solar")	Inhale through the solar (right) nostril, hold the breath, and then exhale through the lunar (left) nostril.
Ujjayi (the "victorious")	Inhale through both nostrils while making a rasping sound with the palate and epiglottis, hold the breath, and then exhale through the left nostril.
Sitali (the "cool")	Inhale through the rolled tongue and exhale through both nostrils.
Bhastrika (the "bellows")	Breathe in and out repeatedly and rapidly through both nostrils before slowly inhaling through the right nostril, holding the breath, and exhaling through the left nostril.
Sitkari (the "whistler")	Make a whistling sound while inhaling through the mouth. Exhale through the nostrils. The yogi becomes like a second god of love.
Bhramari (the "buzzer")	Make a buzzing sound while inhaling and exhaling; this brings about bliss.
Murccha (the "swoon")	At the end of inhalation, apply the chin lock and then breathe out slowly, bringing oneself to the point of fainting.
Plavini (the "floater")	Fill up the abdomen with air in order to float on water.

In Hatha yoga, breath retention was primarily practised after inhalation. The word *kumbhaka* literally means "holding a full pot." As this analogy suggests, the chest is filled with air like a pot, and, by

---

697 Mallinson, James. "Haṭha Yoga" in Jacobsen, Knuth A., et al., eds., *Brill's Encyclopedia of Hinduism*. Vol. III, Leiden and Boston: Brill, 2011, 770-781, p. 777.

applying the root lock (mula bandha) and the chin lock (jalandhara bandha), one "locks" the air or prana inside the trunk. Furthermore, one tries to manipulate various aspects of prana inside the body (for example one tries to push *prana*, situated in the trunk *down*, and pull *apana*, situated in the lower belly, *up*).[698] These "hydraulics" during prāṇāyāma work best if the body is filled with air, i.e., after inhalation, according to the yogis. Therefore, deep breaths were probably inhaled before retention because it is then easier to place the chin on the chest. However, the outcomes of the practices were subtle, and the idea of a spontaneous retention of the breath (kevala kumbhaka) or the breath becoming so subtle that it is almost imperceptible is also found. The technique of holding the breath after exhaling also exists in premodern yoga, but it is more frequently practised in tantric contexts.

Besides breath retention, there are other preliminary breath practices that are, strictly speaking, not part of the prāṇāyāma set. This includes alternate-nostril breathing, in which one inhales through the right nostril, exhales through the left, inhales through the left, and exhales through the right, and so on. An important outcome of the practice is the cleansing of nadis (subtle channels in which prana flows; the ida and pingala nadis end in each of the nostrils), or nadi suddhi/nadi shodhana. (See Chapter Seventeen for more on the nadis.) It prepares one for long breath holding practices. Another cleansing technique is kapalabhati or rapid breathing which involves a controlled form of hyperventilation.

Already in premodern times, prāṇāyāma was practised for health benefits. For example, some practices are said to destroy worms in the intestines (*Hathapradipika* 2.50)[699] and to eliminate excess heat, wind, or phlegm (e.g., through bhastrika, as described in *Hathapradipika*

---

698 Several systems in Hindu tradition divide prana into a varied number of sub-pranas. The most common system is the "five pranas," which are *prana, apana, vyana, udana,* and *samana.* For details, see Zysk, Kenneth G. "The Science of Respiration and the Doctrine of the Bodily Winds in Ancient India." *Journal of the American Oriental Society* 113.2 (1993): 198-213.

699 All references to the *Hathapradipika* are quoted from Digambarji, Swami & Raghunathashastri Kokaje, eds. *Haṭhapradīpikā of Svātmārāma.* Lonavla: Kaivalyadhama S.M.Y.M. Samiti, 1970.

2.65). Ujjayi destroys diseases of the subtle channels (nadis) and within the seven tissues (dhatus). And several Prāṇāyāma s are said to produce heat in the body (particularly suryabhedana).

However, Prāṇāyāma is also a powerful tool in religious contexts, tantric practices, and magic performed by the yogi, as the rich folk tale tradition of India recounts. These so-called siddhis are also frequently mentioned in Hatha yoga texts. Among the most prevalent ones are the idea that the yogi can stop his breath at will for as long as he wants (*Sivasamhita* 3.45),[700] that he is bestowed a beautiful smell, voice, and face (*Sivasamhita* 3.30; *Yogayajnavalkya* 5.21–22) and becomes like a "god of love" (*Hathapradipika* 2.54). If the breath is held for three hours, the yogi can balance himself on his thumb (*Sivasamhita* 3.67). Further magical powers are levitation, power over wild animals (*Dattatreyayogasastra* 75–83),[701] being free of all diseases, conquering old age and death (*Kumbhakapaddhati* 149–150), conquering sleep, hunger, and thirst (*Hathapradipika* 2.55), attaining long-distance vision and hearing, subtle sight, and the ability to enter the body of another person (*Sivasamhita* 3.60). There is also a rich tradition that uses observation of breath to foretell future events including one's own or another person's death (svarodaya or "svara yoga," Hemacandra's *Yogasastra* 5.70–117).

Naturally, the yogis of the modern era also use these accounts of acquiring magical powers to point to the potency of prāṇāyāma. Whether they are regarded as true or fictitious must be decided by each follower of yoga. There is, however, evidence that at least some were also designed to motivate yogis to stick to rigorous practices and strict routines.

Another important outcome of the practice of prāṇāyāma is its role in attaining final liberation. Some Hatha texts state that prāṇāyāma can lead directly to final liberation or moksa (e.g., *Goraksasataka* 8–10).[702]

---

700 All references to the *Sivasamhita* are quoted from Mallinson, James. *The Shiva Samhita: A Critical Edition and an English Translation*. Woodstock: YogaVidya, 2007.

701 Quoted from Mallinson, James & Mark Singleton. *Roots of Yoga*. 2017, p. 156-157.

702 Quoted from Mallinson, James & Mark Singleton. *Roots of Yoga*. 2017, p. 157.

In this, prāṇāyāmaʼs capacity to make kundalini (a female energy (sakti) dormant at the root of the spine) arise is crucial and often considered a prerequisite for higher progress on the yogiʼs path. On the spiritual side of yoga, there is also a huge emphasis on prāṇāyāma for calming, steadying, and transforming the mind. Without these qualities, a yogi cannot proceed to higher practices of yoga which include the ability to effortlessly hold oneʼs breath for long periods (kevala kumbhaka), and the advanced manipulation of prana, meditation, and trance-like states. They also include feats like projecting the self out of the body through the cranial vault (as during death to attain final liberation). Indeed, it is said that prana is linked both to the mind and semen, and all three become steady in the highest practices of yoga, which is samadhi. The yoga scholar David Gordon White explains the significance of this powerful triad that bestows omnipotence to a yogi:

> "When the breath is stable, mind and semen are stabilised; but more important, when through breath control (*prāṇāyāma*) the base of the medial channel is opened, that same breath causes the reversal of mundane polarities. Rather than descending, semen, energy, and mind are now forced upwards into the cranial vault, affecting total yogic integration (*samādhi*), a reversal of the flow of time, immortality and transcendence over the entire created universe."[703]

Mastering prāṇāyāma is a highly intricate process that involves years of study, and, in premodern yoga, it was often stated that it cannot be learned without the guidance of an experienced teacher. The subtle body of the yogi was a universe that could only be conquered by intense and regular practice. Within modern prāṇāyāma, many of these themes, ideas, and practices persist, but several new themes are also on the rise.

Before transitioning to the next important time period, a few remarks on the practices in relation to the overall theme of this book are due. We think the benefit of holding the breath after inhaling is the

---

703 White, David Gordon. *The Alchemical Body: Siddha Traditions in Medieval India.* Chicago and London: The University of Chicago Press, 1996, p. 45.

manipulation of prana within the body. It is really the mechanics of the yogic subtle body that help to explain the practices – but detailed modern research is pending, perhaps due to the immeasurability of the subtle effects that prāṇāyāma has (the occurrence of siddhis has not been proven by modern science either).

The negative side of breath retention after inhaling can be a strain on the heart, so practitioners with heart conditions should avoid it. Breath retention after exhaling (mostly called bahya kumbhaka) is also quite common in modern yoga. Some authors state that it is easier while others state that it is more difficult than normal kumbhaka. However, they agree that unnecessary strain should be avoided and that the safest way to practise prāṇāyāma is to start off with slow, regular inhalations and exhalations. Retention after exhaling often follows kapalabhati or rapid breathing. The hypoxic state that occurs after kapalabhati due to increased CO_2 elimination enables an easy long breath retention with controlled intermittent hypoxia.[704] But practitioners should be cautious about hyperventilation, and it is not part of the original prāṇāyāma set. As late Swami Maheshananda (whom I was privileged to learn from during my stay at Kaivalyadhama) put it, one should know about the difference between an *aftereffect* (i.e., a pleasant easily achieved hypoxic state) and a long-lasting *change* in one's breathing patterns which can only be achieved by a regular and devoted practice.

Generally, in premodern yoga, we find few recommendations for how to regulate breathing in everyday life. The exercises described in texts were designed for yogis who were already "experts," and they focused on brief descriptions of the practices while expounding greatly on the mundane and spiritual effects of prāṇāyāma. Long descriptions of the practices were also unnecessary because prāṇāyāma was supposed to be learned directly from an experienced yogi and not from a written text. Although the texts do not recommend breathing behaviour for a layman's life, one can nevertheless see that the practices *did* influence everyday life, as seen in the health benefits listed above. There were

704 See Section Two of this book "Creating a Breathing Program".

also recommendations to be followed before practising prāṇāyāma, including:

- A good place to practise (a quiet place with a well; a small hut; a place without insects)
- Sitting on a blanket or animal skin during practice
- A moderate diet (mitahara)
- An empty stomach before and during the practice
- And the cleansing of nadis through alternate-nostril breathing without breath retention (*Gherandasamhita* 5.1–45).[705]

Although recommendations for everyday life were sparse, there are some for everyday breathing that suggest that the "preservation" of breath was considered to promote longevity. For example, *Hathapradipika* 2.3 states that one should carefully deal with vayu (i.e., air, here a synonym for prana) in the body, because:

> "There is life so long as Vāyu is working in the body. Vāyu ceasing to work means death. Therefore, respiration should be regulated (so as to minimise respiratory activity)."[706]

Gherandasamhita 5.81–84 expounds even more clearly on that idea. It states that the breath flows from the nostrils at various distances (measured in finger breadths) during different activities. In the natural state, it moves 12 finger breadths. The activities then mentioned are singing, eating, walking, sleeping, sex, and physical exertion. The breath moves, as the text observes, quite naturally more strongly and with increased distance from the nostrils in each of these activities. The text then recommends to *decrease* the length of the breath as it flows from

---

705 All references to the *Gherandasamhita* are quoted from Mallinson, James. *The Gheranda Samhita: The Original Sanskrit and an English Translation*. Woodstock: YogaVidya, 2004.

706 Quoted from Digambarji, Swami & Raghunathashastri Kokaje, eds. *Haṭhapradīpikā of Svātmārāma*. Lonavla: Kaivalyadhama S.M.Y.M. Samiti, 1970, p. 36.

the nostrils in order to *increase* or prolong life; this also means, when the breath is held in, death cannot occur (*Gherandasamhita* 5.83–84).

These texts promote a low tidal volume as in non-exhausting activities, and they state that it is helpful to practise prāṇāyāma to accomplish this. This idea is similarly found in Oxygen Advantage®, in which light, slow, and low breathing is a means to a healthier, more joyful, and peaceful life. In returning once more to Patanjali's idea that the breath becomes "long and subtle" through prāṇāyāma, in modern yoga, this is expounded by Karambelkar, a researcher at the Kaivalyadhama Yoga Institute (on which, see below) in 1986. He defines prāṇāyāma as using "deliberate and prolonged" inhalations, exhalations, and retentions, thus producing a "slackening and consequent prolongation of the process of breathing."[707] He is aware of the concept of CO_2 sensitivity and suggests that the slackening of respiration will "lead to better exchange of gases (O_2 and CO_2) between the blood and the lung alveolar air." He concludes that "one aim of the whole training of prāṇāyāma is to condition the respiratory control centre to bear comfortably the highest possible concentrations of CO_2."

Karambelkar's definition of prāṇāyāma is derived from Patanjali's idea that the breath is made "*dirgha-suksma,*" or "long and subtle." For him, this also means that "rapid breathing during exertion and deep breathing" does not fall under the category of prāṇāyāma in Patanjali's sense. An "alteration of the normal rhythm of breathing" would count as prāṇāyāma so long as the alteration is "finer and slow" breathing.[708] In that sense, Oxygen Advantage® training, with its characteristic light, slow, and low breathing, would, at least for Karambelkar, indeed classify as prāṇāyāma . That such prāṇāyāma would produce a feeling of air hunger (i.e., the feeling of taking in less air than one needs) goes without saying, but Karambelkar also makes clear that the whole organism is trained to gradually accept a finer and slower intake of air.

707 Karambelkar, P. V. "Patanjala Yoga Sutras: Sanskrit Sutra with Transliteration, Translation & Comment." *Yoga Mimansa* 24.4 (1986): 257–296, p. 280, 283.
708 Karambelkar, P. V. "Patanjala Yoga Sutras: Sanskrit Sutra with Transliteration, Translation & Comment." *Yoga Mimansa* 24.4 (1986): 257–296, p. 280, 283.

In fact, that is part of the individual's learning in the prāṇāyāma process. Also, prāṇāyāma's effect on the mind is profound, which was already acknowledged by Patanjali. That is also a major reason for today's yogis and yoginis, as well as practitioners of Oxygen Advantage®, to stick to the practices.

Transitioning to Modern Prāṇāyāma

Modern prāṇāyāma derives important ideas and practices from the premodern era. In the period of early modern prāṇāyāma, starting in 1850, we find accounts in English that report various feats that yogis can perform. An important document is N. C. Paul's *A Treatise on Yoga Philosophy* (first edition 1851).[709] Here is why this is particularly interesting. Paul was a Bengali physician who was aware of the latest medical literature that featured the role of carbon dioxide during breathing, breath retention, and in various weather conditions as well as at varying times of the day.[710] He was also interested in the research on trance-like states that James Braid, the inventor of hypnosis, described.[711] He blended the most recent scientific and medical observations with accounts of prāṇāyāma as taken from the yoga traditions. Inspired by Braid's ideas about trance as a human form of "hibernation," Paul described various accounts of yogis who survived being buried alive for several weeks. Paul claims to have been an eyewitness to one of these events. The yogis who could reduce their breath and heartbeat to a minute amount (hence the idea of "hibernation") could survive in airtight containers for days or weeks. This was apparently accomplished through advanced prāṇāyāma practice and swallowing one's tongue

709 Paul, N. C. *A Treatise on the Yoga Philosophy* (Second Edition). Benares: E. J. Lazarus and Co., 1882 [1851].

710 To be precise, he drew on Karl von Vierordt's *Physiologie des Athmens: Mit besonderer Rücksicht auf die Ausscheidung der Kohlensäure* ["Physiology of Respiration: With Special Remarks on the Expulsion of Carbon Acid"] of 1845.

711 Braid, James. *Observations on Trance: Or Human Hybernation.* London and Edinburgh: John Churchill, 1850.

(khecarimudra) to obstruct the breathing passages and withstand the impulse to gasp for air.

Paul marks the transition from premodern to modern prāṇāyāma because he is aware of the basic biochemical aspects that govern the process of breathing and combines those with traditional knowledge on prāṇāyāma. Indeed, Paul builds a complete theory around reducing CO_2 elimination in the yogi's out-breath. He recommends yogis move slowly to reduce the frequency of their respiration; avoid cold places (in which CO_2 in the out-breath increases); avoid loud speaking, mental labour, and physical exertions; eat less, drink less, and engage in meditation.[712]

However, that it is CO_2 sensitivity that makes us breathe was only discovered about 40 years after Paul's *Treatise* was written.[713] Thus, unlike Karambelkar, Paul did not go into the details of the significance of CO_2 tolerance/sensitivity for breath holding. Nevertheless, yogis with prolonged breath holding time certainly had reduced CO_2 sensitivity. Even if accounts on surviving those extreme experiments were significantly exaggerated (which may well be), any breath holding time over a minute would already point to a reduced chemosensitivity to carbon dioxide. In being true to yoga traditions, Paul suggested that the yogi should stay at high altitudes, which, as we now know, naturally increases the oxygenation of the blood, particularly if it is combined with long breath holds.

A Few Examples from Hygienic Culture

The hygienic movement started to flourish in central Europe in the early nineteenth century and was oriented toward various nature cure practices. A major influence was the ancient Greek medicine of Hippocrates (c. 460–c. 375 BCE) and Claudius Galen (131–201 CE),

712   Paul, N. C. *A Treatise on the Yoga Philosophy* (Second Edition). Benares: E. J. Lazarus and Co., 1882 [1851], p. 2-7.
713   Fitzgerald, S. Robert. "The Regulation of Breathing." in Donald F. Proctor (ed.). *A History of Breathing Physiology*. New York: Marcel Dekker, 1995, 303-342, p. 308-309.

which hygienists aimed to revive. The importance of light clothing, natural environments, fresh air, water baths, and particularly the concept of "light and air" were prominent features closely linked to a hygienist's interest in breath practices.

Hygiene was mainly a movement that promoted self-help techniques, but it also had a medical side, which meant that doctors as well as nature cure experts were part of the movement. In regard to breathing, a main objective was to help fight lethal diseases of the breathing apparatus like pulmonary tuberculosis and to recover from or even prevent them. Deep breathing, particularly filling the lungs up to the clavicles, was said to reduce germs that would breed in these unventilated areas of the lungs. The idea was that "he lives most life whoever breathes most air."[714] The emphasis was sometimes laid on chest breathing and sometimes on belly breathing, and, as a synthesis, some advocates stated that the best way to breathe was the "full breath" that harnessed all three breathing spaces (belly, ribs, and upper chest). This is more understandable if we picture how people lost their loved ones as soon as their breath was barely palpable and their chests dreadfully sunken and stiff. It is in these contexts that the idea of deep breathing started to thrive and spread all over Europe, America, and India by the 1880s.

Hygienic culture also promoted nasal breathing over mouth breathing as it was known that the nasal passages could filter unwanted germs from the air, which was also warmed when breathed through the nose. Good breathing – particularly nasal breathing – was also said to rescue civilised white man from the degeneration of the "race"; promoting right breathing was often interwoven with eugenic thought (as were various forms of physical culture at that time). Catlin's *Shut Your Mouth and Save Your Life* (1870) is an influential early work that promoted nasal breathing over mouth breathing. Along with hygiene, improving everyday functional breathing through the nose was a major concern, but tendencies to overbreathe were also evident in deep breathing contexts.

714 Evans, W. F. *Esoteric Christianity and Mental Therapeutics*. Boston: H. H. Carter & Karrick, 1886, p. 96.

Let's now briefly investigate how these trickled into modern *prāṇāyāma*.

William Walker Atkinson was an American yogi and occultist who also wrote under the pseudonym Yogi Ramacharaka. His highly successful yoga manual *The Hindu-Yogi Science of Breath* of 1904, promoted "yogi-breathing."[715] But his manual is truer to exercises derived from Euro-American contexts than to the yoga traditions. In fact, the only Hatha yogic breathing technique that he adopted was alternate-nostril breathing. In his manual, we see a strong hygienic influence, some occult ideas and practices, as well as exercises derived from New York's voice culture scene.[716]

In all these contexts, the idea of deep breathing – sometimes called "full breathing" – was prominent, and Yogi Ramacharaka promoted it as the "Yogi Complete Breath." For him, it was so central that he regarded it as the "fundamental breath of the entire Yogi Science of Breath." In this practice, one assumes an erect sitting or standing position and fills the lungs gradually from bottom to top. After a brief retention, one exhales through the mouth by first drawing in the abdomen, and relaxes both the abdomen and chest fully after exhaling. The idea behind it is that "the quality of the blood depends largely upon its proper oxygenation in the lungs, allegedly being acquired by the complete breath."[717]

We see some misconceptions already happening here: while inhaling the big breaths advocated may bring more oxygen into the body, that oxygen is not available for use because the reduced carbon dioxide causes haemoglobin to hold on tightly to it. Blood circulation also reduces, making oxygen less available where it is needed. Nevertheless, the influence the book had on subsequent Euro-American and Indian yogis is remarkable. The "complete" breath entered prāṇāyāma curriculums

---

715 Ramacharaka, Yogi [pseud. William Walker Atkinson]. *The Hindu-Yogi Science of Breath: A Complete Manual of the Oriental Breathing Philosophy of Physical, Mental, Psychic and Spiritual Development*. Chicago: Yogi Publication Society, 1904.

716 For details, see Kraler, Magdalena. *Yoga Breath: The Reinvention of Prāṇa and Prāṇāyāma in Early Modern Yoga*. University of Vienna, 2022, p. 282-303.

717 Ramacharaka, Yogi. *The Hindu-Yogi Science of Breath: A Complete Manual of the Oriental Breathing Philosophy of Physical, Mental, Psychic and Spiritual Development*. Chicago: Yogi Publication Society, 1904, p. 31-39.

around the globe. For example, Swami Satyananda Saraswati from the Bihar School of Yoga refers to it in his seminal *Asana, prāṇāyāma, Mudra, Bandha* (1969),[718] and André van Lysebeth mentions it in his *Yoga Self-Taught* (1968).[719]

Few yogis realised that Ramacharaka was not a South Asian yogi, and even fewer opposed his ideas on the value of deep breathing. One of the earliest to argue against overbreathing is Mable E. Todd, a lecturer of "bodily balance" and "bodily economics" at Teachers College, Columbia University, in her generally influential *The Thinking Body: A Study of the Balancing Forces of Dynamic Man* (1937). A passage by Todd on chemical balance is worth quoting in full:

> "The virtue of 'full breathing' has been very much overestimated. In the tidal air of quiet breathing there is all the oxygen needed for the use of the individual under ordinary circumstances. There is always oxygen as well as carbon dioxide exhaled from the lungs. . . . The amount of residual air present in the lungs is sufficient to keep the oxygen balance. . . . When a greater amount of oxygen is needed for the body cells, as in extreme activity, there is deeper and faster breathing, not wider, 'fuller' breathing, unless hysteria is present. When we gasp at a sudden shock, the ribs become rounder and stiffer. But deep breathing in response to the physical and chemical needs of the inner cells of the body is vertical breathing."[720]

Todd was not a yogini, and, although she backed her doctrine scientifically and taught for over 30 years at Columbia University, it

---

718 Satyananda, Saraswati Swami. *Asana, Prāṇāyāma, Mudra, Bandha*. Compiled from Lectures Given During the Nine-Month Teacher Training Course, 1967-68, and the Three Year Sannyas Course, 1970-73, at the Bihar School of Yoga (Double Edition), Monghyr, Bihar, India: The Bihar School of Yoga, 1973 [1969].

719 Van Lysebeth, André. *Yoga Self-Taught: Complete, Easy Instructions for the Correct and Safe Practice of the Great Classics of Yoga*. 1968. Translated by Carola Congreve from the French "J'Apprends le yoga", New York: Barnes & Noble Books.

720 Todd, Mable Elsworth. *The Thinking Body: A Study of the Balancing Forces of Dynamic Man*. Hightstown: Princeton Book Company (Reprint), 1937, p. 240-241.

did not reach the yoga world. Some of the misconceptions about the oxygenation of the blood could have been eliminated already by the late 1930s if the yogis had access to the material and were aware of the importance of internal breathing, i.e., the gaseous exchange in the muscle cells.

Despite the unfortunate tendencies to overbreathe in modern prāṇāyāma classes, hygienic contexts did provide helpful hints on how students of yoga should mind their breath in everyday life. An important feature was the importance given to nasal breathing over mouth breathing and promoted by Catlin, Ramacharaka, and many subsequent authors. This is a new feature since nasal breathing was not specifically promoted in Hatha texts. Authors of hygienic contexts also highlighted the importance of taking in fresh air, the ventilation of rooms, taking air baths, and restoring health at high-altitude sanatoriums that focused on the prevention of pulmonary diseases. A common feature of advice in yoga and hygienic culture was the idea that the out-breath should be longer than the in-breath.

In *modern* yoga, the focus is on "slow, steady, and harmonious breathing"[721] as opposed to the rigorous breath retention of the Hatha Yogis or the deep breathing of the hygienists. Deep breathing was influential (and the idea is still deeply rooted in many), but it did not diffuse all ideas and contexts of prāṇāyāma. It is, however, only in the 1980s, as shown with Karambelkar, that the idea of "long and subtle" breathing gained more currency. It was also practised and taught by the influential yogi T.K.V. Desikachar, son of T. Krishnamacharya.[722] As long-term yoga practitioner Maria Engberg puts it, it is really about the subtle but strong effects that prāṇāyāma can have on the whole system:

721 Basu, Srischandra. *The Esoteric Philosophy of the Tantras: Shiva Sanhita*. Delhi: Cosmo Publications, 2004 [1887], p. xlvi.
722 Soder, Martin & Imogen Dalmann. "Prāṇāyāma: Von Buddha bis Svātmārāma." *Viveka*. 2022. p. 62, 21-22, p. 22, n. 5.

"By long-term practice of prāṇāyāma, one can learn how to skillfully regulate and stretch the breathing pattern, with the aim to slow and to stabilise, tranquillise and harmonise the working of the whole organism."[723]

Early Research on Prāṇāyāma

Hygienic contexts also had a medical side that inspired modern Indian yogis to conduct medical research on prāṇāyāma. Although N. C. Paul was a pioneer in this in the mid-nineteenth century, medical research on prāṇāyāma only started to thrive in the 1920s. Swami Kuvalayananda was a major case in point. He was a yogi who also conducted research in his yoga ashram and research centre, the Kaivalyadhama Yoga Institute which was established in Lonavla, India, in 1924. Not only was he critical to the theory of blood oxygenation through deep breathing that so many yogis of his time promoted,[724] but he was also the first one to conduct extensive laboratory experiments on prāṇāyāma.

In the lab, Kuvalayananda aimed to shed light on the functions of various Hatha-yogic breathing techniques including breath retention. He also emphasised the difference between deep breathing and traditional forms of prāṇāyāma, stating that deep breathing did not involve changes in intrapulmonary and intrathoracic pressure in the same way as prāṇāyāma did due to the factor of retention.[725] The research methods sought to detect the biochemistry of breathing before, during, and after prāṇāyāma or kumbhaka, involved measuring internal pressure in the lungs and intestines and measuring heart rate and blood pressure during various phases of the practice. This was done using microscopes, x-ray machines, blood pressure gauges, spirometry,

---

723 Engberg, Maria. *Spiro ergo sum: The Practice of Prāṇāyāma and the Theory of Relativity.* Notes on Breath, Space, and Energy. Gärsnäs: Turning Pages Förlag, p. 336.

724 Kuvalayananda, Swami. *Prāṇāyāma: Part One.* Lonavla: Kaivalyadhama, 1931, p. 123.

725 Kuvalayananda, Swami. "Pressure Changes in *Prāṇāyāma* " *Yoga Mimamsa.* 4.1 (1930c): 47-64, p. 49.

and the most up-to-date equipment available, such as the Haldane gas analysis apparatus.[726] Research produced at Kaivalyadhama is published in the ashram's journal, the *Yoga Mimamsa*, until today.

Early research on prāṇāyāma and bandhas involved x-ray experiments in which the Swami aimed to determine the relationship between the movements of the ribs in relation to the diaphragm.[727] He challenged the medical doctor J.F. Halls-Dally and the physical culturist J.P. Müller and their understanding of the functions of the diaphragm. The Swami then continued with pressure experiments during prāṇāyāma. Research on CO_2 elimination during prāṇāyāma with specific attention to each phase of the breath followed.[728] These experiments attempted to show differences in CO_2 elimination and O_2 absorption in prāṇāyāma with and without kumbhaka. The results showed that there were only insignificant differences in CO_2 elimination or O_2 consumption directly after breath retention. Kuvalayananda's conclusion was that prāṇāyāma and breath retention was practised for the sake of "nerve culture" and not for CO_2 reduction or O_2 consumption.[729]

Reviewing Kuvalayananda's work, Dr. V. Pratap found that the focus on "nerve culture" meant that the Swami tried to directly impact the autonomous nervous system by reprogramming the respiratory feedback centre.[730] Kuvalayananda explained that, if prāṇāyāma was performed correctly –

"It is capable of improving the oxygen-carrying capacity of the blood as no other exercise is. This is not because during the process

726 Alter, Joseph. *Yoga in Modern India: The Body Between Science and Philosophy.* Princeton and Oxford: Princeton University Press, 2004, p. 77, 85.
727 Kuvalayananda, Swami. "The Diaphragm and the Ribs: Part 1." *Yoga Mimamsa* 3.1 (1928): 18-37.
728 Kuvalayananda, Swami. "CO_2 Elimination in Prāṇāyāma." *Yoga Mimamsa.* 4.2 (1930a): 95-122; Kuvalayananda, Swami. "O_2 Absorption and CO_2 Elimination in Prāṇāyāma." *Yoga Mimamsa* 4.4 (1933): 267-289.
729 Kuvalayananda, Swami. "O_2 Absorption and CO_2 Elimination in Prāṇāyāma." *Yoga Mimamsa* 4.4 (1933): 267-289, 273, n.2.
730 Cf. Alter, Joseph. *Yoga in Modern India: The Body Between Science and Philosophy.* Princeton and Oxford: Princeton University Press, 2004, p. 91.

of prāṇāyāma an individual absorbs a larger quantity of oxygen, but because of the training of the respiratory system which helps the individual for twenty-four hours. The impression that an individual absorbs larger quantities of oxygen in prāṇāyāma is merely a superstition."[731]

Here, the swami points to the effect of prāṇāyāma on everyday breathing. He further notes that during prāṇāyāma one actually inhales *less* air than in normal respiration because of a lower breathing rate. However, as a result of prāṇāyāma practice, the breathing apparatus is so trained "that during the remaining part of the day, respiration is carried on most efficiently" and thus one absorbs more oxygen than one normally would.[732] If this resulted in an altogether lower breathing rate, this would mean that prāṇāyāma considerably altered the chemosensitivity of practitioners. However, this was not the object of Kuvalayananda's experiments in 1931 and 1933. To my knowledge, this only became part of Kaivalyadhama's research interests in the 1980s, as shown above with Karambelkar.

Research on prāṇāyāma that extended into investigations of the composition of air can be read as attempts to explain the nature of prana.[733] According to modern yogis, prana cannot simply be equated with oxygen – its workings were more subtle, more powerful, and more complex. Nevertheless, since prana itself proved to be immeasurable, the swami had to rely on biochemical and biomechanical experiments to explain the efficacy of prāṇāyāma. Whether the experiments conducted by the swami were or are (still) valid cannot be determined here (the investigation of which would need much broader medical knowledge than we can offer), but this highlights the fact that the role of biochemistry in breathing was acknowledged by the yoga community

731 Kuvalayananda, Swami. *Prāṇāyāma: Part One*. Lonavla: Kaivalyadhama, 1931, p. 123.
732 Kuvalayananda, Swami. *Prāṇāyāma: Part One*. Lonavla: Kaivalyadhama, 1931, p. 124.
733 Kuvalayananda, Swami. "Alveolar Air Composition Experiments." *Yoga Mimamsa* 5.1 (1934): 9-38. Cf. Alter, Joseph. *Yoga in Modern India: The Body Between Science and Philosophy*. Princeton and Oxford: Princeton University Press, 2004, p. 90-91.

in India and even abroad. Kuvalayananda's experiments had a pan-Indian reach and influenced various subsequent yogis and yoga-related research institutes outside India.

Ever since Kuvalayananda's efforts in the lab, research on prāṇ āyāma and other yogic practices, including yoga therapy, is on the rise and still thriving. However, in performing research on the margins of the measurable, the subtleties of prāṇāyāma and its effects described in Hatha texts (such as the heating of the body by inhaling primarily through the right nostril) have as yet not been proved in any reliable medical study.[734] From this perspective, Kuvalayananda's research efforts are landmarks in the history of research on prāṇāyāma not in terms of their overall validity but as attempts to understand the complexities of the specific effects of these breathing techniques.

What is more tangible is prāṇāyāma's workings on specific diseases and ailments. At Kaivalyadhama, experiments after Kuvalayananda's demise focused on asthma, among other diseases. A series of studies on asthma were conducted by M.V. Bhole and others who were Kuvalayananda's long-term research associates.[735] Of these, Bhole's (1982) is particularly interesting because it focused on improving lung functions through yogic therapy in asthmatic patients. He applied slow and prolonged inhalations and exhalations, as well as the rapid breathing of kapalabhati with the stress on active expiration enforced by the abdominal muscles and the diaphragm, while the inspiration was

---

734 Telles, Shirley et al. "Body Temperature in Practitioners of a Yoga Breathing Technique Considered to be Heat Generating." *International Journal of Yoga* 13.2 (2020).
   On the (un)reliability of medical studies on *Prāṇāyāma* due to lacking research standards, see also Campanelli, Stephany et al. "Prāṇāyāmas and their Neurophysiological Effects." *International Journal of Yoga* 13.3 (2020). https://www.ijoy.org.in/article.asp

735 These are Bhole, M.V. "Prāṇāyāma and its Rationale." *Yoga Mimamsa* 8.2 (1965): 19-26; Bhole, M.V., Deshpande, R.R. "Effect of Yogic Treatment on Total and Differential Leukocyte Counts in Asthmatics." *Yoga Mimamsa* 20.4 (1982): 1-8; Bhole, M.V. "Effect of Yogic Treatment on Various Lung Functions of Asthma Patients–A Pilot Study." *Yoga Mimamsa* 20.4 (1982): 43-50; Bhole, M.V., Bhagwat J. M., and Gharote, M.L. "Effect of yoga treatment on autonomic balance in asthmatics – A pilot study." *Yoga Mimamsa* 22.1&2 (1983): 73-79.

passive. Aiming at better manipulation of the breathing apparatus, the training also sought to affect the nervous system and the psychological improvement of the patient. After four to six weeks of yogic training, they saw "no significant differences in pulmonary functions," but –

> "the spirograms did show a qualitative improvement of air trapping, smooth and even breathing pattern and a better performance during maximum breathing capacity manoeuvre."[736]

Research on asthmatics in modern yoga goes back to the 1920s, when Shri Yogendra, founder of the Yoga Institute in Bombay, started to work with asthmatics and documented the positive effects of prāṇāyāma. Yoga shares a common interest with Dr. Konstantin Buteyko (an important influence on the Oxygen Advantage®) who, himself successfully worked with patients since the 1950s. In Bhole's research, we see a focus on the improvement of *functional* breathing, for example, the quality of a "smooth and even breathing pattern," which marks the first improvement in an asthmatic's behavioural patterns.

In addition to the curative effects of prāṇāyāma mentioned in Hatha yoga texts, by the 1980s, the acknowledgement of the beneficial effects of prāṇāyāma on overall health, psychosomatic integrity, and well-being had advanced greatly. In *Light on prāṇāyāma* (1981), B.K.S. Iyengar explains that prāṇāyāma helps to improve the circulation of blood and lymph in the lungs, that splenic blood circulation is stimulated, peristaltic movement is improved, and that the sweat-glands act as micro-kidneys during prāṇāyāma.[737] The list of benefits to inner organs could be extended.

Concerning levels of self-knowledge and self-perception, it is noteworthy that Iyengar highlights the sensitivity, elasticity, and receptivity of skin which can be developed through prāṇāyāma so that the skin

---

736 Bhole, M.V. "Effect of Yogic Treatment on Various Lung Functions of Asthma Patients–A Pilot Study." *Yoga Mimamsa* 20.4 (1982): 43-50, p. 47.

737 Iyengar, B. K. S. *Light on Prāṇāyāma: Prāṇāyāma Dīpikā*. With an Introduction by Yehudi Menuhin, London: Unwin Paperbacks, 1983, p. 56-57.

becomes an important "source of perception." Through prāṇāyāma, one develops a quality of deeply "listening" to the breath through the inner ears, which are likened to the "windows of the mind."[738]

738 Iyengar, B. K. S. *Light on Prāṇāyāma: Prāṇāyāma Dīpikā*. With an Introduction by Yehudi Menuhin, London: Unwin Paperbacks, 1983, p. 56-57.

INTERVIEWS WITH PATRICK MCKEOWN & OA® INSTRUCTORS

ROBIN ROTHENBERG: TEACHING YOGA AND THE ROLE OF FUNCTIONAL BREATHING

*Robin Rothenberg is a breath expert and yoga therapist. She is widely respected in the international yoga therapy community for her knowledge of breathing and prāṇāyāma. Her book, **Restoring Prana: A Therapeutic Guide to Prāṇāyāma and Healing Through the Breath**, referred to many times in this book, provides a comprehensive overview of the science behind ancient practices and the way prāṇāyāma should be taught. Robin successfully marries science with tradition, both in her writing and her work with students. Now, she's training a new generation of yoga therapists via her IAYT-accredited certification course. In this interview exclusively for this book, Robin shares her knowledge and optimism for the future of teaching yoga.*

How did you get so deeply involved in the study of breath?

I've had upper respiratory issues my whole life. Even in early childhood, I had ear and adenoid problems. The doctors finally took my tonsils out when I was 17, but I continued to have respiratory problems and low exercise tolerance. By the time I was a young adult, I had chronic fatigue and fibromyalgia-like symptoms.

When I started doing yoga, it helped a lot. I started feeling healthier. I became more discerning about what I was eating and how I was spending my time. More mindful of my life in general. I got much healthier, and a lot of my symptoms dissipated. But then, around 2010, they started flaring up again. I was getting a lot of respiratory infections and a cough that just got worse and worse. None of my yoga or prāṇāyāma practices seemed to make a difference.

In 2015, I got a particularly bad infection. I was coughing what felt like all day and night for three months. I finally went to see my doctor, who prescribed inhalers and told me I had asthma. Nobody had ever said that to me before.

I turned to one of my long-time students, Pippa, who was trained in the Buteyko Breathing Method. Pippa had been a lifelong asthmatic. Before she started the Buteyko Method, she always had her inhaler on her yoga mat. Then she did this breathing method, and she told me how much it helped. At the time, I thought it was wonderful for her. But I had prāṇāyāma, so I didn't need it, but when my doctor said I had asthma, my immediate thought was to call Pippa and ask her to teach me how to breathe. From our first session, my symptoms decreased. And, because of the kind of mind I have, I needed to know more! I started reading.

One of the books I read was *The Oxygen Advantage*. Before I'd even finished it, I had signed up to go to Ireland and study with Patrick. I just had to know what this was about. So, Patrick and I connected. I loved his style of teaching. I loved that I learned so much. And I knew right then that I had to write my book to help yogis to understand what we didn't learn in yoga school. But the physiology is so complicated, I didn't understand it well enough myself at that point. I had to host Patrick a couple of times, to hear it more and more, to study, and read.

When I got back from Ireland, I hit the yoga books. Not the contemporary books, the original texts on prāṇāyāma, and I found that they are all saying, "Breathe less." And it's all about the breath holds, the kumbhaka, not the inhale and exhale. I realised then that it was even more important for me to write my book because we're lost in the middle here. We have this Western physiological perspective, and this Ukrainian doctor saying it's healthier to breathe less. We've got the ancient yogis saying the same thing. In the middle, we're telling people to breathe more.

My publisher says that my book has consistently been one of their top sellers, so people are reading it. I get emails frequently from people saying, "Your book has changed my life," which is awesome.

How is breathing taught in existing yoga teacher training programs?

When I went to yoga training school, there wasn't an emphasis on loud breathing. We were never taught to breathe through our mouths in yoga class. But nobody said we should breathe through our noses when we weren't in class either. Yoga class was probably the only time I nose-breathed because nobody instructed otherwise. Even in my teacher trainings, I only paid attention to my breathing during practice.

Nobody addressed how we should breathe the rest of the time. The thing that's missing is an understanding of what is functional. Within those parameters, obviously, everybody is a little different. But the basics such as how much air to breathe, what's healthy and what's not so healthy, and the fact that it's important to attend to how you're breathing both on and off the mat . . . these sorts of things were not taught. And they still aren't being taught, which to me is a big omission. The yogis were very clear about consciousness around breathing.

When I studied with Pippa and then with Patrick, I learned the importance of practising several times a day. I was reinforcing a pattern and changing my chemistry and my tolerance for CO_2. I'd practise for maybe an hour, but I'd break it up across the day. Then I read in the yogic texts that the prescription for prāṇāyāma is to practise four times a day, spread out from dawn to midnight.

What's being taught now is that you sit down and do 10, maybe 30 minutes of breathing, and that's your prāṇāyāma practice. People do six rounds of alternate nostril breathing, and that's it for the day. They don't really practise making it a habit. There's no intentionality about changing your chemistry or changing the fundamental way your body functions. It's more like, oh, you're stressed, do this technique and you'll calm your nervous system. And it's effective for that. For half an hour or so, you feel chilled out. It's not a bad thing, but the way prāṇāyāma is used is as a quick fix. If you're feeling a little lethargic, you can use prāṇāyāma to bring your energy up. It's like a cup of coffee.

But, in terms of the original intention, it's clear from my studies that the yogis were much more interested in long-term transformation and creating such internal quiet and stillness that they could enter the state of samadhi. The breath is an incredibly powerful tool for doing that, providing that you move in the direction of kumbhakas, specifically suspension after exhale.

The yogis didn't talk about CO_2 or biochemistry, but they knew that kumbhaka quietens the mind more than anything else. They didn't talk about it in the scientific way that Patrick does or the respiratory physiologist would, but they certainly point in that direction. They noticed through their own observation that, when they were able to stay in those kumbhakas for two or three minutes, their heart rate and breathing rate would drop so low that their mind would become very quiet.

It wasn't until I experienced 60-plus seconds of kumbhaka on a regular basis that I understood. I think that's what samadhi is like – there's a deep quiet inside. But it started small, and I didn't discover this through yoga. Buteyko breathing opened me up to that experience, and then yoga provided me with the reference point and language to understand it.

How can we bridge the gap with yoga teachers to help them integrate the science with an understanding of what the ancient texts are saying?

The intention of yoga is to discover, explore, and plumb the depths of that inner stillness. Not to do fancy postures or to hold a handstand or plank pose longer than anyone else. I have this conversation all the time with yoga practitioners who are really steeped in body mastery. It becomes the lens through which they view all of yoga.

Western cultures are not about surrendering. We're about proving our capacity, accomplishing, and producing. Movement is important for our health and wellbeing, and mindful movement can greatly affect how we feel. By attending to the body, we can take a step inward. We can get closer to attending to our breath and to our minds. The physical practice is a huge doorway in because many people in our culture are very disconnected from their bodies. Getting them into their body is critical.

For me, teaching breathing without teaching movement would be like trying to teach with my mouth taped. Because movement affects breath, breath affects movement, both affect the mind. And according to the yoga teachings, the mind is where all the problems are. The body and movement aren't the end point, but they offer a way to connect. It's a way of calming the nervous system, to start to establish the first layer of stillness, and become anchored in your body. As the mind gets still, it creates a feeling of safety, like a safe container. As the nervous system calms down, you can begin to feel present. It all works together very beautifully with the intention to take you into those deeper realms of quiet.

What difference do you think it could make to teaching if yoga instructors used the BOLT score to assess breathing patterns in their students?

There's great value in the BOLT score, but, psychologically, it's not straightforward. Some people get very caught up striving for a number. That can create anxiety for people who are already anxious. It can be a distraction. If someone is extremely competitive, they may be inclined to chase the number instead of attending to the experience. I want people to have an experience of the breath and to come to know themselves through the breath because it's such an incredible mirror. As a practitioner and instructor of yoga, I'm most interested in students coming to know themselves through practice. That's the primary goal rather than performing a pose or achieving a certain BOLT score.

When I work with clients, I'm cautious. I take their BOLT score, but I won't necessarily have them take it on their own. I want them just to practise and to come to know what it feels like when they settle the breath and what it feels like when their breath is unsettled. What's going on in their life and in their mind. How they are feeling in their body. I find that if they focus on those things, when they come back, their BOLT score is better.

I do have some students tracking their BOLT score because they're able to do that without stressing about how high or low it is. But often I don't start there because I've found that people got caught up in it, and all they wanted to talk about was the numbers.

I have the same experience with the yoga teachers at the *Restore Your Prana* training course. Even though I say a hundred times, "The BOLT score is not a practice, it's a measurement," I still hear students say, "I didn't like my BOLT, so I took it again." Would you do that with your blood pressure? The BOLT score is just information. And even though I'm a good teacher, and I find many ways to explain this, the BOLT score is still a sticking point for some. There's something about the mind that just wants to grab onto the number. If I say anything, it will be something like, "You'll probably feel a great difference when your BOLT is somewhere around 20." I try to make it accessible so there's less anxiety. And then, when they get higher than that, it's awesome. I do my best to introduce it in a way to curtail their tendency to strive for it.

My main concern is that there's a level of ignorance in the world of yoga about what constitutes basic functional breathing versus dysfunctional breathing, about how to assess breathing disorders, not just biochemically but the biomechanics of breathing. Even when teachers talk about diaphragmatic breathing, what they're actually teaching is chest breathing or belly breathing – not functional, abdominal diaphragmatic breathing. They don't really understand what they're assessing, and they don't understand the pitfalls of starting with the BOLT score. To me, teaching functional breathing is much more valuable than giving a tool like the BOLT to teachers with very little understanding of the basics and who may take it out of context.

One of my yoga teachers talks about learning in terms of carved blocks. Breathing instructors don't generally have this "carving," this deeply ingrained idea of "yoga" behind them. Most people who become breathing instructors do so because they want to get healthy and help others. They're a blank slate when it comes to understanding the breath.

It's a very different thing from teaching people who think they're experts on the breath because they are yoga teachers when what they know is really very limited and in some ways wrong. They have a whole tool chest of awesome prāṇāyāmas to increase energy or relax the mind, but they don't know what healthy, normal breathing is. The BOLT score is a tool that can potentially do good, but I don't think it's the best tool for new yoga teachers. I think it's best to start by teaching abdominal diaphragmatic breathing because we're body-based practitioners. To start by calming the breath and, from there, move to subtle breathing or reduced volume breathing. And then, once they understand that, breath suspensions. Only then can they talk about increasing the capacity to suspend the breath in a relaxed way and measure it.

When I start working with a client, I assess their biomechanics first. Then, I just say, "Now I'm going to do another breath assessment to get a sense of how comfortable you are in that space where you're not breathing." I don't talk. I write the number down, and I write it down again after practice, so I have it for reference. Maybe, at some point, I'll explain what it's about. But, if they're already anxious or highly competitive and I can see that they're just going to be like a greyhound after a rabbit, I don't go there.

What's your take on using functional everyday breathing in asana practice?

It's very important. With any physical exercise, there can be the belief that the harder the workout, the more you need to breathe. But, if you do your sun salutations with this very light breath, it completely changes your experience.

I'm the queen of open-ended questions. That's my teaching style. I ask one question after another to direct the student's minds to go inside and to name and claim their own experience. This wrong idea that, when we're doing bigger movements, we should breathe harder, and that breathing harder with bigger movements somehow oxygenates us better . . . we must stop teaching that!

Instead, we can have students experiment and explore what it feels like when they **Breathe Light**. For people who want intensity, this is great. The yogis who are interested in Oxygen Advantage® are often competitive personality types. The type of student who is into power yoga and hot yoga. Knowing that, and knowing the psychology of those minds, you can have them practise sun salutations with reduced breathing. Physically, they don't have to do anything more. It still bumps up the intensity because, the more you breathe during a physical practice, the easier the practice will be.

People don't understand the power of light breathing till they experience it. They don't appreciate that it's much harder to **Breathe Light** when you're moving. This is the way in for yoga people – not the theory. Yogis learn through movement, so you need to take the breathing into movement and have them feel the difference.

What's your take on the instruction we frequently hear in yoga classes that you should be able to hear your breath?

I have great respect for all the prāṇāyāmas. They're all useful and intentional when they're applied in the right way. Even kapalbhati and bhastrika are very useful. I mean, Wim Hof is using them all the time! There's value to them, and there's also potential risk with them. You have to know who you're working with.

Ujjayi – which is what people call the Darth Vader breath – that's the most used prāṇāyāma. Again, it's a very useful tool as it's described in the original yogic texts. The texts talk about the felt sense of a slight narrowing at the glottis, which of course will reduce the breath. That narrowing also helps to engage the diaphragm more. There's a direct connection between the closure of the glottis and increased diaphragm recruitment – just like there's a connection between the nose and the diaphragm. It's all connected. It's literally connected through the fascia, connective tissue. But the texts don't talk about the external sound. They talk about the feeling, which is very internal and subtle.

The senses are an inherent part of the yoga teachings. Every single aspect of yoga talks about the relationship between the senses, the mind, the nervous system, and our state of being. A lot of practices use the senses to refine and focus the mind. When you put your attention on the glottis and create that slight constriction, first you notice that, instead of being outwardly focused, you bring your senses inward. You can feel it straight away in the eyes. Then, you have to be really attentive to maintain that slight contraction without letting it turn into a big sound. It's a beautiful practice for people who don't have throat inflammation and irritation.

It is also said in the texts that you shouldn't practise Ujjayi if there's heat in the throat. If you've had COVID and have inflammation in your throat, you shouldn't be practising Ujjayi. But it is a beautiful practice. And it was never about how big the sound could be. I teach that, if you can hear yourself breathe, you're breathing too much. I used that as a teaching cue for myself too. When I practised, I'd be like, "Oh, did you hear that? Robin? You had just gasped . . . Did you hear that? You just sighed . . . Did you hear that? That was a big breath! So, I've really flipped it on its head.

In the Oxygen Advantage® method we teach that, if you lose control of your breathing when you're exercising, slow down. Does the same go for a yoga practice?

Yes. To slow the practice down. Or even to pause and settle your breath, and then come back into the practice less vigorously. By doing this, you find the level of movement that allows you to maintain the functional breathing pattern of a slow, light breath.

I teach breathing with asanas the way Patrick teaches Oxygen Advantage® with athletes. You need to build your tolerance to be able to move more while breathing less.

*When people first practise nose breathing to run, they often
report a runny nose or nasal congestion. How do you deal with
nasal congestion in a physical yoga practice when you want to
Breathe Light?*

If you have congestion and you put your head down into downward dog
at the beginning of your practice, of course, there's going to be more
blood flow. You may have to come up and blow your nose.

But nasal congestion may also be something to do with the state of
your sinuses. Try using a neti pot before you practise. Afterward, put
some oil in your nostrils so they don't dry out. The saline from the neti
pot can be drying, so make sure to moisturise your nose.

You can also try practising the nose clearing exercise— a few breath
holds with movement – at the start of your practice. Sometimes if I'm
feeling congested or lethargic, I'll do some short breath holds while
jogging on the spot or running up and down my hall. That gets me a
little jazzed up and ready to do my yoga practice.

*Why is it that some people never progress from a physical yoga
practice to prāṇāyāma or meditation?*

First off, there's a misunderstanding. I hear it all the time: "Well, I do
yoga and I meditate." But yoga is really about meditation. A lot of people
do yoga, and they go practice Buddhist-style meditation. That's fine. It's
a beautiful practice. But meditation is there in the yoga sutras. There
are 196 sutras, and 190 are about meditation. There are three sutras
about movement, and they don't talk about individual postures. The
posture is just the thing that precedes meditation. The texts talk more
about presence of mind. They emphasise stability of mind and ease –
the lack of tension in the body that allows you to sit and meditate. They
don't talk about downward dog or sun salutations. Then there are four
or five sutras on prāṇāyāma. Again, they're all linked to the drawing
inward of the mind and the senses. So, quite literally, yoga is about
meditation.

But that's not the way it's marketed. We're in a physical culture that is very externally driven. We always want to know what we can get. If we're struggling with feelings, we want something external to make us feel "whole." We go to our yoga class, and the teacher guides us through the movements, and, for that period, we don't think and so we feel better. There's more to yoga than that. But a lot of teachers haven't had that experience. They don't know how to take their students into the deeper practices. They haven't had the training or the internal personal experience of yoga. And that goes back to the way in which yoga is taught – the way it's presented.

The classes that are packed with 40 students – the classes where the teachers can make money – are hot yoga and power yoga. The emphasis in these classes is on who can do which asana . . . who can contort the most . . . who can stay longest in their handstand . . . and who can breathe the loudest. It's externally driven, and that's not yoga.

In my teaching, I stay focused on the people that are hungry and looking for more depth and for that internal experience. People who are interested in the subtle body because prāṇāyāma is all about the subtle body, and prāṇāyāma itself is subtle. The whole process is about less, not more. About needing less and wanting less. About being more at home and content with yourself.

*It's been documented that some mantras are the same length
as the optimal breathing pattern (six breaths a minute).
What are your thoughts about that?*

Mantras are a beautiful way to regulate the breath. The sound is always made on the exhale, so breath control is intrinsic to the practice. At the same time, mantras harness the mind. You direct your mind toward the intention of the mantra – whether it's connecting you to your heart or to God or to a sense of wellbeing. By reinforcing that intention, you can calm the nervous system and the mind. Even if your breathing is intense, the mantra can be a very soothing companion.

I often have people use mantras during their breath holds. It's especially helpful for anyone who is anxious. Sometimes my students have something from their own liturgy that they like to repeat. It helps them connect to God while they practise their mantra. That's very soothing, even though it's intense. When we focus on holding the breath, it's easy to spin out into anxiety, but, with the mantra alongside, it feels safe. You don't feel alone. So, mantras can be very powerful.

Traditionally, prāṇāyāma was taught with mantras because prāṇā-yāma was always about the mind. It was never about achieving certain breathing ratios or breath hold times. In the ancient texts, even the means for measuring time were convoluted. I hinted at this in my book because it makes me laugh at the way the ancient yogis measure time. There are things like, "Circle your finger around your knee," or, "Listen to the cowbell five times." Well, how much is that cowbell going to be ringing? What that tells me is that they weren't really thinking about time or ratios in the precise linear way we do.

A mantra can be regulated to the same pace as coherent breathing. But that does depend on how fast you chant it. It isn't an exact measurement. At the same time, there's an exactness to Sanskrit. Every letter has a beat, and the metre is important. You have to make the sounds in the right way. This means correct mantra practice requires a lot of mental focus and discipline. All that precision is happening with the coordination of the breath and the intention to give your whole being a break from the neurotic circling of your mind. But, ultimately, the magic of mantra happens when you stop the mantra. The vibration of the mantra impacts the body and the focus of the mind in a certain way. There's deep stillness and quiet afterwards . . . and that is what takes you into that meditative state.

How can yoga teachers gain an understanding of functional breathing, correct prāṇāyāma practice, and functional movement?

Most yoga teachers aren't taught the basics of breathing. So, class teaching can be challenging on multiple levels. They're often not taught proper anatomy or functional movement either. Most of them are just taught poses . . . and then they give the same pose to 30 people in a room without being able to assess whether someone is hypermobile or has asymmetries in their movement patterns that are likely to cause potential problems six months or a year down the line.

That's where specialist teaching comes in. In my program, I take those concepts, and, chapter by chapter, we go through the breathing practices in my breathing journal. Then, for each module, there's a practicum where the student will teach those concepts. As they go through the program, it becomes more complex. By the final stages, they get to weave everything together in a four-part yoga series that they script out. Throughout the process, they're mentored, reviewed, and assessed. The feedback I'm getting from graduates who have completed the program is that they feel completely different in how they work. It's a slow process to teach them in this way – to apply the breathing directly to yoga teaching.

It's relevant to how yoga teachers work with people in different demographics too. For instance, the International Association of Yoga Therapy recently hired me to run a nine-hour training on therapeutic breathing for long COVID. It involved taking a client through sessions and follow-up interviews. I was teaching the nose clearing exercise, some small breath holds, and subtle, reduced breathing. Afterwards, I did a follow-up weekend training for yoga teachers and yoga therapists, and there was a lot of curiosity. They were seeing this client getting better, week by week, and they wanted to know how it was possible.

I also did an interview with *Accessible Yoga*. This is a movement started by Jivana Heyman. He has a huge following. Accessible Yoga is really about making yoga accessible for all different demographic types – all different abilities – taking yoga out of the "body beautiful," uber-flexible image and showing that it's for real people. Jivana interviewed me for his podcast, and he asked me to write a blog about breathing for long COVID and to share what yoga teachers need to know. I addressed the big breathing and all the stuff we've talked about, and people were really engaged with it.

I know people are reading my book, so it's filtering through, and that's good news. I think in the last month and a half I've been on four different podcasts, and I talk about the breath. That's what people want me to talk about. I'm very happy to talk about it. I'm always addressing this issue of how yoga teachers are taught.

Things are changing. It's already a different landscape from when I was first consulting with Patrick about writing the book. Several of the people who run yoga therapy programs are doing my certificate course, so they're teaching prāṇāyāma correctly. I have yoga teachers who run teacher trainings who are doing my course, so they can teach prāṇāyāma correctly.

What potential do you feel yoga could offer if instructors were to embrace breathing exercises targeting the three dimensions of breathing?

That's my dream – a breath revolution. My dream is that every yoga teacher training around the world starts with breath. That we start with the concept of functional breathing and dysfunctional breathing, looking at the biomechanics and the biochemistry. And then, from that point, teaching prāṇāyāma, because, if you teach prāṇāyāma, it makes sense that there should be a foundation of understanding the breath.

If people are not functional breathers, you can't have them doing the more extreme prāṇāyāma practices. That just doesn't make any sense. I do have to say, as much as I experienced pushback when I first brought these ideas to the world of yoga, people do see the logic of it. You can't do an extreme breathing ratio when you can't functionally inhale or exhale without gasping. It's the same in a physical practice. If you can't raise your arms above your head, you wouldn't go straight into backbends. There's a process. You have to gradually increase flexibility while simultaneously maintaining stability at the core. Then, the body can withstand the challenge of a backbend safely.

It's no different with prāṇāyāma, but, in the world of yoga, often there's an idea that we can take people where they are and have them do these extreme practices. That's where it becomes dangerous, and people get into trouble. I hear stories, people come to me saying, "I went to a class called 'Gentle Yoga for Beginners,' and the first pose was headstand." This is very unwise. I once spent two years in acute pain because I compressed two discs in my neck from doing a headstand without being given the proper preparation.

In the same way, people don't understand the power of the breath. They don't understand that it's driving our entire nervous system. It affects our physiology – our digestion, our circulatory, endocrine, and lymphatic systems – every system in the body. And the movement of the diaphragm is so much about the power of the breath.

It's not just biochemistry or relaxation. Abdominal diaphragmatic breathing directly impacts our organs. Everything that is above or below the diaphragm is massaged when it moves properly. I have some MRI images of diaphragmatic vs. chest breathing. They would blow you away. You can really see how critically important it is to get the biomechanics straight, to get people out of chest breathing, paradoxical breathing, and "belly" breathing. Many of us lack a real understanding of the many functions of the diaphragm – this is a real miss in yoga teacher training.

People need to be taught why they are doing the breathing, instead of just following instructions. In the United States alone, there are more than 20 million people practising yoga. Multiply that throughout the world, and this could have a huge impact!

You know, one time, I was practising alternate nostril breathing and a friend called. My then ten-year-old daughter brought the phone to me, and I heard her say to my friend, "I don't know what she's doing. She's playing with her nose." And that's what a lot of people do – they play with their nose, but they don't understand the intention – that closing one of the nostrils reduces the breathing volume in half, and that, if you partially close the other side, you've reduced the airflow by three quarters. It means you're taking the breath to a more subtle level. You're really monitoring your breath and navigating it very sensitively through the placement of your fingers on your nostrils. But most people are just "playing with their nose," and they're breathing at the same level they were breathing with both nostrils. Or maybe they breathe even harder.

So, yes, Patrick and I have the same vision for the world. May everyone, every day wake up and breathe functionally. If I were to explain it "Miss America style," that would be the way to world peace! If people were breathing functionally, they just wouldn't be so agitated, anxious, fatigued, depressed, angry, or fearful. If they were practising yoga, they'd have a lot more confidence in themselves because they would feel grounded in their body. They would be examining their own neurotic patterns of mind and taking responsibility. So, yeah, let's do it!

You can find out more about Robin's work
at EssentialYogaTherapy.com.

TIGER BYE: MERGING THE OXYGEN ADVANTAGE® METHOD WITH ANCIENT PRACTICES OF YOGA & AYURVEDA

Tiger Bye is an international yoga instructor, specializing in alignment-based hatha yoga. She is an Oxygen Advantage® Master Instructor and holds a Master of Science in Health and the Public Interest from Georgetown University. Tiger is also the co-founder of Better Yoga, an online yoga studio where people can learn to move, breathe, and feel better with the help of experts in yoga, breath training, and ayurveda.

Tiger believes that functional breathing is public health. Through her classes, workshops, and training programs, she weaves functional breathing techniques, alignment-based yoga, and seasonal practices to promote personal and environmental health. Merging the Oxygen Advantage® method with ancient practices of yoga and ayurveda, Tiger layers profound embodied experiences with scientific underpinnings so that students and clients can grasp the "why" behind the "what" that they feel during practice.

How did your interest in breathing develop?

Sitting for pranayama is uncomfortable for many Western bodies. Due to our sitting culture, our hip flexors are locked short and unconscious and compounding pressure is placed on the lower spine – a poor recipe for functional breathing. In a public yoga class, it's common to see many people rounded forward in a cross-legged pose (sukhasana), sinking into habitual patterns of degraded posture. When told to sit tall to prepare to breathe, people end up muscling through it, elongating the spine with much effort that only puts pressure on compensatory muscle groups, such as the scalenes supporting the neck. Why do I bring this up? Because I used to hate pranayama. And it was because I didn't know how to sit.

It wasn't until I learned how to sit sustainably did functional breathing become accessible, and eventually the central theme of all my movement practices. Once I learned to properly elevate my pelvis above my knees, using a generous amount of props underneath me, it was like my lungs were freed from what was truly my rib "cage".

At that point, I was doing a lot more traditional pranayama, including kapalabhati and variations of bhastrika, with some kumbhaka (breath holds). The main form of yoga I practice, Katonah Yoga®, features lots of this big breathing. I used to conflate feelings of the resulting lightheadedness as glimpses into my spiritual self. It wasn't until I read Patrick's book, *The Oxygen Advantage,* that I realized the feelings I was having were just severe manipulations of my body's biochemistry. My pranayama practice changed dramatically after reading his book.

While I still believe there is a time and place for kapalabhati and bhastrika, I now see them as techniques for specific scenarios, as opposed to the basis of my practice. My practice migrated from the mat into my physical exercise regimen. I was never a runner, but before for cardiovascular exercise I was confidently running 5 kilometers several times a week. When I started only nasal breathing during physical exercise, I could maybe run half a mile. I think at first it was my competitive nature that made me want to improve my functional breathing. However, today, my goal is balance. With a basis of functional breathing, the breathing I do depends on what my body needs in a given moment, day, or season. I tend less toward extremes or mono-method practices. I am interested in breathing as a means to keep the abode of my spirit clean and liveable, like any house ought to be.

As functional breathing and simulating high altitude have become cornerstones of my personal practice and exercise regimen, my teaching has also evolved into a blend of Oxygen Advantage® techniques and traditional pranayama, with an added layer of seasonal attunement to align personal nature with great nature. Combining ancient practices with modern science on a seasonal basis keeps the practice interesting and balancing for the mind-body. I think of my personal practices and teachings like a palimpsest – I get to add new layers of techniques and continue cultivating an authentic and purposeful recipe.

What led you to becoming a yoga teacher and how did you come to practice and teach Katonah Yoga in particular?

I was being dragged to yoga classes by my parents for as long as I could remember. Yoga was never a "woo-woo" thing in our household. It was as common as going to a baseball game.

During university, it was the counterweight to my type-A, competitive personality that earned me a 4.0 and a Summa Cum Laude distinction on my diploma. But after years of burning the midnight oil in New York City, I was absolutely fried. I knew I had to do something for my crumbling mental health, so with encouragement from our families, my boyfriend (now husband) and I enrolled in a 200-hour yoga teacher training at the Kripalu Center for Yoga and Health in Western Massachusetts. I think it was an experience that brought us together as partners because we learned how to have compassion for ourselves.

I never intended to teach yoga, rather just deepen my personal practice. My plan was to do this training, take some time off, and eventually go work for a big firm that would earn me big money. I have to laugh at that now. I knew the moment I met my mentor, Kari Harendorf, that that plan went out the window. She was our anatomy and physiology teacher during our 200-hour, and she was doing something completely magical. I watched as she aligned people's body's, dislodging years of tension and trauma that brought people to tears of amazement. I thought to myself, *now that's yoga. Connecting the mind and body in a way that frees people from pain and gives them more joy.* After the teacher training, I began studying with Kari, and her practice I learned was called "Katonah Yoga". I've learned so much about the body from her. Years later, today we are business partners, seeking to help others move, breathe, and feel better through alignment-based yoga.

How was breathing taught in your yoga teacher training program and how does it differ from your current practice?

We learned three breathing techniques in my 200-hour teacher training program. Dirga, Ujjayi, and Kapalabhati Pranayama. I think the session lasted 1 or 2 hours. I remember having to memorize all the contraindications for kapalbhati pranayama and afterwards felt too scared to teach it.

In my second 200-hour training with the Katonah Yoga Center, I was shocked by how much kapalabhati and variations of bhastrika were taught. We were invited to participate in 45-minute sessions that were filled almost entirely with up-regulating breaths. When I finally learned how to sit for 45 minutes straight, I rather enjoyed the sessions because they were also woven with Katonah Yoga theory, which is fascinating. The combination of Chinese medicine, Taoism, sacred geometry, and attunement to the seasons allowed me to eclipse my personal nature to great nature. I felt part of something greater, and breathing was a big part of that.

However, every time we ended one of these breathing sessions, I was so jacked up that I had to question how many cups of coffee I drank that morning.

It was like I was riding a pranayama pendulum, going from a culture of cautious teaching to participating in completely transcendental experiences. I'm grateful for the plethora of experience I received in both the Kripalu and Katonah domains and would not trade my experience for any other.

Yet, if we think about the body as a car, in Kripalu Yoga, so many safety checks had to be performed that it took the joy out of going for a ride. In Katonah Yoga, I definitely felt like I was finally in the driver's seat, but my foot was a little too pedal-happy. The Oxygen Advantage was like getting a copy of the owner's manual. I took a look under the hood and figured out how everything worked, so that now when I'm driving, I feel much more in control.

What's your take on the instruction we frequently hear in yoga classes to take a deep belly breath?

Most people are unconnected to the lower half of their body. In the West, we have very strong backs and arms, but underutilize our legs. Its why back pain is so chronic. Going into the basement can be scary. It's literally everything that we keep "under the table."

From this lens, cueing people to breathe into the belly can be productive. Dropping the brain further into the body can be soothing, and make the basement less scary. It can allow people to relax in a place that houses fear and anxiety. Many people don't trust their gut because they've spent most of their lives being cut off from its vital information.

Of course, physiologically, we don't breathe into the belly. And it's not something I cue unless guiding something like dirga pranayama which is a specific filling of the belly, ribs, and chest in that order. Even then when you go to fill the ribs, the belly will naturally hollow back. For me, it's a waste of time to fixate on the "wrongness" of belly breathing, because it has helped a lot of people learn to relax. In my classes, I discuss the importance of lateral expansion through the rib cage to project the spine, but I prefer to emphasize that the body is a tensegrity structure – a term coined by Buckminster Fuller which describes an interconnected structure where one element strengthens all others through continuous tensions and compressions in constant equilibrium. Ultimately, the idea is that when we manipulate one area, it is functionally supported throughout the body when muscles, bones, and joints are aligned properly. I encourage students to think of the breathing as a 360° experience, making us more spherical, able to bounce back.

How can yoga teachers gain an understanding of functional breathing, correct prāṇāyāma practice, and functional movement?

Not every teacher is going to care about functional breathing. There, I said it. Unfortunately, yoga can be a very ego-driven practice. Flip through any social media platform and search #yoga, and you're bombarded with guys standing on their head and women doing the splits (and not always with great alignment). The images can be awesome, but asana is a means to an end. Every posture is really for the purpose of being able to sit well. Sitting well is for the purpose of breathing well. Breathing well is for the purpose of meditating well. And meditating well is for the purpose of living well. We do this by severing our obsession with the self. Just as yoga is a "union of the body-mind", it is also a dissociation of self and our true spirit. As such we don't do yoga to be good at yoga. We do yoga to be better at life while we have our brief moment on this earth.

One of my favorite metaphors capturing this is adapted from the writings of Kabir, a 15th-century Indian mystic poet and saint. It goes something like this:

> In a vast ocean, a large swell formed. As the wave grew larger, a drop of water crested off from the wave. "Ah!", the drop spontaneously exclaimed, then asked "Who said that?", before dropping back into the water to become a part of the ocean once more.

It's a metaphor for our brief existence on earth. We realize we have a self and become so attached to our conceptualization of ourselves as singular drops, that we forget we are the ocean. We dread returning to the water, making our lives a fixation on figuring out "who said that".

When we functionally exchange air in and out of the body, the calmness that results can allow us to feel unseparated from the rest of life's big ocean. The breath is a constant reminder that we depend on a larger system outside of ourselves in order to remain alive.

So, the question is really: How do we facilitate people's recognition that they are the ocean? In my opinion, a yoga practice focused solely on asana won't get you there. We need to learn to be good breathers to settle our self-centered minds. We owe a lot to people like Patrick who are spreading the word about learning to breathe better. As much as we can bridge cultures of healing, Western medicine and Eastern practices, I think more and more yoga teachers, and more medical professionals as well, will value the importance of breathing. It not only has the potential to make people healthier physically, but spiritually as well. The world needs both.

What potential do you feel breathing, and in particular functional breathing, in yoga has for helping with mental health/stress/ anxiety/mood issues?

Just as we find ourselves in a breathing renaissance, we also find ourselves in a large-scale mental health crisis–especially among young adults. At its heart, I think Functional Breathing is public health. It's low cost, accessible, and can mitigate stress which makes every disease worse. Cognitive therapies are important, but I believe top-down approaches are more effective when they are coupled with bottom-up approaches. There's a lot of talk right now about "full body mental health", with many therapists emphasizing the importance of nutrition. I am on board with this wave, as many of the building blocks of our neurons are dependent on what kind of nutrients we are getting from the food we eat. However, I think James Nestor captures the topic well, "From what I've learned in the past decade, that thirty pounds of air that passes through our lungs every day and that 1.7 pounds of oxygen our cells consume, is as important as what we eat or how much we exercise. Breathing is a missing pillar of health." The breath is a bridge between the body and the mind. It's kind of like picking up a flower of a Hawaiian lei, eventually, when you lift one flower, the others lift up as well. To get our minds right, we have to look at our breathing, our nutrition, and our spiritual health, which for me involves the community we keep. Breathing is a flower in the lei, and an obvious one to pick up first

What led to your interest in ayurveda? Are there any parallels between this practice and the approaches you take in your Oxygen Advantage® work?

Ayurveda is often described as the "sister science of yoga". While one could consider both yoga and ayurveda as sciences, yoga was never intended as a medical science. Really, it's a spiritual science aimed at alleviating spiritual suffering. While yoga can heal the mind-body in many ways, historically it is not separate from Ayurveda in this domain. Ayurveda is an ancient medical system, which has been espousing the tenets of functional breathing (and hypercapnic, hypoxic training through kumbhaka) for thousands of years. Ayurveda is a huge proponent of nasal breathing. Indeed, for thousands of years, children in India were taught to breathe through their nose during sleep and exercise. Modern Ayurvedic doctors, like Dr. John Douillard, are advocates for nasal breathing, as the traditions of this ancient medical system are now being proofed by modern scientific studies thanks to people like him.

What I like about blending the Ayurvedic principles with the Oxygen Advantage® is that they are already naturally aligned, and their integration simply personalizes breath training even more. While we can get a pretty good sense of what exercises to teach somebody by measuring things like the BOLT score, taking into account one's Ayurvedic constitution (vata, pitta, kapha), one's geographic location, season of the year, and life stage can bring more nuance into healing through breathing. Ayurveda takes the Oxygen Advantage® one step further though attuning people's personal nature with great nature.

You can find more about Tiger's work on her website, **tigerbye.com,** *and you can practice yoga and breathing with her on* **betteryoga.net.**

ALESSANDRO ROMAGNOLI: BREATHING, YOGA, MEDITATION, FIGHTING, AND PSYCHOLOGY

Certified Oxygen Advantage® Master and Yoga for Brazilian Jujitsu instructor, Alex Romagnoli is not only a martial artist since childhood. He is also a psychologist specialising in Cognitive Neuroscience with post-graduate diplomas in Clinical Neuropsychology and Psychosomatic Medicine. In his practice, Alex combines his expertise in sports, yoga, martial arts, psychophysiology, thought processes, mindfulness, and breathing techniques, including Wim Hof and Oxygen Advantage.® And he works with everyone from patients with serious psychiatric conditions, to professional athletes (MMA fighters, wrestlers, marathoners, rugby players, Olympic fencers), and the Special Forces.

Alex talked to Johanna McWeeney about how he came to yoga and breathwork, about bringing together spirituality and the practical science of breath training, and about mindfulness and breathing practices.

How did your interest in breathing develop?

Everything started when I was a kid – with a monk in Madagascar who used to teach me, for example, how to bring your focus onto breathing, how to bring your attention to the breath.

I started meditation while I was living in Africa for more than 15 years. I got introduced to a VIPA meditation by the monk who was a soldier during the Vietnam war, a very old guy, an amazing guy. He saw that I could learn something from that, and he helped me to go forward. And, as soon as I went to university, I decided to specialise in psychology, neuroscience applied to meditation, and then meditation, and mindfulness.

Mindfulness used to be very morally oriented, human-oriented for the wellbeing of someone. Then, mindfulness shifted slowly to a more, we could say, technical aspect as it was used as a tool. If you want to be free, just meditate ten minutes a day. I used to teach mindfulness meditation, especially the body scan exercise, to Special Forces. So, we are not into spirituality anymore, but we are into something technical. We use the tool, just that piece from spirituality and bring it back to the West.

During my thesis, while I was teaching and paying attention to mindfulness, especially from a scientific domain, a student that used to attend my lessons during conferences introduced me to the Wim Hof method. Then, with the Wim Hof method, I had the chance to experience many research protocols. We used to go to the mountains during the breathing exercises and apply them many times. So, I got introduced to breathwork through my university thesis. Everything started from there.

Mindfulness had a kind of peak audience around 2014, 2015 worldwide. We could call it the golden age of mindfulness. But the thing about mindfulness is that it is really made for everyone but not everyone can do it. Second thing – sports athletes – yes, they like it, but I noticed that, in the mindfulness community, among all the users, more women were doing and applying mindfulness meditation, but sports athletes wanted something more challenging, something more sensory. So, with the Wim Hof method, I found something very interesting.

I work as a sports psychologist also, and I teach a lot of professional soccer players or fighters those kinds of techniques. With those kinds of sports athletes, I always start with breathing because they already have the habit of handling and managing their breath.

The thing that I like about the breath is that you can do an active hyperventilation or slower hyperventilation. The way you relate to a certain emotional situation is more manageable than just asking someone to pay attention to their anger. I remember while teaching my first mindfulness classes, I used to say, 'bring your attention to your body'. The CEO of the company got angry by this and just left the lesson.

The approaches are different through mindfulness and through breathing, but you can easily combine them in a very good way. You start from the body, you continue through the breath, and then your mind becomes stable. Working this way is much more manageable.

What you've just said about from the body, through the breath, and to the mind kind of echoes the path of yoga. Many people who practise yoga never look at meditation because they're not interested in that spiritual journey, they just want to feel better. But there are numerous ways into that journey and that journey can be whatever it needs to be for you.

Exactly! You're using your own resources at that moment. And then, you can be led down a spiritual path. For example, you're doing yoga. You start doing yoga because your lower back pain is killing you, but one day, sooner or later, you find yourself paying attention to your breathing during those lessons. And then, you learn a lot about yourself and especially about the resistance that you can have to the positions. And you understand that it's your central nervous system, and then you apply this learning in a spiritual way. Then you find yourself inquiring: What can I do to share all of this in a very compassionate way?

This sequencing is very pragmatic because, if I start to do everything starting from the spiritual side, saying, yes, I want to bring love and compassion to everyone, that would be really mature. But, if you start with the basics from what you have, back pain, for example, then you will do it and stay with your lessons for a long time, and you will gain depth. And this depth will be that you'll radiate that experience and people will feel it. This is why I love to combine yoga and breathing exercises and fighting and psychology together because it teaches you a lot from a metaphysical point of view.

Your yoga teaching is for jujitsu. How did you come to that? And the world of yoga?

Pain, pain, pain is the best teacher. Apart from being a psychologist, I'm also a fighter. So, I train a lot. And the problem is that, in fighting, especially Brazilian jujitsu, you use a lot of your lower back. It's an anti-natural way of moving yourself, so you have to compensate, meaning changing your lifestyle, starting from the way you eat. And also the way you take care of yourself. And, if you don't do some kind of stretching at the end of sparring, for example, you will begin to have some lower back pain.

For me, it all started with lower back pain. I had a hernia and decided to do some yoga. The yoga I did was applied specifically to fighters. The main founder of this yoga wasn't able to sit down because it was too painful, instead, he had to crouch ever so slowly on the chair. This pain led him and his wife, who is a yoga teacher, to found *Yoga for Brazilian Jujitsu*. I practised the program and wanted to go beyond. This led me to rethink some techniques and exercises that helped me during my thesis at university.

There seems to be resistance from the yoga community when it comes to integrating scientific breathing ideas and Oxygen Advantage® ideas. It seems that, perhaps, there's a tendency to want to hold that sacredness of a particular tradition and insist that people follow that path.

Instead of the yoga community, we could be talking about the psychologist community or the mental health community. It's the same thing. But, on the opposite side, it's the same but reversed. Many psychologists won't use it. They have a block against the fact that when many people talk about the breath, they talk about the esoteric side of things. On the other side, with yogis, it's the same problem, but it's more 'this is the tradition, and we stick to the traditions.' So, on one side, we have, 'No, I don't want it because it's too woo-woo.' And, on the other side, 'No, it's mine, it's sacred, and I want to keep my traditions.'

There is a lot of resistance, but we can bypass it by binding together science, and personal practice, and personal experience. For example, the breathing techniques from Oxygen Advantage® can be applied without talking about any kind of sacredness or secular things. They can be explained from a scientific point of view, with scientific language . . . and we can share the scientific evidence, such as those that show breathing techniques can work even better than cognitive behavioural therapy.

What I understand of yoga, whatever your spirituality or religion, it compliments that. So, for me, the scientific breath training would be a step back from that, saying the science compliments whatever your yoga tradition. But it takes a certain amount of openness to accept that.

We have to keep in mind the following thing about the world – we had two big divisions. From a geographical and political point of view, the East and West have been split for many, many centuries with a wall in the middle. So, we just had fragments of knowledge from one country to another in the West, for example, from Italy, Poland, or France, and very little news coming from countries in the East.

Spirituality in the East began to be synonymous with esoteric magic by Westerners. When we talk about the East with someone, from a stereotypical point of view, we have monks meditating inside a cave. We have a lot of stereotypes.

Around the 18th century, we began to translate many books. So, after all those translations, we started with something else. People, especially students, and scholars, started to study the practice of meditation around the sixties and seventies, for example, Dr. Herbert Benson who is mentioned in many books, especially also in the Breath book by James Nestor. And you can see also the videos on YouTube, where Benson assesses the human capacity to influence inner abilities and metabolism at will.

Then around the eighties, Jon Kabat-Zinn founded his first mindfulness protocol and went in depth with it to bring meditation to lay people. And then, we also saw the first appearance of circular, connected breathwork practices such as Rebirthing and Holotropic breathwork. During the seventies, people were not really attracted to it, however, around the nineties, something shifted. We saw the beginning there . . . we saw the first selling of all the self-help and personal development books. And they were booming.

Mindfulness began to be strengthened around 2013-14. This is the beginning, on one hand, of the new breathwork method. And Wim Hof is appearing with his method with his 23, 24, or more world records. And this is attractive to many people, and many identify with Hof, thanks to all the scientific experiments he has done. On one side of the Wim Hof Method, you have spirituality, and, on the other side, you have a very physical practice. You have to expose yourself to the cold. You see people going to Everest barefoot. It means that now, if I identify myself with Hof, I can do it too. So, there was a booming of interest in breath practices, and the Oxygen Advantage® led forward on that wave.

Today, a lot of people, especially sports athletes, are really interested in how to improve their respiration rate with breathing techniques. In the past, there was no one there to help you establish good breathing at the gym. This was my problem. When you ask people who used to go to the gym, they were usually told to breathe in from their nose and out from their mouth. No one ever taught us how to breathe properly.

I work with professional sports athletes, and their first problem is finding out how they should breathe. They want to know how they can reduce their chances of being breathless and how they can increase the amount of time before they become breathless.

Thanks in part to the Oxygen Advantage®, we are now facing a breathing revolution worldwide. We are seeing an interesting mix of mindfulness practices that had a peak around 2014, and on the other side, the Wim Hof method and all those kinds of breathing practices, and the Oxygen Advantage® and we're mixing them all together. And we are binding once again, from one side, a spiritual practice based on mindfulness meditation, with, on the other side, a spiritual practice or personal development practice based on breathing. So, we've travelled a lot of roads from antiquity with Buddha or some Yogi teaching breathing for mindfulness meditation, to today, where you can meditate using an application on your smartphone.

And we're just taking a fragment of it. We've taken a very long road, and everything was really fragmented, but maybe we're seeing less spiritual practice, from one point of view, but the esoteric practice, just mutated. We have the same discipline – I have to go to the gym; I have to be the best version of myself, etc., all those kinds of mantras that we see at this point.

What you said about spiritual practices mutating and about things being a bit woo-woo . . . These things, we kind of know that they work, but then, from the Western perspective, we have to prove it. We come to the point where, within certain schools of yoga, science is almost seen as atheism, whereas spirituality is within the tradition. Yet, all that science is doing is finding out how the techniques work.

The main question that is coming up from student feedback in the Breathing for Yoga *course and when yogi's come to this work with Oxygen Advantage®, is how exactly it equates to prāṇāyāma. If I practise this, is it the same as this? Do you have any thoughts about that?*

Usually, for highlighting a technique from a scientific point of view, I will also use maybe an illustration and affirmation from a spiritual practitioner. I'll share the new spiritual model of a scientific spirituality and how spirituality and science are becoming entwined, but it has to be harmonious. We don't have to fit everything from prāṇāyāma into science and we don't have to fit all the science into prāṇāyāma.

We have to find a good balance. So, for example, the **Breathe Light** exercise gives you a lot of sensations that are well-documented from a scientific perspective. We have the increasing Bohr effect. We have a lot of oxygenation inside of the cells. We have the parasympathetic nervous system which is more activated than the sympathetic one. We have a lot of saliva in the mouth, etc.

But, if we go on the other path, the spiritual one . . . if you **Breathe Light**, you pay attention to your breath. You have to because the air hunger pulls your attention to your breath. Ram Maharshi used to say every breathing technique is prāṇāyāma breathing. Also, bringing your attention to the breath is prāṇāyāma without changing the breath. So, to comfort yoga practitioners who are not really attracted to science, we can mention things like this. We can insist on a breathing technique, find an equivalent thing from a spiritual author, and then bind them together.

On the other side, you have people that avoid yoga that feels too spiritual. They don't feel comfortable with this and prefer things to feel more practical. I can tell you that from my clinical experience perspective, if for example, someone in psychiatry comes to me and tells me, "I don't feel okay," and I answered that it's because of their chakras, I will just bring them another metaphysical problem. And I will be far away from their experience. I want to approach their experience.

So, what do I mean by that? People just want to feel self-sufficient. This is maybe one of the first guidelines that I'm noticing now – is that a lot of people come to yoga to feel self-sufficient. They will do yoga for a practical reason such as to address their back pain or lower their stress, and they're not approaching it for esoteric studies. It's very rare that someone would start out by saying "I have to do yoga to be spiritually awakened". Maybe, this will happen over time but it's that self-sufficiency that I see first.

Also, a lot of yoga teachers that I know are personal trainers, and they approach it from a biomechanical perspective. If I go on Instagram, I can see countless super fit and athletic yoga teachers, but the image they convey doesn't show the spirituality side of the practice. The spiritual aspect has faded away; the discipline remains but it's applied in another domain. The same paradigm as going to the gym to be fit has been applied to yoga. There is an underlying mentality that – I have to do this, this, this, this, this. I have to do those kinds of torsions in position because I'm athletic. It's more picture-perfect and social media oriented . . .

There is a thing that I see with evangelists. They are really strong believers and, for them, doing yoga, knowing the fact that it comes from another spirituality and knowing that the Bible says that you will have only one God, can make it very difficult to practise. And especially if you put yourself in the perspective of someone that considers yoga a religion, they will have an identity bias where they feel ashamed and have a sense of culpability while practising. Evangelist yoga exists because it was a way to bypass that identity challenge. So, now, we are seeing things like Christian yoga or lay mindfulness. People can find themselves because now there are many currents of new identities where people will be able to fit in. But the most important thing that will help people is to, first of all, feel results because in today's society, we are result-oriented.

What I am hearing is that yoga is a practice of identity and that's where the sticking point is – whether we identify as super fit or we identify with the tradition we've come into. So, it's a challenging thing to convey in this book because it's not a book about spirituality, but it has to acknowledge that mindset within this world.

Remember at the beginning we split the world into two poles, the West and the East where the East equals spirituality, in a contemplative culture where contemplation has been an inner experience. On the other side, we have the West where we see everything analysed into parts.

But the East and the West are two sides of the same coin. This is what will be in the middle – a spiritual science that will help us to go forward. Breathwork, from this point of view, is right in the middle of spirit. A lot of contemplative practices are based on breath. On the other side, science has studied the breath. It is also the way to feel self-sufficient. The breath is one of the most important things that combines all the cultures together, and then everyone can work it on its own.

Until recently, most people weren't attracted to breathwork in the modern world. Why should I breathe like him for one hour or 30 minutes? Is it useful? The practice was built on spirituality and the science was lacking, so people weren't willing to commit their time to it.

Maybe the best thing that can illustrate a practical and spiritual science blended together is the Muse device. When you buy it, you just put it on your head, and it calibrates your EEG waves. It can highlight your results on your iPhone, and every time your mind begins to wander, you hear a soothing wave-like sound. This is a wonderful device that offers a new experience, self-sufficiency, and immediate results.

The impression I get is that spirituality is an intensely practical thing, but we want it through different interfaces. Maybe, this is why you've got these two schools – the esoteric and the scientific. And some people are more over here, and some people are more over there . . .
. . . Can you talk a bit about mental health now?

Our program combines all the breathing techniques inside a psychological context.

Let's imagine, you have been left by your partner. You're feeling angry frequently. Of course, it's natural. Then, for example, you come to your breathing expert and the breathing expert says, focus on your breath. Be present, focus on your breath. Don't be angry . . . Of course, you will be angry. You will be super angry!

If you come to me, first of all, I will allow you to be in a bad mood. It's justified. You don't feel okay. It's normal. I don't believe in excessive, positive thinking. I believe that people are facing waves in their life, and we can authorise ourselves to feel bad. We cannot be at 100% all the time.

In psychology, we really need the breathwork. And we don't have it. And then, once the psychological aspect is fading, we can start introducing some small cognitive exercises.

During my clinical experience, I had the chance to apply breathing techniques to different clients. I worked with people with depression, anxiety, schizophrenia, and other mental health disorders. I learned that breathing techniques and mindfulness won't work on most schizophrenics. Some people really don't like the effects of it, so it's better to avoid it. Sometimes psychotropic drugs are the best way to keep people stabilised who have no other choices.

With anxiety and depression, it's the same thing, we have to be careful of what kind of breathing techniques we use – with some people, using just the **Breathe Light** exercise is best. I often use slow breathing just for three seconds in and three seconds out because five seconds in and out would be too overwhelming. It's a delicate matter.

Emotions don't rise up casually. They are always context-related. For example, you won't start to cry for no reason unless you have depression, or you won't start to laugh from nowhere, unless you have some kind of delusion episodes, but, usually, normally, we are emotionally localised. So, for example, we start to laugh at a movie or with some friends chatting in the bar. We have an emotional context where emotions rise up.

When it comes to anxiety, usually when I have a patient who suffers from it and they tell me, for example, "Yes, doc, I have a problem. I feel anxiety". I ask them "When was the last time you felt anxiety?" And I can localise them and deduce a lot of things from their answers. From there, you can give the client breathing techniques. And then, when the client is ready, you can work on the experience and start to investigate their life.

You were going to tell me about the missing piece with prāṇāyāma, how that's dropped out of the practice, and what your thoughts about that were.

We had the translation of the Oriental Renaissance starting from around the 17th century. At that time, they started to apply mainly the yoga posture practices that were in the past quite significant. But people didn't care during this period about the breath work behind the yoga. They cared about the asana and went forward with that. After a while, going back to 1968 and 1969, many people were attracted to the oriental because it maybe was surrounded by this kind of mystical atmosphere. People were wondering what does it mean to be happy? So, all this curiosity was starting.

During the seventies, people were just at the beginning of those kinds of meditation techniques. At the start of the eighties, we saw some different techniques like holotropic breathing – which I advise against doing. I had three patients who had a problem with holotropic breathing. What happened is that, with holotropic breathing, they would start hyperventilating, and this causes a reduced blood flow to the brain which can trigger a sensation of dying.

That is the one where it's prolonged hyperventilation, is that right?

That's right. And it can last for one hour. If you want to do it, do it with a facilitator who has a lot of experience. But I had three patients, one of them developed a tic, where he felt the compulsion to push his tongue against his teeth every second. This lasted an entire day, and it started right after a 30-minute session of Holotropic breathing. Another patient developed a brain problem and experienced paranoia right after the session.

He already had a certain kind of clinical background, but, with those kinds of breathing techniques, we have to be careful who is trying and using them. So, please be careful with the Rebirthing and the Holotropic breathing.

I did the Holotropic breathwork once just for 30 minutes. Physically, it was quite unpleasant, but, at the end of it, I had a proper kind of psychedelic experience. I was lying on the floor, and I had this old Turkish carpet and I could see the carpet in front of my eyes. It's so strange. The patterns. And I thought, oh, that's why these cultures all have these patterns in their textiles because it's what you see when you hallucinate – it's all just a visual pattern.

But did it help you somehow?

No, it didn't. I was fortunate. I didn't go really full on with it,
so I did induce the psychedelic effects, the colours and everything,
but I didn't have any particular after-effects, either good or bad,
though I was conscious that there could be some. They sell this stuff
for trauma and for people who have quite serious mental illnesses
like addiction. I think it's playing with fire, to be honest.

Agreed, I don't like this approach and I don't feel comfortable with it. I would like people to avoid it, because it gives them too much adrenaline, in my opinion. Instead, I recommend nice, slow, gentle breathing, this is especially helpful in our overstimulated world.

It seems like, first of all, you're approaching something that requires
a certain gentleness with basically a sledgehammer. It seems like
what the practitioner is expecting is an easy instantaneous cure.

I'm not really keen on it. It's not for everyone. A lot of people talk about having an emotional release thanks to those techniques. So far, for me, an emotional release can mean a lot of things and nothing at the same time. The concept behind those kinds of techniques is that you have to do something in order to release something else. This is an old concept of psychoanalysis. It's a pattern of healing, of curing. Of course, it can work sometimes. But the problem is they believe that, if you reach the trigger, the trauma itself, you target it by simply discovering it. And by knowing what the problem is, you can put an end to it. And that's not often the case.

So, what do we have to do? We have to change perspective. This is why I like Cognitive Behavioural Therapy because it will give you a tool to adapt in your everyday life and you will go forward with practising it. And that's nice. But my domain of psychotherapy is to help my patients to have a different life experience.

For example, say my partner left me yesterday. I can call someone and tell him, listen, I'm sad because of this blah, blah, blah, blah, or my friend could come and say to me, Ali, you're not okay. Let's go out.

Let's change experience. This is far more helpful. If you want to heal something, you have to keep continuing to do something different in another kind of experience. Even if you don't like it, at least you will have some meanings to absorb, and those meanings will adapt to your previous situation. It will help give you some insight into the problem you have and then offer you a further window of improvement.

If you want to change, first you have to expose yourself to a new experience because the previous experience is giving you the same results. So, if you want something different, you have to expose yourself in a different way. For example, if someone has a phobia of snakes, the best way to solve the problem is to gradually expose themselves to snakes. First week, they look and think about snakes. Second week, they watch snake documentaries on TV. Then they have different therapies. Then they get closer to the vivarium. So, changing happens through different experiences and also constants. There's that saying in psychology that miracles lay in constants. They lay in constants in a structured way where you maintain a certain way of behaving.

And now, to get back to breathwork. There is a breathwork revolution happening at this very moment. You can check it on Google trends.

Some studies about breathwork had already been done around year 2000, but it was just a glimpse. Interest really started to snowball with Wim Hof in 2012, not only because his method was revolutionary and there was a good marketing approach, but also because the method was really working well on autoimmune disease. Hof has also broken many records and stood as an example that everyone can do it. And there is also the ice bath that is not only beneficial for your body but is also a good spectacle that gives a certain image of the warrior.

*That ties in with how we're attracted to the more gross practices.
So, with breathwork, people are more attracted to the interesting
ones, the things that feel more extreme . . .*

*What I'm discovering, when I talk to clients, is that many people
don't think they are stressed, but they are. A friend who's just had
COVID said, oh, I'm generally quite relaxed. I did a couple of
breathing exercises with him, and he could not stop yawning. I said,
you might feel relaxed mentally because you're used to chronic
stress. He had a BOLT score of 10 – which is a sure sign of bodily
imbalance. That is the definition of stress.*

*I also worked with a lady who was one of three women who
worked for the UN peace Corps at NATO. She said, no, no, I'm not
stressed. My job's not stressful. And yet her hair was falling out and
she had hyperthyroidism. She'd been an international-level skier,
and she couldn't walk upstairs without losing her breath. Chronic
stress is a global epidemic, and this is why we need breathwork.*

For someone who comes to me and tells me that they are not stressed, I
would try to put them in a stress condition. Maybe through breathwork.
I will ask the client, okay, hyperventilate in front of me. How do you feel?

There is also another kind of stress that people don't talk about all
that often. It is parasympathetic stress. I've worked with athletes, for
example, that are too nice during competition and seem to be operating
too slowly. This happened to one of my friends recently. He showed
up, was getting ready on the mat, and was having anxious feelings and
thoughts such as "God what am I doing here? . . . I should be drinking
with friends. Why am I here?" The problem here was that his stress
condition was too high. It reached a level that was unsustainable and
everything collapsed because it was too invariable for him. And now
he's just destroyed. He has no energy or drive. This can be caused by a
depletion of, or desensitisation to, adrenaline cortisol from outputting
too much, for too long. When this occurs, it can be incredibly
de-motivating and debilitating.

So, what do we do in these cases? We prepare them gently. We work
on a lot of focused breathing for example. And during the night, when

they're sleeping at a meet, we wake them up at 3:00 AM with a super loud song. We do this to purposefully activate stress and we'll use really harsh songs such as heavy metal to ensure the stress activation level is high. We want them to find their own resources to face that kind of stress. From there, they can develop the ability to cope with certain parasympathetic anxiety conditions.

That's really interesting. When I was studying music, before I went on stage, I would get that feeling of absolute exhaustion and like, what am I doing here? I was so stressed that I just wanted to go to sleep.

Interesting. When high anxiety is present, the prefrontal cortex is overactivated. What you experienced was likely a hyperactivated prefrontal cortex and sympathetic anxiety.

I play the violin. What I've found the most useful has been Breathe Light. I think that old advice to take deep breaths just compounds the activation in the prefrontal cortex because you end up hyperventilating. When I came back to performing after the pandemic, I found Breathe Light really useful. Also, it makes your hands warm. One of the things that's most debilitating with performance anxiety is that you've practised everything with this fine, fine motor control and then your hands are too cold to do it.

Maybe this can help you – it's a very useful tool. A breathing exercise from the Oxygen Advantage® which athletes love is holding the breath after an exhalation to achieve a moderate to strong air hunger. It's a kind of similar to Wim Hof breathing, but not as strong and includes recovery.

While sitting or lying down, take 20 full breaths in and out through the nose (hyperventilation). Then exhale and hold the breath until a moderate to strong air hunger is experienced (breath hold). Resume breathing in through the nose and **Breathe Light** for 3 minutes (recovery). You could repeat three cycles of the above.

You can find out more about Alessandro Romagnoli
at www.oxylab360.com

GRAY CAWS: ANCIENT TRADITIONS AND TEACHING BREATHING

Oxygen Advantage® Master Instructor Gray Caws combines breathwork and Qigong in his work with runners and other clients. Gray came to Qigong and breathing through his running. He explains how he works with the breath in movement and how he tailors breathing to individual students in larger classes.

Like yoga, Qigong is an ancient method that integrates breath, body, and mind. It's part of Chinese medical tradition, and it embraces ideas similar to those behind many yoga practices.

Such concepts underlying Qigong include:

- The relaxation response.
- The effects of meditation.
- The interrelatedness of behaviour, the nervous system, hormones, and immune processes.
- How our behaviours and environment can affect the working of our genes (now called epigenetics).
- Traditional energy theories – the idea of a subtle energy or life force (called Qi in Chinese, Ki in Japanese . . . and prana in the yogic tradition).

The idea of Qi, Ki, or prana pervades different healing traditions throughout the world. There are also plenty of stories of healing through hands in the Bible. More recently, the practice of reiki has emerged and gained popularity. The word *reiki* means *universal life (rei) energy (ki)*.

Such techniques have long been dismissed as "paranormal" by Western science. The healing benefits of Ki or Qi are commonly described in terms of the placebo effect or have been thought to be due to hypnosis. Nevertheless, Ki and Qigong therapies remain popular in Japan, China, and, increasingly, in the Western world.

Over the last 30 years, scientists have worked to quantify this energy and explore its biochemical and physiological effects. It is now recognized as a normal phenomenon that involves emissions that include a small amount of infrared radiation. This is a resource that everyone can learn to use.

One 2006 paper examines Ki through a unique breathing method, the Nishino Breathing Method. It is devised and taught by Kozo Nishino, an Aikido black belt and former ballet dancer with a medical degree. His method has some small similarities with yoga. It combines physical movement to relax, rotate, and stretch the body with a slow, deep breath, the complete cycle of which can last between one and two minutes.

Nishino also practises Taiki, which means "a paired Ki-practice." In Taiki, the instructor and student extend their hands to touch. The student sends Ki through his or her hand to the instructor, who then sends his Ki back toward the student. This practice allows the student to develop their level of Ki relatively quickly.

Nishino can even use his Ki to physically move students – with no visual or physical stimulus. In classes, he can cause the students to run or stop, to twist the legs or rotate the ankles up or down, and even to fall by sending information or energy to them. In one experiment, a student stood in a headstand, facing away from Nishino so she could not see him. He opened his hands, and, in response, she widened her legs. As the researchers explain, "This is a physiological reaction triggered by some mechanism, for which we do not currently have a scientific explanation."[739]

Nishino has taught his method to over 10,000 students over the last two decades. Although he does not offer any specific therapy or healing treatment, practitioners report improvements to their health and to conditions including high blood pressure, osteoporosis, arthritis, and even cancer.[740] Scientists have proven that Nishino's method enhances the immune response and reduces stress.[741] One study reports that practitioners seem able to stay "mentally and physically young and healthy."

Another laboratory study using a reiki-like practice demonstrated that Ki can inhibit cell division in cultured human cancer cells. What's more, research into Ki provides further evidence of the body/mind connection. Scientists suggest that, when an individual receives both Ki-energy and Ki-information during Taiki, they may achieve a mental state called "collective unconsciousness," a deeper state than most people can achieve through meditation. It has been shown that just by sitting down in front of a Qigong healer, brainwave activity can synchronise with that of the healer. All of this suggests that Ki or Qi (or prana) is not just energy, it is information.[742]

739 Ohnishi, Tsuyoshi, and Tomoko Ohnishi. "The Nishino Breathing Method and Ki-Energy (Life-Energy): A Challenge to Traditional Scientific Thinking." *Evidence-Based Complementary and Alternative Medicine* 3.2 (2006): 191-200.
740 Ohnishi, Tsuyoshi, and Tomoko Ohnishi. "The Nishino Breathing Method and Ki-Energy (Life-Energy): A Challenge to Traditional Scientific Thinking." *Evidence-Based Complementary and Alternative Medicine* 3.2 (2006): 191-200.
741 Kimura, Hiroko, et al. "Beneficial Effects of the Nishino Breathing Method on Immune Activity and Stress Level." *Journal of Alternative & Complementary Medicine* 11.2 (2005): 285-291.
742 Ohnishi, Tsuyoshi, and Tomoko Ohnishi. "The Nishino Breathing Method and Ki-Energy (Life-Energy): A Challenge to Traditional Scientific Thinking." *Evidence-Based Complementary and Alternative Medicine* 3.2 (2006): 191-200.

Research shows that, like yoga, Qigong has positive effects on quality of life. It helps with fatigue, immune function, cortisol levels, and mental function.[743] It also improves heart rate variability and blood pressure control.[744] Practice involves slow, mindful exercise combined with breath regulation. It's easy to learn, accessible, and promotes relaxation and cultivates energy through the use of mental intention.

Qigong is very similar to yoga in the way that it's connected with and guided by the breath. When you practise certain flows in Qigong, the breath is just light, soft, slow, and easy. When I started practising Qigong with the Oxygen Advantage® techniques, it just made complete sense because neither is about a big breath in or a big breath out. Sometimes, as in yoga, we will use a cleansing and clearing breath, but most of the time you practise breathing light in movement. This is exactly what we teach in Oxygen Advantage® – **Breathe Light** in functional movement.

Another thing with Qigong is that every movement has an intention behind it. Some of the movements have surprising names. For instance, "tiger" is a squat. The names help give you the intention for the movement. This is important because, with any movement we make, our intention affects the way we breathe.

Imagine you're a runner doing interval training. Your coach tells you to run to the top of a hill. If you run up there with the intention of exercise, it immediately becomes a chore. Your focus is just on running up the hill as quickly as possible. You can do the same activity with a different idea in mind. You can run up the hill just to see what's at the top or to catch the sunset. This gives you a completely different intention.

This intention is important because the mind/body connection influences how you breathe and how you approach physical exercise. If you have an understanding or intention behind any movement, your breathing will change. Without consciously guiding the breath, you can

743 Klein, Penelope. "Qigong in Cancer Care: Theory, Evidence-Base, and Practice." *Medicines* 4, 1 2 (2017). doi:10.3390/.

744 Chang, Mei-Ying. "Qigong effects on Heart Rate Variability and Peripheral Vasomotor Responses." *Western Journal of Nursing Research* 37.11 (2015): 1383-1403.

bring in light breathing in this way, through the mind/body connection. The more I explore this idea of intention in different types of exercise, the more I realise its importance.

Like yoga, most movements in Qigong also have a specific breath phase. As such, you would approach a practice in two stages. The first stage is to physically move your body, to cleanse or clear any negative energy, loosen any tight muscles, and warm up. We do this by shaking the body out or using spine rotations, flexion, and extension. This gets you moving to create that mobility and flexibility and to enliven the body.

Next, once the energy is flowing, you go into the practice. In the flow practice, movement is created with the breath and with the energy that's already moving in the body. It's a nice contrast. You begin with the energetic movement in your warmup, cleansing, and clearing, as you would in yoga. But, once you're in a flow sequence, the movements are done with ease and guided by the breath. When you begin the inhalation, that creates the movement, and, when you feel the need to breathe out, the movement follows that breath. Rather than thinking, "I need to get into that position and breathe into that position," you are very much using the breath to create the movement. One of the benefits of this is that anybody can do it. You can even do most movements if you're sitting. Eighty and ninety-year-olds can do it, and they just go to the point where they're not overreaching because they're following the breath.

Oxygen Advantage® and yoga both teach us that the minute we lose control of the breath, we lose control of movement. It's the same in Qigong. So, if you get to a certain point in a movement, and suddenly you have pain in your lower back or your hip, for instance, we interpret that as the breath saying not to push beyond that point. The breath will always be soft, light, and controlled. And, by leading with the breath, you will always be in a safe place to explore the movement and tune in to what's going on in the body.

Does Qigong have its own tradition of breathing exercises?

The foundation of Qigong flow is breathing in and out through the nose – light, slow, and deep – just as we guide in Oxygen Advantage®. There are specific breathing exercises, very much like Breath of Fire, that use diaphragm activation. You would use this to build energy. There's also soft, light breathing, which is down-regulating the body.

When I use the breath with the Qigong movements, I only use a couple of breathing exercises. This keeps it simple. I like that because it's simple for students too. Quite often, people see breathwork as hard work or something additional they must do, almost like another workout. Ultimately, the result we want is for people to be breathing optimally whatever they're doing, whether they're sitting at their computer or walking to the shops.

Breathwork doesn't have to be done separately. It's also important to have this simplicity in practice because people can get disheartened. They see some of the more advanced yoga poses and think, "There's no way I can do that." As soon as they watch their teacher or a peer demonstrate these poses, they feel inferior. That feeling is going to affect how they breathe and how they feel. If you feel a bit anxious and as though you aren't as good as another person, all the breathwork in the world is not going to change that feeling – that memory creates your present moment.

This idea of empowering someone, making sure they feel safe and comfortable but still feel the benefits, is important to me when I work with clients. I like to work in a way that doesn't feel like exercise. I don't want them to strive, force, or strain. There can still, of course, be challenge, change, improvement, and healthy competition. But, to me, that's the whole principle behind Oxygen Advantage®. It's not about exercise. It's about the breath guiding the movement. That also applies to breath holds. When you are walking and practising **Breathe Light**, it's not about walking and breathing the least amount of air. You allow your walk to be guided by the fact you are breathing very lightly, slowly, and comfortably. Then, if you move into a run, keep the breath light. If you struggle with that, you lose control of the breath, and then you lose control of the movement.

How do you bring the ideas of Qigong and breathwork into more mainstream fitness coaching?

The whole idea behind Qigong is to allow your body to find its natural flow and balance. You can do a very simple flow movement and connect with the feeling as you're doing that movement. You can then be doing a completely different movement, such as running, and you can bring your mind back to how the fluidity of that flow felt. You can bring that into your practice. And that's what I like to help people with. To feel that effortless flow.

If you can't, and exercise feels like a struggle, the breath will tell you that you're doing too much. So again, follow the breath as you go from a walk to a run. If you just breathe effortlessly through the nose, which is what we teach in Oxygen Advantage®, then, by default, you will feel a flow. And, as soon as you get out of breath, you're going to lose that flow.

In this way, you should allow your breath to guide whatever practice, whatever movement you're doing. This might mean you have to slow down a bit at first, but your body will become more efficient. You will work out where you need to be strong and where you can soften and relax. This is another focus in Qigong. We spend time in standing postures asking, "Where can I let go but keep a good structure, so everything's not just collapsed on the floor, but it's not rigid either?" It's all about balance.

To give another example, you often see runners with tight fists and fingers, pulling a face with their shoulders up. That's all an unnecessary waste of energy. The energy you put into this tension uses oxygen. So, you'll be breathing more heavily to maintain the tension in your body. Thinking uses oxygen, so if you're overthinking something while you're running, you'll need to breathe more heavily.

Again, going back to the idea of intention, there was a study that showed runners could improve their performance by around 2% just by smiling![745] That doesn't sound like a big improvement, but, if you think about elite competitive runners, it is. In Qigong, we teach something called the "inner smile." This relaxes the fascial muscles and the whole back line of the body through the fascia. So, having the intention to enjoy your run and smiling while you run helps your nasal breathing because it opens the airways. Whereas grimacing uses energy and tightens the chest and airways.

Tongue position is important in Qigong too because it connects the back energy with the front energy in the body. As you breathe in, the spine extends and the body expands. As you breathe out, the front line of the body softens as the spine stays strong. This tongue position

745 Brick, Noel E., Megan J. McElhinmey, and Richard S. Metcalfe. "The Effects of Facial Expression and Relaxation Cues on Movement Economy, Physiological, and Perceptual Responses During Running." *Psychology of Sport and Exercise* 34 (2018): 20-28.

provides for optimal energy flow. It connects to the vagus nerve as well. So, when the tongue is in a good position, it helps support good vagal tone, which means your nervous system is better balanced.

Going back to the idea of movement, by working with the breath, would you say you're producing a more efficient, functional result?

Yes, it's just that we're working from the inside out. It takes time to be aware of what's going on within the body. For that reason, I start with physical movement when I work with clients. When you work with someone new, and you're introducing them to Qigong or to breathwork, and you start by asking them to feel the energy, it can be off-putting. People don't know what you mean. It's useful to get simple movements going first.

Often, you see people sticking or pausing at certain points in their movement. It's very unlikely that you'll get a smooth, fluid movement to start off with, but this is useful feedback. We practise the movement first, and then we add the breath, working from the outside in. Once they've got the idea, they can feel what's going on inside the body. That's the best way I've found to introduce people to Qigong and to what "energy" means. In your first session, you can't suddenly feel Qi running through your body. You can shake yourself, and then you can feel it. The physical awareness is a good starting point.

What about the BOLT score? Do you use it? Would you start with the BOLT score? And do you find that people who have less freedom of movement tend to have a lower BOLT score?

Most of the time, I won't start off with the BOLT score because straight away you're asking someone to test themselves, and, for me, the BOLT score isn't a test. For me, it's about noticing how soon you feel the first sign that you need to take a breath. If you think about where the BOLT score originated, which is from the Buteyko Method, it was the controlled or comfortable pause. There's a lot of value in the BOLT score, but I don't go in cold with it.

If you think about it literally, you want the first definite desire to breathe to be quite quick because, if it's not, it could mean you have low CO_2. For instance, if you've practised hyperventilation like you do in the Wim Hof method, then you take your BOLT score, you could be able to sit for two minutes before you need to breathe. I don't usually go in straight away with the BOLT score. I use measures like resting heart rate and heart rate variability first. I also do a sitting maximum breathlessness test to see how long they can hold their breath, because this gives a direct comparison with the BOLT.

When I use the BOLT, I almost trick people into it, so there isn't that competitive element. I just ask them to take a normal breath in and out, and then to rest, to enjoy the rest – to just go to a comfortable pause and take a breath in. This allows them to do the BOLT score without it becoming a test, and that's the way I find it works for me and my clients.

But, yes, usually when there are sticking points in terms of movement, the breathing biomechanics may not be so efficient, and this could affect your tolerance to CO_2, your BOLT score, and also your mind/body connection.

How do you approach breathing with different students if you're working with a larger class? How do you tailor the breathing so that the breath can still be a successful point of reference for each student?

Actually, this is easier than doing seated breath guidance because you can see the way people are moving. Say, for example, I give my class an exercise called *Buddha Holds up the Earth*. In this movement, you're just "lifting the earth" above your head and then bringing it down again. What's great from a biomechanical point of view is that you extend the spine and then soften and flex it. You open the rib cage and expand the ribs. And you breathe laterally. There's a lot going on biomechanically. Then, you go with the idea that the breath is going to guide you. So, as you breathe in, you lift the arms, and, as you breathe out, you bring them back down. Once they get into the flow of the movement, I just let them move at their own pace. The breath should just be light and slow, and that's all that I cue.

Then, I stop demonstrating the movement, so that they are not following me. Usually, they find their own rhythm. If they don't, I can see that the breath isn't flowing, and I can guide them. If I'm giving any cues to a group, I will cue the group in general, not single out one student. In this sense, the group guides me as to what cues I need to give to help them with movement. As long as you cue the fact that the breath is leading the movement, it works. It can be as simple as that.

When we get into a balancing pose, I explain that it's not about balancing on one leg. It's about exploring what's happening with the breath. The breath is lifting you and helping you balance. I find it very easy to teach in a group because you can see so easily in the movement what is going on with their breath. Any sign of neuromuscular overload shows up in the breath. If somebody's stressed or in pain, you see it in the breath. If someone is pushing themselves too much, you see it in the breath. It's a very visual signal once you get a group moving.

Actually, when you get a group moving in sync, and they're all breathing light, slow, and deep, there's a real energy about that group. It becomes a unified energy, rather than six or ten individuals doing an exercise.

Some of the physical positions in yoga are really challenging. You're going into a plank and moving through it, and that's not an easy move for someone who's unfamiliar with strength and conditioning coaching. If you put someone who's not comfortable or in control of that movement into that posture, it can potentially be harmful, particularly when you're working in a group class.

If you let the breath guide the movement, you're always going to be in control. You're going to be safe. You see this a lot in *yin yoga*, where you just find your safe comfortable place in a pose and breathe into that place.

I once had a wonderful time in Bali doing some yin yoga with a fantastic teacher. He was literally just getting us to the edge of the pose and then asking us to breathe into it. But we weren't forcing anything.

It was about feeling the movement in the body, in the twist or the reach, and breathing through it because that's what releases.

But I think people often have the idea that exercise is all about pushing yourself. Yes, it's about challenging yourself, but, if you push yourself too much, you'll get injured. Or you'll get disheartened and believe you can't do a certain pose. Then you'll feel like a failure, and you might not say it, but that's what's going on in your mind, and that will affect the breath. That feeling will affect how you are breathing in that position.

When I teach Qigong and breathwork, I want to give clients an understanding of why we are doing it and the benefits you can get from doing it. You can understand the benefits just because you feel better,

but there are also studies to back this up. The mind-body connection is so important. So is knowing why we are doing a certain movement. And there we circle back to the idea we started with – intention.

Just to finish off, there will always be discussions about the origins of Qigong and yoga. Qigong people say Qigong came first and that yoga is taken from our tradition. Yoga people say that it's the other way around. Ultimately, it doesn't matter. Both have their roots in how people move. Back when these practices were developed, people had more connection with nature. Even the names of the Qigong movements tell you that. *Heart to Sky* is about lifting your heart to the sky. If you lift your heart to the ceiling indoors, it's a very different thing. It's a very different experience when you're outside looking at the clouds and you're *Pulling Down the Heavens*. Qigong is very much an outdoor sky and earth energy practice. That balance of heaven and earth, between our physical and spiritual experience, that's what it's all about.

You can find out more about Gray's work
*at **AdventuresInMovement.com***

SIENNA SMITH: BLENDING ANCIENT YOGA PRACTICES WITH THE SCIENCE OF BREATHING

*Sienna Smith is a specialist in yoga, breath, and wellness who has been practising and teaching yoga for 22 years. While many people start yoga for the physical practice, Sienna initially came to it for emotional healing. In the last decade, Sienna has been working to balance ancient yogic practices and philosophy with modern respiratory physiology. Her primary goal is to blend science and tradition in a way that makes sense both scientifically and holistically. She offers yoga and breathing classes, workshops, trainings, and retreats, as well as a six-week online breathing course. She is also the host of the **Breathe Better Podcast**.*

Below, Sienna talks about what drew her to yoga and how she integrates an understanding of the breath with her yoga and yoga therapy students.

I took my first class at a YMCA 25 years ago, and I remember the breath was so powerful. Immediately, it took me to places that I couldn't access any other way. As soon as I started breathing in child's pose, I began crying, and that was my doorway into the deep healing world of yoga and breathing.

When you really look at why yoga was created, it was to stop the fluctuations of the mind. The goal was to obtain liberation. This contrasts with modern-day yoga, which focuses on the physical. The West has flipped yoga on its head. Why is that? Perhaps because we sit at a desk, couch, or in a car many hours a day. In a sense, it's not a bad thing that yoga has moved more towards a physical practice. Part of this shift into the physical nature of yoga is necessary and important. It's what our bodies need. But I do think we've gone too far in that direction. We're ignoring yoga's original premise to the extent that most of the yoga that's out there should just simply be called "exercise." True yoga only happens when we are in the present moment. The breath is one vehicle for accessing the present moment, and hardly anyone is teaching it.

It seems that currently, in society, there is a much bigger yearning for people to develop their inner lives, not just their physical bodies. Do you think this might create the conditions for breathing to be reintegrated into yoga?

Absolutely. I think breathing is the doorway to those deeper issues. It helps us deal with the root causes of suffering by illuminating the underlying causes of our pain, disease, and dysfunction. Western science and medicine are symptom-based. They look at the symptoms of disease but not the root cause.

Yoga addresses the root cause of our problems, such as revealing our negative thoughts, misguided habit patterns, poor alignment, distracted minds, and anxious breathing. Yoga also incorporates the energetic, meditative, and spiritual aspects of practice to help people. Yoga shines when people can get beyond the physical . . . when they can get comfortable in their own skin.

There are a lot of stressors in our world right now, stressors that weren't present even 30 or 40 years ago. That heightened stress is all around us, and it's happening inside us. To break through the stress, people gravitate toward things that are hard and fast. They want something they can really feel. And that's why they turn to more physical and often more extreme practices.

Our sensitivity and attention spans have decreased so much that we can't even spend a few seconds focusing on the breath. It's as if, to wake up, we need to be hit over the head. For many of us, that wake-up-call comes from asana practice. It provides a way to shake us into the present moment.

The practice of breath in yoga is a subtle body practice. Asana (posture practice) is what you might call a "gross" body practice. We are attracted to asana precisely because we can't sit still and focus on the breath. If we try breathwork from this place, we become irritable, and we don't feel any benefit. We certainly don't get the huge shift we're expecting.

This is one reason why Ashtanga and hot yoga have become so popular. I would say they are more extreme and more physical in their approach to yoga. Also, traditionally, you would not introduce heat or any outside force to connect with deeper levels of your being. Yoga is about generating heat from within. You wouldn't necessarily practise in a fast, flowing way either because it may minimise your ability to connect with the subtle energy of your body.

By progressing from asana to breath and meditation, yoga brings us from the gross to the subtle, the refined, and the still. And it's in that stillness we can find wholeness. It is when we slow down and breathe that we see and feel the underlying cause of our pain and suffering and also get in touch with our self-healing capacity.

How much information about the breath and respiratory function is covered during yoga teacher training?

When yoga teachers take their 200-hour certification, 30 hours of the training covers anatomy. Perhaps 3 to 5 hours of that is dedicated to the anatomy of breathing.

The first issue for me here is that, if you want to become a yoga teacher, 200 hours of training is not nearly enough. The second is that, with only a few hours teaching, you're going to retain very little of the information about breathing anatomy unless you apply it.

Most schools of yoga don't focus on the breath because there is so much to cover regarding the poses, anatomy, alignment, sequencing, and teaching methodology in only 200 hours. Plus, when yoga teachers start teaching they don't make a lot of money, and, by necessity, the emphasis tends to be on what people want – which is a very physical practice. And so, we heat the room up, we practise faster and harder, and we push for the difficult poses to satisfy what we think people want. We work at a gross level where there's no room for the breath and the subtle level.

In yoga class, we often get physical adjustments from the teacher, but we never get a "breathing adjustment." Do you think one way to bridge that gap would be to integrate little nuggets about breathing into the teaching rather than to make a big feature of it?

Yes, exactly. Anything tactile or sensory helps. People need something to feel or see. If you just ask them to sit and focus on the breath from the outset, most of us find that too challenging. The mind tells us it's not working and therefore not worth our effort.

What's more, for people to start seeing the benefits of breathing, it must be instructed over and over. As teachers, we can use somatic cues to help with that. We can bring the student's attention to certain parts of the body or place a yoga strap or small sandbag on the body. We can ask them to count, use a mantra, or even do guided visualisations. All these things give the mind something to do. This is important because, if you don't give the mind something to focus on, it will take you away from the breath.

If we just teach someone about the breathing muscles, we don't address the fact that the mind wanders. And, if the student doesn't even realize they're being distracted, they can't build that awareness of how to connect with the breath or how important it is. If we want to integrate breathing successfully, it's essential to look at the whole picture.

Do you give your students information about how to use the breath outside their practice?

Yes, absolutely. I often talk about that when I lead teacher trainings or teach public classes. I might ask, "Here's what we do on the mat. How can you take it off the mat?" I think the more we talk about the breath and the more we feed that into our daily classes, the more impact it will have because of the repeated practice. We must find a way to bring it into every single class – to teach it in a way that blends ancient yoga practices with the science of the breath. That's critical. And I think it has to start with focusing on it in teacher trainings. From there, the teachings can spread to the students.

What's your experience with prāṇāyāma and with the Oxygen Advantage® training?

I've been making my way through the Oxygen Advantage® material for a couple of years. I see myself as a researcher. I love research, which is why I appreciate the Oxygen Advantage®. But you need a certain kind of training to be able to consider and incorporate what the science says, and most yoga teachers don't have science degrees. More often, they come from a gym or fitness background or from the corporate world which makes it more difficult for them to speak about the science of breathing and the proven benefits. Unlike physical or respiratory therapists, yoga teachers aren't required to have a health-based degree. In some ways, that means yoga teachers are teaching things that may be outside their understanding. This includes the implications of certain breathing practices, contraindications, and the effects breathing has on our nervous systems, emotions, and mental state.

When I was taking my advanced teacher training, I remember being asked to do six months of breathing. Every two weeks, I would switch to a different breathing technique. Kudos to my teacher for bringing six months of breathing into the training. But, at the time, my life was very stressful. I had two young children, and my marriage was on the rocks. And, here I was, after 15 days training, being sent home with a list of prāṇāyāmas and the instruction to try each one for two weeks and journal about the results. Every day I did about 20 minutes of practice, and, by halfway through, I couldn't feel my feet on the ground. It was as if I'd been launched out of my body. I started experiencing panic. This level of rigorous training was too much for my body. My "vessel" was not prepared for it.

We're often told we must do many years of asana practice to be ready for prāṇāyāma. But here we are, trying to do it all so we can experience the breathing techniques and gain a sense of what we're teaching. That is a lofty goal because prāṇāyāma has intense energetic effects on the body and mind. And then we try to go off and live our daily stressful lives, and we're not even in the body. There are many stories of people practising too much prāṇāyāma in certain ways, and they have a mental breakdown or all kinds of physical issues. So, the question is how do you become proficient in a practice that can take decades or a lifetime to learn? How do you then feel confident enough to teach it to your students in a way that honours the ancient tradition and the physiology of breathing? That's a very tall order.

To give another example, one of the exercises I learned is called Threshold Breathing. In this prāṇāyāma, you work to maximise the four phases of your breath in whichever way you want. You explore making one breath cycle as long as possible. You then continue with it for ten breaths. My teacher had mastered a 60-second breath cycle. That's one breath per minute for ten breaths. Now, I like to push myself, which as we know, is never a good idea in prāṇāyāma. I got up to 42 seconds, and I was able to repeat the breath ten times. Two things happened. First, I realised how much the mind is part of breathing. Second, I noticed tiny things that happened in my life would impact my ability to reach that goal. The breath is a powerful mirror. It shows you things about yourself. It can freak people out and scare them away from the practice, and it can also help heal and transform in a powerful way. A good teacher is essential.

Because of my experience, I tell my teacher-training students to stick with a handful of breathing techniques. These are all exercises people can tolerate quite well. Through my own mistakes, I learned how not to teach prāṇāyāma. I experienced the repercussions of an improper breath practice – what it can do and how ungrounding it can be. At the same time, when I made these discoveries, I did have a certain amount of training and knew how to take care of myself.

We have students coming to class with very little yoga or breathing experience, and we're instructing them to inhale for five seconds and exhale for five seconds. This is not going to go well for most people. They're going to feel anxious and stressed. It's going to activate their sympathetic nervous system, and it won't be relaxing at all.

Instead, we need to give people permission to breathe at a speed that's possible for them. To inhale for three seconds and exhale for three seconds. Even that could be a challenge because we have such a culture of hyperventilation. But we must decrease our expectations about what people are able to do. And we must increase our instruction around how potent and intense the breath can be. If you remember why I got into yoga in the first place, I sat in child's pose, and I was told to breathe diaphragmatically, and I started bawling my eyes out. That's how powerful the breath is.

The stronger ancient breathing practices, such as long breath holds or super-fast breathing, don't always affect our modern-day bodies and minds in a good way. I don't think most people should be doing them, and I don't teach them, even in my breathing course. A student might take my course and think, "Well, this is actually really simple." But it's not simple if you're doing it right. For instance, let's say the highest ratio

I work with in the course is 5:5. That's a five-second inhale and a five-second exhale, for ten breaths. Can you really focus on your breath for those ten breaths? It's not easy. Then you add the small breath holds. In yoga, the holds are considered the most powerful part of the breath because that's where prana is reabsorbed into the body. When you ask someone to hold their breath, it's like death. Especially when we hold after the exhale. And we need to know whether that's helping or hurting the nervous system. That's why the breath needs to be adapted to the person.

How do we translate this to a group yoga class? First, we need to lower our expectations and increase our discussion about contraindications. To talk more about the physiological effects of changing the breath. Over the years, as I've worked with the breath, I've likened it to a goddess. The goddess doesn't like to be pushed around. The breath is a wild, beautiful, ever-powerful goddess, and she doesn't want to be told what to do. If you look at the breath like that, you'll be a lot less likely to go wrong. Respect the breath as it is, get to know its flow, rhythm, pace, and texture. Slowing down to witness the breath is powerful enough. Eventually, if we want to regulate the breath, make it simple so we don't create more stress in our system.

Do you think in some ways it's helpful to keep the idea of functional breathing separate from the idea of prāṇāyāma?

Not necessarily. But I would also say that most of us aren't clear on the definition of prāṇāyāma. Prana is life force. Yama is lengthening or control. So, prāṇāyāma is breath control, breath lengthening, or guiding the breath in a specific way. And, so, rather than separating the ideas of prāṇāyāma and functional breathing, maybe our definition of prāṇ āyāma needs to be examined. It's better for yoga that we broaden the definition of prāṇāyāma – that we're more honest and real about how we can practise it in a way that benefits our health. It doesn't have to be this advanced, mysterious, or extreme technique. We don't always have to get "bigger and better." We can just say, "Close your eyes, be aware of your breathing, and count to five," and we can call it prāṇāyāma. Because, if you look at the bare root of what prāṇāyāma is, this is the exact definition of it, guiding or controlling the breath.

What's your take on using the BOLT score to assess how advanced students are in their physical practice?

In my experience, it can be helpful. We do need a tool to assess. Plus, the BOLT score is a useful way for students to self-assess so they can make better choices for themselves.

The somatic tools are also helpful. Unless you can learn to feel the breath in a certain part of the body, you can't focus on it for any length of time. And, if you can't do that, you can't direct the mind. If a student can't be present with the breath for three breaths, how can you really teach them anything about breathing?

For me, the first step is awareness. That would be the first thing I assess because, otherwise, people are taking the BOLT score, and they can't identify that first definite desire to breathe. We often have such an egoic, striving nature that we want to get a higher number. Some people are able to be honest and self-reflective and see themselves clearly, and some aren't. When you have a student sitting in front of you, you can watch their body wanting to breathe. And you can see that, while their BOLT score is good, their rib cage isn't moving. The BOLT score would then need to be part of a whole – an arsenal of different assessments.

If yoga instructors were to embrace breathing from three dimensions and exercises to up-regulate and down-regulate the nervous system, what potential do you feel modern yoga could offer?

It would help bring our awareness back to what's happening in our bodies. It would help us become sensitised enough to feel the breath. One thing I know from instructing this is that it's hard to get people excited about their breathing. I sometimes have to give them worst-case scenarios: "This is what's going to happen if you don't do this." People respond to that, but I'd rather inspire students than frighten them.

That's a big question. How do we inspire students? One way is to talk about our own positive experiences with the breath. Another is to inspire teachers to have a breath practice themselves. To do that, it's vital that they experience the benefits from breathing.

It's like working with clients in my yoga therapy clinic. How do we break through those barriers and get people to do what we are asking them to do? We must make it simple. People are so stressed out a lot of the time, so can we make breathing fun? Can we make it interesting? Can we keep highlighting the benefits? Are we telling stories about the breath or even cracking jokes?

This ongoing suggestion in the mind is key. When I teach, I explain the benefits. While the students are in a receptive state, I plant seeds. I open the door just a bit. I give them these little cues throughout their practice and point their awareness in certain places so that they feel what's going on in the body. And they might think, "Oh wow, my heart rate has gone down." I think it takes someone noticing and feeling these changes for it to sink in.

Where do you feel this is all heading? Will yoga instructors receive more in-depth training in the breath in the future?

With books like James Nestor's *Breath* and all the work Patrick's been doing for decades, more people are becoming aware of the breath. I've seen more scientific research coming out too. But I've been wondering – how we can get more doctors, medical professionals, and health practitioners involved? I work at a physical therapy clinic as a physical therapy aid. I watch the physical therapists instructing the breath, and I notice it's impossible to separate the body from the breath. You can't separate healing and make it just physical. But how do we keep making that bridge between body and breath in the medical field?

And I wonder, too, how we teach breathing to children in schools. Because, if they learn about the breath early on, the seed has been planted. I look at this like a garden. How many places can we plant the seeds, and how often can we water them? And it has to be many, many seeds, and many, many times. Because the more people see and hear this message, the more open they will be to practise breathing, whether they are teachers, doctors, therapists, or parents, and to spread that knowledge to others.

You can find out more about Sienna's
*work at **siennasmith.com**.*

ANASTASIS TZANIS': MY JOURNEY TO YOGA & BREATH TRAINING

My lifelong journey to better breathing began when I was 9 years old. Like many, I struggled with seasonal hay fever, insomnia, and difficulty concentrating, all symptoms associated with dysfunctional breathing. I vividly remember staying up late at night, awake in my bed, often with chest pain, performing breath holds to calm my racing mind and alleviate the pain! In the background, I could hear my parents and sister snoring loudly. Looking back, it is safe to say that breathing well didn't come naturally to any of us.

To help me with stress and with a secret hope of improving my concentration, my parents encouraged me to play sports. That was helpful, but my breath still often let me down. After running or sparring, I quickly ran out of breath, which obviously affected my performance. I remember trying – my hands on my knees, legs shaking, lungs hurting, mouth wide open – to catch a breath.

My understanding of the importance of the breath really crystallised when I was 12 years old as I was pushed by a boy and landed flat on my back. I fell so hard my diaphragm collapsed. Decades later, my memory of being unable to breathe is still crushingly vivid.

Without much natural talent in concentration or physical skills but with a lot of stubbornness, I pushed through. By the age of 24, I was serving in the special forces as a paratrooper.

One of the scariest moments of my military career occurred when my unit was due to run another military exercise. Without warning, when we heard the siren, we were to load everything on vehicles and resettle in a different location on red alert. The evacuation was to take no more than six hours. As one would expect, the siren went off at the least convenient time – 3 a.m. Minutes after, a young corporal got into a panic attack and began yelling at the top of his lungs. He was intimidating some new recruits who were unable to carry out their tasks. As his close friend, I tried unsuccessfully to help him relax and calm his breathing. Fortunately, before his behaviour was noticed by the seniors, he lost his voice.

After the military, I got my Masters in International Economics and Finance and began a career in finance, landing a currency deviates trading job at a German investment bank in London. It was during my time in those highly competitive environments that I realised the cost that stress can have on the body! And stress always affects our breathing. While the army was physically competitive, the bank was mentally competitive. In the army, I was deprived of mental stimulation. At the trading desk, my brain was taxed, but it was hard not to slip into a sedentary lifestyle.

I was a junior at the trading desk trying to process as much work as possible – hoping I would keep my job for another week. The more senior members of the team were not particularly jolly either. Half the team had recently resigned and whoever was left was overworked, over-stressed, and probably questioning why they were there. In one of the rare moments when the trading floor was quiet, I heard a snoring noise. It was coming from a colleague sitting two to three metres away. He was fully absorbed in his computer screens, red in the face and breathing as loudly as a galloping racing horse. Another colleague, next to him, claimed that this audible breathing was the norm from the moment he'd come in.

Stress during my years in banking took its toll on my health and affected my weight and digestive system, but my journey into yoga really began in 2008 when laser eye surgery triggered a glandular fever. Instead of a week's recovery, it took two months to get my eyesight back. My manager expected me to show up to work, but my vision was constantly blurry. I spent nine hours a day exhausted, staring at screens I couldn't see, and my stress levels went through the roof. At the same time, the glandular fever stopped me from exercising, and I piled on the kilos.

In my search for help, I adopted a fasting diet, dropped 13 kilos in three months, and got better mental clarity than ever before. After that, I decided it was time to take my health seriously. So, at the age of 30, I began studying nutritional therapy and attending yoga classes. For the next three years, I immersed myself in yoga. In August 2011, I went to a yoga festival in Barcelona, which was hosting some famous teachers from the States. There, I discovered more about the non-physical aspects of yoga and how asana practice could impact all aspects of my life. I then travelled to California to learn from more teachers. By then, it was clear to me that people working in competitive environments like banking get older a lot sooner than yoga teachers do!

My true path opened up to me when I was made redundant. At the time, it felt right to take a break from banking. I never found the desire to go back. Instead, I felt called to share with others the benefits I had experienced. After travelling to Europe, USA, Canada, and Singapore to study with some of the best yoga instructors, I settled in London teaching yoga and offering nutritional consultations to individuals like myself.

Despite my active teaching, I avoided cueing the breath during asana practice. My students often commented that, in contrast to their other teachers, I rarely spoke about the breath. I even refused to integrate ujjayi breathing into a beginner class I was giving. I just didn't think I knew enough about it. I didn't want to teach what I didn't fully understand.

I knew that breathing was important in my practice, and I had learned that different prāṇāyāmas create different results, but prāṇāyāma was not covered in any real depth in my training. Since I was never told *how* these techniques worked, I didn't pay much attention to them.

When I didn't find the answers on breathing in yoga, in 2015, I decided to study with a Dutchman known for his Guinness-awarded achievements in extreme environments. The Wim Hof Method was just becoming popular, opening my eyes to different breathing techniques. What I found was a new passion for Breath Training and a new depth to my yoga teaching.

When a friend I'd met on a Wim Hof course came to London in 2017 to take the Oxygen Advantage® training with Patrick McKeown, I went along for the ride. By midday of the first day of Patrick's workshop, I had learned more about breathing than I had in nine years of yoga practice.

I began applying these new ideas in my yoga teaching, and the emails started to come in from my students. Those who suffered with asthma would tell me that, if they had an attack and they didn't have an inhaler to hand, they breathed the way I taught in class and would be able to stop the attack.

Along the way, I discovered that different breathing methods work for different people. I worked with a 47-year-old man with an arrhythmia that compromises his respiratory capacity. The only thing that would reduce his heart rate during an episode of arrhythmia is slow breathing. A 94-year-old lady who has high blood pressure and asthma is only able to practise breath holds.

These days, most of my work is with people in high-pressure jobs – lawyers and corporate high-flyers. Those who put effort into building their respiratory capacity report better concentration and a new ability to overcome panic attacks. They can confidently control their mental and physical state before public speaking and avoid performance nerves.

It's never too late to begin. I didn't practise yoga until I was 30 years old or breathwork until I was 37. The breath is incredibly powerful. Once you know how it works and really understand how to use it, its potential is limited only by how much work you're prepared to put in – just like any other worthwhile practice.

You can find out more about Anastasis'
*work at **www.atzanis.com/bfy/***

BREATHING FOR COLD EXPOSURE PRACTICE

Many yoga practitioners are interested in a variety of wellness and human optimization methods. We're often driven to be the best we can. That means techniques like ice-water bathing are incredibly attractive. Cold water therapy has been used by humans for centuries. Dr. Buteyko wrote many years ago that, "the organism can be greatly affected by dousing with cold water."

There are many reasons and ways to train for better cold tolerance. Most of us start with a cold shower or by turning the tap to cold for 30 seconds after a hot shower. However, the ice bath is often our end goal.

If you work on your cold tolerance gradually, it can have many benefits. Practitioners report more energy, greater mental clarity, and a deeper ability to handle stress. It is also thought cold-water bathing can reduce inflammation and boost metabolism, helping with weight loss[746].

Research is still limited, but it does seem clear that cold-water bathing could be helpful for mental health. One 2018 case study describes a young woman who suffered from anxiety and depression.[747] After cold-water swimming for four months, she no longer required medication. Recently, there has been a much larger trial, but the results have not yet been published.[748]

The research into cold water therapy attracts debate, but the science does generally support the positive experience of practitioners:

- A randomised study of more than 3,000 people aged 18 to 65 years reported that a cold shower of just 30-90 seconds resulted in 29% fewer sick days.[749]
- Cold water immersion temporarily increases your heart rate, boosting cardiac function.[750]
- Exposure to cold creates adaptations to oxidative stress that result in something called "body hardening." Hardening is a process by which exposure to a natural stimulus (such as cold) results in an increased tolerance to stress and therefore to disease. We also call this resilience.[751]

---

746 Guest, Podcast. "Dr. Susanna Søberg: How to Use Cold & Heat Exposure to Improve Your Health| Huberman Lab Podcast."

747 Van Tulleken, Christoffer, et al. "Open Water Swimming as a Treatment for Major Depressive Disorder." *Case Reports* bcr-2018 (2018).

748 "The Effect of a Sea-Safety Course on Mood, Mental Wellbeing and Inflammation." *Clinical Trials.* Devon Partnership NHS Trust. (August 17, 2021).http://www.clinicaltrials. gov/ct2/show/results/NCT0452485?view=results (Accessed July 6, 2022).

749 Buijze, Geert A., et al. "The Effect of Cold Showering on Health and Work: A Randomized Controlled Trial." *PloS One* 11.9 (2016): e0161749.

750 Mooventhan, A., and L. Nivethitha. "Scientific Evidence-Based Effects of Hydrotherapy on Various Systems of the Body." *North American Journal of Medical Sciences* 6.5 (2014): 199.

751 Siems, Werner G., et al. "Uric Acid and Gluthathione Levels During Short-Term Whole Body Cold Exposure." *Free Radical Biology and Medicine* 16.3 (1994):299-305.

- Cold water immersion after training improves perceived sleep quality.[752]
- Just taking a cold shower can send a burst of electrical impulses from nerve endings to the brain. It is believed this could trigger an anti-depressive effect.[753]
- Cold water bathing increases brown adipose tissue, or "brown fat"[754] which increases metabolic rate, burning more calories.

Ice Bath Training

Unlike the simple cold shower, ice water immersion is a technique that requires gradual exposure and careful training. Many new ice-bathers report panic symptoms as they enter the water. If you are competitive or in a supportive group, it can be tempting to stay in too long, too soon. This risks hypothermia. Cold water shock can trigger arrhythmia and heart attack which can cause you to drown. Once you're out of the water, there's also the risk of "afterdrop," a reaction in which body temperature continues to fall after cold exposure, causing violent shivering and obliterating the benefits of the practice.

The Finnish ice swimmer and Ashtanga yoga teacher, Magnus Appelberg, was a guest on the Oxygen Advantage® podcast in March 2022. He uses breathing exercises, before, during, and after ice bathing to prolong the amount of time he can spend in the water. He teaches others to do the same. Growing up in Finland, Magnus had been ice-water bathing for decades when he discovered that hypercapnic breathing exercises allowed him to swim in the ice.

752 Al Haddad, Hani, Jonathan Parouty, and Martin Buchheit. "Effect of Daily Cold Water Immersion on Heart Rate Variability and Subjective Ratings of Well-Being in Highly Trained Swimmers." *International Journal of Sports Physiology and Performance* 7.1 (2012):33-38.

753 Shevchuk, Nikolai A. "Adapted Cold Shower as a Potential Treatment for Depression." *Medical Hypotheses* 70.5 (2008): 995-1001.

754 Vosselman, Maarten J., et al. "Frequent Extreme Cold Exposure and Brown Fat and Cold-Induced Thermogenesis: A Study in a Monozygotic Twin." *PloS one* 9.7 (2014): e101653.

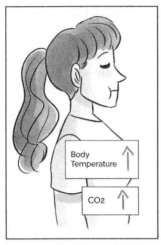

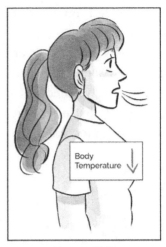

Seven back to back breath holds   Hyperventilation

Remember that it is possible to control body temperature by manipulating levels of CO_2. You can test this by performing seven back-to-back breath holds. Hold the breath after exhaling to 90% of your maximal breath hold capacity. Practise 45 seconds of light, nasal recovery breathing between each breath hold. You should feel your body temperature rising.

On the other hand, if you hyperventilate with your mouth open, you will notice your body temperature drop. If you continue to hyperventilate for some time, you will feel freezing cold.

Many believe that, by adapting to the shock of the cold, we become more resilient to stress, but this adaptation must be approached just as carefully as any breathing exercise that stresses the body. Cold water exposure stimulates the release of stress hormones including cortisol and noradrenaline. It also increases levels of the brain chemical dopamine which is associated with reward. The vagus nerve can be activated by splashing cold water on your face. This slows the heart and relaxes the body and mind.

It is important to understand that if you are already highly stressed, sudden exposure to cold will only amplify the problem. As Magnus explains:

"It's like a medicine. The wrong dose can be toxic. If you tell someone who is really stressed that an ice bath will relax him, he could die. But, if you learn, before you jump in, how to calm down with the breath, then, as the cold shock hits you, you will regain your cool. You discover it's possible to stay there."

For this reason, training for cold tolerance requires a lot of conscious relaxation. You must develop the ability to change states in your autonomic nervous system before you step into the water. This is where breathing exercises come in.

Ice Swimming with Anastasis

My personal experience with cold exposure took place in Iceland. It was a dream come true for me to swim among the icebergs. After travelling for six hours, from Reykjavik on the west coast of Iceland to Jökulsárlón glacier, which is in Iceland's most famous glacier lagoon in the southeast of the island, I parked and headed straight for the water. I was confident of my ability to control my body temperature, and, to the surprise of the other tourists, I was wearing only shorts, a t-shirt, and a scarf. It was February when the temperature in Iceland was around freezing. The experience of swimming for the first time by a glacier was exhilarating, but my girlfriend was concerned and encouraged me to come out of the water after six minutes. I was so pumped up, at that moment, there seemed no better way to celebrate this memorable experience than to do a hundred squats!

On our way back to the car, about 20 minutes' walk away, I started noticing cold blood gradually shifting from my fingertips towards my shoulders. My voice began to break, and, as the afterdrop kicked in, I suddenly felt much colder than I had in the water. I climbed into the car, started the engine, and cranked the heat up to max. It took four and a half hours for my voice and the temperature of my arms to return to normal. Throughout these four and a half hours, I practised ujjayi breathing to help my body warm up.

How to Take an Ice Bath: Anastasis's Protocol

Stage 1:

Stand in front of the ice bath in your swimsuit. Establish a breathing pattern, ideally light, slow, and hypercapnic. When practised correctly, ujjayi breath is effective, but any calm, intentional breathing pattern will do. Look at the ice and visualise entering the cold water.

Stage 2:

On an inhalation, step both feet into the bath. If this is your first time, remain standing. Do not submerge fully. Re-establish the breathing pattern you were working with before you entered the water.

Stage 3:

In stages, over time, you can kneel or squat in the ice water, and then submerge up to your collarbone. Every time you expose more of your skin to cold water, check in with your breath. If breathing is interrupted, breathe more intentionally, and emphasise prolonged exhalations. You may find yourself using your mouth, which, in this instance, is fine. As your mental state shifts from stress to calm, bring your focus to your breath in the following order:

- Breathe in a set rhythm, with no pauses following the inhalation or exhalation.
- Keep your exhales longer than your inhales.
- Breathe through your nose.
- Breathe softly.

What about those hyperventilation exercises that often accompany cold-water bathing? Scientists have demonstrated that hyperventilating before immersing in cold water of 5-10° C (41-50° F) does nothing to offset the respiratory response to cold.[755]

While in the bath, your extremities may become painful. To manage this, you can use the following method:

- Observe exactly which body part is cold. Is it your whole arm, your hands, or just your fingers? Maybe only two of your fingers are cold. Keep monitoring which body parts are painful or burn, as this is likely to change. Avoid identifying with cold. Instead of thinking, "I am cold," be specific. "Three of my toes and my left hand are cold or numb."

---

755 Tipton, M. J., A. Stubbs, and D. H. Elliott. "Human Initial Responses to Immersion in Cold Water at Three Temperatures and After Hyperventilation." *Journal of Applied Physiology.* 70.1 (1991):317-322.

- Observe which parts of your body are hot. While you are in cold water, parts of your body are likely to feel hot due to an increase in blood circulation there.
- On each exhalation, visualise yourself sending heat from the hot areas of your body to the cold areas. You can continue doing this after you leave the ice bath.

Once you leave the bath, practise light breathing or ujjayi breathing to regain warmth. Do not try any vigorous exercise.

How to Take an Ice Bath: Magnus's Protocol

When Magnus Appelberg teaches students who are new to ice bathing, his emphasis is always on long exhalations. When you work with very long exhalations, the parasympathetic nervous system activates. This tells your mind that your body is safe.

Inhaling and exhaling should be through the nose. Nasal inhalations warm the air as it enters the body. They add resistance and slow the breath. As long as breathing volume is not excessive, this helps maintain a healthy level of carbon dioxide in the lungs and blood. CO_2 is important here, as it causes blood vessels near the skin's surface to dilate.[756] This improves circulation in the areas of skin that will meet the ice water. It makes the initial cold shock less painful and helps keep you warmer.

Before getting into the water, spend at least 20 minutes practising breathing exercises with long exhalations. Continue to use this breathing pattern as you enter the water, stepping into the ice on a long exhalation. Once you have a little more experience, you can focus on a light inhalation too. As you step into the water and before immersion, your breathing should follow a pattern of light inhalations and very long exhalations.

---

756 Schaefer, Karl Ernst, et al. "Effect of Chronic Hypercapnia on Body Temperature Regulation." *Journal of Applied Physiology* 38.5 (1975): 900-906.

As you get into the water, you will hyperventilate. Most of us will breathe faster or hold our breath just thinking about going into the cold, so this should not be a surprise. As you step into the ice with one long out-breath, submerge right up to your neck. Magnus explains:

> It can be very painful to stand with water only up to your knees, but when you immerse yourself right up to your neck, the body begins to respond. Thermoregulation starts.

Once in the water, bring your focus back to the long exhalations. Magnus suggests exhaling with sound. This gives you a focus, a distraction from the cold. What's more, the quality of sound in your exhalation gives direct feedback about your stress levels. When you are stressed, the sound will be shorter, higher in pitch, and less resonant. As you relax, you will notice the sound changing.

It's very important here to be in a relaxation mode. If you enter the water in a fight or flight state, you will not adapt. Instead, you will teach your body either to get out of the water or to use willpower to stay in. "That's fight or flight, not adaptation," Magnus says.

You are psychologically teaching yourself this is dangerous, that you have to fight it. And then you lose the whole point. If you can go in and calm down your body, you are not fighting any more. You start adapting.

If you are new to ice-water bathing, it is important not to stay in the water too long. You may practise breathing exercises for more than 20 or 30 minutes and only stay in the ice for two minutes. With practice, and, as your CO_2 tolerance improves, you will be able to stay in the water for longer. However, scientists have shown that just 30 to 90 seconds at 38°F (3° C) is enough to be beneficial.[757]

How to Warm Up After Ice Bathing

The temptation, as Anastasis discovered, is to warm up as quickly as possible. To do some vigorous exercise or jump straight into the sauna. But the process for leaving the water needs to be a careful one. Otherwise, it's easy to make mistakes that cause a dangerous afterdrop and hypothermia.

Do not practise any aerobic exercise as you leave the water. For at least the first five minutes you need to stay cool, warming the body gradually. At this point, the difference in temperature between your

---

757   Buijze, Geert A., et al. "The Effect of Cold Showering on Health and Work: A Randomized Controlled Trial." *PloS One* 11.9 (2016): e0161749.

body's outer tissues and your core is too great. Any exercise that increases your circulation will cause the cold blood to sweep into your body, and you will shiver uncontrollably for a long time.

As his students leave the ice water, Magnus uses static deep squats or planks. These are practised using a breath hold after exhalation. You may also try very slow squats combined with breath holds. To help the process, you can place the palms of your hands and the soles of your feet on a warm surface or in warm water. Static squats performed while standing in warm water are very effective, as the feet have many heat receptors. Hypercapnia can also be enhanced through static muscle activation. When you recruit large muscles by holding an asana or a pose such as a plank, you increase CO_2 production and therefore heat. After 10 or 15 minutes of warming up gradually in this way, it is safe to use the sauna. If you do get the shivers, light or ujjayi breathing will help restore warmth.

Important Things to Know about Cold Exposure

- Do not put your head under water until you have experience with the cold. Never put your head under the water suddenly or dive in headfirst.
- You can splash water on your face. This activates the vagus nerve and slows the heart rate.

- As with any practice, you must build a regular habit to see the benefits. Magnus suggests three times a week.
- To stay safe, have someone with you throughout the practice, and always make sure you can get out of the water easily.
- If you have any medical condition, particularly any cardiovascular disorder or thyroid problem, check with your doctor before trying ice bathing. Do not write off cold exposure as inappropriate for you. Many people with medical issues benefit from cold water bathing.
- Gradual exposure to cold can improve circulation and help build cold tolerance.
- As with breathing exercises, to get the most from the practice, it can be helpful to work with an experienced coach.

Cold Exposure and Your BOLT Score

If your BOLT score is between 10 and 15 seconds, even momentary cold exposure can aggravate inflammation, make you shiver and feel worse, and put you off working with cold water therapy. Do not begin cold water dousing until your BOLT score is 20 or 25 seconds and you feel well. You can warm up using physical exercise or with a hot shower first. Once you have achieved control of your nervous system with your

breath, you will be able to go into the cold without these preliminary steps. The final objective is cold water exposure outside. This is usually accompanied by an intense feeling of vitality and warmth.

Sometimes cold-water tolerance is practised continuously and more energetically than is recommended. Dr. Buteyko recommended starting with just a cold sponging down and dousing of the limbs, before rubbing briskly with a towel. "The organism is ready for cold water," he writes, "If after dousing there is a sensation of an influx of warmth."

One of the most powerful effects of cold tolerance is the sense of achievement that comes from stepping outside your comfort zone. As Magnus puts it:

> To feel comfortable in discomfort enlarges our life. It expands our experience, so we can feel much more appreciation for life, more gratitude, and more love.

In essence, cold exposure works in the same way as a physical yoga practice. By leaning into an uncomfortable asana, we grow. We become more flexible. We expand beyond our limits.

ACKNOWLEDGEMENTS

This book would not have been possible without the coming together of a number of generous and talented people. A special thanks to Dr Catherine Bane for casting her scientific eye to check references, and for writing, proof reading, editing, and helping organise the book's structure.

Thanks are due also to:

- Johanna McWeeney, Megan Ashton and Wendy Maki for proofing, editing and writing – bringing together much disparate information into a digestible format.
- The gifted Oxygen Advantage® Master Instructors: Anastasis Tzanis; Robin Rothenberg; Sienna Smith; Tiger Bye; Alessandro Romagnoli; Gray Caws; and Dr. Paul Sly – for their contributions on teaching breathing in their various fields of expertise. Thanks also to Tom Herron for your words of wisdom and encouragement.
- Magdalena Kraler for contributing a historical perspective on Oxygen Advantage® and prāṇāyāma.
- James Nestor, for writing the forward despite his busy schedule since the publication of his masterpiece; *Breath*. James – it is fantastic to have you introduce the reader to this book. Your contribution and support are much appreciated.
- Bex Burgess, for her unique ability to create easy-to-understand illustrations to support and elevate the text.
- Hans Deprez for reading the proof and making some great suggestions.
- Magnus Appelberg for contributing to the *Breathing for Cold Exposure Practice* Chapter.
- The exceptional team at Oxygen Advantage® and Buteyko Clinic – Ana Mahe, Tijana Krstović, Heather Clarke, Nikki Osthus, Ruth Gibney, Orla Kyne, Ronan Maher and Alessandro Romagnoli.

- All the Oxygen Advantage® and Buteyko Clinic instructors – thanks for joining us on the journey.
- The yogis (old and new) whose teachings and wisdom are quoted throughout the book, and a shout out to my yoga teacher Sinead McKiernan.
- Special thanks to my wife Sinead and daughter Lauren.

Finally, a huge thank you to you, the reader, for supporting this work.

INDEX

Made in the USA
Middletown, DE
25 September 2023

39264641R20309